LECTURES IN ECONOMICS, 3

THE THEORY OF INCOME DISTRIBUTION

HARRY G. JOHNSON

Professor of Economics
London School of Economics & University of Chicago

GRAY-MILLS PUBLISHING LTD
10 JUER STREET
LONDON S.W.11

First edition, 1973
© Harry G. Johnson
ISBN 0 85641 007 1 (*paper*)
ISBN 0 85641 006 3 (*cloth*)

Figures drawn by Bailey & Bailey
97a Albert Bridge Road, London, S.W.11
and printed in Great Britain by
Page Bros (Norwich) Ltd., Norwich

CONTENTS

PREFACE

This book is based on the notes of the course on the theory of distribution and related matters that I have been giving at the University of Chicago for some eight years, under the course description of Economics 302. This course is the second half of the first-year graduate sequence in price theory, the first half being concerned with price and value theory and taught by colleagues. The structure of the course is described in detail in the introductory chapter. Here it may be mentioned that when I took the course over it still had the structure established in the immediate postwar period, with a heavy concentration on the controversial aspects of marginal productivity theory and reliance on the aggregate production function as developed in the interwar period by Douglas, Hicks and others. I have tried in the course to retain this material for the sake of historical perspective but to cut it down to its stylized essentials in order to make room for more recent developments. In particular, I have introduced and applied the two-sector model from the theory of international trade, and devoted considerable attention to models of economic growth.

It is no longer necessary to explain that 'distribution' in theory is to be sharply differentiated from 'distribution' as that branch of economic activity concerned with moving raw materials to factories and factory products to other users and final consumers.

It is, however, probably desirable to call attention to the fact that the contents of the book are concerned with the real theory of distribution, almost exclusively in the context of a full employment situation. This does not preclude consideration of certain neo-Keynesian or anti-orthodox theories of distribution, which typically make the same assumption of full employment but adduce other mechanisms than marginal productivity theory to explain the distribution of the full employment product. It does, however, make the classical assumption that monetary phenomena can be treated as a 'veil' over the operation of real economic forces. This assumption was the focal point of the Keynesian Revolution; but with the success of that revolution, especially in obtaining governmental commitment to the objective of maintaining full employment, it is reasonable once again to use that assumption as the basis for analysis. The assumption though, should be rested on a prior assumption about government success in macro-economic management rather than on the obviously incorrect assertion that the economy will tend automatically to maintain full employment regardless of whatever real or monetary shocks may occur in it.

Concentration on the analysis of the determinants of distribution under full employment conditions obviously excludes two problems suggested by monetary theory. The first, which features large in the Keynesian literature, at least in its earlier phases, concerns the effects of variations in the level of employment in the Keynesian short run (with fixed capital stock) on the distribution of income. The short answer derivable from a traditional model of the kind presented here is that as employment increases the relative share of labour as contrasted with property income will rise or fall according to whether the elasticity of substitution between labour and capital is greater or less than unity. Because rentier incomes are fixed in money terms and a rise in employment implies a rise in money prices (given the Keynesian assumption of wage rigidity) the real income of the rentiers (both absolute and relative) must vary inversely with the level of employment. A more interesting and relevant version of this question in contemporary times concerns the effects of maintaining alternative rates of unemployment as the normal or average condition of the economy, on the distribution of income; but to answer this requires a more careful and elaborate analysis, bringing in theories of the incentives to save and to invest, than can be offered here.

The second problem is the effects on the distribution of income of sustained price inflation or deflation. The function of money in a neo-classical full employment world is to serve as a numéraire or unit of account and a store of value, and theory usually assumes that its general purchasing power is constant. It is clear that unexpected inflation or deflation imposed on a situation of expected stability of prices will alter the real values of all bargains involving the future, and so redistribute income and wealth from those who have contracted to sell for money to those who have contracted to buy for money. The more interesting question is whether, once inflation or deflation has gone on long enough to be expected, it will influence the distribution of real income. This has been a highly controversial issue in monetary theory, for a fuller discussion of which the reader is referred to other works of mine.[1] Suffice it to say at this point that the initial Keynesian finding that inflation would tend to raise the long-run equilibrium stock of capital per head, and therefore redistribute real income from capital to labour, was derived from an excessively simple view of the role of money in the economy, and the outcome of more general models is that what inflation does to income distribution will depend on the precise parameters of the analytical system employed. One further specific thought might be mentioned: if inflation leads to a substitution for the use of money of other methods of effecting transactions, and these methods are relatively labour-intensive (e.g. more frequent wage-payments and more frequent trips to the shops) inflation will increase the labour-intensity of overall economic activity and hence tend to redistribute income towards labour (other things being assumed equal, of course, which they probably will not be).

In conclusion, I should like to thank W. H. Bruce Brittain and Stephen T. Easton for their careful work in taking down and writing up the notes for the course as it was presented during the Spring Quarter of 1971. I am grateful to David Stanton, Richard Layard and Stephen Glaister for some later comments. The notes have been revised and rewritten by myself to

---

[1] Harry G. Johnson, *Essays in Monetary Economics*, London: Allen & Unwin, 1967, chaps III and IV; *Macroeconomics and Monetary Theory*, London: Gray-Mills Publishing, 1972, chaps 19 and 20. The controversies in monetary theory, it should be noted, have been concerned primarily about consumption per head, rather than the distribution of income; but one can easily transform the analysis from consumption to distribution by using the positive relation between output per head and the marginal product of labour.

correct and clarify them and to incorporate new material introduced during the 1972 presentation. In addition, I have appended the final examinations for the course for the past six years, and annotations on the answers to the most recent examination and the past three Core examinations in Price Theory at Chicago in which I have participated.

The University of Chicago   *Harry G. Johnson*
April 1972

1

INTRODUCTION

Traditionally, real economic theory has been divided into two branches, the theory of value and exchange and the theory of production and distribution — the latter being the theory of the distribution of the national income among the factors of production or the agents that produce it. In turn, two aspects of distribution theory may be distinguished: (1) the personal distribution of income among individuals of a society, which depends on the ownership of the factors of production, and (2) the functional distribution among factors. For the most part, economic theory has been concerned with the theory of functional distribution although some economists of the twentieth century have been interested in the distribution of income or of wealth as a descriptive and statistical problem rather than as a problem of economic analysis. Consequently, the bulk of theory concerns the functional distribution of income. Nevertheless, we shall touch on the theory of the personal distribution of income developed especially within the last seven or eight years under the impetus of the 'War on Poverty'.

Distribution Theory in Historical Perspective
The division between distribution and value theory originated in the work of the classical economists (Smith, Ricardo, J. S. Mill) as distinct from the neoclassics (Walras, Jevons, Marshall) or the marginalists. The work of the classics strongly influenced the structure of theory as regards distribution. In turn, their approach was determined by the social and economic environment of the time. Agriculture being the dominant activity, a distinction was made between landlords and tenants that easily suggested a distinction between rent and wages. As the industrial system developed, so did a class of industrial entrepreneurs whose contribution to the productive process was through the ownership of capital: their return was through profits. Only late in the nineteenth century was the system developed enough for analysts to make the distinction between interest as the pure return to capital and profits as the return to whatever the entrepreneur did.

In the classical environment there were three classes of individual — landlords, capitalists and labourers — and it was considered important to distinguish among the shares in income of these groups in any theory of distribution. The important point about the classical theory that survives in modern times (in Marxian theory) is that distribution theory concerns the disposition of income among social classes. Thus we have equivalence between functional and personal distribution theory as the factors, land, labour and capital, are conceived of as corresponding to three broad social groups. It was natural then to seek to explain distribution in terms of the characteristics of the factors, although this analysis was often confused with the characteristics of the people who owned the factors.

Initially, an *ad hoc* system of theory was developed that had a different explanation for each of the factor incomes and involved assigning a residual role to one or more factors' shares. It was the major contribution of the marginal productivity school to point out that the theory of factor prices and distribution of income is only one aspect of the general theory of pricing and one aspect of general equilibrium theory. Hence, the *ad hoc* approaches are unsatisfactory from the standpoint of economic theory. Even so, the development of marginal productivity theory was hindered by the retention of the institutional ideas and preconceptions of the classics.

For example, the Austrian School's formulation of marginal productivity theory was strongly influenced by Marx's use of elements of physiocratic and Ricardian analysis to develop a theory in which labour was the source of all value and other shares the result of the exploitation of labour. That theory emphasized cost of production as the source of value; the Austrians instead threw the emphasis on the utility of the final product to consumers as being the source of the value of the factors used in producing it. The problem of distribution was the process by which value was imputed from the utility of the product to the earnings of the factors. This stood the classical concern with costs of production on its head, and equally obscured the general equilibrium nature of the problem.

The English neoclassical position was largely attributable to the work of Marshall. His theories retained at least two key classical ideas: (1) that there was a basic element of real cost expressed in terms of utility analysis: wages are determined through the disutility of labour while the rate of interest is determined by the disutility of 'abstinence' or 'waiting' (in the sense of foregoing consumption). These ideas are thus behind determining the supplies of labour and capital. Subsequently, the idea of opportunity cost, the amount of production of one good that would have to be given up to obtain a certain amount of another good, was seen as the relevant concept. (2) That the rent of land is a surplus from the point of view of the society as a whole (the Ricardian view) rather than a cost of production attributable to the employment of a particular factor. Further, by failing to state the marginal productivity theory in a form strong enough to contrast fully with the classical theory, Marshall was too deferential to the classical position.

In any case, the marginal productivity theory was a step forward from the explanation of distribution in terms of the supply characteristics of factors toward putting it in the context of the general theory of prices. But in the transition we run into the problem of consistency that bothered economists into the 1930s. In the literature, the debate centres around 'the adding-up problem' of which the essence is: if one assumes that factors are paid according to their marginal productivity, will payments more than exhaust, just exhaust, or less than exhaust the product? The answer to this problem has been obscured by the belief that its resolution depends on assumptions regarding the characteristics of the production function. Rather, the problem may be solved by our assumption of perfect competition. It is interesting to note that the same type of problem occurs in Marxian analysis. Inasmuch as the theory concerns value and prices, we have to determine how values expressed in labour terms may be translated into prices. Since the laws of competition require only that the rate of profit in all activities be equalized it is not necessary that the prices so determined correspond to the labour inputs. As the theory asserts that labour is the source of value of commodities, we have the problem of how the value of labour is transformed into prices of commodities by the workings of the capitalist system. This problem turned out to be solvable mathematically.

With the marginal productivity theory, distribution ceases to be a problem of class distribution and merges into the general theory of pricing. As understanding of the pricing process progressed, the classical model, resting as it did on differences regarding the supply of different factors, ceased to be convincing. For example, the classical theory assumes land is in rigidly fixed supply and that labour breeds to the level of subsistence. However, we are aware that the creation and destruction of land are both possible — the former through exploration and development, the latter through such things as erosion, neglect and excessive use. Thus land may be considered an economic variable, its supply being governed by economic incentives. Similarly with labour, empirical evidence controverts breeding to subsistence and recently economists have begun to be successful in couching explanations of varying fertility rates in incentive terms.

The Case For Distribution Theory
On the basis of this kind of development, one might wonder whether there should be a separate theory of distribution. One might include distribution in the general theory of prices, making the appropriate restrictive assumptions for varying market considerations. In fact, the analogy between maximazation of utility and minimization of cost (or maximization of profit) may be drawn quite exactly. Physical technology parallels the consumer's utility function and the budget constraint for producers may be expressed as an earnings constraint governed by the demand curve that exists for their product. Further, one may allow the individual to vary his labour input according to the structure of incentives to parallel the producer's use of factors. Again, the removal of the social element from distribution theory and the similarities between utility and profit maximization cast doubt on the need for a distinct distribution theory.

We may justify pursuing the subject on four grounds. First, a literature exists containing many special problems and pieces of analysis. Second, from a historical and cultural point of view, a folklore of distribution theory has grown up, particularly associated with the Marxian tradition, with which economists frequently have to deal. Third, economists have recently become interested in the problems of economic growth and capital accumulation — the *locus classicus* of theoretical work on these problems has been distribution theory. Fourth, economists have recently become concerned with problems of inequality of personal income distribution and poverty.

Whereas classical theorists took capital to be actual physical structures and implements, and assumed labour to be homogeneous, contemporary theorists see part of a given capital stock as being embodied in a non-homogeneous labour force. Currently, capital is thought of as appearing in three forms: as material capital (the classical view), as human capital (skills acquired by training and education) and as intellectual capital or knowledge in general, not necessarily embodied in any individual.

Another major difference between the classical and contemporary theorists is in their approach to growth, accumulation and the distribution of income. The classics held that nature imposed a limit to the possibilities for economic expansion through fixity of the supply of land. All their models look at the economy as approaching the stationary state where all growth grinds to a halt. There is a limit to the growth process through diminishing returns from the expansion of labour and capital with respect to land.

Although contemporary growth theory has a different set of assumptions (exogenously given rates of technological progress and population growth) it still contains the diminishing returns phenomenon. As the economy keeps increasing the amount of capital relative to population, output is not increased proportionately. In dynamic long-run equilibrium one finds the exact equivalent of the classical stationary state; for where the economy is growing at a steady rate over time, a cross section of the economy reveals that everything is constant in 'per effective labour unit' terms. The theory of distribution provides the origin for this form of analysis.

At the same time, however, there are rival approaches to the issues of growth and capital theory — the orthodox, neoclassical approach and the Keynesian (or more accurately, Cambridge, England) approach. The first assumes that the production function relationship — in terms of a relation between inputs and outputs — is a useful empirical tool and, in particular, that the assumption that factor shares depend on marginal productivities is valid. The difficulty with the approach is that capital is a produced factor of production and that its value in any period depends critically on variables that we wish to explain, i.e. various rates of return to factors. The second approach involves arguing that the production function cannot be constructed because of difficulties with the definition of capital and, as a corollary, that marginal productivity theory makes no sense. Although there are different versions of the second approach (cf. Kaldor, Robinson) all interpret the marginal productivity theory as saying that shares are determined through knowledge of the production function and amounts of the available factors without reference to individual preferences. It will be demonstrated, however, that when we assume the existence of different production functions for different goods, the marginal products are not determined uniquely by technical considerations but by demand conditions as well in the context of a general equilibrium approach to price determination.

Currently, then, distribution theory concerns functional distribution — which in contemporary theory is handled in a growth context — and personal distribution through recently generated concern with the alleviation of poverty and the stimulation of growth in the less developed countries.

The Reading List

My book on the two-sector model of general equilibrium encapsulates and synthesizes methods and applications developed in the course over the years. Its structure, however, is different from that of the course, since it is concerned only with the development and application of one set of the techniques employed, and obviously cannot cover all the literature or topics covered in the course itself. Students are probably best advised to read it quickly and then use it for a reference at appropriate points in the course. Bronfenbrenner's book is a unique and compendious treatment of the subject, extremely useful for reference.

Section I of the following Reading List contains some surveys of the theory of distribution, which should probably be read in reverse order.

Section II contains general materials on the theory of marginal productivity. Some of this is replete with dead controversies, especially some reflecting the lack of mathematical sophistication of economists in the 1930s, but these issues have a habit of recurring in more sophisticated form.

Section III takes us into the traditional structure of distribution theory, as concerned with the distribution of income among rents, wages, interest and profits.

The traditional theory of rent (section A) is by now pretty cut and dried; however, there have been some interesting new developments, notably concerned with such questions as conservation, common-property resources, pollution and the effects of land-tenure systems.

The theory of wages (section B) has also been fairly cut and dried, as regards the determination of relative wages, but there are interesting new developments in the analysis of the effects of unionization, the application of the human capital concept to the supply of labour in relation to wage differentials and the supply of population itself.

The theory of capital, interest and investment (section C) involves some of the most difficult issues in economic theory, issues which cannot really be resolved but can be understood. The three sections deal with the nature of capital and interest, the theory of investment of the firm and (very briefly) with the theory of profit. Profit poses a difficult problem: socially it is the name of a share of income going to the owners of enterprise, but in economic theory it has to be not an income share on a flow basis rewarding a contribution to the on-going production process, but a capital gain reflecting an improvement in production technique and hence an increase in the value of ownership.

Section IV, on the theory of economic growth, mixes some pieces of straightforward technical theoretical analysis with some of the classic articles on economic growth as a broader social process. It also provides a few references to empirical studies that attempt to apply economic theory to the explanation of growth in actual economies.

Section V is concerned with a special problem that emerged from J. M. Keynes's seminar in Cambridge in the 1930s (though elsewhere too, of course): the question of the apparent constancy of the share of labour in the national income and whether this constituted an empirical regularity unaccountable for by traditional marginal productivity theory. Section V presents empirical evidence and theoretical argument. Section VI represents the work of those who have considered neoclassical theory disproven by the apparent constancy of relative shares and attempted to develop an alternative theory of distribution on 'Keynesian' lines.

Section VII is concerned with the personal distribution of income and the poverty problem. Section A is primarily concerned with theoretical approaches to the explanation of differences in the personal distribution of income.

Section B is concerned specifically with poverty and policies for dealing with it. This Section dates from the days of President Johnson's 'War on Poverty', but the issues are still with us and likely to remain so, though over the intervening years interest has tended to shift from poverty to inequality in income distribution.

Any reading list, but especially one prepared for a one-quarter course in elementary theory, necessarily represents a compromise among several desiderata: the time for reading available to students, the need to balance classical contributions against new approaches, and the search-time available to the instructor to assess new contributions and weigh them against old ones. As such, it is a sketch-map for hunters, not a pin-point guide to where the treasures lie buried. The student is expected to use reading list and lectures together to achieve his own understanding of the subject, and naturally both to read and to think on his own about the problems involved.

APPENDIX: Reading List

General Texts

Johnson, Harry G. *The Two-Sector Model of General Equilibrium* (Chicago: Aldine-Atherton, Inc., 1971; London: George Allen and Unwin, 1971).

Bronfenbrenner, M., *Income Distribution Theory* (Chicago: Aldine-Atherton, Inc., 1971; London: Macmillan, 1971).

I   *Introduction*

*Johnson, Harry G., 'The Political Economy of Opulence', *Canadian Journal of Economics*, vol. 26, no. 4 (November 1960), pp. 552–64. Reprinted as chapter XV in *The Canadian Quandary* (Toronto: McGraw-Hill, 1963).

*Kaldor, N., 'The Theory of Distribution', *Chamber's Encyclopaedia*, vol. 4 (1950), pp. 553–56.

Clark, J. M., 'Distribution', AEA *Readings in the Theory of Income Distribution* (Homewood, Illinois: R. D. Irwin, Inc., 1951, pp. 58–71).

Stigler, G. J., *Production and Distribution Theories*, (New York: Macmillan, 1941).

II   *Demand for Factor Services and Marginal Productivity*

Marshall, A., *Principles of Economics*, 9th ed., book IV (London: Macmillan for the Royal Economic Society, 1961), chapters I–III and book V, chapter VI.

Stigler, J., *Production and Distribution Theories* (New York: Macmillan, 1964), chapters iv and xii.

Allen, R. G. D., *Mathematical Analysis for Economists* (London: Macmillan, 1947), chapters 11.8, 12.7, 12.8, 12.9 and 13.7.

*Knight, F. H., *Risk, Uncertainty and Profit* (Hart, Schaffner and Marx Prize Essays, no. 31).

Samuelson, P. A., *Foundations of Economic Analysis* (Harvard University, Harvard Economic Studies, vol. 80), (Cambridge: Harvard University Press, 1947), chapter iv.

*AEA *Readings in the Theory of Income Distribution*, (Homewood, Illinois:

Richard D. Irwin, 1951). Articles by J. M. Cassels (103–18), G. Stigler (119–42), E. Chamberlin (143–57), F. Machlup (158–74) and D. H. Robertson (425–60).

Allen, R. G. D., *Mathematical Economics* (London: Macmillan, 1956), chapter XVIII, pp. 608–53.

Ozga, S. A., 'The Two-Sector Model: A Geometrical Note', *Economica*, (NS) vol. XXXV, no. 140 (November 1968), pp. 368–84.

III   *Theory of Factor Incomes*
A.   *Theory of Rent*
*Robinson, J., *The Economics of Imperfect Competition* (London: Macmillan, 1933), chapter viii.

Bunce, A. C., 'Time Preference and Conservation', *Journal of Farm Economy*, vol. 22 (August 1940), pp. 533–43.

Gordon, H. S., 'The Economic Theory of a Common-Property Resource: The Fishery', *Journal of Political Economy*, vol. 62, no. 2 (April 1954), pp. 124–42.

Turvey, R., 'A Finnish Contribution to Rent Theory', *Economic Journal*, vol. 65 (June 1955), pp. 346–48.

Cheung, S. N. S., 'Private Property Rights and Share Cropping', *Journal of Political Economy*, vol. 76, no. 6 (November–December 1968), pp. 1107–22.

Coase, R. H., 'The Problem of Social Cost', *Journal of Law and Economics*, Vol. 3 (October 1960), pp. 1–44.

B.   *Theory of Wages*
i.   Relative Wages
Smith, A., *The Wealth of Nations*, book I (London: Harmondsworth, 1970).

Marshall, A., *Principles of Economics*, 9th ed., (London: Macmillan, 1961), book VI, chapters I–V.

*Hicks, J. R., *The Theory of Wages*, 2nd ed., (London: Macmillan, 1963), chapters 1–6 and relevant appendices, especially the review by G. F. Shove.

Friedman, M. and S. Kuznets, *Income from Independent Professional Practice* (NBER), pp. v–x, 81–95, 118–37, and 142–61.

Lewis, H. G., *Unionism and Relative Wages in the United States* (London and Chicago: University of Chicago Press, 1963), chapter V.

Stigler, G. J., 'Domestic Servants in the United States: 1900–40' (NBER: Occasional Paper no. 24).

Johnson, Harry G. and P. Mieszkowski, 'The Effects of Unionization on the Distribution of Income: A General Equilibrium Approach' *Quarterly Journal of Economics*, vol. 84, no. 4 (November 1970), pp. 539–61.

ii.   Human Capital
*Schultz, T. W., 'Investment in Human Capital', *American Economic Review*, vol. 51 (March 1961), pp. 1–17.

Investment in Human Beings, Journal of Political Economy, vol. 70, no. 5, part 2, Supplement (October 1962). Especially contributions by T. W. Schultz, G. S. Becker, J. Mincer, and B. Weisbrod.

Becker, G. S., *Human Capital: A Theoretical and Empirical Analysis, with Special Reference to Education* (NBER: Columbia University Press, 1964).

iii.   Population

Becker, G. S., 'An Economic Analysis of Fertility', in *Demographic and Economic Change in Developed Countries* (NBER, 1960).

Leibenstein, H., *Economic Backwardness and Economic Growth* (New York: John Wiley and Sons, 1957), especially chapter iii, pp. 15–37; viii, pp. 94–111; xii and xii, pp. 185–217.

Jorgenson, D. W., 'The Development of a Dual Economy', *Economic Journal* vol. 71 (June 1961), pp. 309–34.

Spengler, J. J., 'Malthus's Total Population Theory: A Restatement and Reappraisal', *Canadian Journal of Economics*, vol. 11 (February and May 1945), pp. 83–110 and 234–64. Reprinted in J. J. Spengler and W. R. Allen, *Essays in Economic Thought: Aristotle to Marshall* (New York: Rand McNally, 1960), Chapter XIV.

C.   *Theory of Interest, Capital and Investment*
i.   Capital, Interest and Income

*Wicksell, K., *Lectures on Political Economy*, vol. I, part 2 (London: G. Routledge & Sons, 1946).

*Fisher, I., *The Theory of Interest* (New York: Macmillan, 1930).

Knight, F. H., 'Capital and Interest', *Encyclopaedia of the Social Sciences*. Reprinted in AEA *Readings in the Theory of Income Distribution* (Homewood, Illinois: R. D. Irwin, 1951), pp. 384–417.

Lerner, A. P., 'On the Marginal Product of Capital and the Marginal Efficiency of Investment', *Journal of Political Economy*, vol. 61, no. 1 (February 1953), pp. 1–14.

Dorfman, R., 'A Graphical Exposition of Böhm–Bawerk's Interest Theory', *Review of Economic Studies*, vol. 26 (February 1959), pp. 153–58.

Dorfman, R., 'Waiting and the Period of Production', *Quarterly Journal of Economics*, vol. 73 (August 1959), pp. 351–72.

Lange, O., 'The Place of Interest in the Theory of Production', *Review of Economic Studies*, vol. 3 (June 1936), pp. 159–92.

Knight, F. H., 'The Quantity of Capital and the Rate of Interest', *Journal of Political Economy*, vol. 44, nos. 4–5 (August and October 1936), pp. 433–63 and 612–25.

Lutz, F. A. and D. C. Hague (eds.), *The Theory of Capital* (London: Macmillan, 1961). Especially chapters I, III, X, XI, and XII.

Metzler, L. A., 'The Rate of Interest and the Marginal Product of Capital', *Journal of Political Economy*, vol. 58 (August 1950), pp. 289–306; 'A Correction', *Journal of Political Economy*, vol. 59 (February 1951), pp. 67–68.

ii.   Theory of Investment of the Firm

Hirshleifer, J., 'On the Theory of Optimal Investment Decisions', *Journal of Political Economy*, vol. 66 (August 1958), pp. 329–52.

Bailey, M. J., 'Formal Criteria for Investment Decisions', *Journal of Political Economy*, vol. 67 (October 1959), pp. 476–88.

*Haavelmo, T., *A Study in the Theory of Investment* (Chicago: University of Chicago Press, 1960).

Arrow, K., 'Introduction' in Arrow, Karlin, and Scarf (Eds) *Studies in*

Applied Probability and Management Science (Stanford: Stanford University Press, 1962).

iii. Theory of Profits

*Knight, F. H., 'Profits', in AEA *Readings in the Theory of Income and Distribution* (Homewood, Illinois: R. D. Irwin, 1951), pp. 533–46.

Knight, F. H., *Risk, Uncertainty and Profit* (Hart, Schaffner and Marx Prize Essays, no. 31).

Schumpeter, J., *The Theory of Economic Development* (Cambridge: Harvard University Press, 1934). Especially chapter IV.

IV *Theory of Economic Growth*
   A. Theory

*Hahn, F. H. and R. C. O. Matthews, 'The Theory of Economic Growth: A Survey', *Economic Journal*, vol. 74 (December 1964), pp. 779–902.

*Harrod, R. F., *Towards a Dynamic Economics* (London: Macmillan, 1948). Especially chapter III.

Harrod, R. F., 'Second Essay on Dynamic Theory', *Economic Journal*, vol. 70 (June 1960), pp. 277–93.

Corden, W. M., 'A Brief Review of Some Theories of Economic Growth', *Malayan Economic Review*, vol. 6, no. 1 (April 1961), pp. 1–12.

Domar, E., *Essays in the Theory of Economic Growth* (Oxford: Oxford University Press, 1957), chapter I.

Lewis, W. A., 'Economic Development with Unlimited Supplies of Labour', *Manchester School*, vol. 22 (May 1954), pp. 138–201.

Rostow, W. W., 'The Take-off into Self-Sustained Growth', *Economic Journal*, vol. 66 (March 1956), pp. 25–48.

Johnson, Harry G., 'The Neo-Classical One-Sector Growth Model: A Geometrical Exposition and Extension to a Monetary Economy', *Economica*, vol. 33 (August 1966), pp. 265–89. The corrected version of the monetary section appears in chapter IV of *Essays in Monetary Economics* (London: George Allen & Unwin, 1967; Cambridge: Harvard University Press, 1967).

Laing, N. F., 'A Geometrical Analysis of Some Theorems of Steady Growth', *Journal of Political Economy*, vol. 72 (October 1964), pp. 476–82.

*Swan, T. W., 'Economic Growth and Capital Accumulation', *Economic Record*, vol. 32 (November 1956), 334–61. See also 'Comment' by Joan Robinson, *Economic Record*, vol. 33 (February 1957), pp. 103–08.

*Solow, R. M., 'A Contribution to the Theory of Economic Growth', *Quarterly Journal of Economics*, vol. 70 (February 1956), pp. 65–94.

Solow, R. M., 'Investment and Technical Progress', in Arrow, Karlin, and Suppes (eds.), *Mathematical Methods in the Social Sciences: 1959* (Stanford: Stanford University Press, 1960).

*Phelps, E., 'The Golden Rule of Accumulation: A Fable for Growthmen', *American Economic Review*, vol. 51 (September 1961), pp. 638–43.

Meade, J. E., *A Neo-Classical Theory of Economic Growth*, revised edition, (London: George Allen & Unwin, 1962), especially appendix II.

Borts, G. H., 'Professor Meade on Economic Growth', *Economica*, vol. 29, no. 113 (February 1962), pp. 72–86.

Barnett, H. and C. Morse, *Scarcity and Growth* (Baltimore: Johns Hopkins Press, 1963), chapter V.

Bensusan-Butt, D. M., *On Economic Growth: An Essay in Pure Theory* (Oxford: The Clarendon Press, 1960).

Johnson, Harry G., 'Trade and Growth: A Geometrical Exposition', *Journal of International Economics*, vol. 1, no. 1 (January–March 1971), pp. 83–102.

B.   *Empirical Studies*

Fabricant, S., *Basic Facts on Productivity Change* (NBER: Occasional Paper, no. 63).

Denison, E. F., *The Sources of US Economic Growth* (Committee for Economic Development, Supplementary Papers, no. 13).

Denison, E. F., *Why Growth Rates Differ* (Washington, D.C.: Brookings Institute, 1967).

Nelson, R. R., 'Aggregate Production Functions and Medium Range Growth Projections', *American Economic Review*, vol. 54 (September 1964), pp. 575–606.

V   *Functional Shares*

Johnson, D. G., 'The Functional Distribution of Income in the United States, 1850–1952', *Review of Economics and Statistics*, vol. 36 (May 1954), pp. 175–82.

Kravis, I. B., 'Relative Income Shares in Fact and Theory', *American Economic Review*, vol. 49, no. 6 (December 1959), pp. 917–49.

Bronfenbrenner, M., 'A Note on Relative Shares and the Elasticity of Substitution', *Journal of Political Economy*, vol. 68, no. 3 (June 1960), pp. 284–87.

Solow, R. M., 'A Skeptical Note on the Constancy of Relative Shares', *American Economic Review*, vol. 48 (September 1958), pp. 618–31.

Douglas, P. H., 'Are There Laws of Production?' *American Economic Review*, vol. 38 (March 1948), pp. 1–41.

VI   *Alternative Theories of Distribution*

Kalecki, M., 'The Distribution of the National Income', AEA *Readings in the Theory of Income Distribution* (Homewood, Ill.: R. D. Irwin, 1951), pp. 197–220.

Boulding, K. E., *A Reconstruction of Economics* (New York: John Wiley, 1950), chapter xiv.

*Kaldor, N., 'Alternative Theories of Distribution', *Review of Economic Studies*, vol. 23 (1956), pp. 83–100.

Tobin, J., 'Towards a General Kaldorian Theory of Distribution', *Review of Economic Studies*, vol. 27 (February 1960), pp. 119–20.

Robinson, J., 'The Production Function and the Theory of Capital', *Review of Economic Studies*, vol. 21, no. 2 (1954), pp. 81–106.

VII   *The Personal Distribution of Income and the Poverty Problem*
   A.   *The Personal Distribution of Income*

Roy, A. D., 'Some Thoughts on the Distribution of Earnings', *Oxford Economic Papers*, vol. 3 (June 1951), pp. 135–46.

*Friedman, M., 'Choice, Chance and the Personal Distribution of Income', *Journal of Political Economy*, vol. 61, no. 4 (August 1953), pp. 277–90.

Miller, H. P., *Trends in the Income of Families and Persons in the United States*, 1947–60 (US Bureau of the Census: Technical Paper no. 3, 1963).

Mincer, J., 'Investment in Human Capital and Personal Income Distribution', *Journal of Political Economy*, vol. 66, no. 4 (August 1958), pp. 281–302.

Becker, G. S., *Human Capital and the Personal Distribution of Income: An Analytical Approach*, W. S. Woytinsky Lecture no. 1 (University of Michigan, Department of Economics, Institute of Public Administration, 1967).

Reder, M. W., 'A Partial Survey of the Theory of Income Size Distribution', in *Six Papers on the Size Distribution of Wealth and Income*, (NBER: Studies in Income and Wealth, no. 33, 1969).

B.   *The Poverty Problem*

Fishman, L. (ed.), *Poverty Amid Affluence* (London and New Haven: Yale University Press, 1966). Especially contributions by T. W. Schultz (pp. 165–81) and H. G. Johnson (pp. 182–99).

Galbraith, J. K., *The Affluent Society* (London: Hamish Hamilton, 1958).

Schultz, T. W., Lampman, R. J. and Batchelder, A., 'The Economics of Poverty', *American Economic Review*, Papers and Proceedings, vol. LV (May 1965), pp. 510–20, 521–29 and 530–48.

Johnson, Harry G., 'Minimum Wage Laws: A General Equilibrium Analysis', *Canadian Journal of Economics*, vol. II, no. 4 (November 1969), pp. 599–604.

*   Required reading

2

THE RICARDIAN APPROACH TO
DISTRIBUTION AND GROWTH

Introduction
Ricardo's theory of distribution constitutes the background to contemporary
theory (including Marxian theory) with respect to both distribution of
income and the effects and motivations of economic growth. Because of
his status as a major classical figure, there exists a vast literature of interpretation and criticism of his work, which it is not possible to go into here. It
should be noticed however that interest in his work has been stimulated
since the end of the Second World War by the long-awaited Sraffa edition
of his collected works, and by the discovery that he was the first linear
programmer (cf. two articles by Samuelson in the *Quarterly Journal of
Economics* in 1959, and Sraffa's book on *Production of Commodities by Means
of Commodities*).

Here we will not attempt to deal with either the historical or the more
recent literature, but instead present a sort of 'idealized picture' of the
Ricardian model intended to bring out its main features. Specifically, we
ignore two problems important in the literature, Ricardo's quest for an
absolute standard of value and the difficulties associated with the distinction
between variable and fixed capital. These latter difficulties should however
become apparent in due course.

Ricardo's contribution and achievement starts from the fact that Adam
Smith had no real theory of distribution; instead, he dealt with factor prices
as costs which added up into the costs of production, which is no theory of
distribution at all, though within that framework Smith displayed a great
deal of empirical common sense about the details of the analysis. Ricardo
was the first to apply rigorous abstraction and theoretical analysis. Although
what emerged was still very much a group of special theories for particular
factors, he did succeed in applying the marginal productivity principle to
the special case of the application of labour (and capital) to land; and his
method of doing so raised problems of capital theory that have been with
us ever since.

Schumpeter's Treatment of Ricardo
We approach the problem first from the insights of J. Schumpeter (*The
History of Economic Analysis*). Ricardo examines the laws determining the
distribution of the national dividend (D) among the rents to land (R), the
wages of labour (W), and the profits to capital (P) from the basic assumption
that:

$$D = P + R + W$$

Our system involves one equation in four unknowns, and so is indeterminate.

(i) Abstracting from the determination of the nation's output, assume that D is fixed and equal to $\overline{D}$. This is a common assumption of modern theory.

(ii) Assume output proceeds to the margin of production on the land, i.e. where there is no rent, so that marginal output is just equal to the cost of the variable factors (labour and capital) required to produce it. Thus the sum of wages and profits equals marginal output on the land,

$$d = p + w.$$

(iii) Introduce the Malthusian law of wages, that the population breeds to the level of subsistence, hence,

$$d = p + \overline{w}$$

or

$$p = d - \overline{w}$$

(profits equal the marginal product of labour minus the subsistence wage rate). (Actually, Ricardo modified the Malthusian law to be consistent with observations that wages were higher than the subsistence level. This renders the theory untestable: populations breed to subsistence except when they don't.)

(iv) To deal with an industrial society, he relates sectors by assuming that the agricultural sector dominates. The rate of profit in industry is determined by that in agriculture. This neglects, however, the general equilibrium problem of the allocation of capital between the sectors and the influence of this on the rate of profit. Just as, in some instances, the small country assumption in international trade theory and the assumption that firms act as price takers is empirically justifiable, so is this Ricardian assumption by virtue of the fact that industry played an insignificant part in generating the national dividend at the time his work was being done.

(v) Note that two of three incomes shares are residuals. Rent is the residual after labour and capital have received their returns and is the excess of total output on intramarginal land over the cost of labour and capital. Profits are a residual after labour is given its subsistence wage.

This presentation of Ricardo's theories reflects his shortcomings as a mathematician without pointing out his achievement as an economist.

Two things are important in understanding the Ricardian theory: (1) the dominance of agriculture at the time, which explains the dominance of agriculture in the theory; and (2) what was meant by capital. Here, capital is a stock of food (wheat) that is used to support the labour force during the period of production and is supplied by the capitalist. In return for advancing labourers food and providing the means for their support during the year, the capitalist gets the total of the workers' product (this is at the margin of production). There are two features of the analysis that should be noticed: (1) Capital is the same as product and no problem of valuation arises as between capital goods and consumption goods. This same advantage is exploited in one-sector growth models where it is assumed that output can be used as capital or as a consumption good. This permits a clear and precise rate of return to be calculated on the capital stock on a purely technological basis without requiring a valuation of capital goods in terms of consumption goods. (2) The period of production is fixed by nature — there is no possibility of subsituting a less or more time-intensive technique of production. Actually, we know that procedures such as crop rotation are available to alter the effective timing of inputs and outputs in the agricultural production process. (These Ricardian notions are fundamental to a great deal of subsequent capital theory. That is to say, capital is presumed to involve the application of original resources over periods of time in a productive process.) Using the assumption of a fixed production period, we avoid the problem of evaluating techniques involving varying lengths of time, although the problems in it are manifest when moving to an industrial society where inputs and outputs are variable in time-intensity.

These qualifications have been much criticized in that they may also be construed as being destructive of the model's relevance. The model has also been criticized for propagating the labour theory of value when, in fact, as Stigler points out, it is an empirical theory with the problems being posed in the context of an economy where labour is the primary source of value and where the problems of capital theory in relation to the industrial process are not central (*American Economic Review*, June, 1958).

A Ricardian Model of the Agricultural Sector

It is important to the understanding of Ricardian theory to note that capital appears only indirectly, in that none is used in the productive process. Labour does all the work, and only labour and land enter the production function; but capital enters indirectly by supporting labour during the production period.

The basis of the theory is that at any time there is a given stock of wheat available to feed workers (the 'wages fund'). In the short run, the actual wage rate is the wages fund divided by the number of workers and may be greater or less than subsistence. The number of workers determines the marginal product of labour, and profits are the difference between this marginal product and the actual wage rate (see Diagram I). In the longer run, labour breeds to the level of subsistence and the given wages fund in conjunction with the subsistence wage determines the number of workers, the marginal product of labour, and profits (see Diagram II).

The difference between Diagram I and Diagram II is that in the former the wages fund is fixed but the number of workers variable, so that we can obtain different equilibria for the same wages fund; in the latter the size of the wages fund determines the quantity of labour according to subsistence-breeding, and different equilibria require different sizes of the wages fund. In the diagrams, y is average output of food per head, p the marginal product of labour (which includes the profit on the wages fund), and w and w_s respectively the actual wage rate and the subsistence wage rate; hence Ow is the real wage, wp profit per man per year, and py rent per man per year. Note that since agriculture is assumed to have a one-year period of production, the ratio of profits to wages is also the rate of profit on capital.

In this model, distribution is determined by the amount and fertility characteristics of available land, the technology for working land, the size of the wages fund and the number of workers (short run) or the subsistence wage (long run.) Capital does not enter the production function directly,

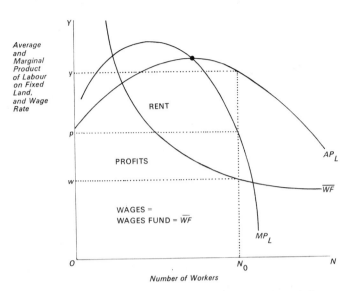

Note: The wages found curve (WF) is a rectangular hyperbola

DIAGRAM I: THE SHORT-RUN RICARDIAN MODEL

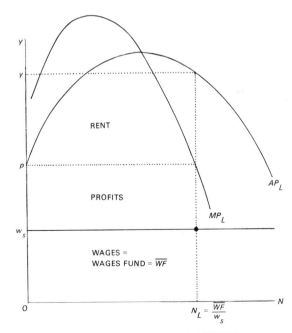

DIAGRAM II: THE MEDIUM-RUN RICARDIAN MODEL

but through the support of labour. (One could also construe the labour as really being capital, since capital is necessary to support it.) If the average product of labour curve is interpreted, at least past its maximum point, as deriving from employment of workers on successively less fertile units of land, it is clear that the marginal land earns no rent; and intramarginal land earns rent because its output exceeds the cost of working it at the competitive wage. If, instead, it is assumed that the same land is worked more and more intensively, the intramarginal units of labour produce more than they cost and hence yield rent to the landowner.

The wages fund is accumulated by the savings of capitalists. In the still longer run, it is assumed that capitalists will accumulate capital as long as the rate of profit exceeds some minimum rate acceptable to them. As they do so, the rate of profit must fall, squeezed between the diminishing marginal productivity of increasing labour applied to a fixed stock of land and the constant subsistence wage. It is obvious from Diagram II that the share of wages must rise as accumulation proceeds. Absolute rent must increase; but whether the share of rent will rise or fall depends on the elasticity of substitution between land and labour — a point to be taken up later. Note, however, that with a Cobb-Douglas production function, the relative shares of rent and of wages-plus-profits would be constants (implying a rising share of wages and falling share of profits) and that for the rent share to rise over time (as the classics tended to assume) requires an elasticity of substitution below unity, which might be a long-run, empirically justifiable assumption.

It is interesting to note that this approach casts the landlords as the opponents of progress. Smith felt that they were for progress as it would seem to raise their rents. Malthus favoured landlords for another reason: increased landlord income would lead them to spend more employing the labour force.

Several questions arise at this point. We have determined the size of the agricultural labour force, but not the total labour force or economic population. First, the total population will include landowners and capitalists and will depend on their numbers, which, in turn, are equal to their total incomes divided by their average incomes. Second, landlords and capitalists will presumably not eat all their incomes, but use some part for employing servants; landlords for example, have a choice between keeping servants and keeping horses to exhaust a stock of food. Third, if we introduce an industrial sector, supported by food from rent and profits, preferences will determine its size and hence the size of the non-rural labour force. Moreover, as capital (food) accumulates, the price of manufactures in terms of food will fall owing to the fall in the rate of profit. Hence, the model abstracts from some important relationships. However, it is applicable to less developed countries as an approximate approach to some important questions.

A final problem involves the nature of the industrial sector, which cannot be assumed to have a fixed, one-year pattern of production. As capital accumulates and the interest rate falls, changes in the prices of industrial goods relative to each other and to food may be produced and so destroy the simplicity of the subsistence wage assumption.

3

POST-RICARDIAN THEORY: THE ADDING-UP PROBLEM

The major advance made by Ricardian theory over that of Adam Smith was the application of the marginal principle to distribution theory. The model envisaged capital as subsistence for the support of labour during the production process, only labour and land directly entering the production process. In particular the theory assumed a fixed stock of land which must impose diminishing returns as additional 'doses' of labour-cum-capital are applied. In the short run, the supply of labour available for employment by a given wages fund can vary accidentally, but in the long run, it is fixed by the principle that labour breeds to the level of subsistence.

The essence of the theory is that capital earns a return that is contingent upon the difference between the marginal productivity of labour in agriculture and the wage rate. The marginal productivity of labour determines the amount and rate of profit, given the breeding-to-subsistence theory of population. However, the theory implies a special law for the incomes of each of the factors and determines two of them in a residual fashion: the share of land is what is left over after labour-capital has been paid its marginal product, and the share of capital (profit) is that which is left after labour has been paid either its wages-fund-share wage or the subsistence wage.

Subsequent developments in distribution theory transcended this reliance on the explanation of income shares as residuals and instead applied the marginal principle to the determination of the rewards to all factors. (This generalization of course applies to the main stream of economic theory; Marx adhered to the concept of surplus and translated it into the language of exploitation, and though his theory of profit is basically a marginal productivity theory he stressed what is a moral and not a theoretical theme, that the owners of capital are not entitled to their profits.) In addition, of course, the marginal principle was applied to the demand side of the analysis, with marginal utility taking the place of marginal product in the analysis of price determination.

Marginal Productivity and Varying Factor Proportions
One of the major contributors to this development was Wicksteed, who perceived that variation in the ratios of the factors, and not in the absolute amount of one of them, was critical in determining the marginal products. He realized that while Ricardian theory held the amount of land fixed, and varied the amount of labour applied to it, this really involved a variation in the land-labour ratio, which could equally well be thought of as a variation in the quantity of land relative to a fixed quantity of labour. In effect, the Ricardian diagram was actually a function in three dimensions (land, labour and output) with a cross-section taken arbitrarily across the land axis;

Wicksteed realized that the cross-section could equally well be taken across the labour axis.

This meant that the Ricardian distinction between labour income determined by marginal productivity and land income received as a surplus was purely arbitrary: either factor's income could be regarded either as marginal product or as surplus. But this posed a new problem: if all factor incomes could be explained by marginal productivity, what was to ensure that the incomes so determined would exactly exhaust the product? (This problem does not arise if one factor is assumed to receive, or possibly to pay, whatever is left over after the others' marginal productivity claims have been satisfied.)

Wicksteed's answer was the assumption of constant returns to scale. A proof, on geometrical lines but actually employing the disregard of second-order effects of the differential calculus, can be provided with reference to Diagram I. In the diagram, capital is disregarded and only labour and land

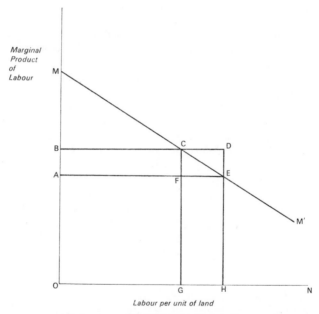

DIAGRAM I: THE ADDING-UP PROBLEM

are assumed to take part in production; for simplicity the marginal product of labour is assumed to be a linear function of the number of workers employed on land. Land is assumed to consist of a fixed number of exactly identical tracts, the diagram representing the marginal product of labour as increasing quantities of labour are applied to any given piece of land. (This assumption of homogeneity of land removes the problem of the external margin of cultivation, and guarantees constant returns to scale, since an equal multiplication of the quantities of labour and land would increase total output in the same proportion.) The initial equilibrium at E represent a given number of workers and a given number of the identical pieces of land. There are two ways of establishing the proposition that, for small changes and in the limit, the rent earned by an additional unit of land will just equal both the rent earned by the existing land and the total increase in national product due to the addition of that land. The latter proposition — that an additional unit of land just earns its marginal contribution to total output — solves the adding-up problem.

Geometrical Proofs of Adding-up Property

(i) Assume that labour is abstracted from each of the existing pieces of land to the extent required to cultivate the new piece of land in the same way as the pre-existing land has been cultivated. The new land earns the rent of existing land, and the labour employed on it earns the same wage as in the pre-existing situation. However, on the old land, labour employed falls from OH to OG, and output falls from area $OMEH$ to area $OMCG$, a loss of $GCEH$. Of area $GCEH$, the rectangle $GFEH$ represents the earnings that the abstracted labour is earning on the new piece of land, while the triangle FCE, multiplied by the pre-existing number of units of land, represents the net loss of output on the pre-existing units of land due to the shift of labour to the new unit. Both the base and the height of this triangle are determined by the number of workers shifted off each pre-existing piece of land, and this varies inversely with the number of pre-existing pieces of land, while the total loss of output is the size of the triangle multiplied by the number of pre-existing pieces of land. It is therefore obvious that the larger the number of pre-existing pieces of land the smaller is the loss of output on pre-existing land to be deducted from the rent of the new land to arrive at the net increase in output due to the addition of the new land. In the limit, the net loss of output on the old land approximates to zero, and rent of the new land is equal to the total increase in output resulting from its addition.

Mathematically, let $m = -\partial M/\partial n$ be the slope of the marginal productivity curve on a single piece of land with respect to the number n of workers employed on it, and Δn be the reduction in number of workers per existing unit of land required to man the new piece of land at the old labour-land ratio. Then the net loss of output per unit of pre-existing land will be the area of the triangle, i.e.

$$\tfrac{1}{2} \cdot \Delta n(m \cdot \Delta n) = \tfrac{1}{2}m(\Delta n)^2$$

and the total net loss of output on all units of pre-existing land

$$A \cdot \tfrac{1}{2}m(\Delta n)^2,$$

where A is the number of pre-existing units of land. Δn itself will be simply N/A, where N is the total amount of labour available. Hence the total net loss will be

$$\tfrac{1}{2}m\left(\frac{N}{A}\right)^2$$

which will vanish as A approaches infinity.

(ii) Assume instead that labour is reallocated so as to equalize its marginal product on the new and the old pieces of land. Labour per unit of land falls from *OH* to *OG* (note that *GH* is smaller in this case than in the previous one, since the new land is not fully manned up to the pre-existing standard), the wages of labour rise from *OA* to *OB*, and rent per unit of land falls from *MAE* to *MBC*. On the pre-existing land, output falls from *OMEH* to *OMCG*; of the smaller output, *ABCF* is redistributed from land-owners to labour. The net loss of output per unit of pre-existing land is *GCEH*; but the labour abstracted now earns *GCDH* in wages, so that there is a net gain for labour of *CDE*. Hence the new land has added its own rent *MBC* to national product, but also a net gain for labour consisting of the triangle *CDE* multiplied by the number of pre-existing units of land. Its rent now therefore understates its total contribution to the increase of production. However, again by increasing the number of pre-existing units of land, the size of the triangle *CDE* can be made negligible. And since its size is proportional to the square of the number of workers reallocated to the new piece of land, whereas the total additional output accruing to labour and not counted in the rent of the additional unit of land varies only proportionally to the quantity of pre-existing land, a sufficient increase in the number of pre-existing units of land will make this additional gain in output negligible and the rent of the additional unit of land approximate the total contribution it makes to increasing the output of the economy.

Euler's Theorem

Contemporary economic theory establishes the exact exhaustion of the product by marginal productivity payments to factors, much more simply, by the use of Euler's Theorem, though it should be noted that this theorem makes use of the same disregard of small secondary effects as has had to be argued in the preceding analysis.

Let $X = f(L, C)$ be a general production function relating output X to inputs of labour and capital. Then, if there are constant returns to scale, an equi-proportional change in the inputs will change the output in the same proportion, i.e.

$$\lambda X = f(\lambda L, \lambda C).$$

Let $\lambda = 1/L$; then $X/L = f(1, C/L) = g(C/L)$ since 1 is a constant; and $X = L . g(C/L)$.

The marginal products of the factors are

$$\frac{\partial X}{\partial L} = g(C/L) - g'(C/L)C/L$$

$$\frac{\partial X}{\partial C} = g'(C/L)$$

and $L\dfrac{\partial X}{\partial L} + C\dfrac{\partial X}{\partial L} = L . g(C/L) - C . g'(C/L) + C . g'(C/L)$

$$= L . g(C/L) = X.$$

Economics of Constant Returns to Scale: The Debate

Payments by marginal productivity, however, only exhaust the product exactly if there are constant returns to scale. The 'adding-up problem' then became the question of whether it is reasonable or not to assume that there are constant returns to scale in production, since this is an empirical question not intuitively obviously to be answered in the affirmative. There has subsequently been much controversy over the realism of constant returns to scale; this however is a spurious issue, as will be explained shortly. It may be noted in passing, however, an argument popularized by Samuelson and others, that from a technical point of view decreasing returns to scale can be ruled out and constant returns regarded as the limiting case of increasing returns to scale, since at worst the scale of production could be increased by duplicating existing production techniques; hence diminishing returns to scale must represent a limitation on the supply of one or more factors (which limitation may be suppressed into the form of the production function rather than represented in its arguments).

Knight, and following him Stigler, noticed that constant returns to scale are required to explain distribution only in the case of perfect competition: in conditions of monopoly, the monopoly profit is a surplus that can absorb any excess of total product over factor payments, or in the case of increasing returns monopolistic price-fixing will ensure that factors do not receive the values of their marginal products. Under conditions of perfect competition, they argued, there must be constant returns to the individual firm, because if there are increasing returns to scale for the firm one firm will become a monopoly and the conditions of competition will cease to apply, whereas if there are decreasing returns to scale firms will become infinitesimally small, a condition inconsistent with the facts of empirical observation.

This solution to the problem left some problems that are apparent but not real. First, with constant returns to scale the size of the firm is clearly indeterminate; but this is not a real problem, since under competitive conditions the size of the firm is irrelevant, it is the size of the industry that is determined by demand and supply and is the object of economic interest. Second, for the same reason, it would seem that a firm would have an incentive to grow until it produced all the output of the industry, and could then proceed to charge monopoly prices; but this is inconsistent with the assumptions of the model, since any effort on its part to do so would bring in new firms enjoying the same costs as itself and able to undersell it. Third, there is the problem that any chance variation from the equilibrium price would either eliminate all output or induce an infinite output from the constant-cost firms; this source of instability of output and price, while familiar in agriculture in the 'cobweb' or 'corn-hog' cycle theory, can be disposed of by reference to time-lags in adjustment and to the availability of information on an industry-wide basis, though it is true enough that in oligopolistic large-firm industries there are cycles of over-investment and under-investment in new capacity.

Economics of Constant Returns to Scale: The Solution

The fundamental solution to the adding-up problem has been provided subsequently by Hicks and Samuelson. The basic point is that the requirement of 'adding-up' has nothing to do with the technology of production. It is a requirement imposed by the assumption of market conditions of perfect competition, which implies the absence of both profits and losses. If the logic of factor-utilization choice implies payment by marginal productivity, and the logic of perfect competition implies zero profits, the competitors in the market must choose points on their production possibility technology such that both requirements are fulfilled.

Mathematically, we have the perfect competition condition that value of product must equal cost of production, i.e.

$$pX = \sum_i w_i q_i$$

where the w_i are factor prices and the q_i factor quantities. We also have the marginal productivity principle of employment of factors,

$$w_i = p \cdot \frac{\partial X}{\partial q_i}.$$

Hence it follows that

$$X = \sum_i \frac{\partial X}{\partial q_i} q_i,$$

in other words that marginal productivity payments must exhaust the product under perfect competition.

The same point can be made with reference to the standard price and cost-curve analysis of the equilibrium of the firm under perfect competition, illustrated in Diagram II.

Competition ensures that any firm that remains in the industry will be producing at the minimum point of its average cost curve, the cost curve

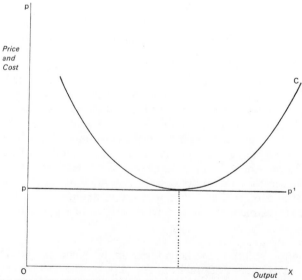

DIAGRAM II: PERFECT COMPETITIVE EQUILIBRIUM OF THE FIRM

itself being U-shaped on the assumption that the firm is constrained by its entrepreneurial capacity in one way or another. At the minimum average cost point, the cost curve indicates local constancy of returns to scale of output, so that the requirements of the adding-up problem are fulfilled.

There are two points to notice about this last argument. First, if firms are assumed to be of different efficiencies, those of superior efficiency will have cost curves lying below those of the others and will enjoy a surplus of price over cost, i.e. a profit. Their output will be determined by the intersection of marginal cost and price, and their costs will be above minimum potential average cost, according to standard marginal analysis of output determination. They therefore will appear to be subject to diminishing returns, their profits representing the excess of price over marginal productivity payments to the factors they employ. However, these profits can be regarded as marginal productivity payments to whatever factor of production enables the firm to earn these profits; and under competitive conditions that factor (be it scarce managerial talent or superior technology) could be rented out to another firm for the same price as the rent it earns in this firm. Consequently, the cost curve of this firm, including both hired-in factors and the rental value of the superior-efficiency factor or factors it owns itself, will also be a U-shaped curve tangent to the price line.

The second point is that the conclusion that marginal productivity payments to factors will exactly exhaust the product under conditions of zero-profit competition can readily be extended to conditions of imperfect or monopolistic competition provided that competition among the firms involved eliminates monopoly profits. All that needs to be done is to re-define p in Diagram II as marginal revenue and the cost curve as the cost of earning additional revenue.

4

POST-RICARDIAN THEORY: THE GENERALIZATION OF THE CLASSICAL INCOME CATEGORIES

As explained in the preceding chapter, it was gradually recognized that the theory of distribution must be regarded as an application of the general theory of determination of price by supply and demand, in the form of the marginal productivity principle. At the level of formal analysis, this raised the question of the consistency of the results with exact distribution of the social product — the 'adding-up problem' — a matter over which there was considerable confusion until it became generally accepted that the problem was imposed by the assumption of perfect competition and that with that constraint the choice of output had to conform locally to constant returns to scale.

The extrication of the theory of distribution from its classical setting of identification of individual factors with social classes also cleared the way for the development of analytical rather than sociological distinctions among the classical categories of income — though it must be acknowledged that large bodies of the contemporary economic literature continue to identify factors with social classes, and this is especially true of the advanced mathematical models of economic growth (with which we shall be concerned later on).

A great deal of this development, as regards the main body of the English-language literature at any rate, is due to Alfred Marshall, whose massive *Principles of Economics* was used world-wide as a textbook for almost half a century, until it was replaced by the contemporary champion textbook, Samuelson's *Economics*. That replacement reflects both the transfer of leadership in the field from England to the United States, and the fact, previously mentioned, that out of deference to his predecessors Marshall disguised the importance of some of his new ideas and failed to follow others through to their logical conclusion. (In addition, for reasons which reflect both the social structure of Victorian England and Marshall's obvious desire to differentiate his product from those of some of his brilliant contemporaries, such as Jevons and Edgeworth, he addressed himself to a presumptive audience of intelligent businessmen and civil servants, anxious for truth and impatient of theoretical niceties, rather than to professional colleagues interested in the methods and techniques of the subject and capable both of spotting errors and improving on the analysis — a methodological mistake a number of English economists still continue to make.)

The Theory of Rent

Marshall's major contribution, in the context of the Ricardian model, was to jettison the special position of the rent of land, regarded as the demand- or price-determined income of a factor of production in fixed supply, and to call attention to the fact that each of the specific factors used in the production process may be in fixed supply temporarily, for a shorter or longer period, so that their incomes constitute a 'quasi-rent' (in contemporary language, a sort of rent); and consequently the rent of land proper is merely 'the leading species of a large genus' (abandoning the biological terminology characteristic of Marshall, Veblen and others, in the post-Newtonian physics phase of economic analysis, land rent is only an extreme case of a generally-observable phenomenon). However, Marshall's exposition of this basic point still remained deferential to the classical position on the special place of land, as is indeed reflected in the nomenclature of 'quasi-rent' to describe the rents earned by other factors in temporarily fixed supply such as industrial equipment or skilled labour. In particular, he attempted to maintain the classical position that land rent is a surplus and not a cost from a social point of view, at least in old countries. This position assumed the validity of the Ricardian view that there are 'original and indestructible properties of the soil', which a great deal of recent work on reclamation, depletion, and the effects of fertilization shows to be invalid. It also ignores the point that, if one considers the total economy, the earnings of the existing stock of capital or labour force constitute a surplus and not a cost in exactly the same way, since the supply would respond only over time to a change in price. And it disregarded the fact that from the standpoint of the individual agriculturalist the rent he pays for his land is very definitely a cost, the cost of attracting that land out of alternative uses into his own employ.

Profits and Interest: The Nature of Interest
A second major development was the separation of the concept of profits from the concept of interest. In the classical model the two were identical, 'profits' being a rate of return on capital of the same dimensions as the rate of interest. This treatment virtually completely ignored the role of the entrepreneur in a dynamic world, and regarded him simply as providing the capital for production and, by virtue of this fact, assuming control of the management of enterprise. Marshall clearly recognized a difference between profits and interest, and treated interest as the return on money capital. (Once this money capital had been invested in concrete form, machinery and structures and so forth, its return became a quasi-rent.) But he carried on the classical tradition, in the sense of attempting to deal with entrepreneurship and the resulting profits as a fourth factor of production, identified to some extent with a fourth social class, and distinguished between that part of the earnings of the entrepreneur which could be attributed to contributions of labour and of pure capital, and that part that was attributable to a fourth factor entering the production function, i.e. 'management'. The attempt to identify 'management' as a fourth factor of production additional to labour, land and capital reflected on the one hand Marshall's loyalty to the classical tradition, in which productive contributions had to be identified with factor inputs into the production function, and on the other hand his desire to write for businessmen considered as a social class, in terms that they could understand and would consider appealing.

For Marshall, interest was the return on pure money capital, and profits the return on an amalgam of money capital and routine administrative labour input and a special productive service called 'management'. This view of management as a special kind of input still survives in the literature; but it misses the economic essence of profit. Similarly, the Marshallian view of interest as a payment for money capital misses the essence of the nature of interest.

To take the latter point first, while various Continental writers had a much clearer view than Marshall of interest as the payment for the use of resources over time (resources, not just 'money capital'), the major breakthrough in economic understanding came with the work of the American Irving Fisher on the relation between capital and interest. On the Fisherian view, income is a stream of contributions to output yielded by a source; and capital is the value of that source, arrived at by capitalizing the value of the stream of productive contributions produced by means of the current rate of interest. Interest is simply the relation between income flows and the capital values of the resources that produce them. Anything that yields a contribution to output is capital and has a capital value. (However, the determination of the rate of interest that should be used to relate income flow to capital value is itself obviously a theoretical problem which will be discussed later.) This view involves a major departure from the Marshallian — and preceding Ricardian — view that capital and interest are to be identified with a particular social class of income recipients, a particular role in the production process, and a particular item in the national income accounts. Its fuller implications will be discussed later in this book.

The Nature of Profits

Turning to profits, the classical view regarded these (which were not distinguished from interest on capital) as the flow reward for a contribution to the flow of production. The Marshallian treatment of them simply sought to distinguish that contribution from the pure provision of money capital at interest without risk on the one hand, and the pure provision of routine labour services on the other. At least, however, Marshall sought to identify a distinguishing contribution; a variety of contemporary theories, ranging from Marxian theories on the one hand to 'institutional' theories on the other, seek to identify profits with the institutional facts of ownership. (My one-time Cambridge tutor, the Communist Maurice Dobb, produced a brilliant Ph.D. thesis at the beginning of the 1920s which argued plausibly, but not convincingly in the light of hindsight, that regardless of the observed phenomena of entrepreneurship the ownership of capital was its essence; little if any modern work has reached Dobb's understanding of the theoretical issues involved, regardless of what one thinks of his own answer to the problem.)

If profits are to be distinguished from interest on capital, it cannot simply be because they are derived from a mixture of interest on capital and other flow productive inputs; it must be because of a difference in the nature of the contribution that the recipients of profits make to production, as distinct from the contribution of the recipients of interest on capital. That difference has to do with the fact that the recipients of interest on capital — like the recipients of rent on land and the wages of labour — normally receive a contractual income, whereas the recipient of profits is the individual who contracts to give incomes to others in return for specified services, and assumes the risk that his net receipts from the sale of their products will be less than the value of his time and efforts, in return for the possibility that these net receipts will exceed the alternative opportunity cost of his time and effort and therefore yield him an uncovenanted benefit. Thus profit (and loss) are associated with differences in both perceptions about the future and the willingness to take risks between those who prefer a contractual income and those who are willing to take the risks of entrepreneurship in the face of uncertainty about the future.

This point was recognized in the nineteenth century in the Continental literature, in the theoretical propositions that the owners of any one of the factors of production as conventionally defined could be the entrepreneurs, and that competition would tend to eliminate profits as a category of income. This view is to be contrasted with the Marshall-Cambridge School view that entrepreneurs are a distinct social class deriving their role from the possession of capital, and that the effect of competition among them is to produce a 'normal rate of profit' which represents the summation of the value of their administrative labour, the interest on their capital, and a risk premium. The point is of considerable contemporary importance, because the popular theory of capitalism stresses that only capitalists in the conventional sense, i.e. those who already possess material capital and are prepared to risk it, are competent to manage a capitalist system, whereas it is perfectly possible, and indeed characteristic of many 'non-capitalist' economies, that either the consumers, in that capacity through co-operatives or as tax-payers through nationalized enterprises, or the workers through 'worker-controlled' enterprises, assume the entrepreneurial role. Capital can be provided, not only by subscriptions from those who possess it in money form, but by loan and loss guarantees through the power of the state to levy taxes on the national income, by a guaranteed flow of purchases and willingness to accept a variable consumer dividend by the members of co-operatives, and by a willingness of workers to accept a minimum wage rate plus a variable share of the profits of the enterprise. And there is no *a priori* reason to think that the selection of the management and the efficiency of the enterprise will be significantly better under the money-subscription form of capitalism than under the tax or income or wages subscription systems, though it must be admitted that empirically there is reason to think that the tax-subscription system and the income-subscription system lead to inefficiency both because consumers, either as consumers or as taxpayers, are unwilling to pay as much as the job of management is worth, and because as typically small-income-earners they attempt to impose on the enterprise the obligation of paying above-market-equilibrium wages under the impression that this will help to better the lot of people like themselves.

While the notion of profit as in some sense a return for the willingness to take risks in a dynamic environment helps to fit profits into the framework of static equilibrium analysis, as a payment for a flow contribution to the production process, it misses the essence of the economic nature of profits, which are not an income flow but a capital gain associated with the exploita-tion of the possibilities of dynamic change in the economy. As mentioned, the entrepreneur (whatever his character, which has been discussed in the previous paragraph), contracts to pay the regular flow-productive-service-producing factors of production a fixed income, necessarily based on their current marginal productivity elsewhere and their alternative opportunity cost, in the expectation that by employing them he can achieve a value of sales greater than his contractual payments and so earn a profit (more specifically, the profit has to exceed what he could himself have earned by hiring himself out on contractual terms to another entrepreneur — though it is possible that he can exercise his entrepreneurial talents in his leisure time, in which case the prospective income needed to make entrepreneurship attractive is the alternative opportunity cost of his leisure).

Seminal Theories of Profit

There are two seminal contributions to the theory of profits, both departing from the late nineteenth-century view of the economic process as a static equilibrium system. The first is that of J. A. Schumpeter, who depicted entrepreneurship as a process of disturbing an established static equilibrium of prices and factor rewards by an innovation in productive technology. The result in the longer run was a new static equilibrium in which all incomes were imputed to existing factors. The gain of the entrepreneur was not a continuing flow of profits, but an increase in the income and therefore the capital value of some factor or factors that he happened to own — the increase of income perhaps or perhaps not appearing as an increase in 'profits' conventionally defined — the increased productivity of the factor or factors in question being 'imputed', on the lines of Austrian theory, to the factors of production by the competitive process. Schumpeter's theory of profits is clearly strongly time-bound by his fascination with the Walrasian theory of general equilibrium, which obliged him to cast his theory in terms of static general equilibrium states interrupted by bouts of entrepreneurial innovation, after which the economy settles down to a new static general equilibrium. It is also influenced by the Marxian view that interest is a purely monopolistically-determined claim on the income achieved by entrepreneurship. (This view, incidentally, gave rise to a long-standing dispute among Harvard economists over whether in the long run the rate of interest would tend to zero, as Schumpeter claimed, or whether it would approximate to the rate of time preference, as neoclassical theory claimed.) Nevertheless, the Schumpeterian analysis has important implications for contemporary theory, both in the sense that profits in the true meaning are a capital gain from innovation and not a flow of income, and in the sense that innovations eventually become transmitted into factor incomes and the return gained by making them disappears from the measured income of the economy. This last point is of particular importance in relation to the contribution of scientific research to the growth of real income per head, since while in the early stages research and development expenditure can be patented or protected by commercial secrecy, thus yielding a return measurable in royalties or abnormal profits, basic scientific research yields its returns in the form of contributions to a general pool of knowledge out of which commercial enterprises can draw without paying anything for the privilege. (This particular problem is covered later by the theory of common property resources, though students may have difficulty in making the intellectual connection.).

The other seminal contribution to the theory of profits is F. H. Knight's *Risk, Uncertainty, and Profit*. Knight distinguishes between risk, which can be pooled on an actuarial basis, and genuine uncertainty which cannot be. The competitive system will pool the risks via one or another form of insurance; but someone has to bear the uncertainties. This means that someone has to bear the burden of hiring the factors of production at contractually-fixed prices, in the expectation of making a gain by predicting the outcome of an uncertain future more accurately than his competitive entrepreneurs can do. The general proposition that emerges is that if entrepreneurs of this type are limited in number, restricted in resources, and fairly accurate in their predictions, they will make positive profits. If on the contrary they are many, well-endowed, and not very prescient, they will as a group make losses. Knight is rather pessimistic about the relative probabilities of aggregate gains and losses, and the example of restaurants and other small businesses tends to bear him out. Adam Smith called attention to the fact that, in the business of law, a few large prizes attracted people who on the average earned less than they could have earned in other more regular professions; and it is quite possible that on the whole society devotes more resources to entrepreneurship than are adequately recompensed, regardless of the earning of a few large fortunes, especially as all current income tax systems offer higher rewards for income accruing in the form of capital gains on successful entrepreneurship than for income earned by a steady regular input into the production process of either labour time or the services of capital.

A Generalization of the Classical Income Categories

It will be apparent from the foregoing discussion of the evolution of the theory of distribution since Ricardo that the classical identification of income categories with social classes is no longer tenable. Any specific factor may earn a rent, and in fact if it is fixed in supply its earnings will be demand-determined. Similarly, the earnings of any factor can be regarded as interest on the capital value of its prospective services; and any factor-owner may be a profit-or-loss-making entrepreneur, in either of two senses. First, the owner of that factor may undertake the entrepreneurial task of hiring the other factors at contractual payment rates and assuming the residual responsibility for losses in return for the possibility of making profits. Second, a point implicit rather than explicit in the preceding discussion, the owner of any factor that has been created by past investment (such as labour skill) or that will yield its services only over a succession of periods in the future (again such a labour skill) stands to make a profit or loss on actual future earnings by comparison with the expected earnings that prompted the creation or acquisition of the factor in the first place. In other words, every factor income can be thought of as involving elements of wages, rent, interest and profits.

Nevertheless, it is possible through insight to make use of the classical categories of income, if one regards them as angles of analytical approach to factor incomes rather than as income categories distinguishing factors of production one from another. The key useful ideas are the distinction between 'wages' as a necessary cost of production, and 'rent' as the demand-determined price of a factor in fixed supply, or more generally as a surplus over the necessary costs of production; and between 'interest' as the normal reward for past investment in the acquisition of a factor of production, and 'profit' as a surplus (and 'loss' as a deficiency) of the reward earned by past investment in relation to the contractual costs involved in that investment.

To use these concepts and distinctions, it is necessary to distinguish between analysis of the economy at a point of time, when the supplies of factors in specific form may be assumed to be either fixed or elastic only because their owners are prepared to withdraw them from productive employment if the market price for their services is unsatisfactory, and analysis of the economy over time, when factor supplies may be assumed to be to some extent at least elastic with respect to expected earnings over time.

At a particular point of time, assuming for simplicity that the supplies of factors of specific qualities — land, buildings, types of skilled labour — are given, the competitive process will allocate these supplies among uses in a general equilibrium for the economy as a whole. Each factor will receive a price for its services, which will be determined by its relative quantity and the general-equilibrium interaction of demand and supply. Of this price, in any particular employment, part will represent the opportunity cost of this factor in that employment, i.e. the price it could earn in the next-best-paid employment, and part (which may be zero) the excess of that price over the alternative opportunity price. Clearly, the division between the opportunity cost or 'wage' element and the surplus over necessary cost or 'rent' element depends on the size or the level of aggregation of the particular factor considered. For example, a particular piece of land may be earning no more rent when used for market-gardening than it would earn if devoted to housing; but if all demand for the services of land were to disappear, the land would still exist, so that in that context the alternative opportunity cost of land would be zero and all its actual earnings rent. Similarly, a machine-tool operator in a particular plant might earn only the going wage for machine-tool operators in the economy; but machine-tool operators as a group might be earning well above the wages they could earn if a change in demand forced them to revert to the status of semi-skilled workers. (This is the ultimate position of the Marshallian theory of rent as developed by G. F. Shove and exposited in Chapter 8 of Joan Robinson's *The Economics of Imperfect Competition*.)

From the longer-run point of view, all specific factors can be considered to be the result of the investment of resources in the past in a specific form. This proposition includes not only buildings and capital equipment, but labour skills, which can be created by education and training, and land itself, which can be 'created' by the construction of transport facilities, irrigation and electrification, and the longer-run use of fertilizers. Factors can also be decreased in supply by letting the existing stock depreciate without replacement: machines can be scrapped, workers allowed to grow old and retire without replacement by new entrants, and land can be allowed to erode and become idle. The current earnings of a specific factor can accordingly be regarded as a return on the past investment involved in creating it or maintaining its productive existence. Conceptually, the 'quasi-rent' involved can be divided into two components which parallel the distinction between necessary cost and surplus in the short-run analysis. The first is interest at the prevailing market rate on the past investment that created the factor; the second is a surplus or deficiency of the actual income in relation to that imputed interest charge, representing under-estimations or over-estimations of the actual returns when the initial investment in the specific factor was undertaken. Of course, this notional difference between expected and actual income flow will not be observed in the market-place; instead, since the market will continually revalue the expected income flow from existing productive assets at the current rate of interest, the difference between expected and actual returns will typically appear as a capital gain or loss for the owners of the factors in question. (The exception is human capital in the form of labour skill, for which no explicit capital market exists, though an implicit market exists in the sense that the wage or salary employee can borrow against his future earning power in such forms as house mortgages and instalment credit for consumer durables.) Nevertheless, people do commonly make comparisons between their actual and their expected incomes from their own labour and their assets.

To summarize, we can represent the classical income categories as involving a four-fold categorization of aspects of the income of a particular specific factor of production, on the one hand between necessary costs and surplus (or, in the case of profit and loss, possibly deficit), and on the other hand between current income as determined by demand and factor availability and current income related to past investment in the creation of the existing supplies of factors of production. This categorization can be summarized in Diagram I.

	Necessary payment	Surplus or deficiency
Current income receipts	WAGES	RENT (always non-negative)
Current income receipts related to past investment	INTEREST	PROFIT (or loss)

DIAGRAM I: THE CLASSICAL CATEGORIES OF INCOME

5

PROBLEMS IN THE APPLICATION OF MARGINAL PRODUCTIVITY THEORY

The marginal productivity theory of distribution has been discussed so far in the aggregative terms characteristic of the classical concern with the distribution of income among social classes. Once one begins to disaggregate the economy and look at the application of the principle to the earnings of particular groups of factors, and especially of different groups of labour, various problems and complications arise. Some of these complications and problems are spurious, and arise from two *a priori* non-scientific attitudes. The first, essentially religious in origin, is the strong aversion of the ordinary man and particularly the intellectual to regard labour service as an economic object with a market value determined by demand and supply. Scientific questions of the determination of the market value of labour thus become confused with the ethical evaluation of the resulting distribution of income. It must be admitted in this connection, however, that some of the marginal productivity theorists, especially the American contributors of the late nineteenth and early twentieth centuries, tended to present wage-determination by marginal productivity as not merely a positive but also a normative principle. The view of the majority of contemporary economists is that the fact that income distribution is determined by factor ownership has nothing to do with the fairness or otherwise of the distribution of factor ownership itself, and that factor ownership distribution rather than the pricing process should be the focus of concern about inequality of incomes and the poverty problem. The second source of spurious problems is the natural tendency of 'practical' people to focus on the facts of nature as they see them — which appear to entail rigidity in the ratios of productive factors one to another in any particular production process — and thus to fail to comprehend the infinite possibilities of substitution both among factors in particular production processes and between production processes themselves and the commodities they produce, on which the operation of the marginal productivity principle depends. It should be noted at this point, however, that there is a subtle difficulty of a fundamental kind involved in the notion of substitutability between capital and labour, arising from the fact that 'capital' as used in the production process is not an 'original' factor but itself the product of past capital and labour, so that substitution in the aggregate between capital and labour involves a change in the rate of interest (by which the cost of production of capital is cumulated over time into the relative cost of capital goods). This problem, which is not the one that ordinary minds have with the concept of substitutability between capital and labour, involves deep questions concerning the nature of capital and will occupy us in great detail later in the course, will be reverted to briefly later in this lecture.

Once we begin to disaggregate and distinguish many factors, the major problems that arise concern questions of imperfections in the markets for particular goods and factors; determination of wages through non-competitive processes such as collective bargaining and administrative wage (and price) fixing; and immobility of factors among occupations and firms. There is also the problem that the use of a particular factor in a particular firm or industry may generate positive or negative 'externalities', i.e. positive or negative contributions to output elsewhere in the economy which are not captured by the employer and therefore by the owner of the factor in question. Such externalities, however, pertain mainly to the normative questions of whether competition results in the achievement of a social maximum output, and whether factors earn exactly their contribution to the social output, rather than to the positive theory of distribution.

The implications of market imperfections, in both the product and the factor markets, occupied a great deal of attention following the 'imperfect-monopolistic competition' revolution of the 1930s, which substituted for the perfect-competition assumption of parametric product and factor prices to the individual firm the assumptions that product price must fall as sales increase and factor price may rise as quantity employed increases. In consequence, the value of the marginal product of a factor (physical marginal product multiplied by product price) will exceed the marginal value product of the factor (physical marginal product multiplied by marginal revenue), since in order to sell the extra product produced by a marginal increment in employment of a factor the employer must reduce the price. Similarly, the marginal cost of employing an additional unit of a factor will exceed the price of the factor, because the price paid to all factor units must be increased.

Market Imperfections

The general condition that emerges from these considerations, for the maximization of employer profit from the use of factors of production, is the equality of marginal revenue from the use of a factor and the marginal cost of employing it, i.e.

$$\left(1 - \frac{1}{\eta}\right) p_x \frac{\partial x}{\partial a} = p_a \left(1 + \frac{1}{\varepsilon_a}\right)$$

where η is the elasticity of demand for the product, p_x is the product price, $\partial x/\partial a$ is the physical marginal product of the factor A, p_a is the price of the factor A, and η_a is the elasticity of supply of that factor. Note that if both perfect elasticity of demand for the product and perfect elasticity of supply of the factor are assumed, the equation reduces to the traditional equality of value of marginal product and price of factor. Note also that if we assume that competition, in the general form of free entry into the industry, prevails and eliminates abnormal profits, marginal value productivity payments to the factors of production will exactly exhaust the product.

Since the 1930s' flurry of enthusiasm about market imperfections, it has come to be recognized that such imperfections make little difference from the point of view of positive economics. That is, it remains true, as under the assumption of perfect competition, that an increase in demand will tend to raise both price and quantity produced, and a fall in factor prices to lower price and increase quantity produced. The exceptions arise where there is oligopoly or oligopsony (Chamberlin's 'small group' case) and even there contemporary theory argues that self-interest will lead oligopoly and oligopsony industries respectively to behave like monopolists and monopsonists, in which case the same qualititative conclusions about the response of quantities and prices to changes in demand and supply data will follow, as follow under the assumptions of perfect competition. The precise quantitative magnitudes of the resulting changes will of course depend on the relevant empirical parameters.

The main implications of market imperfections for economic analysis, as J. R. Hicks recognized early on in a percipient survey article in *Econometrica*, concern normative analysis or welfare economics as contrasted with positive economics. In the 1930s, Joan Robinson, Richard Kahn and others viewed imperfect competition as involving the 'exploitation' of the factors of production by the employers, because payment by marginal value productivity meant payment of less than the value of the marginal product. To arrive at this position they had to ignore the productive contribution of the entrepreneur, who, according to the general theory of marginal productivity payment under imperfect competition, would also receive less than the value of his marginal product. In the general version of the theory, all factors including the entrepreneur are 'exploited' in the same sense. If everyone is exploited more or less equally, it would appear that no-one is really being exploited at all, or that if someone is being exploited, it requires an empirical knowledge of the parameters in question to determine who it is.

Attention then shifted to the more interesting question, still fascinating to radicals, or at least to the more amateur economists among them, of whether society could not be made better off by reducing the scope of product differentiation and forcing the industrial system to supply a smaller number of varieties, or only one variety, of each product, thereby enabling the consumer to purchase that product at a lower cost of production. The essential problem here is that consumers are willing to pay for variety; further, given the competition between the brand-named products and the store-named products (such as Sears in the United States and Marks & Spencer in the United Kingdom offer their customers) there is no real reason to assume that consumers are forced to choose among branded products only, so that there is an interference with market competition requiring social action. The 1930s' solution was to weigh the total consumers' surplus enjoyed on the differentiated products against the cost saving that could be accomplished by standardizing production, i.e. integrate the areas under the demand curves for the differentiated products and subtract the cost of production, then compare the results with the area under the demand curve for the standardized product minus the (lower) cost of producing it. Contemporary economics, following the work of Kelvin Lancaster and others, has produced a different approach, according to which each differentiated 'product' is a bundle of characteristics — such as power, braking capacity, speed, comfort, radio and other accessories, and style in the case of an automobile — and competition tends to be perfect in terms of the supplies of the characteristics even though it appears to be imperfect in terms of the competition among commodities embodying different bundles of characteristics.

Collective and Other Forms of Bargaining

It is a fact of common observation that frequently the price attached to the services of a factor is determined by bargaining, either individual or collective. Individual bargaining can be readily understood as a consequence of the fact that each specific factor has its own characteristics, differentiating it from other specific factors belonging to the same general class (cf. Hicks' *Theory of Wages*), and that bargains can always be renegotiated. A further consideration is that not everything involved in an employment contract can be negotiated simultaneously: for example, a university may be willing to pay an above-market price for an assistant professor, in the expectation that if he does not live up to his promise it will not have to raise his pay in subsequent years or promote him; and an assistant professor may accept a salary lower than his apparent market value in the expectation that he will learn enough at the university he contracts with to increase his future earning power by more than he loses through accepting a below-market salary.

Collective bargaining, as represented by negotiations between trade unions and employers, or administrative fixing of wage levels, can be thought of as fixing the price dimension of the contract rather than selling the quantity for its market value. At a superficial level, i.e. taking the price fixed as arbitrarily given, the quantity employed will adjust to the price so that the equality of marginal productivity with factor price will be attained, not by price, but by quantity, adjustment. At a more sophisticated level, the bargaining process may be thought of as a way of assembling the kind of market information about product demand and factor supply that in theory a perfect market would supply. While economics possesses theories of bargaining, in the form specifically of the economic theory of games, these theories to be interesting have to assume that there is some kind of undistributed joint monopoly power which the bargaining process is used to distribute; and, as in the case of oligoply or oligopsony, one would presume that there exists a bargain that will maximize the welfare of both sides to the bargain, taking account of the overall economic situation. In other words, theories of bargaining power have to assume a situation of partial ignorance on the part of at least one party to the process, because only in a situation of ignorance can strategy, personality, forcefulness and the other elements of what is normally thought of as bargaining power be effective in achieving otherwise unwarranted gains for one of the parties. (It might be noted that in a situation of overall inflation proceeding at a variable rate, both sides to a wage bargain must be under considerable uncertainty about the real value or cost to them of a decision fixing the money rate of wages; in this case, 'bargaining power' may well become a relevant consideration.)

Immobility of Factors

Immobility of factors of production, occupational and geographical, will give rise to differences in the earnings of the same factor of production, because demand will be relatively larger in relation to supply, and supply relatively larger in relation to demand, in some areas or occupations than in others. Not all observed differences in the earnings of apparently identical factors reflect the presence of immobility, however. Differences in skill associated with differences in formal training and/or experience, the latter typically reflected in higher earnings for more senior employees, may account for differences in pay, as may preferences regarding certain kinds of employments.

Immobility is associated with the fact that mobility geographically and occupationally has costs, which exceed in value the benefits to be gained from mobility as envisaged by the individual. Hence earnings differentials due to immobility do not necessarily constitute a source of economic inefficiency. They will do so, however, if the costs of mobility to the individual — in the form of migration from one place to another, or training for a different type of employment—exceed the true social costs. (The opposite case is of course possible.) One source of inefficiency arises from the inefficiency of capital markets in making available personal loans to be repaid from future earnings. On the other hand, free or publicly-subsidized education and re-training programmes may lead to economically wasteful mobility, with the total private and social cost exceeding the private gain.

We shall return to this kind of question when we come to the theory of wages. For the time being, however, we shall proceed on the basis of a highly aggregated model of the economy.

The Problem of Capital

As already mentioned, if we attempt to treat capital, not as a collection of specific pieces of equipment, structures, etc., which earn Marshallian quasi-rents, but as an aggregate factor of production, earning interest, we encounter the major problem that capital as it enters the production function is a produced and not an original factor of production.

This fact is embodied in the Ricardian model, in which both labour and land are regarded as original factors of production, land being assumed fixed in total supply and possessing 'original and indestructible' properties and labour being assumed homogeneous in quality and 'produced' biologically at a constant subsistence wage. (Note that neither assumption is realistic, and that the classical economists, including Marx, had difficulty both with the subsistence assumption for labour and with the explanation of differences in wages according to labour skills.) Capital in the Ricardian model, on the other hand, is food, the product of the production process: the stock of capital is the stock of food accumulated by the capitalists in the past, and the rate of return on it depends on the quantity of labour available for it to support and on the marginal productivity of labour in production relative to the wage rate.

Once we move to a modern industrial economy, with many different specific types of capital equipment, the stock of capital can be measured only by placing a value on each item of capital available, and aggregating (in contrast to the Ricardian model case, where capital is homogeneous food). But to do this requires a set of prices for capital goods, and this requires the use of a rate of interest either to cumulate the past costs of production of the items or to discount their future earnings streams into a present value. But since the object of the exercise is to determine the marginal product of capital and therefore the rate of return (interest rate) on it, we seem to be involved in a hopelessly impossible circularity. The question of whether or not it is possible to construct an aggregate production function including capital as an argument and according it a marginal product has been the focus of a twenty-year debate between the Cambridge (England) and the Cambridge (American) schools. The upshot of that debate, which will be discussed later, has been that it is not always possible mathematically to perform the feat, though it is possible in a large number of cases to do it with enough general equilibrium mathematics; but that no important issue in economics depends on this conclusion, since if one can define the problem one can find the answer with enough mathematical labour.

That is of course a personal judgment. In my view the Cambridge (England) school has been carrying on by modern mathematical–theoretical means the debate inherited from the early days of capitalist industrialism over whether profits are socially justified by the productive contributions of capital; and to my mind the positive theory that factors derive their incomes from their contributions to the productive process should be sharply distinguished from the question of whether the owners of factors are ethically entitled to own them, or whether their returns would be different if ownership or preferences were different. The Cambridge (England) school, bluntly speaking, has misinterpreted 'orthodox' theory (in their terms) because it has misunderstood it. Specifically, if, as will be shown later, one leaves out the demand side of the general equilibrium model or insists on regarding it as arbitrarily determined, one will not arrive at a determinate theory of distribution on marginal productivity lines. This is not to deny, however, that the Cambridge (England) school has contributed a great deal to the development of formal capital theory, both itself and through its provocation to the Cambridge (America) school and others.

Meanwhile, we proceed with post-Ricardian models of distribution. To justify these, we need to assume that capital is 'malleable', i.e. that its physical form can be changed in adaptation to changes in the relative quantity of labour without cost. An extreme form of this assumption, embodied in the Ricardian model, is the assumption that capital and output are the same thing. (This assumption is employed in the so-called 'one-sector model' of economic growth.)

We also need to recognize that in so far as we are concerned with a static equilibrium model in which capital is simply assumed to exist, the product being consumption goods, the earnings of capital have to be regarded as a rental on the existing stock; we can only transform them into a rate of return if we introduce from the outside a valuation of the capital stock to which the rental earnings can be related as a percentage. (Alternatively, we could assume a prevailing rate of interest at which the rental of capital is transformed into a capital value.) If we assume instead that capital goods are being currently produced, we can take the marginal productivity of capital in producing capital goods as an instantaneous rate of return with the dimensions of an interest rate. However, if we assume the economy to be changing over time, so that the instantaneous rate of return is changing, we still have the problem of transforming the varying instantaneous rate of return over time into a current interest rate representing the life-time return on current investment.

6

THE ONE-SECTOR MODEL OF INCOME DISTRIBUTION

The model of distribution developed in the late 1920s and early 1930s by Paul Douglas, J. R. Hicks and others made use of an aggregate production function for the economy as a whole, with labour and capital as its arguments. The central concept employed was the elasticity of substitution, definable as the elasticity of the ratio of the factors employed with respect to their relative prices or relative marginal productivities. The concept was a novel one, and, for that period, a sophisticated mathematical one, and its interpretation and clarification consumed an inordinate number of journal pages, especially in the newly-established *Review of Economic Studies* (Also see p. 53 below).

To avoid problems in the analysis, capital is assumed to be the same stuff as output and to be malleable. Further, it is necessary to distinguish between the services of factors sold in the market (having the dimensions of quantity per unit time) and the quantities of the factors themselves. It is assumed that the flow of services deriving from a factor is strictly proportional to the size of its stock — at the same time, it is recognized that in reality factors may be constant in quantity terms but that the intensity of their use may vary. For example, in a recession the existing quantities of labour and capital are not fully utilized; conversely, in a boom, factor services may be provided at a higher rate than normal.

A production function for the economy as a whole is postulated, relating total output to the quantities of the factors employed. It is assumed that there are constant returns to scale in production, i.e. that the production function is linear homogeneous. This latter assumption generates the result that the ratio of marginal products of the factors depends only on the ratio in which they are employed or in a graphical representation, that the isoquants of the function have the same slope along rays drawn from the origin. Assuming that competition ensures that the factors are paid their marginal products, the price ratio between factors will correspond to the slope of the isoquant at the point located by the given amounts of factors — say, labour and capital (L and C respectively).

The Geometry of Income Distribution
Such a construction allows depiction of the distribution of income. The existence of price ratios between the factors enables us to measure total output (income) in terms of the total quantity of either factor that output could buy, i.e. total output is represented by its value in terms of one of the factors. Income shares may be described in these terms as well (see Diagram I). In particular OC_0 is the value of capital's share in terms of capital and OM is total output in terms of capital. The slope of the price line drawn through

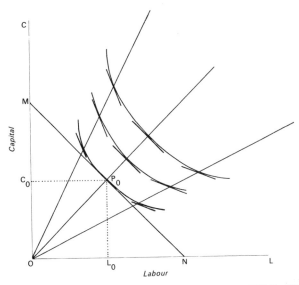

DIAGRAM I: THE ONE-SECTOR MODEL OF INCOME DISTRIBUTION: THE ISOQUANT
MAP

the given amount of labour and capital (C_0, L_0) multiplied by the amount of labour gives labour's share of income in terms of capital, MC_0. The share of capital in total income is OC_0/OM and the ratio of the income of capital to that of labour is $(OC_0/OM)/(MC_0/OM) = OC_0/MC_0$.

Another way of showing the distribution of income involves taking a cross section of the isoquant map at a given level of the capital stock. This is equivalent to examining the product of successive units of labour applied to a fixed capital stock. It is obvious from Diagram II that the marginal product of labour must decrease as more of it is applied to a given stock of capital (this can be seen by looking across the isoquant map for a given stock of capital and increasing quantity of labour). The value of labour's income in terms of output is the marginal product of labour (the slope of the cross-section curve at the point corresponding to the amount of labour, i.e. the slope at point R for labour L_0) multiplied by the quantity of labour $OL_0 = P_0R$, giving labour's income as P_0Q. Total output is OP_0 and OQ the earnings of capital. The relative share of labour in output is P_0Q/P_0O and the relative share of capital is OQ/OP_0. By similar triangles, the relative share of labour is OL_0/TL_0. Note that the slope of the tangent at R is the marginal product of labour and can be measured by RL_0/TL_0; the average product of labour is RL_0/OL_0; hence labour's share in total output is its marginal product divided by its average product. Since every elasticity is defined as the division of a marginal by an average relationship, labour's share is the elasticity of total output with respect to labour. Hence if this elasticity remains constant as the quantity of labour increases relative to the quantity of capital, the relative share of labour will also be constant.

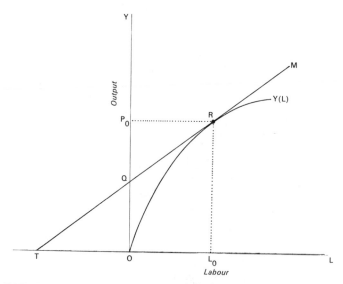

DIAGRAM II: THE ONE-SECTOR MODEL OF INCOME DISTRIBUTION: CROSS-SECTION OF PRODUCTION FUNCTION FOR FIXED CAPITAL STOCK

Effects of Changes in the Quantities of Factors

The ultimate purpose of setting up economic models is to examine the effects on the equilibrium values of the dependent variables of changes in the 'givens' or exogenous variables of the system. In the present case, the questions of interest concern the effects of changes in the quantities of the factors available for employment in the aggregate production function, and changes in the production function itself, on the relative and absolute shares of the factors in the total product (the absolute share is the total income of the factor, the relative share the absolute share divided by the total product.) It may be noted in passing that the isoquant diagram (Diagram I) only displays relative shares, while the cross-section diagram shows both.)

It is evident that increasing the quantity of one factor must increase the marginal product and therefore the absolute income share of the other factor, since that factor becomes relatively scarcer. What happens to the absolute share of the augmented factor and to relative shares depends on the characteristics of the aggregate production function (it is trivially obvious though that if the augmented factor's absolute share falls its relative share must fall also). So far as changes in factor quantities are concerned, with a given aggregate production function, the analysis can be formulated in a variety of ways. If the interest lies in the absolute income of the augmented factor, what happens to this can be formulated, rather tautologically it is true, in terms of the elasticity of demand for that factor derivable from the production function: if the elasticity of demand for it is unity its absolute income is unchanged, if greater than unity increased, and vice versa. If the interest is in the relative income of the augmented factor, the cross-section diagram gives an easy answer: the relative share will increase, be constant, or decrease, depending on whether the elasticity of output with respect to that factor increases, decreases, or remains constant. Alternatively, that factor's share will rise or fall according to whether the elasticity of substitution between the factors is greater or less than unity, with a unit elasticity of substitution constituting the dividing line of constant relative shares. (The analysis leading to this conclusion is developed below.) If the augmented factor's relative share falls, its absolute share may, but not necessarily will, fall.

Harking back to the Ricardian model of distribution, it is easy to see that while an increase in the labour force working on the given stock of land (which entails an increase in the wages fund) must raise the absolute amount of rent, the share of rent in the total output of the land will increase only if the elasticity of substitution between land and labour in the agricultural production function is less than unity, or the elasticity of agricultural output with respect to labour falls as the quantity of labour applied to the given amount of land increases.

It should be noticed that the question of the effect of a change in the quantity of labour employed, relative to the stock of capital, which originated in the long-run context of growth in a full-employment economy, arose subsequently in the context of the Keynesian short-run variable employment model. In that context, the question is the effect of an increase in the amount of labour employed to work a given capital stock on the relative shares of labour and property income (it is obvious on the classical assumptions Keynes used that the real wage rate must fall), and the answer can be put either in terms of the elasticity of substitution or in terms of the direction of change of the elasticity of output with respect to labour. To complete a Keynesian distribution model, one must assume a class of rentiers who provide money capital at fixed interest rates (and presumably also land at fixed money rents) to the entrepreneurs who operate the existing stock of capital equipment. On the Keynesian assumptions of a rigid money wage rate and a diminishing marginal productivity of labour as employment increases with a given capital stock, increased employment must reduce the absolute real income of the rentier class, transferring part of their share of the profit in real terms to the entrepreneurial class.

The Elasticity of Substitution

While other analytical approaches exist and have been mentioned above, the standard approach to the effects of factor-quantity changes on distribution is via the characteristics of the isoquants of the production function, and employs the concept of the elasticity of substitution. As already mentioned, this concept evoked a vast literature in the 1930s, partly because of the rudimentary knowledge of mathematics possessed by the economists of the time, and partly because Hicks in his *Theory of Wages* used the concept to tackle big issues, especially the effects of technical progress on the welfare of labour, which the classical economists had debated hotly but the analysis of which had been left in a theoretically very unsatisfactory state.

Before we proceed to discuss the concept and its application to income distribution, some general points should be made. First, the elasticity of substitution, as employed in distribution theory, is a tautology, in the same way as the Marshallian concept of elasticity of demand is a tautology when employed in such statements as 'if the elasticity of demand is greater than unity, the amount spent on a product will increase as its price falls, and vice versa'. In both cases, the economic problem is measurement, not statements about the implications of hypothetical measurements. Second, the definition of the elasticity of substitution is clear-cut only in the two-factor case to be considered below; if there are three or more factors, there will be alternative definitions, according to what is assumed about the behaviour of the prices or quantities of the other factors when the price or quantity of one is changed. Third, as applied to an aggregate production function assumed to include capital as an argument, it raises all the problems of capital as a produced means of production discussed in the previous chapter and to be discussed later on — which is the basis of Shove's critique of the *Theory of Wages* and led Hicks to leave it out of print for some thirty years.

Refer to Diagram III, which reproduces Diagram I. Initially, equilibrium

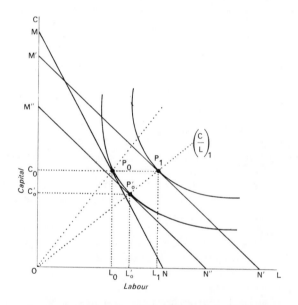

DIAGRAM III: EFFECTS OF INCREASED LABOUR SUPPLY

is at P_0, with capital OC_0 and labour OL_0, the relative share of labour being MC_0/OM or OL_0/O_n. An increase in the quantity of labour to OL_1 changes production to P_1 and reduces labour's relative income share to $M'C_0/M'O$. It could alternatively have increased labour's share (note that in the former case labour's absolute share might even have fallen). What happens to labour's relative share clearly depends on both the increase in the total output, reflected by the movement from P_0 to P_1, and the change in labour's relative marginal productivity or price, which is reflected in the change of slope between MN and $M'N'$. But owing to the assumption of constant returns to scale, the change in the relative prices of labour and capital, and therefore in their relative shares, is the same as if capital had been reduced to C_0' and labour increased to L_0' so as to keep output on the original isoquant but to establish the same factor-utilization ratio as prevails on the new isoquant. This fact permits a symmetrical treatment of the effects of changes in the quantities of the two factors, since what matters for relative shares is their ratio, which may be changed by changing the quantity of either. Obviously, also, the effect of an increase in the relative quantity of labour depends on the curvature of the isoquant in the neighbourhood of P_0. This determines how the slope of the MN line changes as the capital–labour ratio changes, and therefore how the ratio of MC to MO, which reflects the relative shares, changes as the capital–labour ratio changes.

The relevant parameter, however, is not the curvature of the isoquant, but the elasticity of substitution, which is the reciprocal of the curvature multiplied by a constant determined by the initial position on the isoquant map. The elasticity of substitution, diagrammatically, is the elasticity of the capital–labour ratio C/L with respect to the tangent slope MN. That slope can be thought of as the ratio of either the marginal product of labour to that of capital, or the price of labour to the price of capital (both prices of course being expressed in terms of the product, since there is no money in the system, though if there were it would not matter). If the elasticity of substitution is unity, the change in relative price just compensates for the change in relative quantity and relative shares are unchanged; if the elasticity of substitution exceeds unity, the change in relative quantity of a factor is less than offset by a resulting change in relative factor prices, and the income share of the augmented factor increases; and vice versa.

The concept is most simply understood by charting from the isoquant diagram, on to a new diagram whose co-ordinates are the relative prices of the factors and their relative quantities, the explicit relationship between these two variables implicit in the isoquant diagram. See Diagram IV, which

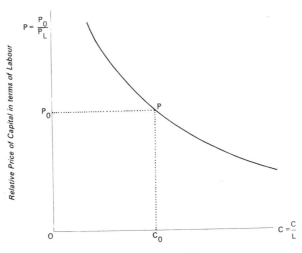

Ratio of Capital to Labour

DIAGRAM IV: THE ELASTICITY OF SUBSTITUTION

charts the relative price of capital $p_C/p_L = p$ against the ratio of capital to labour $C/L = c$. The share of capital divided by the share of labour is $p_C C/p_L L = pc$, which is the area under the functional relationship. Just as with an ordinary demand curve, that area will increase as the quantity increases, i.e. pc will increase as c increases, if the elasticity of the functional relationship is greater than unity and vice versa. The elasticity of the functional relationship is the elasticity of substitution, i.e.

$$\sigma = -\frac{p}{c}\frac{\partial c}{\partial p}$$

(the sign being altered to make σ positive).

The elasticity of substitution is best adapted to the study of the effect of changes in relative factor quantities on relative income shares. All we can say about absolute shares is that if a factor's relative share declines sufficiently, its absolute share will decline as well. This possibility is illustrated geometrically in Diagram V, where P_0 represents the initial and P_1 the final equilibrium point when the labour supply increases from L_0 to L_1, and MN and $M'N'$ the corresponding factor price ratios. Using the constant-returns-to-scale property, total output can be measured by the distance along the ray OP_0 extended of the isoquants for the initial and final levels of production, i.e. respectively by OP_0 and OP'_1. The absolute shares of labour in the two situations can then be measured by drawing $L_0 E_0$ parallel to MN and $L_1 E_1$ parallel to $N'P'_1$. As shown in the diagram, OE_1 is less than OE_0.

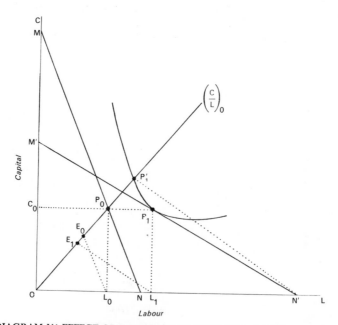

DIAGRAM V: EFFECT OF INCREASED LABOUR ON ABSOLUTE SHARES

Technical Progress

As mentioned, one of the most difficult problems that concerned the classical economists was whether technical progress could be disadvantageous to labour. The issue still comes up in relation to such phenomena as the automation of factory work and the computerization of clerical work. Considering such progress as exogenous to the system, one may handle it in either of two ways. Either one may consider the production function as alterable for given supplies of factor inputs, or one may regard the production function as given but the 'effective' supply of factor inputs available from a given quantity of factors alterable by technical changes that increase their 'quality'.

Technical Progress in Output

On the first approach, technical progress involves shifting the isoquant map in towards the origin, so that more output is obtainable from any given stock of factors. There are three types of shifts, which may be defined either only for the immediate neighbourhood of existing factor supplies on the production function, or for the whole isoquant map. For simplicity we consider only technical changes of the second type, since only such changes are independent of the original supplies of the factors. Such shifts may be of three types.

First, the shift may increase the physical marginal products of the two factors in the same proportion. In this case, the isoquant map looks the same after as before the technical progress, and can be represented simply by re-indexing the isoquants of the original map for the increased productive capacity of any given stock of factors. The effect, with given factor supplies, is to increase the absolute share of each factor in the same proportion as total output, and to leave relative shares unchanged. The effect on distribution is neutral. Such technical progress is now, however, referred to as Hicks-neutral technical progress, because of its assumption of fixed factor quantities. In contemporary growth models, it is assumed that if the rate of return on capital temporarily rises, due to technical progress, capital will be accumulated until the rate of return on it is brought down to its original level. In terms of the preceding analysis, capital will be accumulated until its marginal product returns to the initial level. If, after this has occurred, the relative share of capital is unchanged, the technical progress in question is referred to as Harrod-neutral technical progress. (In fact, this is the only kind of technical progress consistent with steady growth of the economy in response to and at the same rate as an assumed exogenously given rate of growth of the effective labour force.) It should be noted that Hicks-neutrality and Harrod-neutrality coincide only when the production function is of the Cobb–Douglas variety $(X = AL^{x}C^{1-x})$ since only then is the share of a factor in the total product independent of its price.

In the Hicksian analysis, technical progress is said to be biased when it changes the relative marginal productivities of the factors other than equiproportionally. Specifically, technical change is described as *capital-saving* if it raises the marginal product of labour more than that of capital, proportionally, and *labour-saving* if it raises the marginal product of capital more than proportionally to that of labour. The reason behind the description is that, with fixed factor supplies, the effects of the technical change on relative factor prices are the same as if the factor described as 'saved' had been increased in relative quantity: a capital-saving invention has the same effect on the relative (though not absolute) marginal productivity of capital as an increase in the relative quantity of capital, and vice-versa for a labour-saving invention.

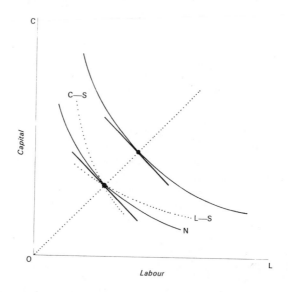

DIAGRAM VI: TYPES OF TECHNICAL PROGRESS SHIFTING PRODUCTION FUNCTION

Diagrammatically, a labour-saving invention can be thought of as making the slope of the isoquant for any given quantity of labour and capital less steep with reference to the labour axis. and a capital-saving invention as making the slope of the isoquant for given factor quantities more steep with reference to the labour axis (see Diagram VI).

Technical Progress in Inputs
The alternative approach is to regard the production function as given by nature and technical progress as increasing the effective quantities of factor services supplied by the stocks of factors measured in natural units. Consider as an example a model of production in which one man uses one tractor to produce a crop, and assume that the education and skill of the man and the quality and performance of the tractor increase. On the previous approach we would regard the increase in output as an increase in the output obtainable from one man and one tractor; on the alternative approach we would consider that there is a given production function employing human services and machine services to produce output, and that technical progress has increased the human services supplied by the man and the machine services supplied by the tractor. Mathematically, the first approach would be expressed in the general production function

$$X = Ag(C, L, T) = Af_T(C, L)$$

where A is a constant that can be eliminated by appropriate measurement of X; and T is a technology shift factor, altering the function relating X to C and L only. The second would be expressed by the general production function

$$X = Af(K, W)$$

where K and W represent inputs of capital services and labour services respectively and $K = g(C, T)$ and $W = h(L, T)$, where in each case C and L are quantities of capital and labour measured in natural units and T represents the level of technology.

On this alternative approach, the isoquant map is unchanged by technical progress, but the axes are redefined to measure effective available inputs of labour and capital services. Neutral technical progress increases the effective inputs of the two factors' services equi-proportionally; capital-saving technical progress increases the effective inputs of capital services more than proportionately to the increase in the effective inputs of labour services; and vice versa for labour-saving technical progress (see Diagram VII).

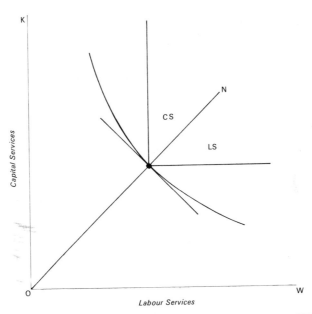

DIAGRAM VII: TYPES OF TECHNICAL PROGRESS AUGMENTING EFFECTIVE FACTOR
SUPPLIES

It follows by definition that with labour-saving technical change the ratio of the marginal product of labour to that of capital falls, and since factor quantities are fixed the relative share of labour falls; conversely for capital-saving technical change. But the absolute share of a factor may still increase, however, even though its relative share declines, because of the general increase in productivity due to the technical improvement. A smaller relative share of a larger total output may entail either an increase or a decrease in the absolute income of the factor.

The foregoing analysis takes the source of technical change as exogeneous. But the knowledge involved in technical change is, as previously explained, a form of capital that can be created by investment. The question naturally arises, for those interested in the distribution of income between capital and labour, whether technical progress is biased in the labour-saving direction. One question here concerns knowledge of the production function. Specifically, the production function may be known only in the neighbourhood relevant to existing factor prices, and what appears to be technical innovation may consist only in the discovery of new ranges relevant to a different range of factor prices — this possibility has been described as 'induced' innovation, and is really not a genuine change in the production function itself, Another question concerns the incentives to invest in labour-saving as contrasted with capital-saving inventions. My one-time teacher, E. H. Chamberlin, used to argue that because labour constitutes about 75 per cent of total cost, inventions would be directed towards labour-saving. But this proposition clearly takes no account of the costs and potential returns of different kinds of invention. Also, it is not actual costs but prospective increases in costs that should motivate the desire to economize on a particular input. Considerable high-powered mathematical work has been done, in the context of growth theory, on the question of arriving at a plausible proposition regarding the equilibrium allocation of investment in research and development between labour-saving and capital-saving kinds; but no strong propositions have emerged.

The Assumptions of the Marginal Productivity Theory
A few remarks on the nature of the assumption embodied in this formulation of the production function are in order. First, to write the production function in this fashion there must exist the possibility of substitution between factors at all times and every substitution must change the relative productivities — a continuously diminishing rate of substitution between factors. This has been subject to criticism on the grounds that these alternatives in production are not always possible. Typically criticism of this sort selects only one man tending one machine, ignoring the broader possibilities for substitution such as maintenance men, office workers and the like offered within a larger production process.

Second, a contrary assumption would be that there are fixed proportions in production and that the first assumption is invalid. A defence of the first assumption against this criticism takes two main lines.

One must take a broad look at the productive process and, recognizing that fixed proportions may exist in every industry, there are still substitution possibilities between labour and capital generated by the possibility of simultaneously increasing the output from other capital (labour) intensive activities and decreasing output from other capital (labour) intensive activities. Thus there may exist substitution between factors through substitution in consumption.

Alternatively, following on the lines of linear programming, one may assume that while technology involves fixed proportions between the factors, society has a choice among a number of technologies each involving fixed proportions, and each subject to constant returns to scale, i.e. infinitely divisible (see Diagram VIII). Some of these technologies will be inefficient,

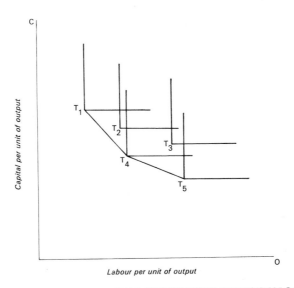

DIAGRAM VIII: FIXED FACTOR PROPORTIONS IN TECHNOLOGY

in the sense that they require more of both inputs than either some other technology by itself, or by an appropriate mixture of two other technologies. A production frontier, equivalent to an isoquant but consisting of straight-line segments connecting adjacent efficient technologies, can be formed. In this case, depending on factor supplies, production takes place either at a point — only one technique being utilized — or on a segment — a mix of two techniques being employed. On the segments, there is a determinate factor price ratio; at the points, the factor price ratio can lie anywhere between the slopes of the adjoining two line segments, and is indeterminate within those limits. The existence of the segments is more important than the existence of the points, from a general economic point of view, because it ensures that factor prices will be constant under non-negligible changes in relative factor quantities. (In the diagram, T_2 and T_3 are inefficient techniques, since mixes of T_1 and T_4, and of T_4 and T_5, respectively, will enable the output to be produced with less of both inputs; $T_1 T_4 T_5$ forms the locus of efficient production, with factor marginal productivities being determinate in the ranges $T_1 T_4$ and $T_4 T_5$.)

   This discussion also has relevance to the theory of capital. In the production process it has been assumed that capital enters as a physical entity — a machine, etc. — and in this sense it is timeless. Clearly, however, capital deteriorates and has a lifetime of finite length. Hence, although the marginal productivity of the machine in the productive process may not be affected, the value of the machine will certainly be altered. The quantity of capital as a certain amount of value must be distinguished from the quantity of capital that enters the production process in the determination of marginal product, etc. (A machine producing 100 units of output per week that totally collapses at the end of a week is not worth the same as a machine that produces 100 units of output per week for a year.) If we wish to obtain a production function which contains the value of capital as an argument, we must as a beginning assume a balanced stock of capital among the different ages. Even so, the value of a balanced stock of capital will depend on the rate of interest — though it is possible to get around that problem in most cases but not in all by chain-indexing quantities of capital as the rate of interest changes. Then, too, the marginal product of the machine in the productive process must be distinguished from the rate of return on the machine. Depreciation must be subtracted from the gross marginal product to arrive at the net marginal product or rate of return. If human beings are assumed to last forever (so we can ignore interacting depreciation) while capital equipment does not, and marginal product is calculated as before, then there are two techniques of adjusting for depreciation, depending on how we assume depreciation to take place. One assumption is that over its life time a machine steadily loses a fixed proportion of its productive power — the so-called 'evaporation assumption': In that case, the value of a new machine is either

$$V = \sum_{t=0}^{t=\infty} \frac{q}{(1 + i)^t (1 + d)^t}$$

or

$$V = \int_0^\infty q\, e^{-(i+d)t}\, dt = \frac{q}{i + d}$$

depending on whether discrete or continuous mathematics are applied, q is the annual or immediate rate of output of a new machine, i is the rate of interest, and d is the rate of depreciation by evaporation.

The alternative assumption is that a machine remains equally productive over a finite working life and then collapses completely — the 'one-hoss shay' assumption. In this case the value of a new machine is either

$$V = \sum_{t=0}^{t=T} \frac{q}{(1 + i)^t}$$

or

$$\int_0^T q\, e^{-it}\, dt = \frac{q}{i}(1 - e^{-iT})$$

again, according to whether discrete or continuous mathematics are employed. T is the fixed life of the machine, and q its fixed rate of yield over that life.

Appendix: Mathematical Notes on Relative and Absolute Factor Shares

Let $x = f(a, b)$ be the aggregate production function, assumed to be linear homogeneous. This implies $f_{ab} = -(a/b) f_{aa} = -(b/a) f_{bb}$, and $x = af_a + bf_b$, and σ (the elasticity of substitution) $= f_a f_b / x f_{ab}$ [R. G. D. Allen, *Mathematical Analysis for Economists*, pp. 317 and 343].

Define $K_a = af_a$, $K_b = bf_b$, the absolute shares; and $k_a = (af_a/x)$, $k_b = (bf_b/x)$, the relative shares.

$$\frac{\partial K_a}{\partial a} = f_a + af_{aa} = f_a\left(1 - \frac{bf_{ab}}{f_a}\right) = f_a\left(1 - \frac{bf_b}{x}\frac{1}{\sigma}\right)$$

$$= f_a\left[\frac{\sigma - k_b}{\sigma}\right] = f_a\left[\frac{\sigma + k_a - 1}{\sigma}\right]$$

$$\frac{\partial K_a}{\partial b} = af_{ab} = \frac{af_a f_b}{x}\frac{1}{\sigma}$$

An increase in the amount of one factor must increase the absolute share of the other; it will increase the absolute share of the factor itself unless $\sigma < k_b$, that is, unless the elasticity of substitution is less than the share of the other factor.

$$\frac{\partial k_a}{\partial a} = \frac{1}{x^2}[bf_b(f_a + af_{aa}) - af_abf_{ab}]$$

$$= \frac{1}{x^2}(bf_bf_a - b^2f_bf_{aa} - abf_af_{ab})$$

$$= \frac{1}{x^2}bf_af_b\left[1 - \frac{(af_a + bf_b)f_{ab}}{f_af_b}\right]$$

$$= \frac{1}{x^2}bf_a\left(1 - \frac{1}{\sigma}\right) = \frac{1}{x^2}bf_af_b\left(\frac{\sigma - 1}{\sigma}\right)$$

The relative share of a factor increases as its quantity increases if the elasticity of substitution exceeds unity, is constant if $\sigma = 1$, and falls as its quantity increases if $\sigma < 1$.

Consider technical progress as increasing the 'effective quantities' of factors. Let $da/a = k\,(db/b) = k\lambda$, where λ is the proportional increase in the effective quantity of b due to technical progress.

$$dK_a = f_a\,da + af_{aa}\,da + af_{ab}\,db$$

$$= \lambda(f_aak + f_{aa}a^2k + abf_{ab})$$

$$= \lambda(f_aak - abf_{ab}k + abf_{ab})$$

$$= \lambda[af_ak - abf_{ab}(k - 1)]$$

$$= \lambda a f_a \left[k - \frac{b f_b f_{ab}}{f_a f_b} (k - 1) \right]$$

$$= \lambda K_a \left[k - \frac{b f_b}{x} \frac{1}{\sigma} (k - 1) \right]$$

$$= \lambda K_a \left[\frac{k\sigma - k_b(k - 1)}{\sigma} \right]$$

Progress reduces the absolute share of the factor if $k\sigma < k_b(k - 1)$; this requires $k > 1$ and $\sigma < k_b$. The full condition is $\sigma < k_b(1 - 1/k)$ [if $k < 1$, the right-hand side is negative and the conditions cannot be fulfilled].

7

THE TWO-SECTOR MODEL OF
INCOME DISTRIBUTION

The Hicksian one-sector model of income distribution produces simple results, but it has the great disadvantage of implying that distribution is determined by the technology and the factor supplies of the system with demand playing no part, whereas in full general equilibrium demand, and therefore the distribution of income among demanders, plays an integral part in determining distribution itself. The two-sector model represents an improvement over the Hicksian one-sector model because it necessarily introduces demand conditions into the determination of income distribution.

The two-sector model assumes that each commodity requires the use of both factors, in production functions characterized by constant returns to scale. Commodity X is assumed to be relatively capital-intensive, and commodity Y relatively labour-intensive, in the sense that at any given factor-price ratio, the cost-minimizing ratio of capital to labour in the production of X is greater than the corresponding ratio of capital to labour in the production of Y. To make the model theoretically interesting, it is assumed that labour and capital are owned by separate groups in the population, these groups having different preference systems. (This assumption follows the Ricardian-classical convention of identifying factor owners with social classes, and is not realistic; but one could adapt the model to the assumption that different groups owned factors in different ratios, or that while their ownership shares were identical their tastes differed among commodities.) The model may be developed in terms of two alternative diagrammatic techniques, the Lerner–Pearce diagram and the Edgeworth–Bowley box diagram.

The Lerner–Pearce Diagram
The assumption of constant returns to scale allows each production function to be represented by a single isoquant, X and Y respectively in Diagram I. Choose a particular factor price ratio, represented by the slope of C_0, and define commodity quantities such that a unit of each costs the same amount OC_0 to produce at the initial factor price ratio. The minimum cost optimal factor ratios in production at the initial factor price ratio are R_x and R_y.

Now lower the relative price of labour in terms of capital to that represented by the slopes of C_x and C_y. The cost of producing a unit of X becomes OC_x, and that of producing a unit of Y becomes OC_y. In other words, a fall in the price of labour reduces the relative price of the labour-intensive good and raises the relative price of the capital-intensive good. Conversely, a rise in the price of labour would shift the tangency points north-west, and raise the relative price of the labour-intensive good. There is thus, as an

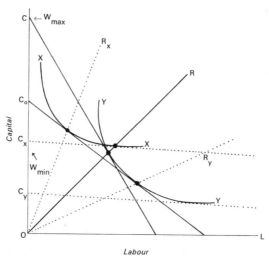

DIAGRAM I: THE LERNER–PEARCE DIAGRAM — COMMODITY PRICE, FACTOR PRICE, AND OUTPUT RELATIONS

implication of the technology, a monotonic relationship between the relative price of a factor and the relative price of the commodity which uses it intensively in production. (While the proof above relates only to the neighbourhood of the factor-price ratio implicit in the slope of the C_0 budget line, commodity units can be redefined for each new factor price ratio to give equal production costs, and the proof be repeated.)

Now introduce the fixity of supplies of factors, expressed as an endowment ratio OR. For full employment of factors, OR must lie between OR_x and OR_y, for production of both goods to be feasible, and production must be allocated between X and Y in such a way that R_x and R_y average out to R. As the price of labour falls, substitution of labour for capital lowers both R_x and R_y, until eventually R_x and R coincide, at the factor price ratio given by the slope of C_x; simultaneously, the economy specializes on the production of X. The slope of C_x, which is the slope of the X isoquant where it crosses the endowment ratio line OR, is therefore the lowest price of labour and highest price of capital the economy can have, consistently with full employment. Conversely, if the price of labour is raised (or capital reduced), R_x and R_y increase as the result of substitution of capital for labour, until R_y corresponds with R; at that point the economy becomes fully specialized on the production of Y. The corresponding factor price ratio, the slope of the line marked W_{max}, is the highest price of labour and lowest price of capital the economy can have, consistently with full employment of the factors.

Diagram II approaches the same point in a rather different way. In that diagram, the slope of MN is the arbitrarily-selected factor price ratio, and its location in the diagram is such that it passes through the endowment point of the economy (its absolute amounts of labour and capital) $\bar{R}$; the XX and YY isoquants are selected to be tangent to MN and thus represent the total outputs of the two goods that the economy could produce with its available factor supplies if it were free to trade one for the other at the given factor price ratio as required. By completing the parallelogram with corners at O and R and sides parallel to OR_x and OR_y, we obtain the actual production points for X and Y, respectively P_x and P_y, necessary to employ all available supplies of each factor (i.e. by vector addition of OP_x and OP_y we reach the endowment point $\overline{R}$).

It is easily seen that if we rotate OR_x and OR_y clockwise, to represent the effects of an increase in the price of labour, the production of the labour-intensive good represented by P_y must shift back towards the origin and that of the capital-intensive good represented by P_x must shift outwards from the origin; and vice versa for a counter-clockwise rotation induced by a rise in the relative price of capital. That is, a rise in the relative price of a factor is associated with an increase in the relative and absolute production of that good, and vice versa. The limits of feasible price variation are set when the parallelogram collapses into a line coinciding with the capital-labour ratio in one of the industries, and the economy becomes completely specialized on production of one of the goods.

In contrast to the one-sector model, in which factor quantities determine distribution of income uniquely, relative factor quantities in the two-sector model determine a feasible range of income distributions. Which one of these will be the equilibrium one will be determined by the interaction of distribution with demand for commodities, and the equilibrium condition that production and consumption must be equal for each commodity (by Walras's law, equality of demand and supply for one commodity implies equality for the other.)

It can be easily shown, by sketching in a higher overall capital to labour ratio, that an increase in capital relative to labour will raise both the minimum and the maximum feasible wage rate, and lower both the minimum and the maximum return to capital; and conversely for an increase in labour relative

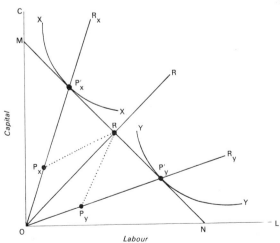

DIAGRAM II: THE LERNER–PEARCE DIAGRAM — FACTOR ALLOCATIONS

to capital. But this does not imply that an increase in the quantity of one factor relative to the other will necessarily reduce the per unit earnings of that factor, as is necessarily the case in the one-commodity model; reference must be made to the demand conditions to analyse this question.

To complete the analysis in general equilibrium terms, demand conditions need to be introduced. Although a mapping of factor inputs to commodity outputs is not given explicitly in the diagram, note that a pattern of demand in terms of labour and capital may be derived given the unique relation between relative commodity prices, relative factor prices and capital—labour ratios in the two industries. The groups owning labour and capital have preferences over goods — these may be used to derive preference systems over the factors that produce the goods. Diagram III is the same as Diagram II but with the

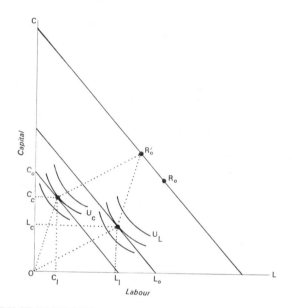

DIAGRAM III: DISTRIBUTION AND DEMAND FOR OUTPUT

production side left out. Given an initial factor price ratio that implicitly defines the value of capital in terms of labour, budget lines may be drawn for labour and capital from C_0 on the capital axis and L_0 on the labour axis parallel to the overall budget constraint defined by the arbitrary factor price ratio drawn through the point R_0. Utility functions (defined over labour and capital) of the owners of labour and capital are drawn with O as the origin. At the initial price ratio C_c, L_c and C_L, L_L are derived demands for capital and labour by capital and labour. By vector addition, total demands for labour and capital amount to R_0'. This represents an excess demand for capital and an excess supply of labour. Assuming that such a situation forces the price of capital to fall, consumers will be led to substitute capital intensive goods for labour intensive goods in consumption, but income will be redistributed towards labour; if labour has a strong marginal propensity to consume labour intensive goods, and capital, a strong marginal propensity to consume capital intensive goods, the excess demand for capital may increase. However, assuming that both labour and capital want to consume some of both goods, if this process exists there is a limit to it, such that both the price of labour and the price of capital are positive. Although there is no theoretical justification for restricting demand or production conditions to generate a unique stable equilibrium, we assume that one exists.

The Edgeworth–Bowley Box Diagram
Implicit in the analysis of Diagrams I–III is a determinate combination of outputs of the two commodities, and a distribution of income between the two factors of production, for each given relative factor price and corresponding relative commodity price. Analysis of the general equilibrium determination of income distribution could proceed by using the output combinations and corresponding income distributions, and introducing the tastes of the factor owners, equilibrium requiring that the demands of the factor owners, given their tastes, the distribution of income, and the relative commodity prices associated with that distribution, for commodities should just absorb the factor supplies. It is, however, desirable to know how the transformation curve representing alternative feasible outputs with the given factor supplies and technology, and the distribution of each total output between the factors, can be derived from the technology and factor supplies.

The left-hand rectangle of Diagram IV is the familiar Edgeworth–Bowley

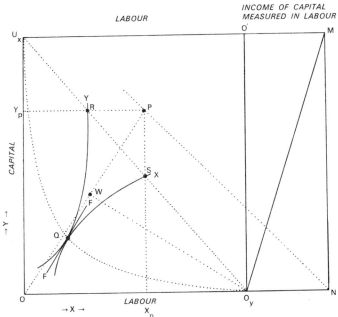

DIAGRAM IV: THE EDGEWORTH–BOWLEY BOX DIAGRAM — PRODUCTION AND
INCOME DISTRIBUTION

contract box: the given quantity of capital is measured on the vertical side of the box, the given quantity of labour on the horizontal side. Isoquants of the production function for X are inserted in the box from the origin O_x, isoquants for Y from the origin O_y. The tangency points of the two sets of isoquants trace out the contract curve $O_x Q O_y$, which is a locus of efficient production, i.e. of factor allocations which maximize the amount of one good that can be produced, given that a specified amount of the other must be produced. FF, the common tangent to isoquants for the two goods at the point Q, represents the equilibrium factor price ratio at that point, i.e. for that combination of feasible outputs. Note that as Q moves along the contract curve in the direction of O_y, FF becomes less steep with reference to the horizontal, because such a movement involves substitution of labour for capital along isoquants of the production function for X, i.e. the equilibrium factor combination travels north-east along the X isoquant.

Because of the assumption of constant returns to scale, the quantity of X produced can be measured, for any production point in the contract box, by the distance cut off by the corresponding isoquant along any ray from the origin O_x. Thus the output of X at point Q can be measured by the distance $O_x S$ along the diagonal $O_x O_y$ cut off by the corresponding X isoquant. $O_x S / O_x O_y$ is the proportion of the maximum quantity of X that the economy can produce, that is being produced at Q. By projection, the output of X can be measured along the horizontal axis, by reference to the origin O, output of X at Q being $O X_p$. Similarly, output of Y at Q can be measured along the diagonal from the origin O_y, and projected on to the vertical axis with origin O, the output in question being $O Y_p$. X_p and Y_p can then be used to plot the point P, which shows the quantities of X and Y produced at point Q. Similar plotting of the corresponding points P as Q moves along the contract curve yields the transformation curve $O_x P O_y$, with reference to the origin O. For

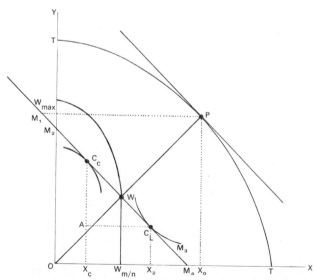

DIAGRAM V: THE EDGEWORTH–BOWLEY DIAGRAM — GENERAL EQUILIBRIUM

diagrammatical simplicity, this curve is not drawn in the figure. The factor price ratio at point Q is given by the slope of FF. The value of capital in terms of labour can be measured by drawing a line through O_y with the same slope as FF, to intersect O_xO' produced at M. O_xO' represents the income of labour, measured in terms of labour, and $O'M$ the income of capital, measured in terms of labour ($O'O_y$ is the quantity of capital, and the slope of FF with reference to the vertical axis gives the number of units of labour a unit of capital will buy). Drop MN perpendicular to OO_y produced, to transfer the division of income to the bottom axis. Draw a line joining N to P, and draw a parallel line through O_y to intersect OP at W. W then divides OP into the two segments OW and WP, which correspond to the division of the total output represented by P between labour and capital respectively. Repetition of the exercise for other points Q and corresponding P will trace out an income division line $W_{max}W\,W_{min}$, where W_{max} will be on the Y axis and W_{min} on the X axis.

Since, as the output of X expands from zero to the maximum possible, the capital to labour ratio must fall in both industries, and the marginal product of capital in terms of both products rise and of labour in terms of both products fall, the income distribution curve must have the property that as W moves south-east down it, successive budget lines through W with the slope of the price ratio between the commodities for the corresponding P must lie inside one another.

The transformation curve and the income distribution curve derived in Diagram IV are reproduced in Diagram V. For the production point P, labour's share of income is OW and capital's WP. The line through W with the same slope as the tangent to the transformation curve at P (which is the commodity price ratio) is the budget line for labour with respect to the origin O (labour's budget line is M_2M_4) and for capital with respect to the origin P (capital's budget line is M_1M_3). Insert indifference curves for labour with origin O, and for capital with origin P. The tangency of an indifference curve with the relevant budget line will show for each factor the quantities of the two goods demanded by that factor. The desired consumption point of labour is C_L, and for capital is C_C. Adding together the desired consumption quantities of goods by the two factors, and comparing them with the total amounts produced by the economy as shown by point P, it appears that in the diagram the desired consumption of X exceeds production, while production of Y exceeds desired consumption. Excess demands for X is AC_L, excess supply of Y is AC_C. (To illustrate, labour desires to consume OX_L of X, capital desires to consume X_OX_C of X, but when total output OX_O is subtracted there is a deficiency of supply relative to demand of X_CX_C.) General equilibrium will only be achieved at a production point P, and corresponding commodity and factor price ratios and income distribution, such that C_C and C_L coincide.

It is possible alternatively to use two income distribution curves, that for capital being obtained by subtracting labour's from the transformation curve; start indifference curves for both factors from the origin; determine each factor's consumption point; and by vector addition determine the total consumption demand on the budget line tangent to the transformation curve at P. Since this exercise has been carried out for the Lerner–Pearce technique, it will not be repeated here.

A Note on the Existence of Equilibrium and the Possibility of Multiple Equilibria
There must always be an equilibrium, as is obvious from the assumption that owners of both factors always wish to consume some of both products but that in fact variations of the income distribution involve moving from specialization on producing one commodity only to specialization on producing the other commodity only. But there may be multiple equilibrium. These points can be illustrated by considering the loci of C_L and C_C as income distribution changes between W_{max} and W_{min}. Diagram VI represents the two

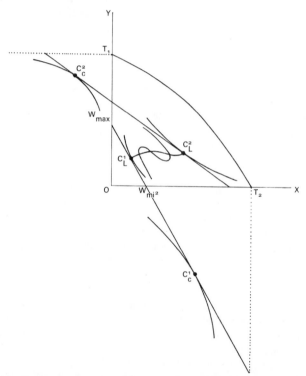

DIAGRAM VI: THE POSSIBILITY OF MULTIPLE EQUILIBRIUM

extreme income distributions and the corresponding locations of C_L and C_C. The loci of desired consumption points must join C_L^1 and C_L^2, and C_C^1 and C_C^2, by curves lying in the space between the two budget lines; hence the loci must intersect at least once in that space. But since there is no restriction on the shapes of the loci, because consumption indifference curves cannot be restricted as narrowly as can isoquants, there is no reason why the loci could not intersect more than once, though they must intersect an odd number of times, with the intersections representing alternatively stable and unstable equilibria. Such a possibility is indicated on the diagram though it is quite possible that the actual drawing violates some constraint on the paths the loci may take.

It can be shown, however, that the conditions required for multiple equilibrium are extremely restrictive. For multiple equilibrium there must be an unstable equilibrium. This requires that an increase in the price of a commodity produces an excess demand for it. The transformation effect in production and the normal compensated substitution effects in consumption must tend to produce an excess supply. Hence instability must depend on a redistribution effect coming through the change in factor prices associated with the rise in the price of the product; and for that redistribution effect to tend to create excess demand, the factor used relatively intensively in producing the good whose relative price has risen must have a relatively stronger preference at the margin for that good than does the other factor, i.e. must have a higher marginal propensity to consume it out of income. Further, since these marginal propensities to consume are both fractional (assuming both goods normal, neither inferior in consumption) the redistribution of income must be greater than the increase in the value of output of the good whose price has risen. Now, if the elasticities of substitution in production for the two goods are both unity, the amount of income redistributed will be only (approximately) the difference between the shares of the factors in the total income generated by the two industries multiplied by the change in output, and since these shares are fractional so will be the income redistributed as a fraction of the output increase in the industry where the price has risen. For that fraction to be greater than unity, the elasticities of substitution must in some average sense be less than unity, so that the factor whose price increases obtains an increased share of the income generated in each industry.

Relaxation of Assumption About Substitutability
It is possible to relax the assumption of continuous substitution in consumption and production. With no substitution in production (see Diagram VII), isoquants are right angles and the contract curve is consistent with full employment of factors at only one point — where the rays from the origins representing the fixed capital to labour ratios in the two industries intersect. We could move in either direction from the point A in order to produce more of X or Y but either the price of capital (producing more X) or the price of labour (producing more Y) would fall to zero. The production possibility frontier corresponding to fixed coefficients in production is shown in Diagram

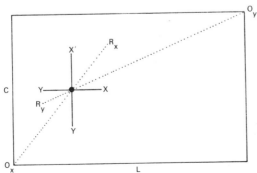

DIAGRAM VII: NO FACTOR SUBSTITUTABILITY IN PRODUCTION

VIII. When demand considerations are introduced, three possibilities for final equilibrium exist: (1) Demand is such that equilibrium is along AB, the price of capital and capital's income are zero. The only relevant indifference curve is labour's and AB is the relevant budget line; (2) Demand is such that equilibrium lies along BC — labour's income and price are zero; (3) both factors receive an income and production is at B. Letting l_y, l_x, c_y, c_x represent the fixed amounts of labour and capital required to produce units of Y and X,

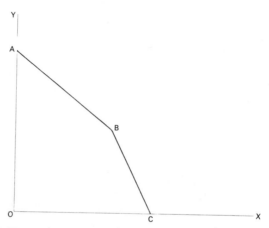

DIAGRAM VIII: TRANSFORMATION CURVE WITH NO FACTOR SUBSTITUTABILITY

we know that competition will generate product prices that equal costs of production per unit of output. Setting the cost of a unit of Y to 1 and defining the price of X in terms of Y as P_x, we may derive the associated distribution of income from the following:

$$w \cdot l_y + r \cdot c_y = 1$$

$$w \cdot l_x + r \cdot c_x = P_x$$

where $P_x = P_x(X, Y, w, r)$, X and Y are the amounts of the commodities produced, w and r being fixed such that distribution of income in conjunction with the preferences of the factor owners leads the market to absorb X and Y produced at B. A range of prices of X will exist such that w and r are positive. In this model distribution has to be made consistent with production.

The above model is similar to Kaldor's model of distribution. Consumer goods and producers' goods are produced in a ratio that is determined by entrepreneurs and does not change. Entrepreneurs and workers save different proportions of their incomes and the distribution of income has to be such that total savings equals total investment. In this analysis, if the production possibilities frontier exhibits continuous possibilities for substitution in production, problems are encountered. Given a point on the frontier, marginal productivity theory predicts a particular distribution of income, in line with the contribution of each of the factors to the total product. This distribution may conflict with the one Kaldor would predict, i.e. the one that generates consumption of the two goods indicated by the initial point on the frontier.

Alternatively, it may be assumed that there is no substitutability in consumption. If the community has a single set of tastes, the production point A is fixed as in Diagram IX. The distribution of income adapts passively to correspond to payment of factors according to their marginal product and does not feed back on the production process. Assuming two classes of people, each with a different set of tastes (Diagram X), limits on production of X and Y may be established on the assumption that each group wants to consume some of both goods so that neither factor's share can fall to zero.

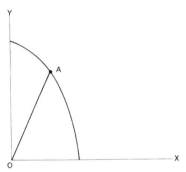

DIAGRAM IX: EQUILIBRIUM WITH NO SUBSTITUTABILITY IN CONSUMPTION, SINGLE TASTES

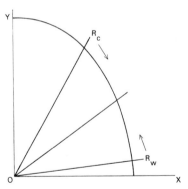

DIAGRAM X: POSSIBLE EQUILIBRIA WITH NO CONSUMPTION SUBSTITUTABILITY, DIFFERING TASTES OF FACTOR OWNERS

8

THE TWO-SECTOR MODEL CONTINUED

Changes in Factor Quantities

The two-sector model has been developed to examine the effects of changes in underlying conditions such as the availability of factors and the available technology. The approach begins with a temporary assumption that factor prices are constant and determines what happens to the excess demand for one of the products, given a change in the quantity of factors. The constant factor price assumption has the advantage of allowing the increase in income to accrue solely to the factor whose supply is increased — the analysis will then show that the demand for each good will increase by less than the amount of the total increase in income. Further, effects are divided between demand effects and supply effects — on the demand side, consumption of both goods will increase; on the supply side, production of one good will increase and production of the other will decrease. Bringing the two sides together it will be shown than an increase in the supply of a factor will cause demand for the good using the factor intensively to rise relatively less than production at constant factor prices — thus, excess supply of the good is generated, its price and the price of the factor used intensively in its production must fall. Symbolically (and assuming that the factor prices ratio is unity in order to deal only in terms of quantities):

In consumption, for a given change in factor availability:

$$dX_C > 0$$

$$dY_C > 0$$

$$dX_C + dY_C = dM \quad \text{(where } X \text{ is intensive in the factor}$$
$$\text{augmented)}$$

in production:

$$dX_p > 0$$

$$dY_p < 0$$

$$dX_p + dY_p = dM$$

therefore, $dX_p > dX_c$, where dM is the change in total income.

The point is established in terms of the Edgeworth box diagram in Diagram I. For factor prices to remain the same after an increase in capital shifts the origin from O_x to O_x'. the capital to labour ratio in both X and Y production must remain the same. This implies a shift in production from P to P' involving a decrease in Y production (moving back along $O_y R_y$) and an increase in X

production (production at P' is greater than production at P by $P'' - P'$). As output of Y has fallen, the output of X must have risen more than in proportion to the increase in income at constant factor prices. The same point is made in the Lerner–Pearce diagram (Diagram II) where the increase in capital is represented by a shift in the overall factor endowment from R to R'.

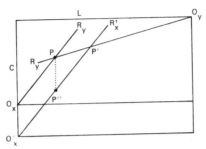

DIAGRAM I: INCREASE IN QUANTITY OF CAPITAL (A) EDGEWORTH–BOWLEY DIAGRAM

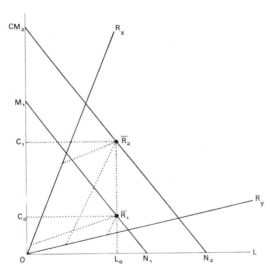

DIAGRAM II: INCREASE IN QUANTITY OF CAPITAL (B) LERNER–PEARCE DIAGRAM

Diagram III illustrates that the possible range of relative price variation shifts to the left from $R_A R'_A$ to $R_B R'_B$ with an increase in the availability of capital, with X being capital intensive in production at all factor price ratios. While the range of variation shifts to the left, it cannot be proved conclusively that the relative price of X will fall without introducing demand conditions — the set of price ratios may, in fact, move from A to B implying an absolute reduction in Y production.

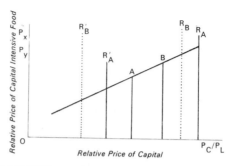

DIAGRAM III: SHIFT IN POSSIBLE RANGE OF RELATIVE FACTOR PRICES AS CAPITAL INCREASES

Technological Change

In considering the effects of changes in technology for a closed economy it is convenient to assume that factor prices initially remain constant and ask what happens to demand and supply in the factor markets on the assumption that technological change reduces the price of the product proportionally to the degree of the improvement. Note that the effects of technological progress may be interpreted in two different ways: (1) commodity prices stay the same. At the given factor price ratio, the cost of production is lower than its value. The change that restores equilibrium is an increase in the price of the factor used intensively in the production of the good produced in the industry experiencing the change; (2) the price of the commodity falls and the benefits of the improvement are absorbed by consumers — this introduces a difficulty in terms of the distinction between welfare and income. That is, labour and capital may have the same income in terms of money or in terms of the good whose price has not fallen — but their welfare is increased by the fact that the price of one of the goods that they consume has fallen.

Consider a Hicks neutral technological improvement in the capital intensive (X) industry (see Diagram IV) such that the ratio of the factors' marginal productivities does not change — each marginal productivity rises in proportion to the technical improvement. With a constant factor price ratio, the capital labour ratio in each industry stays the same but the price of X falls in the same proportion as the degree of the improvement. To maintain full-employment at the same factor price ratio, the output of X must expand in proportion to the degree of the improvement. Whether this will be a position of equilibrium depends on the overall, uncompensated price elasticity of demand for X. For consumers to demand an increased amount of X in the same proportion as the fall in price, this price elasticity must be unity. If it is greater than unity there will be excess demand for X; if it is smaller, there will be excess supply. In the instance that the elasticity is unity, relative prices of labour and capital will not have changed and factors will experience increases in welfare to the extent that they consume X — marginal productivities in terms of Y stay the same and rise in terms of X. Where the elasticity is different from unity, changes in the price of X will be generated by conditions of excess demand or supply — this will cause redistribution towards labour

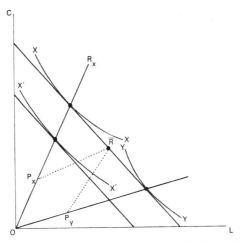

DIAGRAM IV: HICKS-NEUTRAL TECHNICAL PROGRESS IN CAPITAL-INTENSIVE
INDUSTRY

(elasticity below unity and P_x falls) or towards capital (elasticity above unity and P_x rises).

If the X industry experiences capital-saving technical progress, the marginal product of labour is reduced at the old capital–labour ratio. Alternatively, with a constant factor–price ratio, the capital–labour ratio in X falls — by completing the parallelogram in Diagram V we can conclude that X production will be increased and Y production decreased (P'_x is a greater distance

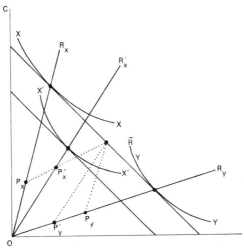

DIAGRAM V: CAPITAL-SAVING TECHNICAL PROGRESS IN CAPITAL-INTENSIVE
INDUSTRY

along OR'_x than is P_x along OR_x, and P'_x represents greater output along OR'_x after technical change than before it). In proportional terms, the increase in X production is greater than the degree of technological change. In this instance, the elasticity of demand for X must be greater than unity in order for the unchanged factor price situation to be an equilibrium position. Technological change in this instance may be conceived of as involving a neutral change plus an increase in the amount of effective capital — the X industry must then expand and the Y industry contract to absorb this increase. The technological change will be unfavourable from the point of view of capital unless the price elasticity of demand for X is something greater than one.

With labour saving progress in the X industry, the capital–labour ratio rises in X at constant factor prices. This implies an increase in Y production and a decrease in X production (see Diagram VI). The decrease in X production is not as clear-cut as the decrease in Y production in the previous

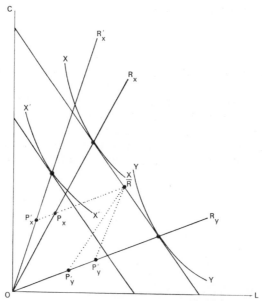

DIAGRAM VI: LABOUR-SAVING TECHNICAL PROGRESS IN CAPITAL-INTENSIVE INDUSTRY

example — at the point P'_x, the index of production is greater after the technical change than was the index used to evaluate production at P_x. This situation can be seen as a neutral technical change plus an increase in the effective supply of labour that must be absorbed by expanding the labour intensive industry and contracting the capital-intensive industry. At unchanged factor prices, the price elasticity of demand for X must be something less than unity in order for this to be a position of final equilibrium.

The results obtained so far may be summarized as follows: if neutral technical progress occurs in one industry, the relative price of the factor used intensively in that industry will rise, be unchanged, or fall, according to whether the uncompensated elasticity of demand for the product of that industry is greater than, equal to, or less than unity. If the technical progress is biased towards saving the factor used relatively intensively in that industry, the critical value of the uncompensated elasticity of demand that determines the outcome will be something greater than unity; and if the technical progress is biased towards saving the factor used relatively unintensively in that industry, the critical value of the uncompensated elasticity of demand that determines the outcome will be something less than unity.

An Alternative Approach to Technical Progress

The preceding analysis of technical progress kept factor prices constant, reduced the price of the product in which progress occurred in proportion to the progress and examined whether the resulting production equilibrium would be consistent with the effects on demand of the reduced price. An alternative technique is to keep the relative prices of commodities unchanged. In this case, the factor price ratio must adjust so that costs remain consistent with the (temporarily) fixed commodity price ratio. This means that the relative price of the factor used intensively in the innovating industry must rise and that of the factor used intensively in the other industry must fall. Moreover, since productivity in the other industry has remained unchanged, and also relative commodity prices, the price of the factor used intensively in the non-innovating industry must fall in terms of both products, and that of the factor used intensively in the innovating industry must rise in terms of both products, so that more than all of the increase in social income produced by the innovation accrues to the factor used intensively in the industry that produces it, the owners of the other factor losing in absolute income. If the factor used relatively intensively in producing the product where the technical change has occurred has relative marginal preference for that good (i.e. higher marginal propensity to consume it), the value of it demanded may increase more than the increase in the national income due to the technical progress.

What happens on the supply side depends on the nature of the progress. If it is Hicks-neutral, the rise in the relative price of the factor used intensively in producing the product must lower the ratio of that factor to the other employed in both industries, thereby requiring an increase in the output of the innovating industry by more than the total increase in the value of output due to progress and reducing the output of the other industry. This is illustrated in Diagram VII, where to maintain the equality of costs and prices after an innovation in the X industry, the factor price ratio has to shift from MN to $M'N'$, and the factor-usage ratios from R_x and R_y to R'_x and R'_y. This implies expansion of X production and contraction of Y production to maintain full employment of the factors, as can be seen by mentally filling in the standard parallelogram. Thus it is only in the probably very exceptional case of a strongly positive redistributionary effect on demand that there will not be excess supply of the product in which the innovation occurs at the original commodity price ratio and consequently that its price will rise rather than fall.

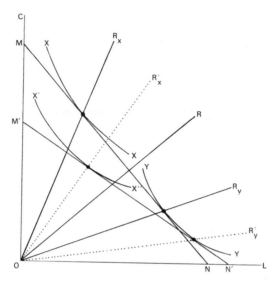

DIAGRAM VII: FACTOR-AUGMENTING TECHNICAL PROGRESS

This conclusion will be stronger in the case of technological progress that saves the factor used intensively in the innovating industry, since such progress will tend to reduce the cost-equalizing factor-utilization ratio in that industry even more than under neutral technical progress. On the other hand technical progress that saves the factor used unintensively in that industry will tend to raise the utilization ratio for the factor used intensively in that industry, and this effect may outweigh the substitution effect against that factor in that industry, and if it does so sufficiently, so that the effect on factor allocation among the industries outweighs the effect of the reduction of the utilization ratio for that factor in the other industry, the other industry may expand rather than contract. In that case, even without a positive redistributionary effect of the type described above, there might be excess demand for the product in which the technical change has occurred and a need for its relative price to rise rather than to fall in order to restore equilibrium after the innovation.

Application to General Growth
The preceding analysis has taken up each possible source of growth in turn. The results can be put together for combinations of sources of growth, e.g. growth of capital and labour together, or technical progress occurring in both industries simultaneously. To take only the simplest cases, if both factors are growing at the same rate, or neutral technical progress is occurring at the same rate in both industries, relative commodity and factor prices will remain constant only if demand for the two commodities grows at the same rate, that is, if the income-elasticity of demand for each is unity. If the income elasticities differ, the commodity with the above-unitary income elasticity will rise in relative price, and the factor employed relatively intensively in producing it will also rise in relative price as compared with the other factor.

This point, in the specific case of technical progress going on at the same pace in both sectors, has an application to the falsification of the predictions of the classical economists concerning the growing scarcity of, and rise in the rent on, land as population grew and technical progress occurred. That prediction assumed either no or negligible technical progress in agriculture. The stylized facts have been that technical progress has proceeded at about the same pace in agriculture as in industry, but the low income-elasticity of demand for agricultural products relative to manufactured goods has meant a fall in relative farm incomes. This fall has been accentuated by the relatively low price elasticity of demand for farm products. The result has been the introduction of social policies designed to raise farm incomes by raising farm prices. These policies in turn have tended to benefit the owners of agricultural land rather than farm workers, because of the relative inelasticity of supply of the former as compared with the latter; and this result has been compounded by the resort to policies designed to take agricultural land out of production.

Application to Capital and Growth Theory
These subjects are reserved for later detailed treatment, but the stage of analysis reached naturally suggests some remarks on them.

Thus far, the analysis has assumed two commodities being produced, and two factors in existence, with no necessary connection between them. In order to construct a system which contains capital as a produced means of production, and not merely an existing stock of a particular factor of unexplained origin, it is necessary simply to make one of the commodities produced capital itself. It simplifies matters to assume that once capital is constructed it lasts forever. Once one good is identified as capital or investment goods, it follows that the distribution of income among owners of capital and labour will depend on the demand for investment goods, that is on the rate of growth of the capital stock desired by savers. (The rate of growth of the capital stock is simply the current rate of production of capital goods divided by the existing stock.)

The returns on investment in this model appear in two forms: as a rental rate for capital used in producing the consumption good, equal to its marginal productivity in the consumption goods industry, and as a rate of return on investment, equal to the marginal productivity of capital goods in producing capital goods. (One must recall, though, that if this marginal productivity is changing over time it is not necessarily easily translated into a rate of return on investment in the form of a rate of interest.)

The effects of changes in the rate of investment on the current rate of return on investment depend on whether capital goods are relatively capital-intensive or relatively labour-intensive. If the latter, the current rate of return will fall as the rate of investment rises; and vice versa for the former. Hence if capital goods are capital-intensive, the share of capital will rise with the rate of investment; and vice versa if capital goods are labour-intensive. The former case gives rise to a possibility of unstable equilibrium, if it is assumed that saving is governed by fixed ratios of saving to income higher for capitalists than for workers. But this, as demonstrated earlier, is only a condition of local instability; and the conditions required for it also involve the elasticities of substitution in production being on some sort of average less than unity. The possibility of instability is more serious if saving is assumed to be motivated by a minimum rate of time preference, because then if capital goods are capital-intensive in production any chance increase in the rate of investment will increase the rate of return on saving and motivate still more saving and investment.

It should perhaps be remarked that the extension of the model in this direction assumes a neo-classical world in which the credit market functions so that all savings are translated into investment; and that this is in contrast to the Keynesian models in which whatever investment entrepreneurs want to do is translated into saving through some sort of multiplier process.

9

ASPECTS OF THE THEORY OF RENT

Introduction: The Special Place of the Environment in Popular Thought
Previous lectures have referred to the special place occupied by land, and by
the rent of land, in classical economics. This special place is bound up on
the one hand with the political-social environment of that time, which was
characterized by the identification of factor ownership with social classes, and
on the other hand with the structure of the Ricardian theory of distribution.
Adam Smith was very definitely a 'landlord's man', having made his early
living and started his investigation of economics as tutor to the son of the
local lord; and Malthus also favoured the landlords on the grounds, suggested
by his undercomsumptionist theories of unemployment, that by spending
their 'unearned' rents they provided a demand for labour. Ricardo, as
previously explained, simplified the problem of distribution into manage-
ability by associating rent with what he called 'the original and indestructible
properties of the soil' and treating it as the residual output (surplus) left over
after labour, applied to the land with the support of capital in the form of
the wages fund, had been paid its marginal product. In this analytical system,
the landlords appeared as the enemies of progress, because economic growth
would eventually be brought to a halt by the fall in the rate of profit resulting
from diminishing marginal productivity of labour on the land in connection
with the fixed subsistence wage. This view of the anti-social role of the landlord
led in particular to the movement for free trade in food and the repeal of the
'Corn Laws' (laws protecting domestic British agriculture against foreign
competition by means of a rather complicated tariff structure designed to
maintain the level of domestic prices, very similar in some respects to present-
day agricultural support price policies).
    The Ricardian treatment of distribution meant a sharp differentiation
between land, a factor assumed to be in absolutely fixed supply, and the other
two factors — labour, whose supply was governed by the subsistence wage,
and capital, whose supply in the long run was governed by the willingness of
capitalists to accumulate capital in response to the rate of return on it. This
differentiation had a strong influence on the subsequent development of
distribution theory. In particular Alfred Marshall, as a loyal student of the
work of the classical economists, retained important elements of it in his
own analysis, even though he laid the basis for the modern theory of rent by
recognizing that the earnings of any factor in fixed supply are a rent, and by
introducing the concept of 'quasi-rent' to apply to the earnings of a factor
which is in fixed supply in the short run but not in the long run.
    For both reasons — the social position of land-owners, and the analytical
position of rent in the traditional theory of distribution — land, and the rent

on it, have always enjoyed a special place in academic and especially in lay thinking about public policy, particularly in the realm of taxation. In the context of taxation, land appears as an especially fit object of taxation, on the grounds that rent is 'unearned' by effort on the part of the land-owner. Thus Walras, in his role as a socialist philosopher, proposed that the existing system of taxes should be replaced by one in which the government owned the land and derived its revenue from the rents thereon. He proposed to make the transition to the new system of public finance through governmental purchase of land at fair market prices, arguing that the private market tended consistently to underestimate the prospective increase in land values, so that eventually the government would receive a surplus of rents over the interest on the money required to buy the land in the first place. (Incidental facts: Walras submitted this idea in an essay contest sponsored by the Swiss canton of Vaud, did not win the prize, but so impressed the judges that he was offered the Chair at Lausanne — which gave him academic rescue from a long career as an outcast socialist French journalist: to this day the city of Lausanne derives a substantial part of its revenue from its ownership of an extensive local vineyard.) More important in this connection was the American Henry George and his single-tax-movement, a feature of late nineteenth-century economics. The single tax was a tax on land rents to support local government. The idea gained considerable practical acceptance in the mid-west of the United States and Canada, where it proved both an important source of disturbance during the post-1929 depression when the prices of agricultural products fell drastically, and a limitation on the powers of local governments to finance public expenditures desired by the voters after the Second World War. It had an important influence on the British Fabians also, and hence on the British Labour party: the idea that both land rent and increases in land values are peculiarly 'unearned' and therefore morally especially fit objects of taxation has exercised an important influence on Labour Party thinking, specifically in the form of policy proposals to nationalize the land and to charge 'fair' rents for housing within the means of the ordinary man. In this connection, the notion that rent is 'unearned' dovetails with another popular notion of ordinary thinking, that a speculator who makes money by buying up property which is being used inefficiently or for a low-yield purpose and converts it to a higher-yield purpose is performing no useful social function and should either be stopped by legislation or taxed as far as possible out of his ill-gotten gains.

The fiscal notion that taxes should be levied on rents rather than the income from effort is a mixture of theoretical wisdom and practical ignorance. Theoretically, an optimal tax system should fall on rents, and not distort marginal choices in the allocation of resources. The practical problem is to devise taxes that accomplish this, since the income on which taxes are usually levied almost invariably involves an element of marginal choice; also, even if one could specify a source of pure rent for taxation purposes, there would be no guarantee that that source would suffice to finance government's needs for revenue. Specifically, the identification of the land as a unique and ubiquitous source of rent ignores two facts. First, land is not fixed in quantity, as the Ricardian view would have it, but instead is variable in both physical and economically relevant quantity. One can invest in producing it — for example, Northwestern University found it cheaper to create new campus space by filling in a bit of Lake Michigan than by buying adjacent land in Evanston — in which case a tax on land rental value will influence decisions to invest in the creation of new land and so create allocative distortions. Also, the effective quantity of land is changeable by technology. This includes the discovery of new land, the reclamation of land by draining and filling in swamps, the use of fertilizers, the building of glass-houses and the exploitation of hydroponics. Second, other factors than land enjoy rents or quasi-rents, in the sense either that their available quantities are fixed for at least some period of time, or that the quantities available are fixed within some range of possible price variation. Witness the considerable variations in the real incomes of academics that have occurred over the postwar period, which have not induced the majority of academics to abandon their profession or, on the contrary, induced large numbers of non-academics to become such. In short, the principle is correct, but its practical application is extremely difficult and cannot be efficiently achieved by concentration on systems of taxing the rent of land or capital gains from the ownership of land.

Another and less subtle way in which the classical tradition of regarding land as a special case appears in popular thought is what used to be known as the 'conservation movement' and has more recently become known as the movement for the protection of the environment. The fundamental idea is that man has an environment on which he is dependent for his existence, but which he can destroy irrevocably by his own carelessness; hence, it is necessary for public policy to take pains to prevent men from wantonly destroying their environment, through measures to 'conserve' natural resources and/or to prevent pollution of it. This attitude neglects several important economic considerations. First, certain aspects of the environment may be economically valuable at one point of time but cease to be so in the course of time as the result of technical progress. For example, Chilean deposits of guano (accumulated bird excrement) were valuable as fertilizer only until the development of chemical fertilizers; agricultural land is valuable in a community dependent on farming for its existence, but reservation of land for agricultural purposes becomes a nuisance and a distortion of resource allocation in an industrial society in which people want land on which to build factories or houses. Second, it may well be economically rational to use up the wealth provided by the natural environment and convert it into other forms of wealth. (Early settlers in Ontario customarily cut down the tallest trees on their land allotments, floated them down-river, and sold them as masts for the British navy, in order to acquire cash to buy food and seeds for the next crop year; the less-developed countries of contemporary times sell off their oil, tin and other mineral deposits for royalties from which they finance education and industrial investment.) Third, it is almost invariably possible to re-create the environment by investment of resources; also, if re-creation becomes desirable and profitable, the technology required to do it will itself be created by investment. (Witness, as only one example, the landscaping efforts of urban developers in modern cities.) Fourth, the incentives to deplete or to augment the environment are dependent on economic circumstances and particularly on the production and consumption aspects of economic growth. The descendants of the Ontario settlers who cut down the trees for masts and firewood are now investing in the planting of trees for shade and amenity and the construction of swimming pools to replace the swimming facilities in local rivers and lakes lost through the effects of forest denudation on water flow and pollution by industrial wastes. Less-developed countries will now sacrifice the environment for the sake of better-paying industrial jobs, but like the developed countries now will eventually wish to improve the environment at the expense of higher costs of industrial production.

Finally, as suggested by the foregoing arguments, the important question from an economic point of view is what kinds of spoliation of the environment are efficiently remediable and what kinds are not. Conservationist or environmentalist writers typically spoil whatever case they have by choosing for examples either forests or landscape — which are flow supplies of production or utility gains easily capable of improvement by investment — or exhaustible mineral deposits whose exploitation gains can be re-invested in other forms of productive capital and/or which can — and, if their prices rise enough, will — be substituted for by alternatives produced by technological progress, or else eked out by re-utilization and re-cycling of the existing stock. The law of conservation of matter applies in full force here. Consider for example the possibility that the world will eventually run out of deposits of iron ore: already a large part of current steel production is based on the utilization of iron and steel scrap, and at a high enough price every school-child would be scrounging around his environment in search of old tin cans. In addition, the pressure of scarcity would lead to cash payments for the return of used tin cans (they are mostly steel, the tin component being very small) sufficient to induce purchasers of commodities packed in tin cans to treat them as capital goods rather than perishable consumption goods; there are numerous alternative materials from which to construct packaging material, a number of which are provided by flow production rather than by the use of depletable mineral deposits. The real problem is that there are some forms of preventable pollution that appear irremediable within the bounds of contemporary or foreseeable technology, such as the pollution of the upper atmosphere of the Earth by jet-plane-combustant-discharges. (Another apparently irremediable problem concerns joint pollution of water, air, etc. by neighbouring states and provinces; but this is actually a remediable mis-allocation or mis-specification of the property rights of the citizens of the independent political units, and will probably be corrected eventually by political co-operation.)

A related source of popular concern, especially evident in recent years, is the Malthusian fear that unrestrained population growth will exhaust the limits of the capacity of the Earth to supply food for its people. In fact, technology has had little difficulty, on a global basis, in achieving an over-production of food, in the sense of producing more than is or would be consistent with farmers earning incomes comparable with the incomes of industrial workers of similar skill. The population problem is not a problem of food production *per se* (though this is the strong implication of the classical tradition in economic theory) but a problem created by the necessity for countries with growing populations to accumulate capital proportionally or more than proportionally to population growth simply to keep income per head of population from falling. Even this apparent problem is usually created and dramatized by the prediction of pupulation trends from past and current demographic data in disregard of the feedback from poverty, recognized by Malthus and his contemporaries, induced by excess population to marital and procreative customs and mores. Modern theory suggests that people's decisions about marriage and child-bearing are economic decisions, given the availability of knowledge of contraceptive techniques, and that therefore the population problem will solve itself in time.

Classical Rent Theory and the Availability of Inferior Land
Classical rent theory assumed a fixed quantity of land, specified in terms of fertility, in response to the application of other factors to it in the production process, and assumed that these other factors could be treated as homogenous. Rent was the surplus of output over the cost of production, or the surplus of the average product of the other factors over their marginal product when applied in agriculture. See Diagram I, which graphs the average and marginal

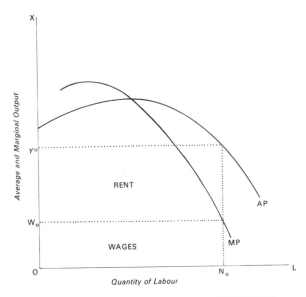

DIAGRAM I: THE CLASSICAL THEORY OF RENT

products of labour applied to land; for a given quantity of labour N_0 the marginal product is W_0, which determines the wage rate, the average product is Y_0, and rent is the difference between the two, multiplied by the quantity of labour. Classical theory envisaged two ways in which the use of more labour could increase output from the land, albeit subject to diminishing marginal productivity. The first was by resort to inferior land (the 'extensive margin' of cultivation), the use of which would become profitable as the wage of labour fell; the second was by more intensive cultivation of existing land (the 'intensive margin' of cultivation) which would become profitable under the same circumstances. In either case, the fall in the value (marginal product) of labour would increase the rent earned from the existing level of application of labour to the land.

The association of the earning of rent with the necessity of resorting to inferior land generates a confusion, characteristic of some expositions of the theory of rent, and one which must be avoided, namely the attribution of rent to the existence of inferior land. On the contrary, rent is due to the scarcity of existing land, and the availability of inferior land sets a limit to the rent that can be earned on the best quality land. This point is illustrated in Diagram II. Assume for simplicity that there is a fixed coefficient between

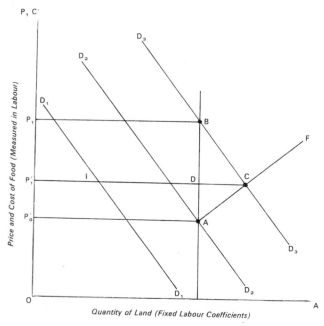

DIAGRAM II: RENT AND THE AVAILABILITY OF INFERIOR LAND

the amount of land and the labour required to till it, and that society has a fixed stock of land of constant fertility available to it. With a small population, represented by the demand curve $D_1 D_1$, not all of the land will be required for food production, the price of food will be the labour cost of production, and there will be no rent. But as population increases, the demand for food will shift to the right, and at a demand curve position $D_2 D_2$ all the land will be required for production. Further population increase, represented by the demand curve $D_3 D_3$, will result in the emergence of rent (the rectangle $P_0 P_1 B A$); and still further increases in population will raise rent without increasing the total production of food, until eventually the population will presumably reach an equilibrium determined by the fixed total supply of food production. Now introduce the availability of land of inferior quality, represented by the continuation of the supply curve or cost curve of food AF

beyond the original curve P_0A. With the demand curve D_3D_3, rent will be the area $P_0P_1'CA$ rather than the area P_0P_1BA. The rent on the best quality land will have fallen by $P_1'P_1BD$; total rent will have fallen by this amount and risen by the triangle ADC, so that the net effect of the availability of inferior land on total rent will be uncertain and dependent on the slopes of the demand and the supply curves. The essential principle is that total rent is determined by the scarcity of land, a matter of the interaction of demand for and supply of land, and that the availability of inferior land constitutes an increase in the supply.

An alternative approach to the theory of rent is that of von Thünen, who divorced the theory of rent from questions of land quality by constructing a model in which all land is of equal quality and situated in a flat plain surrounding a city. The fertility of land in this case is a matter, not of the inherent properties of the soil, but of the distance of its location from the city. At the margin, the cost of food delivered to the city must include both its cost of production on the land location, and the cost of delivery (transport) to the city. Land located near the city will command a rent equal to the difference in transport costs between it and the city and between marginal land and the city. This model, which makes rent a function of distance and transport cost relative to a market centre rather than of the inherent properties of the land itself, is far more useful than the classical model for the study of the important problems of rent theory in contemporary society, which are primarily concerned with the determination of urban land values, location of urban population in relation to the city centre, and the effects on these of technological changes or applications of them such as the construction of rapid-transit commuting train-routes and expressways for automobiles.

This approach is illustrated in Diagram III, which assumes all land of equal quality and fixed coefficients between labour and land in production. The direct cost of production is the horizontal line CC; the cost of transport to market per unit of distance is represented by the slope of the curve P_eP_e. (Actually, transport costs are more complicated than this, involving both a distance charge and a terminal loading-unloading charge, but this makes no difference to the general principle.) The quantity of food output demanded is assumed to require production of food at a maximum distance from the urban centre of D_e; land located at that distance is just worth cultivating, the urban price P_e just paying the cost of production and the transport charges to the market. Land located closer to the urban centre earns a rent equal to the difference between the transport cost from the marginal farms and the transport cost of its own product to the city, total rent as a proportion of cost being the ratio of P_eQC to CQD_eO. (This is put in terms of a ratio since, on the assumptions given, land in agricultural use will be contained in a circle circumscribed about the urban centre and not lie in a straight line along a road starting from the urban centre as the diagram implies.) The diagram, obviously, can easily be adapted to the assumption that what is produced on land is not food but accommodation or living space for city dwellers or workers, and that the transport cost is the cash and time cost of commuting between a suburb and the city centre. Thus we would predict that land values in a city would generally vary inversely with distance from the city centre. But for a fuller understanding of the economics of urban land

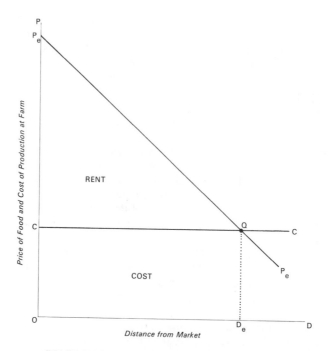

DIAGRAM III: THE DISTANCE THEORY OF RENT

use, we would have to take account of the long lag between changes in land values and the adaptation of building construction to these changing values, which is typically reflected in the overcrowding of old buildings located near the city centre (slums and ghettoes) and the eventual replacement of these old buildings by high-rise apartments, as suburbanites begin to find commuting costs more expensive in terms of time-cost of commuting than the saving in cash rental costs that they permit.

Aggregate Rent and Economic Growth
The central proposition of the classical theory of distribution according to Ricardo is that as capital accumulates and the population increases the amount of rent must rise due to the increasing scarcity of land. This will occur whether growth entails resort to increasingly inferior land (the extensive margin of cultivation) or resort to increasingly intensive cultivation of existing land (the intensive margin of cultivation). In either case the rise in rent is due to the principle of diminishing marginal productivity as more of one factor is applied relative to the quantity of the other — the so-called 'law of varying proportions'. (This principle is straightforward in the case of the intensive margin of cultivation; in the case of the extensive margin, one must recognize that it is the effects of the law of varying proportions that make it economic to resort to use of the inferior land.)

What about the effects of growth on the relative share of rent? As already seen, if one confines the analysis to a one-sector model, that is, treats agriculture as the only activity of the economy, the relative share of land may rise or fall as the amount of other factors increases. There are two alternative statements of the condition for the share of rent to rise: (1) the elasticity of substitution between land and the factors whose quantity is increasing is less than unity; (2) the elasticity of output with respect to the growing factors falls as their quantity increases. Note that, to maintain the proposition that as growth goes on the relative share of rent must rise we must assert either that eventually the elasticity of substitution between land and other factors becomes less than unity, or that the elasticity of output with respect to other factors falls, as their quantity increases. (These are of course equivalent propositions.)

In the context of a two-sector model, in which the two sectors are agriculture and industry and production is assumed to require land and labour, agriculture being land-intensive relative to industry, an increase in the available supply of labour at constant commodity (and therefore factor) prices would, by the Rybcynski theorem (p. 173 below) shift resources out of agriculture and reduce agricultural output. The price of agricultural products would have to rise relative to the price of industrial products to restore equilibrium, and this would raise the rental price of land. The fall in the price of industrial products would, however, induce their substitution for agricultural products, and this would have a similar effect to an increase in the elasticity of substitution between labour and land in agricultural production, in tending to reduce rather than raise the relative share of land in the total income of the economy.

A parallel problem concerns the effect of innovations in agriculture on the relative and absolute share of rent in national income; this has been covered in previous analysis. In a single-activity model, the effect of innovation on the relative share of rent depends only on whether the innovation is land-saving or labour-saving, if we identify the innovation with a shift in the production function; in the former case land's relative share decreases, in the latter it increases. Note that the result does not depend on the elasticity of substitution. If on the other hand we treat innovation as augmenting the effective supplies of land and labour for use within a given production function, the relative share of land will fall either if the innovation is relatively land-augmenting and the elasticity of substitution is below unity, or if the innovation is relatively labour-augmenting and the elasticity of substitution is more than unity; and conversely for a rise in the relative share of land. If the innovation is sufficiently land-saving in the former case, or if the elasticity of substitution differs from unity in the required direction by a large enough amount in the latter case, the absolute as well as the relative share of land will fall.

In a two-sector model, technical change in agriculture will increase or decrease the relative share of land, assuming it is the factor used relatively intensively in agriculture, if the elasticity of demand for agricultural products exceeds or falls short of a certain critical constant; this constant is unity for Hicks-neutral technical progress in agriculture, greater than unity for land-saving innovations, and less than unity for labour-saving innovations.

These are theoretical possibilities. But there is a great body of empirical evidence to the effect that both the income and the price elasticity of demand for agricultural products are substantially less than unity in developed countries. This suggests the conclusion that technical progress in agriculture will as a matter of fact tend to reduce the share of rent in national income, unless such progress is strongly labour-saving. This has something to do with the failure of the classical predictions about the effects of growth on the rent share, and the eventual halting of growth by a fall in the rate of profit. A full treatment would require analysis of the type of technical progress and the industry to which it applies, as well as of the effects of the growth of other factors relative to land. Previous analysis shows that the growth of the other factors, assuming that agriculture is land-intensive, would tend to raise rental value of land per unit, though the effect on the share of rent in total income is indeterminate. If neutral technical progress occurred at the same rate in the agricultural and industrial sectors, at constant factor prices, outputs in both sectors would rise in the same proportions; but with a less than unitary income elasticity of demand for agricultural products, the relative price of land would have to fall, and with it the relative share of rent in total income. This in fact seems to have been what has happened historically — technical progress in agriculture has gone on at more or less the same rate as in industry — and the result, given the low income and price elasticities of demand for agricultural products in conjunction with the immobility of labour off the land, has been depressed farm incomes relative to industrial incomes and a chronic problem of agricultural poverty.

Fertility and the Pattern of Land Settlement
There was a classical controversy between Mill and Carey over the pattern of land settlement. Mill, following Ricardo, maintained that the order of exploitation of land in a new country would occur in decreasing order of the fertility of land (this following the theory of the extensive margin of cultivation), the land first exploited yielding the highest rent and the largest output. Carey on the contrary maintained that the most fertile and highest-yielding land, in terms of both rent and output, would be settled later. The Finnish economist af Heurlin has provided the solution, which is illustrated in Diagrams IVa and IVb; the central point is that fertility is not necessarily equivalent to least cost of immediate exploitation, nor is high rent necessarily equivalent to least cost of immediate exploitation. In the diagrams, C_1 and C_2 represent the minimum costs of production on land of types 1 and 2, and C_1C_1' and C_2C_2' are the cost curves per unit of output from a given amount of the two types of land. Obviously, land of type 1 will be settled first, because the cost of production on it is lower for small amounts of output. Land of type 2 will be settled only when the price of the product rises above C_2. If the cost curves of increasing production are related to each other as in Diagram IVa, with cost of production on land type 1 always below the cost of production on land type 2 for any given level of output, it is clear that land type 1 will always be more fertile, in terms of the optimal level of production given the price of the product, than land type 2, and will always bear a higher rental value (areas $A + B$ rather than A only). But if the cost curves for increasing production are related as in Diagram IVb, rent on land type 1 will be $A + B$ and rent on land type 2 will be $B + C$;

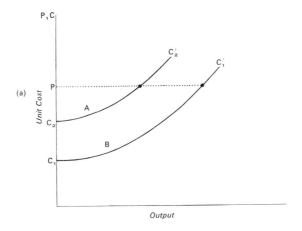

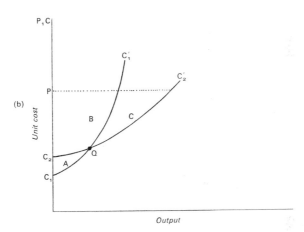

DIAGRAM IV: RENT AND SETTLEMENT

at a price for the product corresponding to the point Q, land type 2 becomes more fertile than land type 1, in terms of optimal total output; and with a high enough price of the product such as P, C is greater than A, so that rent on land type 2 is greater than rent on land type 1. Diagram IVa is Mill's case; Diagram IVb with a high enough price of the product is Carey's.

Farm Price Support Policies
Suppose that society becomes concerned about the low incomes of farmers, and decides to raise them by raising the prices of agricultural products and providing for the absorption of the resulting increase in quantity supplied by restriction of quantities of imports, stock-piling, subsidized sales to the poor via food stamps, or some other means. If the supply of farm labour is perfectly elastic, there will be no effect on the wages of farm labour and, therefore, in relieving the poverty of rural workers. The only effect will be

84

an increase in the rental value of land. This will be capitalized into the price of agricultural land, giving a capital gain to existing owners of land but making it still more expensive for rural workers to become land-owners. Moreover, the gain will be greater for the land-owners, the more land they own or the more fertile (in the sense of output per acre) is the land they own. Thus a price-support programme benefits not the rural workers, but the rural land-owners, and is more favourable to them the more wealthy they are already. Further, if the price support programme threatens to lead to an embarrassingly large surplus of farm output, and policy responds to this threat by placing quotas or acreage restrictions on the use of land for production of the price-supported crops, the effect is to reduce the amount of land available per unit of rural labour, and this could even have the effect of reducing the wage rate of such labour below what it would have been in the absence of price supports and the accompanying restrictions on land use.

Share-Cropping and Efficiency
Share-cropping — the system by which the tenant farms the land in exchange for delivering a fixed proportion of the output to the landlord — has generally been regarded in the economic literature as an inefficient system, on the basis of the apparent analogy with a tax per unit on the tenant's output. Stephen N. S. Cheung, however, has shown that share-cropping should be as efficient as fixed-rent tenancy.

The argument is illustrated by Diagram V, where MP_L is the marginal product of labour applied to a given quantity of land and $(1 - r) MP_L$ is the tenant's net receipts after paying the crop-share rental r. It appears that the optimal amount of labour for the tenant to supply, given his alternative

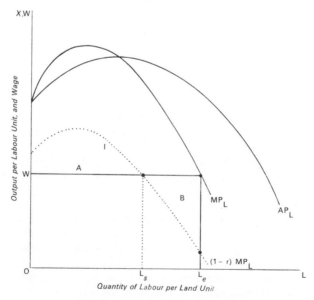

DIAGRAM V: SHARE-CROPPING

opportunity wage W, is L_s, which falls short of the quantity of labour that would maximize the owner's rent, L_e. This is the per-unit-tax analogy. But there is a flaw in the argument: if the tenant rented the land on these terms, he would be obtaining a rent for himself measured by the area A, over and above the cost of his labour (alternative opportunity cost); this would be inconsistent with the assumption of perfect competition in the labour market. The landlord could try to insist, as part of the tenancy contract, that the tenant provide labour in the amount of L_e, which would maximize the landlord's rent for this piece of land and the specified landlord's share of the crop. However, this would only be acceptable to the tenant if the area B were equal to the area A, i.e. if his total net receipts under a contract specifying both the landlord's share of the crop and the amount of labour he has to provide were just equal to the alternative opportunity cost of his labour. If area B exceeds area A, the landlord's optimizing strategy should be to increase the amount of land offered to the tenant and decrease the rental share, while still specifying the amount of labour required for the tenant to supply; and vice versa. In short, the landlord can obtain the same rent-maximizing results that he would obtain under a competitive fixed-rental system with a share-cropping system, provided that the share-cropping system allows him to fix both the amount of land per tenant and the amount of labour that the tenant is obliged to put in in tilling the land. It follows that, given freedom of contract with respect to land size and tenant labour input, share-cropping is as efficient as a fixed-rental system. It also follows that conversion from an efficient share-cropping system to a fixed-rental system will not improve efficiency, and may reduce it if the conversion is accompanied by arbitrary fixation either of rents or of tenant land allocations or both. This proposition is a particular application of the 'Coase theorem', which says that if property rights and obligations are clearly defined legally, and contracting and litigation are relatively costless, the externalities and distortions with which much of contemporary welfare economics has been concerned will be 'internalized' by the economic system and cease to create welfare problems.

Common Property Resources and the Pollution Problem

Common property resources are environmental resources which are scarce but which, for institutional reasons, are not charged for to the person who uses them. The result is that their utilization is carried beyond the socially optimal point, since the costs of utilization, not being charged for, are disregarded in the profit-maximizing calculations of the users. Common property resources in the form of grazing rights on common land played an important part in the enclosure movements in pre-industrial British economic history, which essentially recognized the inefficiencies that resulted from such rights and sought to internalize them; similar rights to let one's livestock graze on common property constitute an important problem in some less developed countries today, where such grazing prevents the growth of trees necessary to the conservation and control of water supply. In recent times and recent literature, however, common property resources have been identified with fishing rights in lakes and oceans, and the relevant theory has been developed in that context.

The problem of common property resources is illustrated in Diagram VI. The curves graph the average and marginal products of resources applied to exploitation of common property resources, and the cost of these resources, assumed for simplicity to be constant. If the common property resource were charged for, production would be carried up to the point of application of N_o of other resources, which would maximize the rent on the common

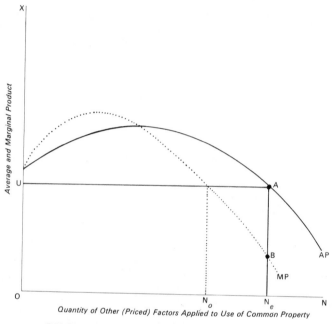

DIAGRAM VI: COMMON PROPERTY RESOURCES

property resource. But if the common property resource is not charged for, production will be carried to the point where the average product of application of other factors to the common property resource is equal to the marginal cost of applying the other factors, which is a quantity of application N_e yielding an average product of $N_e A = W$ and a marginal product of $N_e B$ less than the average product and cost of the other factors W. Thus the common property resource will be utilized beyond the point of optimality or maximum efficiency. Note that this would not happen if the common property resource were clearly owned by someone, and appropriately charged for.

This analysis leads us into the contemporary concern about the problem of pollution of the environment by industrial waste and noxious discharge of effluents. The pollution problem arises because the environment is a common property resource the use of which is not charged for, so that polluters do not have to pay the costs to others of their pollutant activities. The economically appropriate solution, however, is not to prohibit pollutant activities entirely: as Diagram VI shows, there is a socially optimal level of usage of common property resources which could be achieved by charging an appropriate rent for the use of the environment; and this rent would normally not be so high as to preclude any use of the environment whatsoever.

The problem is to establish property rights in the environment, so that the use of the environment will be properly charged for. Who actually possesses the property rights will influence the distribution of income, but not the achievement of optimization (e.g. it will make a difference to income distribution whether industrial firms have the right to pollute local rivers and citizens can bribe them not to do so, or whether citizens have the right to unpolluted rivers and firms can bribe them to accept pollution; but the results of free contracting should be the same, allowance being made for the income effects of the distribution of property rights in the environment). The catch is that the argument assumes that the transactions costs, and possibly also the litigation costs, of private contracting over property rights in the environment are negligible. If the transaction and litigation costs are not negligible, the assignment of property rights in the environment will make a difference to the equilibrium outcome.

The central point in the previous paragraph is the Coase theorem. If property rights are clearly defined, and transactions and litigation costs are negligible, society will arrive at a Pareto-optimal position in spite of externalities, because externalities will be internalized through the process of contract and litigation. The assignment of legal rights will affect matters only through income or wealth effects. And there will be no case for public intervention and regulation to prevent pollution, etc., unless either property rights are not clearly defined and need to be re-defined at the discretion of the state or the private costs of transactions in contracts (including litigation) are so high that state definition of rights and obligations would be substantially cheaper.

Economic analysis also suggests that if the state does intervene in the matter of pollution of the environment, its best strategy is not outright prohibition of pollutant activities, but auctioning off of the right to pollute to the highest bidder. This would enable those who dislike pollution to buy up the rights to pollute and not use them if they disliked pollution enough.

The Modern Theory of Rent

The foregoing sections have been concerned with the rent of land or, more generally, of the environment. This follows the classical association of rent with land, as the factor fixed in available supply to society. But available supplies of land are not fixed: land can be invested in, or disinvested in. On the other hand, the supplies of other factors, for example, skilled labour of a particular grade, may be fixed, at least for a period of time long enough to be economically relevant; and where this happens the theory of rent is applicable to them as well. In fact, the theory of rent is applicable whenever the supply of a factor is imperfectly elastic in the relevant economic context.

For any factor which is completely fixed in supply, the price it commands will be determined by the demand for its services, and neither its alternative opportunity cost in other uses nor its cost of original production will play

D

any part in determining its price. (Of course, its owners may have 'reservation prices' representing the alternative value of the factor in private, non-market use.) All the earnings of the factor, above zero (or above reservation price) will be a rent or surplus — and, as such, amenable to taxation that will not distort resource allocation.

If a factor is in imperfectly elastic supply, and conditions are competitive, an increase in demand for its services will have to raise its price in order to attract additional supply; the rise in price will, due to the assumption of competition, apply to all units already in employment. Thus the units that would have chosen the employment at a lower price will earn a rent — a surplus over their 'transfer price', i.e. the price at which they are indifferent between transferring into or out of some other type of employment.

A question arises concerning the determinants of the transfer price, and the characteristics of the 'marginal man'. Consider a particular occupation, such as the teaching of economics in universities, which employs individuals of varying qualifications and abilities, and with varying alternative opportunities. The marginal man, the one with the highest transfer price, who would shift out of the occupation if demand fell and into it if demand rose, might be either a man of low quality with few alternative opportunities, or a man of high quality with plentiful alternative opportunities. Specifically, when the demand for university teachers of economics increased sharply in the early 1960s, some of those attracted into teaching from the outside world were extremely able economists who had previously been able to earn higher incomes (or incomes plus non-pecuniary advantages) outside the universities, and now found the higher level of university salaries attractive; others were individuals who had not before been considered good enough to merit a university post. This is an important point to remember in a variety of contexts, i.e. that the marginal man may be marginal either because he is better or because he is worse than the average. As one example, it is not necessarily true that an expansion of the number of places available in higher education will mean a deterioration of the quality of the students in university (or the faculty teaching them, for that matter).

The most important points are that the incomes received by all factors may contain an element of rent above the price necessary to keep the factor in its current employment; and that the division of the price between necessary price and surplus depends on the perspective. For example, labour employed by a firm in a competitive industry may earn no rent, in the sense that it could readily transfer to employment with another firm in the industry at the same wages (though a particular individual may be earning a rent if he can provide services specifically useful to the firm that employs him but not useful to other firms). Yet all the labour employed in the industry may be earning some rent, in the sense that if the industry closed down the workers would have to accept substantially lower wages to obtain employment in other industries. Similarly, if we consider all the labour in an economy at a particular time, all or most of its earnings is likely to be rent, in the sense that if the economy were to cease operations the alternatives would be migration, starvation, or retreat into self-employed search to obtain subsistence. This last point is rather far-fetched, but it has an application to the economics of wartime devastation and also of postwar economic recovery. (That is, postwar poverty does not necessarily or even usually mean absence of productive skills, whose earning power can be fairly quickly restored with time and possibly a modicum of outside aid resources).

10

ASPECTS OF THE THEORY OF WAGES

Introduction

We move on to consider the theory of wages and the peculiarities of labour as a factor of production. These differences have largely to do with supply considerations and the fact that labour, unlike land or capital, has to have its owner present when services are rendered.

First, the return to labour includes a cash return plus a return of utility or disutility to the owner derived from his presence in the workplace. Marshall's law of equalization of net advantages took account of this and states that the cash return plus the money value of the utility flow will be equalized across occupations — of course, this point will hold only to the extent that workers share common tastes in their work preferences. If tastes are not similar, people will tend to gravitate to occupations they prefer and cash rewards will tend to converge. Differences in wages will reflect the marginal worker's valuation of the utility flow associated with the employment.

Second, the fact that workers are generally hired in large numbers for work in the same location requires us to recognize that there will be elements of social interaction and group formation. Workers, unlike other factors, will be able to band together in, say, trade unions in order to pursue their common interests. Further, the amount of labour service actually rendered will depend on the physical and social conditions in the work place.

Third, the provision of time is not an element of any other factor's decision as to how much service to provide. Apart from considerations of depreciation, the owner of capital does not mind how much his capital is used. The worker's choice is traditionally that between labour and leisure time — the implicit assumption being that leisure time has scarcity value. The standard analysis of the 1920s recognized that a rise in the wage rate would have two effects: an income effect and a substitution effect, the latter causing the worker to provide more labour time, the former causing him to provide less. Development economists have had a tendency to espouse the view that in developing countries the adverse income effect will predominate. They assume that farmers will produce less for the market as the price of agricultural produce rises. This led to a recommendation to keep agricultural prices down in order to provide the industrial sector with low cost foodstuffs and to maximize the marketable surplus of agricultural output. Empirical evidence suggests that the development economists are wrong and that the substitution effect predominates.

The more complex analysis of the provision of labour time developed since the 1950s involves recognizing that using leisure time involves using various kinds of equipment (commodities). The choice is thus not between labour and leisure but between earning more to buy commodities and having the time to use them. This reflects on a once standard theory of taxation. It was held that taxation of income was a more efficient way of generating government income than excise taxation as it left the margins of choice between labour and leisure undistorted. Friedman and Little pointed out that the margin of choice between labour and leisure was being distorted by the income tax — in effect, leisure was being given a subsidy. Corlett and Hague argued that the optimal tax structure would involve a differential tax on commodities, lower on substitutes for and higher on complements for leisure. The problem is, of course, to find a reasonable classification of goods that are 'complementary'. This scheme is not the 'best' from an efficiency point of view — the best being a tax on potential income (actual cash income plus a valuation of leisure time at the market wage).

It is clear that the progressive income tax provides disincentives for work — the social value of an hour worked is greater than its value to the individual. A lump sum tax would leave margins undistorted and would thus be efficient. One might however, wish to consider questions of equity. Is it 'just' to tax someone at the flat rate of $4000 per year when all he earns is $3500? Progressivity suggests itself and we are back at our initial problem.

More recently, Becker has examined the problem of leisure choice. We can summarize the theory as saying that optimal behaviour is a rationing problem. In purchasing goods people are faced with two budget constraints and two sets of relative prices. The one involves cash income and money prices, the other involves available time and the time costs of purchasing and consuming the goods in question. This analysis leads to a number of results that differ from the usually accepted ones. Technological progress may cause the relative prices of goods in terms of time to change. Rather than causing individuals to work less, this may have the effect of causing individuals to work more as the time price of leisure activities is lowered. Note that the provision of time choice is made in a number of different dimensions — people may alter the length of their vacations, they may enter the work force sooner and leave it later, and so on.

Fourth, the owner of the factor labour may be restricted in the amount of time that he can spend searching out new opportunities. This gives new support to the Keynesian hypothesis that in the short run wages are rigid or sticky. The process of search in which an unemployed labourer must engage involves a fair amount of time. Surveying the market and determining that a new, lower wage is appropriate may take enough time for the unemployment to increase sharply without driving wages down.

Fifth, individual liberty dictates that each man has control over the disposition of his own time. It is thus very difficult for those lacking the financial wherewithal to engage in binding contracts for the purpose of financing accumulation of human capital — individuals are unlikely to invest in other individuals unless there are guarantees to capture a reasonably certain return. It is also argued that accumulating human capital is done in the absence of complete information. The long lags involved in the adjustment of supply to demand make the future uncertain. Several circumstances mitigate the seriousness of the limitations on the funds to finance human capital. Individuals may invest in their children without formal contracts — they may treat the investment as a means of endowing their children or they may impose non-contractual moral obligations. In the aggregate, the return on human capital may equal the return on other forms of capital while distortions take the form of systematic exclusion of certain groups from the educational process.

Sixth, capital is held to be accumulated according to the rational rule that as long as the present value of the returns exceeds the present value of the costs, capital will be accumulated. On the other hand, it is held that population does not grow according to these precepts — this may be blamed on transitory social conditions, and it may be held that as knowledge regarding the means and devices to control the size of families become available and widespread, and when individuals are charged the full social costs of having children, population growth will behave as any other economic variable. In any case, the theory presents a happy alternative to those of Ricardo and Malthus who postulated that workers bred to the level of subsistence set by pestilence and famine (while, of course, the capitalists did not). Recently economists have returned to the idea that family size is a variable of rational choice.

The Principle of Derived Demand
The most interesting problems in labour economics occur on the supply side, but we begin the analysis with the demand side, because certain aspects of the general theory of factor pricing can be conveniently dealt with in this context. While factor pricing is a general equilibrium problem, Marshall's partial equilibrium approach is a reasonable first approximation. We concern ourselves with labour of a certain specified type, or labour used in a particular industry.

The principle of derived demand (which is very similar to the Austrian principle of 'imputation' of value of product to the factors used in producing it) starts from the point that productive factors are demanded, not for their own sake, but for their services in producing final products. This is implicit in the marginal productivity principle: the value of the productive service rendered by a factor is the value of its contribution to output. (Note that this is only true if the firms using the factor face a perfectly competitive product market; otherwise, the factor price is equal, not to the value of its marginal product, but to its marginal value product, i.e. marginal physical output multiplied by marginal revenue to the firm. Also, the VMP or MVP curve is only the demand curve for the factor, and has to be brought into relation with factor supply to determine price; if employers face a competitive market for labour VMP or MVP will be made equal to factor price, but if the employer has monopsony power in the labour market he will equate demand price with marginal cost of labour, which will be above the price of labour if the supply curve of labour is upward-sloping. These points modify the marginal productivity theory as a theory of distribution, and have implications for the efficiency of the competitive system in allocating labour among alternative uses.)

The principle of derived demand implies that the demand for the services of a particular factor — the location and slope of the demand curve for it — depends not only on the possibilities of substitution between it and other factors in the production function for the production of a given output, but also on the effects of a change in its price in changing the price of the final product and inducing substitution between that product and other products. A further element considered in the literature is the elasticity of supply of other factors of production as the quantity of them demanded changes in response to a change in the price of this factor; this influence will not be considered here.

On the basis of the principle of derived demand, Marshall developed four propositions about the demand for labour; one of these was incorrect and was subsequently corrected by Hicks in his *Theory of Wages*. The first three (including the corrected one) are contained in the formula for the elasticity of demand for a factor, which can be found in R. G. D. Allen's *Mathematical Analysis for Economists* (ch. 14.8). The elasticity of demand for a factor with respect to its own price is, in a two-factor model, and assuming constant price of the other factor,

$$\frac{E_a}{E_{pa}} = -(k_b\sigma + k_a\eta)$$

the elasticity of demand for the other factor with respect to a change in the price of this one is

$$\frac{E_b}{E_{pa}} = k_a(\sigma - \eta)$$

where E_a/E_{pa} and E_b/E_{pa} are not corrected in Marshallian fashion to make the own-price elasticity a positive number, but σ (the elasticity of substitution in production) and η (the elasticity of demand for the final product) are so corrected, and $k_a(=1-k_b)$ is the share of factor a in total cost initially. Marshall's four propositions, the third being corrected according to Hicks, are as follows:

1. The elasticity of demand for a factor will be greater, the greater the elasticity of substitution in production.
2. The elasticity of demand for a factor will be greater, the greater the elasticity of demand for the final product.
3. The elasticity of demand for a factor will be greater, the greater the share of the factor in total cost, *provided that the elasticity of demand for the final product exceeds the elasticity of substitution*. (The Hicksian proviso can be easily established by re-writing

$$\frac{E_a}{E_{pa}} = -\sigma - k_a(\eta - \sigma)).$$

4. The elasticity of demand for a factor will be greater, the greater the elasticity of supply of the other factor. (This is too obvious to require proof, or modification of the algebra to include the elasticity of supply of the other factor.)

Note in passing that an increase in the price of a factor will increase or decrease the quantity of the other factor demanded according to whether σ is greater or less than η.

A note of caution about these propositions is necessary, because the results are somewhat different for a production function with more than two factors, because this case raises the question of definition of 'the' elasticity of substitution. Allen's definition of the elasticity of substitution (ch. 19.6) produces the following formulae, which leave the first two propositions intact but remove the proviso from the third:

$$\frac{E_{a_1}}{E_{pa_1}} = k_1(\sigma_{11} - \eta) \text{ where } \sigma_{11} \text{ is necessarily negative;}$$

$$\frac{E_{a_2}}{E_{pa_1}} = k_1(\sigma_{12} - \eta) \text{ where } \sigma_{12} \text{ can be positive (a substitute) or negative}$$
$$(\text{a complement}).$$

The elasticity of demand for a factor is relevant to the questions of whether, if the quantity of a factor increases, its total income will rise or fall, and whether, if its price rises (for example as the result of union action) its total income rises or falls. For example, if a union is interested in maximizing its revenue from union dues, and these are a fixed proportion of the total wage bill, the union should set wages at the level at which the elasticity of demand for labour is unity.

Criticisms of the Marginal Productivity Theory of Wages
The marginal productivity principle as applied to the determination of wages has aroused much controversy, some of it ignorant or prompted purely by a reluctance to accept the proposition that if the wages of a particular category of labour are low this is because that wage is all the labour in question is worth to society, some of it prompted by concern over the realism of the theory (its correspondence to the observed or allegedly observed facts of reality), and some of it concerned, whether consciously or not, with fundamental problems about the nature of capital (as the factor with which labour co-operates in production).

Some of these criticisms are dispelled by the recognition that marginal productivity is merely the demand side of the picture, and that it is necessary to bring in the supply side to arrive at the determination of wages. For example, the contention that wages are determined by 'custom' or by collective bargaining is not inconsistent with the marginal productivity theory: if the price is fixed, demand determines the quantity employed. But this contention raises the deeper issue of why custom or bargaining should fix wages at the levels at which they are fixed: both may represent simply a rule-of-thumb institutionalization of longer-run economic forces, in particular the training costs of different types of labour and the monopoly power that a particular union has created for itself.

Other criticisms are countered by the recognition that the theoretical analysis of marginal productivity theory is an abstraction from the real world of forces working over the long run to influence wage determination. Much of Hicks' analysis in the *Theory of Wages* is concerned with reconciling theoretical abstraction with empirical reality. A specific problem is that workers are seen to receive standard wages even though their labour performance differs in quality. The standardization of wages for labourers of different quality is a convenience for company accountants and a comfort to the workers' desire for apparent equity. But workers' incomes tend to be adjusted to their performance through other dimensions of the employment contract — regularity of employment, overtime work, prospects for promotion to a higher grade, etc. As a case in point, in the United Kingdom all lecturers (and assistant lecturers, a grade recently abolished) receive the same pay, which is a base rate increased according to seniority; but when I was a professor in Manchester in the late 1950s, the economics department appointed a lecturer in applied economics who had only one year of post-B.A. experience, at the same time as the economic history department appointed an assistant lecturer who had twelve years of post-B.A. experience, with three published books to his credit. The alternative to standard wages is individual bargaining between employer and worker; here the principle, according to Hicks but going back to Böhm-Bawerk's theory of 'marginal pairs', is that the limits to the price fixed in the individual bargain are the higher price required to employ a better-quality worker and the lower price that will suffice to attract a poorer-quality worker.

The aspect of marginal productivity theory most difficult for the layman to swallow is the notion of substitutability of capital for labour. This difficulty mixes naïveté of observation with fundamental theoretical difficulties. The naïveté results from the observation that production techniques in use usually involve apparent fixity of the ratio of men to machinery, and specificity of the machinery; it therefore appears that subtraction of the men would bring the whole operation to a stop, so that the marginal productivity of the men is the whole output, or, alternatively, that an additional man would add nothing to total output. But this is naïve because, first, in the short run some way could usually be found by which most of the output lost through the absence of a man could be retrieved, and an extra man could be utilized to increase output (e.g. by carrying water and sandwiches for the others); and, second, in the longer run equipment could be re-designed to accommodate varying numbers of men. For example, in the United States it takes only one man to drive a truck delivering Coca-Cola; in India, it takes three men: one to drive, one to load and unload, and one to keep the books on deliveries and receipts. The difference is due on the one hand to a big difference in the price of labour relative to the cost of the truck, on the other to the fact that American labour is skilled in more dimensions than Indian labour.

The fundamental theoretical problem, which arises from D. H. Robertson's contemplation of the choice between eleven men spelling each other in the use of ten shovels of a specified size and eleven men using eleven shovels of smaller size representing the same quantity of capital, is the meaning of the concept of a fixed quantity of capital in relation to a varying quantity of labour and the consequent necessity to adapt the physical specification of the capital equipment to suit the needs of maximum production. For the individual firm in a competitive market, there is no problem: constant quantity of capital can be identified with constant cost of capital equipment, regardless of its physical specification, since the market provides prices at which one specification can be translated into another. But this answer will not work for a major sector of the economy, or for the economy as a whole, because for these cases the cost of items of capital equipment cannot be regarded as parametric. The reason is that capital equipment is a means of production produced by the use of other factors (labour, and capital equipment itself) and its cost in terms of labour will not be parametric but instead dependent on wage and interest rates. Specifically, if the wage rate rises in money terms, without a change in the rate of interest, the prices of all goods will rise equi-proportionally and there can be no induced substitution of labour for capital. Substitution between labour and capital requires a rise in the real and not merely the money wage rate and, correspondingly, a fall in the rate of interest. (This was the essence of G. F. Shove's criticism of Hicks's theory of wages, which led the latter to keep his book out of print for nearly thirty years.) But a change in the rate of interest will change the relation between the value of capital in terms of its purchasing power over consumption goods, and its quantity viewed as an input into the production process. This problem is taken up later, in connection with the theory of capital. For the present, note that it is a real and fundamental problem.

The result of these considerations is that there is a real dilemma in the application of marginal productivity theory. In the short run, there appears to be fixity of capital-labour coefficients that deprives the principle of sub-stitution of plausible empirical validity (this is not necessarily true, as mentioned, but the substitutions involved entail varying the labour utilized with a fixed specification of capital equipment which is not necessarily optimal for the relevant price of labour). In the long run, the specification of the capital equipment can be varied to suit relative factor prices, but this raises the question of the meaning of a fixed quantity of capital. Most economists have been prepared to live with the fuzziness of the concept of a fixed quantity of capital, and to assume that the problem can be taken care of with sufficient ingenuity in the statistical measurement of the capital stock. However, a group of theorists centred on Cambridge University in England have con-vinced themselves that the difficulties involved in measuring the quantity of capital are so great as to make the whole structure of marginal productivity theory a nonsense. (This question will be dealt with in later chapters.)

A final point in this connection is that marginal productivity theory suggests that unemployment must be attributable to workers insisting on a level of real wages that is too high to permit all workers to be employed. This would be true, if wage bargains fixed real wages. But — and this is one of the important contributions of Keynes's *General Theory* — workers bargain for money wages and not for real wages, though of course the money wage bargains are influenced by expectations about the purchasing power of the money wages so achieved. Unemployment may result because the money wage bargains imply a real wage higher than is consistent with full employment, even though the workers do not intend this result — as may happen if there is a drastic deflation of the money supply but workers do not appreciate the implications of this for the equilibrium level of money wages. In the face of a monetary deflation, a lowering of money wage rates may be necessary to restore full employment and such a lowering will imply a reduction in real wages relative to those that would prevail at less-than-full employment, because less-than-full employment with a given stock of capital implies a rise in the marginal productivity of labour. But it would be more efficient, given the resistance of workers to a lowering of money wages, to restore full employment by reflation of the money supply rather than by waiting for money wages to fall sufficiently to restore the real value of the money supply to what is consistent with full employment. In short, unemployment must be associated with real wages being fixed at too high a level; but the reasons for this situation may and usually do reflect monetary influences rather than worker intransigeance. It should, however, be noted that popular contemporary theories of 'cost-push' inflation assume that the workers typically demand real wages higher than are consistent with full employment, and that the policy-makers are, or feel themselves, obliged to maintain full employment by systematically robbing the workers of their expected increases in real wages by allowing inflation of prices to reduce the real value of wage increases.

The Effects of Unionization

The effects of unionization will be given only a very sketchy and partial treatment here. A full examination would require reference to political and sociological aspects; even the economic aspects would have to comprise treatment of labour as human capital and of the union as a means of protecting and increasing the value of the workers' human capital. The analysis to be presented deals with the short-run effect of unionization on distribution, on the assumption that total supplies of labour and capital are fixed. It must be recognized, however, that in the longer run these distribution effects will influence the supplies of factors; but these effects are ignored in this analysis.

Starting with a partial equilibrium analysis one can make the usual assumptions that the sector under study is so small that the effects of any changes in this sector will not alter prices or marginal products elsewhere in the economy. Thus, if unionization raises wages in a particular industry, this acts as a tax reducing the output of that sector and causing factors to shift into other areas. Hence, this tax will cause the release of factors into the economy in the proportions in which they were employed in the now unionized sector. The conclusion then follows that if the elasticity of demand for labour is less than unity, with appropriate final demand and substitution elasticities, there will be an increase in total income earned by the unionized workers — which of course will be shared by a smaller number of employees, although those who have left the industry since unionization could be compensated by those remaining. This is not necessarily a welfare maximizing solution for those no longer in the industry. If the elasticity of demand for labour is greater than unity (again with the other appropriate elasticities) there will be a reduction in both total income for those who started in the now unionized industry and for the number still employed in that industry — although there is still an increase in income per head of those still in the industry. Since partial equilibrium analysis does not worry about the general level of wages, unionization does not hurt those who have to leave the industry since they will receive the same wage elsewhere (the wage which they initially earned). The only damage they suffer is as consumers of the product now produced at a higher price in the unionized industry. Thus there is a transfer from those who purchase the product with the higher price to those workers working for a higher wage in the unionized industry. Indeed, one might argue that the benefit to those workers that remain employed is greater than the loss to those employed elsewhere because property owners also purchase the unionized product.

The problem with the partial equilibrium type of analysis is that it is confined to small sectors of the economy and fails to consider repercussions on the relative earnings of labour and capital in other sectors. But, given the prevalence of unions in the economy, what is really needed is a general equilibrium analysis so that these restrictions can be dropped.

The particular assumption that will be used in this general equilibrium analysis of unionization is that unions establish a wage *differential* between labour in the unionized sector and labour in the non-unionized sector. An alternative approach might assume that the effect of unionization is to establish a minimum level of real income but if unions do this, then, with a given level of real income, union members are automatically better off and the interesting question then becomes what happens to real income outside the unionized industry. The wage differential approach also has the advantage of fitting in with problems of international trade — questions of factor market distortions and tariffs to offset them — and public finance — the incidence of taxation (Harberger, *The Incidence of the Corporation Income Tax*). In the case of taxation, the union may be viewed as a distortion in the labour market equivalent to a tax on labour in the unionized sector. The only difference is that, in the case of the union, the tax is collected by the unionized labour.

The analysis may be illustrated through the use of the Edgeworth–Bowley box diagram (see Diagram I) in which there is a contract curve and an initial

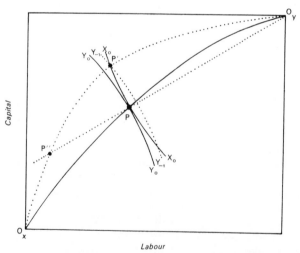

DIAGRAM I: UNIONIZATION IN THE CAPITAL INTENSIVE INDUSTRY (X).

production point P which satisfies the Pareto efficiency criterion that the marginal rate of substitution of labour for capital in each industry is the same and hence production is at a maximum with the given inputs. Now, if the wage differential is introduced in the capital intensive X industry (unionization) output must now take place at a suboptimal level $(Y_{-1}Y_{-1})$. The cost of producing the initial quantity of X (at point P') is now higher than at point P, measured in terms of Y foregone. Clearly, the same result could be brought about in different ways. For example, either labour in Y could be subsidized or capital in X could be subsidized. Attention here, however, will be confined to the 'tax' on labour. This has the advantage of allowing capital to be used as a numéraire since the marginal product of capital in both industries will be assumed to remain equal.

The introduction of the wage differential and the move from P to P' has two effects: production takes place at a less efficient point; and prices facing consumers of the product no longer reflect the social opportunity costs. The production effect of the wage differential in terms of the transformation curve is to shift the transformation curve in toward the origin at all points but the end ones. In terms of the contract curve, it is apparent that the marginal rate of technical substitution in X is not equal to that in Y. Consumption of the product X will also be distorted since the rise in the relative price of X does not reflect the social opportunity cost of production. That is to say, a move of one unit of labour from Y to X involves loss of the marginal product of labour in Y, but the cost to the employer is the price of labour in X which is greater than the marginal product in Y.

In the opposite case, when unionization takes place in the labour-intensive Y industry, (see Diagram II, where P_u, C_u is the equilibrium with unionization

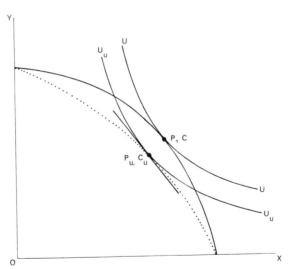

DIAGRAM II: EQUILIBRIUM WITH UNIONIZATION IN THE CAPITAL INTENSIVE INDUSTRY (X).

and P_1C the equilibrium without it) the relative capital to labour ratio must rise in the Y industry. Clearly, it is possible for a factor intensity reversal to take place and for the transformation curve to become concave to the origin. The dividing line is a wage differential that equates the capital labour ratios in the two industries. Using the Savosnick technique (*Economisk Tidskrift*, Sept. 1958), this can be shown. When unionization takes place in the capital intensive X industry, locally concave-to-the-origin transformation curves are also possible.

The basic proposition that emerges when unionization occurs is that, regardless of the gain to some groups, since production is at a suboptimal level, there must be a net loss. As the distribution of income changes as a result of unionization, there will be three important groups to consider: labour in the unionized sector, labour in the non-unionized sector, and the owners of capital. Second, we might also be concerned whether labour on the whole gains or loses, and similarly for the capitalists; but with distortions, it is not always clear that there exists a clear answer without consideration of the utility functions of the groups. Thus it will be assumed that demand is normal — a reduction in real income will reduce the demand for both goods at constant prices, and a fall in the relative price of one good will cause an increase in demand for that good. This is a rather strong assumption since it was apparent in an earlier lecture that a rise in the price may actually increase the demand for the good if the factor that is used intensively in producing a good has a strong preference for it. The following analysis will yield only qualitative answers, because of the lack of detailed specification of demand conditions.

Starting with unionization in the capital intensive X industry the impact of unionization on the distribution of income can be traced (see Diagram I). Let P be the initial production point — the optimal one. Then, with unionization, if the production of X is kept constant, production would move to P'. P' is located on a locus of points consistent with the given wage differential and must represent a fall in the production of Y. At this point P_x/P_y has risen due to the increase in labour costs with constant output. This can be rigorously demonstrated with the aid of the Lerner-Pearce diagram (see Diagram III). Begin by establishing equal factor costs in both industries. Now, as the price of labour rises in X and is kept the same in Y, the cost of X rises from $C_x = C_y$ to $C''_x > C_y$, in terms of capital (the necessary numéraire, since union and non-union labour have different prices). But a rise in the price of labour in the X industry induces an increase in the capital-labour ratio in that industry from OR_x to OR'_x, which would be inconsistent with full employment of the existing capital and labour stocks represented by the endowment ratio OR. To keep production of X at its initial level, the relative price of capital must rise (the two tangents become flatter); and as X is the capital-intensive good its relative price must rise as a result. We therefore have the result that if X production is kept at its original level, production of Y and, therefore, real income must fall, while the price of X must rise. But these two things — a fall in real income and a rise in the relative price of X at a constant level of consumption — are not consistent with equilibrium according to the posited demand conditions. The production point must therefore shift back from P' towards O_x along the new contract curve depicted in Diagram I. As it does so, the capital-labour ratio rises in both industries, raising the real marginal product of labour in the unionized industry in terms of the product of that industry, raising the real marginal product of labour in the non-unionized industry in terms of the product of that industry,

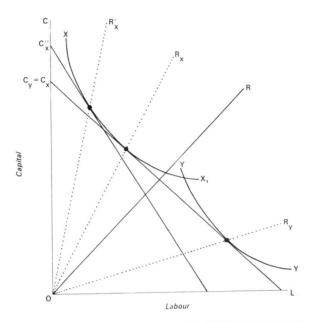

DIAGRAM III: UNIONIZATION AND PRICES IN THE CAPITAL-INTENSIVE INDUSTRY.

and lowering the real marginal product of capital in terms of the products of both industries. Note that at the point P' the real marginal product of capital is lower in terms of X and higher in terms of Y than at P; the real marginal product of unionized labour is higher in terms of X, and also higher in terms of Y because the price of X in terms of Y has risen; and the real marginal product of non-unionized labour is lower in terms of Y, and also lower in terms of X because the price of Y in terms of X has fallen. Hence, if production stayed at point P', we would have unambiguous conclusions for the effects of unionization on the welfare of unionized and non-unionized labour — an unambiguous gain for the former and loss for the latter — while the effects on the welfare of capital would depend on how capital spent its income as between X and Y. As the production point shifts back along $O_x P' O_y$ towards O_x, however, the real incomes of both unionized and non-unionized labour increase, while the real income of capital falls, by comparison with the position at P'. P'', the point on the new contract curve at which the capital-labour ratio in Y is the same as it was at the original production point P, is a sort of dividing line between two possible outcomes. At P'', non-unionized labour has the same purchasing power in terms of Y as it had originally, and so does capital; if either spends any of its income on X, it will be worse off than it was originally, if it does not it will be exactly as well off as originally. To the southwest of P'' capital must be worse off than it was originally, while non-unionized labour may be better off, since its gains in purchasing power over Y may offset the relatively higher cost of X. Where the actual equilibrium point will fall depends on demand conditions, which we have not specified fully enough to permit a definitive statement; loosely, we can say that the more income and price elastic is the demand for X, the more likely will it be that unionization will improve the welfare of the non-unionized labour at the expense of the capitalists. In any case, unionization of the capital-intensive industry must increase the welfare of the unionized labour; it may increase the welfare of the non-unionized labour as well.

The next case to consider is that of unionization in the Y or labour-intensive industry. As pointed out previously, unionization here gives rise to the possibility of oddly shaped transformation curves. If, however, attention is focused on the case in which the labour intensity is only somewhat reduced (see Diagram IV), then the essence of the analysis can be brought out without

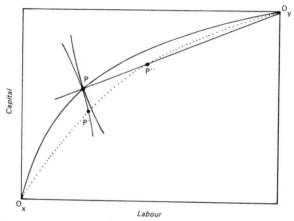

DIAGRAM IV: UNIONIZATION IN THE LABOUR-INTENSIVE INDUSTRY (Y).

undue complication. Keeping production of Y temporarily constant, movement would then be to P', a less efficient point than P. Is it possible for labour in the non-unonized sector to become better off? Since the 'tax' raises the price of Y and lowers real income, production must shift towards less Y. But to get to the initial capital-labour ratio in X production of Y would have to be expanded and this cannot happen. The capital-labour ratio in X must always lie below the initial ratio. Non-union labour is unambiguously worse off. The capital-labour ratio in Y begins to fall, which erodes the initial gain in real income generated by unionization. Production moves back along the new less efficient contract curve from P' toward O_y. As this continues, the capital–labour ratio falls in both industries further hurting the welfare of non-union labour. At P'', the marginal products of labour and capital are the same in Y as before unionization and the marginal product of capital in terms of X is higher and that of labour lower. As production moves further toward the O_y origin from P, labour in the unionized industry may become worse off than without unionization. Thus, if unionization occurs in the labour intensive industry, (1) non-unionized labour is unambiguously worse off, (2) unionized labour may be either better or worse off — if union workers consume only the unionized product then P'' is the dividing line;

otherwise to the right of P'' they may be better off in terms of X while worse off in terms of Y. Capitalists at P' find that the marginal product of capital in X has risen as compared to that at P, while in Y it has fallen. However, as production moves toward O_y, the marginal product in both sectors begins to rise. At P'', the marginal product in Y is back to its original level and the gains from unionization to labour have been eroded.

This proposition can be seen from another point of view (see Diagram V). If C_x is the original factor cost for both X and Y, when the price of labour in

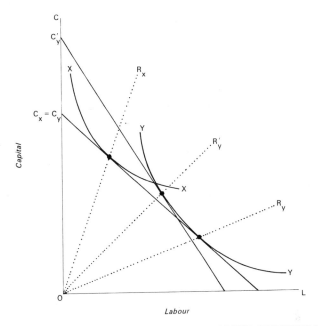

DIAGRAM V: UNIONIZATION AND PRICES IN THE LABOUR-INTENSIVE INDUSTRY.

Y rises, to the slope yielding the cost C_y, the price of Y must also rise — the capital-labour ratio moves to R'_y. To maintain full-employment with an increased capital-labour ratio in Y, output of Y must expand. Since there is less capital per unit in Y than X, the movement of resources from X to Y has left some capital unemployed. It is this capital combining with labour in Y that raises the capital labour ratio and expands output of Y. This cannot occur! With the reduction of real income engendered both by the less efficient production of Y and the rise in the price of Y, the demand for Y must fall. The Y industry must contract and the price of labour in Y must fall below what it was at P'. Indeed, the marginal products of labour in both X and Y must fall as the Y industry contracts.

The basic economics of this process can be seen in the operation of a tax on the product of an industry. If X is taxed, then demand shifts away from X to Y — this implies a decrease in the production of X. This releases factors in the ratio in which they are used in X for use in the increased production of Y. The increase in the demand for Y raises the prices of the factors used in the production of Y and changes the marginal products as they are absorbed in the different ratio. If X is capital-intensive, excess supply of capital and excess demand for labour induce a fall in the earnings of capital and a rise in those of labour (cf. Johnson-Meiszkowski, QJE '70).

The Economics of Minimum Wage Laws

In the previous section dealing with unionization, it was mentioned that unions might be treated as attempting to establish a minimum wage in real terms for their members. On this interpretation, unionization and the legislation of minimum wage laws constitute the same analytical problem and, in fact, constitute alternative political means for attempting to secure the same empirical result.

It is a familiar notion to the economist, though not to the general public apparently, that minimum wage laws, though they benefit those who are successful in obtaining employment in the industries subject to them, tend to create unemployment or else to drive a number of workers into the equivalent of the 'subsistence sector' of the economy, i.e. the sector not covered by the minimum wage law. This conclusion is derived from the elementary partial equilibrium theory of demand and supply as applied to policies of price supports. However, it is worthwhile to investigate the problem in a general equilibrium context. It emerges that, contrary to the results of partial equilibrium analysis, there are possible circumstances in which a minimum wage law that applies to only a part of the productive activities of the economy may benefit workers in all sectors. On the other hand, if the minimum wage law applies to all sectors, or to all sectors except those regarded as constituting a 'subsistence sector', the traditional conclusion can be rigorously demonstrated.

Before commencing the analysis, it is relevant to note that minimum wages are invariably legislated in terms of money, and that while they may have been originally intended to raise real wages above the level prevailing under competition, the intention may have been frustrated, and the minimum wage have become ineffective, through the joint influence of price inflation and increasing productivity resulting from technical progress. This fact is disregarded in the ensuing analysis, in which it is assumed that the minimum wage is effective in raising the real wage of labour. It is further assumed, for purposes of analysis, that the minimum wage law is intended to raise the marginal product of labour in the industries to which the law applies in terms of the product of those industries.

For the purposes of the analysis, the economy is initially divided into two sectors, producing two commodities with the employment of two factors of production. Commodity X is assumed to be relatively capital-intensive by comparison with commodity Y; both are assumed to be produced subject to constant-returns-to-scale production functions. The three Diagrams (VIa, VIIa and VIII) all depict the standard Edgeworth–Bowley production contract box, the endowment of the economy with capital being represented by the vertical side of the box and the labour endowment being represented by the horizontal side. The isoquants (for simplicity not depicted) for commodity X

start from the south-west corner and those for commodity Y from the north-east corner of the box.

In Diagrams VIa and VIIa, $O_x P'' P O_y$ represents the contract curve under conditions of competition. P is the point on the contract curve that would prevail under competition. It is assumed that this equilibrium is unique — the redistribution of income between labour and capital that occurs as production shifts along the contract curve is assumed not to result in the possibility of multiple equilibrium. In other words, it is assumed (for both these diagrams and Diagram VIII) that an increase in the relative price of a

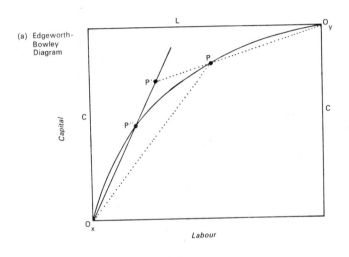

(a) Edgeworth-
    Bowley
    Diagram

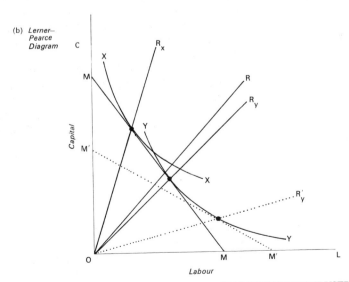

(b) *Lerner–
    Pearce
    Diagram*

DIAGRAM VI: MINIMUM WAGE IN THE CAPITAL INTENSIVE INDUSTRY

commodity reduces the excess demand for it, through the usual income and substitution effects, regardless of the redistribution effect.

Diagram VIa represents the case in which the minimum wage law is imposed on the X industry, the capital-intensive industry. The effect of the law is to increase the capital-labour ratio in the X industry from the slope of O_xP to the slope of $O_xP''P'$, and to make the economy's new contract curve consist of the curved section of the old contract curve between O_x and P'' and the straight line section $P''P'$ extended.

As production moves from O_x to P'' along the old contract curve, the relative price of X in terms of Y must increase. The same holds true as production of X continues to increase along $P''P'$ extended. This is proved by reference to Diagram VIb. In the diagram, units of X and Y are chosen to have equal costs of production at the factor price ratio prevailing with production at P'', their common costs of production being given by the budget line MM. The overall endowment ratio of the economy is represented by OR, and the optimal factor utilization ratios in the two industries by OR_x and OR_y respectively. In order to increase the production of X, with the fixed factor utilization prevailing at P'' and set by the minimum wage law, it is necessary to free the relevant capital required by reducing the capital-intensity in the Y industry, the new ratio of capital to labour in that industry being represented by OR'_y. The new factor price ratio in the Y industry will be $M'M'$. Since capital is mobile between the two industries and its price unrestricted, competition will equalize the price of its services in the two industries; hence capital can serve as the numéraire for measuring the effect of the production change on relative commodity prices. And since M' lies below M on the C-axis, the relative price of X must rise.

Returning to Diagram VIa, at P'' both the production of X and the price of it in terms of Y are necessarily lower than at P; hence P'' cannot represent a possible equilibrium, which equilibrium must lie to the north-east of P'' on O_xP' extended. At P', the quantity of X produced must be lower and of Y produced higher than at P; the price of X in terms of Y must be higher than at P (this can be proved by considering the effect of an increase in R_x in Diagram VIb). With a lower quantity produced and a higher relative price of X, P' could be an equilibrium position. If it is, the marginal product of labour in the Y industry is unchanged, while its marginal product in terms of X (through exchange in the market) must be lower than at P. Hence, if P' is the new equilibrium position, labour in the Y industry can at best be no worse off (if it consumes no X) and generally will be worse off than at the competitive equilibrium position P. If the demand for X is sufficiently inelastic, P' will represent an excess demand for X, and the equilibrium with the minimum wage will lie to the north-east of P'; in this case the marginal product of labour in Y will be lower than before in terms of both products, so that such labour will be unambiguously worse off. But if the demand for X is sufficiently elastic, the new equilibrium of the economy with the minimum wage law in effect will lie between P' and P''; the capital-labour ratio in the Y industry must rise as compared with competitive equilibrium, while the relative price of X in terms of Y must fall by comparison with P'. The marginal product of labour in the Y industry must rise in terms of Y, and may even rise in terms of X; and, depending on the preferences of the owners of labour in consumption of the two goods, labour in the Y industry may be made better off than it would have been under competitive equilibrium in the absence of the minimum wage. This possibility constitutes the exception to the standard conclusion.

Diagram VIIa illustrates the case in which the minimum wage law seeks to raise the real wage of labour in the labour-intensive sector in terms of the

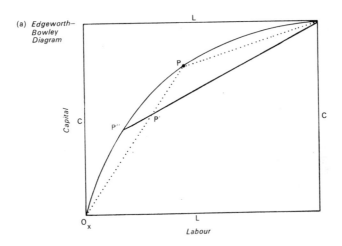

(a) *Edgeworth–Bowley Diagram*

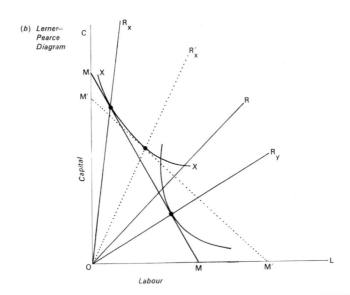

(b) *Lerner–Pearce Diagram*

DIAGRAM VII: MINIMUM WAGE IN THE LABOUR-INTENSIVE INDUSTRY

product of that sector. The new contract curve consists of the segment O_xP'' of the competitive contract curve, and the straight-line segment $P''O_y$ determined by the minimum wage law. Diagram VIIb shows that as production of X increases from P'' along the straight-line segment, the relative price of X in terms of Y must fall. At P'', the point of division of the segments of the new contract curve, production of X and its relative price in terms of Y are both lower than at P; hence P'' cannot be a position of equilibrium. Nor can P', since at P' both production of Y and its relative price in terms of X are higher than at P. The new equilibrium of the economy must lie somewhere on the straight-line segment of the new contract curve between P' and O_y. The ratio of capital to labour employed in the X industry must be lower than it was under competitive equilibrium in the absence of the minimum wage law. Hence the marginal product of labour in the X industry must be lower than under competitive equilibrium; since the price of X must also be lower in terms of Y, labour's marginal product in Y transformed into terms of X through conversion at the commodity price ratio must also be lower than under competitive equilibrium without the minimum wage law. Hence the minimum wage law must necessarily make labour in the non-included industry worse off than it would be in the absence of the law.

Diagram VIII illustrates the case in which the minimum wage law is imposed in both industrial sectors (assumed either to exhaust the economy,

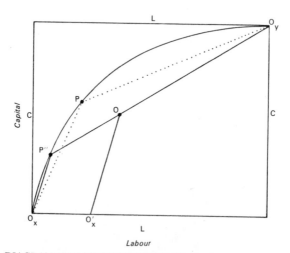

DIAGRAM VIII: MINIMUM WAGE IN BOTH INDUSTRIES.

or to comprise the non-subsistence sectors of it), raising the capital-labour ratios in them from O_xP and O_yP to O_xP'' and O_yP'' respectively. Production at P'' involves a smaller quantity and a lower price of X and hence is incapable of being an equilibrium point. There is an excess demand for X and an excess supply of Y. Reallocation of the economy's resources towards X and away from Y, maintaining the capital-labour ratios required by the minimum wage law, releases more labour from the Y industry than can be absorbed in the X industry, given the relative capital-intensity of the X industry, and necessarily creates unemployment (or, where there is assumed to be a subsistence sector, forces part of the labour force to retreat into that sector). The resulting equilibrium of the economy is depicted by the point Q (which may involve more or less production of X than point P, since the relative price of X as the capital-intensive good must have fallen by comparison with Y, the labour-intensive good). $O_xO'_x$, the shift of origin for the production of X, represents the amount of unemployment created by the minimum wage law.

Relative Wages and Wage Differentials

In the analysis thus far, wages have been treated as the price of a homogeneous input labour, and the questions considered have been questions of differentiation or market distortion introduced by unionization or minimum wage legislation. We now treat labour as composed of different kinds and qualities, and consider the determination of the differentials among rates of pay for different kinds of labour.

Treating labour as a non-homogeneous input, the question arises as to what determines wage differentials among different forms of labour. One would expect that their marginal productivities would depend not only on the amount of factors co-operating with the particular forms and amounts of labour but on the distribution of demand among commodities as well. In the short run then, relative wages would be determined by marginal productivity schedules in conjunction with supply functions of labour. Over the course of time, however, one would expect the quantities of the various forms of labour to adjust to the differentials in wages. The form of this adjustment has many dimensions including: labour mobility among industries; retraining programmes; migration of labour from depressed to growing regions; and entry of new participants to the labour force — this tending to be the dominant form of adjustment in a rapidly growing economy where rates of growth are not equal in all industries. One would expect, in line with Marshall's idea of the equalization of net advantages, that wages would tend to equality over all occupations after correction for differences in training costs. That is to say, that as workers are assumed to maximize their cash income plus a money equivalent of the utility flow from their occupation, and as the work force is a depreciating asset that is continuously replaced, wages would tend to equality over all occupations. It should be noted that the process of disinvestment in declining industries may be slow and that there are imperfections in the provision of some forms of labour services — these factors would tend to perpetuate wage differentials.

Human Capital

In developing a comprehensive theory of wage determination, one must also take into account the varying costs of investment in human capital. Here it is possible to distinguish costs to the individual and costs to the society. Further, when considering education as the means of forming human capital, one must distinguish between formal institutions such as schools and universities, where at least part of the costs are budgeted, and informal institutions such as apprenticeships and on-the-job training plans where many of the costs are implicit. Costs of formal schooling involve payments by governments and individuals for the provision of the teaching service, and the income foregone by individuals who withdraw from the labour force to enhance their earning power. There are costs from the social point of view as well, in the form of smaller tax bases and decreased national product while individuals are being trained. The same costs are involved in the informal institutions but are not as readily observable — for example, individuals in on-the-job training programmes receive less than what they would earn when fully trained but are, in the meantime, still earning something; costs, such as output foregone by firms who train individuals of temporarily lower productivity, are implicit and not budgeted. In others of the informal institutions for investing in human capital (migrating and consumption of medical services, for example) costs would involve: in the case of the former, absorbing a capital loss on a house, say, by moving from an area where housing of one quality was inexpensive, to one of higher cost housing of that same quality; and, in the case of the latter, foregoing earnings while the medical treatment is administered.

A further complication is one that has been mentioned earlier — given perfect capital markets, individuals could borrow funds to finance human capital formation when the rate of return justified it. But with imperfect capital markets, some groups of individuals may be systematically excluded from access to capital. This may prevent rates of return on all forms of capital from being equalized.

The essential notion of human capital is that of the choice between alternative income streams, and this is the problem of investment in the Fisherian sense of choosing between alternative consumption streams. Diagram IX describes the choices that are involved in choosing between the alternatives: (1) starting at time t_0 — say, the minimum age at which one can leave school, and entering the labour force directly to receive income y_0 over the course of one's working life t_0 through t_n; and (2) undergoing further training over the period t_0 through T, and receiving income y_1 for that time, and receiving income y_2 from T through t_n. The investment decision involves comparing

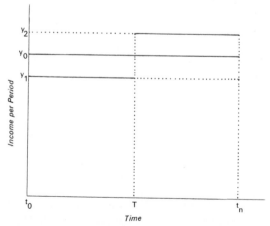

DIAGRAM IX: INVESTMENT IN HUMAN CAPITAL.

the attractiveness of the two alternatives — investment, itself, being the sacrifice of consumption in the initial period in order to attain a higher level of consumption in the later period. To compare the streams of income, their present values are:

P.V. of income stream 1:

$$PV\,(1) = \sum_{t=1}^{t=n} \frac{y_0}{(1+i)^t}$$

P.V. of income stream 2:

$$PV\,(2) = \sum_{t=1}^{t=T} \frac{y_1}{(1+i)^t} + \sum_{t=T+1}^{t=n} \frac{y_2}{(1+i)^t}$$

If the present value of stream 2 is greater than that of stream 1, the investment is worthwhile. Note that it is necessary for a known interest rate or discount rate to exist for these calculations to be made.

Viewed as an investment opportunity, the appropriate criterion for undertaking the training would be whether it increases the capital value of the individual involved: present value of the investment opportunity is

$$V = \sum_{t=1}^{t=T} \frac{y_1 - y_0}{(1+i)^t} + \sum_{t=T+1}^{t=n} \frac{y_2 - y_0}{(1+i)^t};$$

if the present value is greater than zero, undertake it.

A third way of evaluating the opportunity is to calculate an internal rate of return on the investment — the criterion for investing involving a comparison of this rate with the going market rate of interest: set $V = 0$ and solve for r, the notional rate of interest that would leave us indifferent between the alternatives. Alternatively, one could set

$$\sum_{t=0}^{T} \frac{y_2 - y_1}{(1+r)^t} = \sum_{t=T+1}^{t=n} \frac{y_2 - y_0}{(1+r)^t}$$

in order to calculate the rate of return that made the present value of the costs equal to the present value of the returns. If the notional rate is greater than the market rate, the project is worthwhile. The problem with the internal rate of return criterion is that solving for the rate involves solving an equation of high order. It is only under certain circumstances that the equation will be well enough behaved to give us unambiguous results. Further, use of the internal rate rule makes the implicit assumption that one can borrow or lend indefinitely at the notional rate of interest (see Chapter 13).

The above has important implications for predictions concerning the income streams of various individuals once net advantages are equalized. One would predict that individuals with education would have different time profiles of income than those without — income would rise faster and to higher levels for those with education, incurring larger costs would yield greater returns, and undertaking longer training periods would yield greater returns.

Here it has been assumed that individuals incurred the costs of their own education. We may distinguish between the return to the 'natural' unit of labour and the return to the investment of capital 'embodied' in the skilled worker in the form of his training and consider the question of who pays for the worker's education and who receives the returns. Further one can distinguish general training, or training that may be used in a wide range of occupations, and specific training that is of use within one firm. It will never be in the interest of firms to absorb costs of training workers in general skills due to the risk of workers leaving after the training period to obtain the full value of their marginal product elsewhere. Institutions such as apprenticeship plans have arisen in order to ensure that the individual incurs the full cost of his general training. In the case of specific training, two equally efficient systems for training the worker are possible: (1) the worker receives a lower income for the training period and subsequently receives the full value of his increased marginal product; or (2) the employer pays a constant wage, incurring costs of training in the initial period but receiving the returns from increased marginal product in later periods. In the first case, the worker — who is also doing the investing — receives the return to the natural labour unit and the return to the investment; in the second case, the worker receives the payment to the natural unit of labour and the employer, who incurred the investment costs, receives the return to that investment. Of course, there exists the possibility of splitting costs so that both worker and employer obtain part of the investment return.

The determination of which system will result depends on the risks involved — on the one hand, when the employer pays, there is the risk that the worker may quit; on the other hand, when the worker incurs the costs, there is the possibility that he may be fired — and thus on the subjective probability judgments regarding quitting and firing. Possible inefficiencies exist in that probability judgments may differ as between employers and workers and, as well, that those estimated probabilities may be wrong.

Note that if the employer pays the costs of the training of the worker in a specific skill, the worker will be receiving less than the marginal product of his labour input after he has been trained. This might suggest that he is being 'exploited'; but this is not so. He is receiving the market value of his own contribution to the production process — the raw labour which the employer has trained — and the excess of his marginal product over the value of that input is accruing to the employer as a return on the investment in his training that the employer has financed.

Some Economic Aspects of Population Growth
The classical economists based their analysis on the so-called 'iron law of wages' according to which population would tend to breed to the level of subsistence. The concept of subsistence was itself ambiguous, and the 'law' was so clearly not fulfilled in the nineteenth century that economists dropped it and began to build their models of the economy on the assumption either of a constant population or on the assumption that the rate of growth of population was exogenous. Recently, however, partly but not wholly because of the increasingly widespread availability of contraceptive knowledge (not wholly, because Malthus and his contemporaries, and the Roman Catholic Church, were fully aware that the easiest way to avoid having a child is to behave so that there is no risk of having one), economists have begun to look at family size and the associated rate of population growth as

economic variables determined by individual choices. These choices include both age of marriage, which has an influence on probable fertility in the bearing of children, and number of children sought for after marriage (which has become less and less dependent for fulfilment on age of marriage).

There are two economic concepts of major importance relevant to the question of the economics of population growth. The first is the distinction between children viewed as a production good and children viewed as a consumption good. In agricultural societies, particularly primitive ones, children are a production good: it is not long before they become old enough to contribute at least as much to farm output as they take from it in consumption, and the main problem for parents is that when they mature they want to become independent and 'self-supporting' (which usually means that they want to control the spending of their own productive contributions rather than pay a substantial part of them in taxation to their parents). Children are also a form of social insurance and property protection: one's children, at least the males, are available as a police and military force as one grows older, richer, and less capable of defending oneself against aggression by others; they are also available, however grudgingly, as a source of income support in one's old age. In more advanced industrial societies, on the other hand, children are a form of consumption good: one does not need them for protection or insurance, and in fact they contribute little if anything to family production, cost money to support, and divert resources away from provision for one's old age. Their existence has to be justified by the pleasure they give to life, and by their potentialities as monuments to one's own personality traits and as providing a second chance at more worldly success than one has oneself accomplished. Whatever happens to one's children, they at least provide some form of immortality, which is generally comforting in an age that does not really believe in a life after death. (It takes a great deal of self-assurance to be content with leaving posterity an inheritance in the form of physical structures, charitable foundations, or ideas rather than in the form of natural offspring, even though more dead citizens are remembered for the former than for the latter.)

The second point is that the procreators never bear the full social costs of their child-bearing. (Nor do they reap the full social returns, if the net returns are positive.) A major reason is that many of the costs of child-bearing are borne by the state, through public responsibility for the costs of education, medical care, etc., including the costs of dealing with criminal activities in which the offspring may indulge. Once launched into life, a child increasingly acquires claims on the social income, whether it or its parents are contributing enough to social income to meet those claims or not. There is therefore a tendency towards excessive population growth, which could only be remedied by changes in both the institutions and the mores of society.

Appendix: Some Elementary Notes on Factor Market Distortions
Let $X = f(L_n, K_n)$ and $Y = g(L_y, K_y)$ be the two goods, Y the numéraire, p_n the price of X, w the wages and r the rental of capital, with subscripts representing the goods.

$$w_n = p_n \frac{\partial X}{\partial L_n} \qquad r_n = p_n \frac{\partial X}{\partial K_n}$$

$$w_y = \frac{\partial Y}{\partial L_y} \qquad r_y = \frac{\partial Y}{\partial K_y}$$

Let the distortions be δ_{LX} and δ_{KX}, where δ can be positive or negative, and $w_n = (1 + \delta_{LX}) w_y, r_n = (1 + \delta_{KX}) r_y$

$$p_n = (1 + \delta_{LX}) \frac{\dfrac{\partial Y}{\partial L_y}}{\dfrac{\partial X}{\partial L_n}} = (1 + \delta_{KX}) \frac{\dfrac{\partial Y}{\partial K_y}}{\dfrac{\partial X}{\partial K_n}}$$

The price of X is given by the ratio of the cost of a small increment in the production of X to the increment in the quantity of X

$$p_n = \frac{w_n \, dL_n + r_n \, dK_n}{\dfrac{\partial X}{\partial L_n} \, dL_n + \dfrac{\partial X}{\partial K_n} \, dK_n}$$

$$= \frac{(1 + \delta_{LX}) \dfrac{\partial Y}{\partial L_y} \, dL_n + (1 + \delta_{KX}) \dfrac{\partial Y}{\partial K_y} \, dK_n}{\dfrac{\partial X}{\partial L_n} \, dL_n + \dfrac{\partial X}{\partial K_n} \, dK_n}$$

The transformation curve slope is

$$\frac{dY}{dX} = - \frac{\dfrac{\partial Y}{\partial L_y} \, dL_y + \dfrac{\partial Y}{\partial K_y} \, dK_y}{\dfrac{\partial X}{\partial L_n} \, dL_n + \dfrac{\partial X}{\partial K_n} \, dK_n}$$

Call this slope, with sign reversed, the social cost of X, and denote it by S_n. Then

$$\frac{p_n}{S_n} = \frac{(1 + \delta_{LX}) \dfrac{\partial Y}{\partial L_y} \, dL_n + (1 + \delta_{KX}) \dfrac{\partial Y}{\partial K_y} \, dK_n}{\dfrac{\partial Y}{\partial L_y} \, dL_y + \dfrac{\partial Y}{\partial K_y} \, dK_y}$$

The market price ratio is distorted from the social cost ratio so long as

$$\frac{p_n}{S_n} \neq 1.$$

The transformation curve is distorted inwards so long as $(1 + \delta_{LX}) \neq (1 + \delta_{KX})$ — if they are equal

$$\frac{\partial Y}{\partial L_y} \bigg/ \frac{\partial X}{\partial L_n} = \frac{\partial Y}{\partial K_y} \bigg/ \frac{\partial X}{\partial K_n}$$

and the marginal productivity conditions are fulfilled.

Note that if $\delta_{LX} = \delta_{KX} \neq 0$, the transformation curve is undistorted but the price/cost ratio is, being equal to $(1 + \delta)$.

Note also that for the price/cost ratio to be undistorted while factor markets are, δ_{LX} and δ_{LY} must be of opposite sign, which necessarily implies a distorted transformation curve.

Now simplify the problem by assuming a positive distortion δ_{LX}, with $\delta_{KX} = 0$

$$\frac{p_n}{S_n} = \frac{(1 + \delta_{LX})\dfrac{\partial Y}{\partial L_y}\,dL_n + \dfrac{\partial Y}{\partial K_y}\,dK_n}{\dfrac{\partial Y}{\partial L_y}\,dL_y + \dfrac{\partial Y}{\partial K_y}\,dK_y}$$

$$(1 + \delta_{LX})\frac{\partial Y}{\partial X}\Big/\frac{\partial L_y}{\partial L_n} = \frac{\partial Y}{\partial X}\Big/\frac{\partial K_y}{\partial K_n}$$

There are four tax-subsidy policies that might be used to correct the factor-market distortion

(1) subsidize labour in X: $w_n = (1 + s_{LX})\,p_n\dfrac{\partial X_n}{\partial L_n}$

$$p_n = \left(\frac{1 + \delta_{LX}}{1 + s_{LX}}\right)\frac{\dfrac{\partial Y}{\partial L_y}}{\dfrac{\partial X}{\partial L_n}} = \frac{\dfrac{\partial Y}{\partial K_y}}{\dfrac{\partial X}{\partial K_n}}$$

$s_{LX} = \delta_{LX}$ eliminates the distortion in the factor market and makes $c_n/s_n = 1$

(2) tax labour in the Y industry $w_y = \dfrac{1}{1 + t_{Ly}}\dfrac{\partial Y}{\partial L_y}$

$$p_n = \left(\frac{1 + \delta_{LX}}{1 + t_{LY}}\right)\frac{\dfrac{\partial Y}{\partial L_y}}{\dfrac{\partial X}{\partial L_n}} = \frac{\dfrac{\partial Y}{\partial K_y}}{\dfrac{\partial X}{\partial K_n}}$$

$t_{LY} = \delta_{LX}$ eliminates the distortion in both the factor market and the commodity market

(3) tax capital used in the X industry $r_n = (1 + t_{KX})r_y$

$$p_n = (1 + \delta_{LX})\frac{\dfrac{\partial Y}{\partial L_y}}{\dfrac{\partial X}{\partial L_n}} = (1 + t_{KX})\frac{\dfrac{\partial Y}{\partial K_y}}{\dfrac{\partial X}{\partial K_n}}$$

let $t_{KX} = \delta_{LX}$; this eliminates factor-market distortions but makes

$$p_n/s_n = 1 + \delta_{LX} = 1 + t_{KX}$$

(4) subsidize capital used in the Y industry $r_y = (1 + s_{KY})\, \partial Y/\partial K_y$

$$p_n = (1 + \delta_{LX})\frac{\dfrac{\partial Y}{\partial L_y}}{\dfrac{\partial X}{\partial L_x}} = \frac{(1 + s_{KY})\dfrac{\partial Y}{\partial K_y}}{\dfrac{\partial X}{\partial K_n}}$$

set $s_{KY} = \delta_{LX}$; this eliminates factor market distortions but makes

$$p_n/s_n = 1 + \delta_{LX} = 1 + s_{KY}.$$

Source: Fishlow and David, *JPE*, 1961.

11

CAPITAL AND INTEREST:
THE WICKSELLIAN MODEL

Introduction

The theory of capital, interest and investment is probably the most difficult branch of economic analysis, not merely because it involves some difficult pieces of technical analysis but because of the variety of approaches employed by different theorists, each of which usually contains some insight into the problem but not the whole truth applicable to every case, and the variety of questions with which different theorists are concerned.

Much of the difficulty goes back to the historical origins of distribution theory in the Ricardian model, which involved both a specific model of the production process based on primitive agriculture, and the identification of categories of income with specific social classes. The production model entailed fixed proportions between capital and labour, and capital that consisted of the same stuff as final output, thereby ruling out substitutability between capital and labour and problems of the valuation of capital in terms of final product. It also suggested that what the capitalist contributed to production was time. The identification of wages, rent, and profits with social classes made the theory of distribution one with political overtones and raised the question of the social justification for the receipt of profits, since the capitalist seemed to collect his profits merely for letting labour and land work together. The classical answer was that profits were the reward for 'abstinence', or in Marshall's later phrase, 'waiting'. This was easily subjected to ridicule at a superficial level, since the capitalist was popularly viewed as able to indulge himself in the consumption of many things that the worker could not afford, and he drew his income from current production just like the rest; nor could he 'consume his capital' in the physical form in which it was directly embodied. The point is simply that it is the creation of the stock of capital by the foregoing of current consumption, and not the use of the income that the stock provides, that involves the abstinence, and that so long as the stock is scarce it will have a positive marginal product giving rise to a current income; also, once the stock is created, the income from it will appear as a continuous flow simultaneous with inputs of the services of labour. The focal point of social criticism should be the justice of ownership of capital by those who own it or of the processes by which they have acquired and retain it. Nevertheless, economists of socialist persuasion from Marx down to the leaders of the contemporary Cambridge (England) school have attempted to provide apparently scientific underpinnings for their social convictions by efforts to develop theories of distribution in which the returns on capital are not explainable economically by its contribution to production but are somehow determined arbitrarily.

Another source of confusion stemmed from the fact that rent is conventionally reckoned as a payment for the services of land, and wages as a payment for the services of labour, per time period, i.e. as a rental rate for a physical unit of input, whereas profits are reckoned as a rate of return on investment, thus suggesting a difference in kind between the former two and the last category of income. As mentioned earlier, Irving Fisher was the first to see clearly that interest is the factor that relates a stream of income (rentals) to the capital value of the source of that stream, and that from that point of view land and labour are 'capital' in the same sense as material capital. Nevertheless, the identification of the concept of capital with material capital earning a rate of return, as distinct especially from labour earning real wages, continues to dominate the Anglo-Saxon tradition of economic theory.

A source of real difficulty, avoided in the simple construction of the Ricardian model, is that capital equipment is a produced means of production, produced with the aid of other factors along with capital equipment itself. This appears to pose an insuperable circularity, but it can be handled with sufficient mathematical general equilibrium analysis. The problem then arises, however, that a model of the production process is required for this, and any number of models of that process and of the specific functions of capital goods in it can be constructed. (For example, in constructing growth models, one can assume either that, once installed, capital equipment can be used only with a fixed complement of labour, or that there is still substitutability; and either that technical progress gets embodied only in new capital equipment, or that it affects the productivity of old equipment as well.)

Further difficulties are encountered in the empirical application of capital theory. The usual situation with which pure capital theory works is that of a balanced stock of capital, such that the quantity of capital in some sense, its productive capacity, and the depreciation on it remain constant; also such that the cost of production of a new piece of equipment is equal to the discounted value of its future stream of contributions to production, and the value of an old piece of equipment is equal to the depreciated value of a new piece. With growth and change going on in an erratically growing economy, these equalities will not hold, and there arises the question of how to measure the quantity or value of the capital stock the society has.

The Wicksellian Model of Capital

We proceed with a simple neo-classical model of capital, following on the contributions of Wicksell. In this model, scarcity of land by itself plays no part — though the limited bounty of nature does — operating by creating diminishing marginal returns to an increase in capital relative to labour. Wicksell's own model involved the ageing of wine, older wine fetching higher prices in the market; this model is somewhat unsatisfactory because the prices paid for older wine are dependent on tastes and presumably influenced by relative quantities of the different vintages produced. Instead, we construct a sort of termite economy in which labour is expended in planting a tree, the tree grows by itself with no further inputs other than what nature provides, but according to a law by which eventually its rate of growth declines continuously, and the harvesting of the timber costs nothing (termites consume on the spot). Technically, this is described as a 'point-input, point-output' production system. The first problem is to determine the optimum age at which to harvest a tree. Obviously if there were no constraints on economic activity, the optimum age would be that at which the tree reached its maximum content of wood. So we must introduce a constraint. This can be done in a variety of ways; the important point to realize is that one constraint is sufficient to specify an equilibrium. Three possibilities are shown in Diagrams Ia, Ib, and Ic, where in each case $x(t)$ represents the quantity of wood as a function of the age of the tree.

The first possibility (Diagram Ia) is that labour is available at a fixed wage

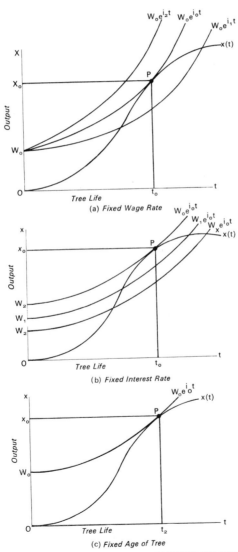

DIAGRAM I: THE WICKSELLIAN MODEL OF CAPITAL.

rate W_0. The curves $W_0 . W_0 e^{it}$ represent the cumulated value of the investment in the wage of the labour required to plant the tree at different interest
rates over successive time periods. Competition among workers for employment will enable the owners of capital to maximize the rate of return on their
investment, the age of the tree being determined by tangency of the tree's
growth function with the highest attainable cumulation-of-value curve,
point P.

The second possibility (Diagram Ib) is that capital is available at a fixed
rate of interest. The curves $W . W e^{it}$ represent the cumulated values of investments at different levels of wages and the given interest rate i at successive
points of future time. Competition among capitalists will enable workers
to drive wages to the highest level at which capitalists can still earn the rate
of return i, again a point of tangency between the tree's growth function and
the highest attainable cumulation-of-value curve.

The third possibility (Diagram Ic) is that, for some reason we need not go
into at this stage, there is a fixed age at which the tree can be harvested. There
will be one combination of a wage rate and an interest rate which will make
this fixed age optimal under competitive conditions in the capital and labour
markets, and this will be determined by finding the interest rate curve tangent
to the tree's growth function at the point P and following the curve back to
the vertical axis.

It should be noted that in each case the condition for equilibrium is
tangency of the cumulation-of-value curve to the tree's growth function.
This implies equality of the interest rate with the rate of growth of the tree
at that particular age, or the rate of return over cost on investing further in
allowing the tree to grow bigger. Also, x_0 is the total wood produced, and
$x_0 - W_0$ the net gain of wood obtained by the capitalist.

We now move from the problem of optimization in the choice of lifetime
for a single tree to the case of an ongoing production process in which trees
are continually being planted and harvested. In this case, the growth function
up to the point P cut off by t_0 represents the constant profile of standing trees,
and the area under them, the amount of physical capital in the sense of wood
standing on the ground that is necessary to enable a sustained unit input of
labour to produce a sustained flow of output x_0. (Note that we now have a
capital stock of wood, through which trees flow as they mature which, in
co-operation with the labour inputs, produces the flow of output.) The area
OPt_0 is the economy's stock of material capital; but the value of that stock
is greater than its physical quantity, because each growing tree will be valued,
not by the wood it actually contains, but by the value of the wood it will
contain when it reaches the age of harvesting, discounted back for the number
of years it still has to grow. Hence the value of the stock of capital will be
given by the area under the cumulation-of-value curve, OW_0Pt_0.

Again, to determine t_0 — or, more generally, to determine t, x, i, and W
simultaneously — we need to impose a constraint, and can do this in alternative
ways. As before, we could select either the real wage rate W or the interest
rate i; but this would imply perfectly elastic supplies of the relevant factor,
which could only be justified for certain special circumstances (e.g. a classical
subsistence-wage economy, or a long-run neoclassical economy in which
accumulation had driven the rate of return on capital down to the minimum

rate of time preference). For .shorter-run analysis, it is more interesting to impose the constraint in the form of fixity of the stock of capital. But there are two measures of the stock of capital, the physical stock which enters into the production process and can be thought of as material capital, and the value of that stock which can be thought of as the material wealth of the community, i.e. the physical capital stock valued in terms of its equivalent in purchasing power over consumption goods.

The Wicksell Effect and the Ricardo Effect
In this particular model, an increase in the physical capital stock will always increase the value of the capital stock by a larger amount, because, by lowering the interest rate, it will increase the value of the pre-existing physical capital stock. Alternatively, a fall in the rate of interest will increase the value of the capital stock by more than it increases the physical quantity, or an increase in the value of capital is accompanied by a smaller increase in the real capital stock. This is shown in Diagram II, where value of capital stock increases

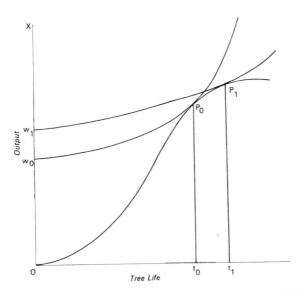

DIAGRAM II: VALUE OF CAPITAL STOCK AND REAL QUANTITY OF CAPITAL.

from $OW_0P_0t_0$ to $OW_1P_1t_1$, while the real capital stock increases by $t_0P_0P_1t_1$, the difference being (approximately) $W_0W_1P_0$. The difference is the increase in the capital value of the existing real capital stock due to the associated reduction in the rate of interest; with the fall in the rate of interest also goes a rise in real wages from W_0 to W_1. The former change, the increase in the real stock of capital, has come to be known as the 'Ricardo effect' of a fall in the rate of interest, the latter, the increase in the value of the existing capital stock, as the 'Wicksell effect' of a change in the rate of interest.

With a continuous tree growth function, the two effects always go together; but with a discontinuous tree growth function (suppose trees grow only in the spring), they alternate (see Diagram III). With the cumulation curve touching t_0 and t_1 and corresponding to W_0, the accumulation of capital between t_0 and t_1 involves no change in the interest rate, the real wage rate, or the value of existing capital, and only the physical capital stock grows. The same holds true of the cumulation curve touching t_1 and t_2 and corresponding to the wage rate W_2. But for any interest rate lying between these two, there is no change in the real capital stock, only a change in the value

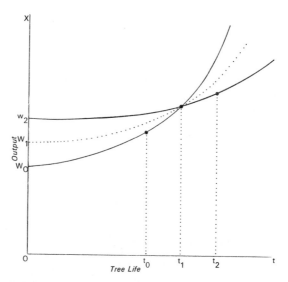

DIAGRAM III: THE WICKSELL AND RICARDO EFFECTS

of the existing capital stock, and a change in the wage rate. In other words, as we reduce the interest rate from that corresponding to W_0 to that corresponding to W_2, there is no increase in the real stock of capital, only a redistribution of income from capital to labour. But for these two interest rates, real capital accumulates without altering the wage rate and therefore the absolute share of labour, while the absolute income of capital rises, so that the relative share of capital rises. (Whether the relative share of capital tends to rise or fall over a sequence of alternations of these two processes depends on the equivalent in discrete-model terms of the elasticity of substitution.)

The presence of the Wicksell effect as well as the Ricardo effect makes the change in the value of capital associated with a change in the interest rate different from the change in the amount of real capital so associated (in this model the value always increases by more than the amount, as the rate of interest falls, but in a more general model in which capital equipment is different from output and its value in terms of output may fall, the difference may go either way). This raises the question of what is meant by the marginal product of capital. Two 'marginal products' may be defined: the marginal product of real capital, and the marginal product of the value of capital.

In the discrete tree growth function case, the marginal product of the value of capital alternates between zero and a positive value, and this raises problems in the analysis of the process of capital accumulation, because at any discrete production point (age of tree) the marginal product of the value of capital is positive in one direction and zero in the other. On the other hand, the marginal product of real capital is always defined, and continually decreasing; but an increase in the value of capital does not always bring about an increase in real capital. This fact constitutes a part of Joan Robinson's criticism of the production function approach to distribution theory, though her criticism is primarily based on a two-sector model in which there is a problem of valuation of capital goods in terms of consumption goods (or, as she actually constructs her model, valuation in terms of labour). But so long as one recognizes the problem, one can take care of it by a more detailed specification of the model. In particular, one must recognize that it is the classical and neo-classical framework of analysis in terms of an aggregate production function containing capital and labour as arguments, combined with the notion that capital is augmented by saving, that makes the differences between real capital and value of capital a source of difficulty. The value of capital is not necessarily a relevant concept for analysis, and resort to it can be avoided by constructing appropriately disaggregated models.

The possibility of two definitions of the marginal product of capital can be misleading. To illustrate, Lloyd Metzler, an acknowledged brilliant theorist, published in the *Journal of Political Economy* in 1950 an otherwise excellent article in which he identified the marginal product of the value of capital with its social marginal product, and argued that because the Wicksell effect made this generally different from the marginal product of real capital, and because savers and entrepreneurs could be expected to govern investment by the private return to capital accumulation, the marginal product of real capital, the stock of capital would not in general be socially optimal. This was an error, pointed out to him by two of his students and acknowledged later by himself. The Wicksell effect is a capital gain (or loss) on the value of the existing stock of capital equipment, involving no social cost or gain, and the social rate of return on capital is equal to the rate of interest, which is the marginal product of real capital measured in terms of itself.

Other Issues in Capital Theory
The first issue is, what is the function of the stock of capital in production? In the simple tree model, the forest just stands there. Output is made possible by the existence of the capital stock of trees and through the ageing process. Once the trees have been planted, no further use of resources is called for to obtain the final output. Although labour is usually thought of as entering into the production function by doing something that involves effort, the function of capital does not necessarily involve an obvious input. (Beware, for example, of the superficially attractive notion that capital earns an income because it eventually wears out during the production process — all this fact does is to ensure that capital must contribute enough to the production process to provide for its own depreciation and replacement.) For example, inventories serve to make production more efficient; but it is the existence of the stock of inventories at any time, not the fact that the individual items

in the inventory turn over and disappear from the stock, that makes the inventory useful to production. (The forest is an example of an inventory.)

Second, once a balanced stock of capital exists, input and output are simultaneous. Further, any owner of capital can buy the stock and immediately proceed to receive an income. The classical and neo-classical notions of the return on capital as having been earned by 'abstinence' or 'waiting' therefore appears superficially to be nonsensical. But abstinence or waiting is implicit either in the process of building up the stock of capital in the first place, or in the process of acquiring the money to buy such a stock, or both. It is also implicit in the process of holding the stock in order to enjoy the income from it, rather than running it down or selling it off in order to increase current consumption.

The Period of Production

Both the Ricardian model and the Wicksellian model entail the notion that 'capital' is a produced means of production that essentially involves the investment of resources over a period of time. In particular, as shown earlier, the Wicksellian model can be summarized in the determination of the optimal time for which labour, the original factor required to plant trees, should be left to mature in the form of the growth of the trees. It is a natural step from such a model to regard 'capital' as consisting of the employment of original resources in a production process requiring a certain period of time, or 'period of production', and to attempt to measure a society's stock of capital by the period of production that it permits.

The classic, or more accurately neo-classic, work on this approach to capital theory is that of Böhm–Bawerk, who conceived of capital as summarized in the period of production and of an increase in capital as consisting of a lengthening of the period of production — in other words, as consisting of the adoption of more 'roundabout' methods of production.

Unfortunately, the notion of a 'period of production' breaks down as soon as one gets away from a single point-input, point-output production process, because with more than one such process or with other types of production processes the determination of the average period of production necessarily involves the rate of interest itself, and hence is not independent of it. The source of the difficulty is the necessity of compounding interest over the period.

To see this, consider the problem of averaging two production processes requiring equal (unit) inputs and taking t_1 and t_2 periods for the inputs to mature into outputs. At simple interest, not compounded, the interest earnings would be

$$it_1 + it_2 = 2i\frac{t_1 + t_2}{2}$$

that is, the interest receipts would be the interest rate multiplied by the labour input multiplied by the average period of production. But with compound interest, the interest earnings would be

$$y_1 = (1 + i)^{t_1} - 1 + (1 + i)^{t_2} - 1$$

whereas the earnings on a two-unit investment for the same average period would be

$$y_2 = 2(1 + i)^{t_1 + t_2/2} - 2$$

Using the binomial expansion

$$y_1 = it_1 + \frac{t_1(t_1 - 1)}{2} i^2 + \ldots + it_2 + \frac{t_2(t_2 - 1)}{2} i^2 + \ldots$$

$$y_2 = (t_1 + t_2)i + 2 \frac{\frac{t_1 + t_2}{2} \left(\frac{t_1 + t_2}{2} - 1 \right)}{2} i^2 + \ldots$$

$$y_1 - y_2 \approx \frac{1}{2} i^2 \frac{(t_1 - t_2)^2}{2} > 0.$$

(The interest income is higher with investment for two periods of different length than with investment of the same amount for a period equal to the average of the two periods.)

If, instead of taking the average of the two periods, we attempt to find a period (T) for the single investment that will yield the same interest, we obtain (using the binomial expansion again as an approximation)

$$2Ti + T(T - 1)i^2 = i(t_1 + t_2) + \frac{t_1(t_1 - 1) + t_2(t_2 - 1) + t_1 t_2}{2} i^2$$

or

$$T^2 + \left(\frac{2}{i} - 1 \right) T - \frac{1}{i} \left(t_1 + t_2 + \frac{t_1^2 - t_1 + t_2^2 - t_2 + t_1 t_2}{2} i \right) = 0$$

This obviously makes the average period of production equivalent in its interest-earning capacity to t_1 combined with t_2 a function of the rate of interest itself.

The point is illustrated simply in Diagram IV, where $V(t)$ charts the cumulated value of a unit investment as it gathers compound interest over time, V_B is the average value of two investments with periods t_1 and t_2, V_A is the value of a single investment of period $(t_1 + t_2)/2$ and $T > [(t_1 + t_2)/2]$ is the period for which such a single investment would have to run to have the same value as the combination of investments for periods t_1 and t_2 respectively.

It is obvious that a similar problem arises when, instead of the point-input, point-output case, we have either inputs or outputs or both distributed over time. Then we cannot find an average period of production without needing the interest rate to calculate the contributions of inputs (or outputs) occurring at different points of time. Thus suppose we have one input at $t = 0$ and another at $t = t_i$, the cumulated value of the investment at time t will be $(1 + i)^t + (1 + i)^{t - t_i}$ and a point-input investment with the same value would have a production period T determined by $2(1 + i)^T = (1 + i)^t + (1 + i)^{t - t_1}$.

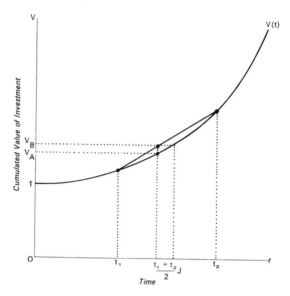

DIAGRAM IV: THE AVERAGE PERIOD OF PRODUCTION

The extreme case of this problem arises when production is considered to involve the use of capital equipment and labour, the capital equipment having been produced by past labour and capital equipment, the past capital equipment having been itself produced by previous use of labour and capital equipment, and so forth in an infinite regression back to the time of Adam and Eve. To evaluate the average period of production in this case, we obviously require a price for the capital equipment currently in use; but such a price necessarily involves the interest rate at which past capital used to produce currently-used capital goods has been cumulated into the determination of their prices.

The Negative Wicksell Effect
In the tree model employed previously, a fall in the rate of interest (rise in the wage rate) is always associated with a rise in the value of capital; a rise in the value of capital is always associated with an increase in the physical stock of capital and a lengthening of the period of production. But this association is a consequence of the identity of capital equipment (standing timber) with the consumption good (wood). If capital equipment is a different physical substance than consumption goods — say, for example, it consists of axes for cutting down trees — the accumulation of physical capital may reduce the value of capital equipment in terms of consumption goods.

This possibility is illustrating in Diagram V, where it is assumed (quite unrealistically) that the production of capital goods is a point-input, point-output process of fixed period. Accumulation raises the wage rate from W_0 to W_1 and lowers the interest rate from i_0 to i_1. The value of a capital good falls from V_0 to V_1, and the stock of capital used in producing capital

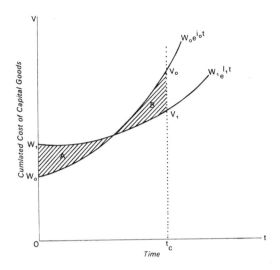

DIAGRAM V: THE NEGATIVE WICKSELL EFFECT

goods falls by the difference between area B and area A. The fall in the cost of the capital good may outweigh any increase that may occur in the quantity of it used in producing consumption goods, so that the value of the total capital stock falls with the fall in the rate of interest and rise in the wage rate.

This possibility of a negative Wicksell effect and a fall in the value of capital as the interest rate falls has played an important part in current controversies about capital theory and the theory of accumulation. We would like to be able to assume a monotonically declining relationship between the rate of return on capital and its value, parallel to the assumption of a declining marginal product of capital as its physical quantity increases relative to the quantity of original factors of production, because we view accumulation of capital as involving foregoing the consumption of current goods and services. But the value of capital may rise, then decline, then rise again as the rate of interest falls. This means that the same value of capital will be consistent with three different interest rates (there are two stable and one unstable equlibrium interest rates) and that as physical capital accumulates the value of capital first increases, then decreases, then increases again — which poses serious problems for an orderly process of capital accumulation (see Diagram VI). This problem is known in the literature as the 'double-switching' problem. Joan Robinson and her followers regard it as disposing conclusively both of the concept of an aggregate production function and of the viability of the capitalist system. Their critics argue on the contrary that no important problems depend on the ability to construct an aggregate production function for the economy as a whole, and that analysis can be conducted safely (on Fisherian lines) on the basis of the marginal rate of return on investment. Note that essentially the same problem recurs with the use of the 'internal rate of return' criterion for the evaluation of investment opportunities (see chapter 13) in the form of the fact that the present value of an investment opportunity does not necessarily rise monotonically (from negative to positive levels) as the rate of interest falls; instead it may rise above zero for a certain range of interest rates and then fall below zero again as the rate of interest declines.

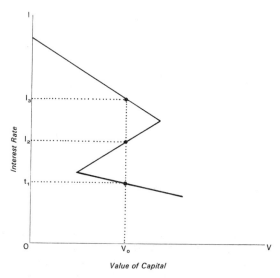

DIAGRAM VI: THE 'DOUBLE-SWITCHING' PROBLEM.

Relation to Marginal Productivity Theory
In the Ricardian model, the marginal product of labour on the land pays both the wages of labour and the profits of the capital (wage fund) used to support labour during the period of agricultural production. In the Wicksellian tree model, the total product is divided between wages, and interest on the capital involved in waiting for planted seeds to mature into optimal-aged trees. In both cases, it is a natural simple logical step to consider the wage as the marginal product of labour, discounted back from the time of production of the output to the time at which the wage is paid; the capitalist can be thought of, by analogy with the discounting of bills of exchange or the making of bank loans, as 'discounting' the future value of the product of labour by the current rate of interest, and living on the difference between the actual and the discounted value of the worker's marginal product. In a more general system using a variety of original and produced factors of production, the factors will be paid the discounted value of their marginal products, and competition will equalize the discounted marginal productivity of each type of factor between its various uses. For a period in the 1920s and 1930s, a number of textbook and other writers took great care always to describe marginal products as '(discounted) marginal products'; but that fashion seems to have died out. The approach is in any case clumsy to use, as it is simpler to think of production as a flow process using inputs and producing outputs simultaneously, rather

than to keep remembering that if the process were started up from scratch there would necessarily be an interval of time between the initiation of inputs and the delivery of finished outputs.

The Accumulation of Capital

The Wicksellian model analyzed so far is a static equilibrium model so constructed as to abstract from many of the difficult problems involved in getting to grips with the process of accumulation in the real world. Note especially that if 'accumulation' is defined in a broad Fisherian sense to include the augmentation of stocks of income — producing assets of all kinds, two of the most important sources of growth in the modern world are excluded by the assumption of a given technology and homogeneity of the quality of the labour force. These sources are, respectively, improvement of technology and of productive knowledge generally through experience and through investment in the creation of useful knowledge in the form of basic and applied research and development expenditure (accumulation of intellectual capital); and improvement of human skills and capacities through investment in formal education and in 'on-the-job' training (accumulation of human capital). In addition, the assumption of a balanced stock of capital abstracts from problems associated in a growing and changing world with the building up and running down of productive operations, which obviously make the static 'production function' relation between inputs, including capital, and outputs inapplicable without considerable modification in the direction of attaching a time-profile to the process. Finally, in a world of change, unless everyone had an impossibly perfect degree of foresight — expressed, say, in a set of interest rates for all future points of time expected with certainty — and reflecting the impact of all the decisions people will take on the basis of these interest rates, there will be bound to be errors in decision-taking, resulting in capital gains for some and losses for others, and in differences between the cost of production or reproduction of items of capital equipment and their market values. To put the same point another way, in a colourful phrase of Joan Robinson's, there will be 'fossils' in society's stock of capital equipment resulting from erroneous past investment decisions.

All these mean that theoretical models of growth and accumulation (including the contemporary growth models to be discussed later in chapters 14 and 15) are very unsatisfactory approximations to a stylization of economic history. However, in this section we discuss what may be described as a neo-classical model of accumulation.

Recall first the Ricardian model, in which accumulation of capital (which in that model is also growth of population) is brought to a halt by the fall in the rate of profit due to its being squeezed between the fixed subsistence wage and the diminishing marginal productivity of labour on the land. Accumulation ceases when the rate of profit becomes too low for it to be worthwhile for capitalists to continue accumulating.

Now return to the Wicksellian tree model, and recall that to obtain a determinate equilibrium it is necessary to fix one of the following: the interest rate, the wage rate, the physical quantity of capital, or the value of capital. It is a logical extension of the model to the analysis of accumulation to start from some arbitrary initial equilibrium, and to assume that if the interest rate is above that at which the community is just satisfied to maintain its existing stock of capital intact, consuming all its current output, the community will devote part of its current output to increasing its stock of capital. We can envisage this process as going on in a series of small steps, from one static equilibrium to another, thereby ignoring the problems of transition between them.

(Note the artificiality of the construction, both in ignoring transition problems and in disregarding the fact that people's behaviour in the short run will be influenced by their expectations about the long run. In particular, it would be senseless to reorganize a static equilibrium for a transition to a higher capital stock, reorganize it again for that static equilibrium, then reorganize it again for another transition to a higher capital stock. Yet this is the logical structure of Schumpeter's theory of economic development — though he concentrated on technological innovation rather than capital accumulation, innovation being motivated by entrepreneural high spirits, and entertained a Marx-like view of interest as a monopoly rent captured by the financiers. It is necessary to observe once more the limitations of the analytical tools available to our predecessors, which they had to render applicable to the problems that interested them by considerable exercise of ingenuity, and to recall that economists did not have the mathematical tools for dynamic analysis until the 1930s and, effectively, the 1940s.)

The analysis in question is presented in Diagram VII. In the diagram, the physical stock of capital is graphed on the horizontal axis (note that it is assumed, contrary to the burden of much previous analysis, that we can ignore Wicksell effects and construct a quantity index of capital despite changes in its physical form as accumulation proceeds). MPK graphs the marginal physical productivity of capital, which is also the rate of return on capital if we measure it in units of capital, not consumption goods. Note that

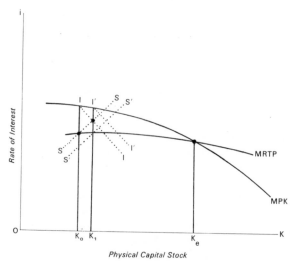

Physical Capital Stock

DIAGRAM VII: A NEO-CLASSICAL MODEL OF CAPITAL ACCUMULATION.

the marginal productivity of capital is explicitly defined for a static equilibrium situation in which the capital stock is kept intact from period to period; otherwise the rate of return on capital would vary somehow with the allocation of production as between consumption and (net) investment or disinvestment. It must fall as the stock of capital rises, assuming of course a static population and technology.

$MRTP$ is the marginal rate of time preference of the community, defined as the rate of return on capital at which the population would just be content to hold the existing stock of capital intact from period to period, alternatively to consume the net output of the economy after provision for depreciation of the capital stock. Note that this is a different definition of the marginal rate of time preference than we will come across in the next chapter on the work of Irving Fisher (in the Fisher model, capital enters only implicitly as a way of transferring consumption possibilities from the present to the future, and individuals' and the social marginal rate of time preference reflect the interaction of preferences with the time profile of consumption possibilities). Note also that the $MRTP$ relation may slope in either direction (in the diagram it slopes downward, indicating that with greater wealth the public will keep the capital stock intact for a lower rate of return on it).

An admittedly crude model of the process of accumulation can be constructed as shown in the diagram. K_0 is the initial stock of capital. Through the MRTP curve runs a savings curve SS which must be upward-sloping, because in order to save people have to sacrifice more and more current consumption for the sake of establishing a higher level of future output and potential consumption than they now enjoy. (The marginal utility of present consumption rises relative to the marginal utility of future consumption, or, in Fisher's terms, the (short-run) marginal rate of preference for present over future consumption rises as savings rise.) Through the MPK curve runs a similar relationship II describing the effect on the rate of return on new investment as production of capital goods rises above the replacement level for the initial stock of capital. This relation, described as 'the marginal efficiency of investment' relation between the amount of investment and the rate of return on it, is usually held to fall below the MPK curve to the right of the initial capital stock on the assumption of a rising supply price of new capital goods as the rate of production of the latter rises, in relation to a fixed stream of rentals on capital goods. However, it is possible, and will be so if capital goods production is capital-intensive (and we assume mobility of factors among capital-goods and consumption-goods producing industries) that the rate of return on existing capital will rise as investment increases, so that the II curve is upward-sloping. Note also that, if we assumed that the economy is used to accumulating capital over time, the II curve would start falling below the MPK curve from somewhere right of the initial capital stock, corresponding to the normal rate of production of investment goods. (These remarks indicate the crudity of the apparatus, which by-passes the problems involved in the short-run equilibrium of savings and investment.)

The intersection of the II and SS curves determines the stock of capital K_1 the economy starts with the next period — with new $S'S'$ and $I'I'$ curves determining the next initial stock of capital. Thus the economy slowly works its way to the long-run equilibrium stationary state with capital stock K_e, determined by time preference and the marginal productivity of capital. This is the neo-classical equivalent of the long-run equilibrium of the Ricardian model, the limit on growth being diminishing marginal productivity of capital as it accumulates relative to labour, rather than of labour as it accumulates relative to land.

Both of the basic assumptions of the neo-classical growth model (or, more accurately, model of the long-run stationary state), diminishing marginal productivity and positive time preference, are subject to critical objections.

Diminishing Marginal Productivity
The notion of diminishing marginal productivity of other factors as more are applied to a fixed quantity of land variable in fertility either at the intensive or the extensive margin of cultivation is plausible enough, though it does raise the question of technical progress as a means of raising the effective quantity of existing land either by improving its fertility or discovering or creating more land by investment. A model which neglects the limitation of available land and is based on diminishing returns to capital as its quantity is increased relative to the quantity of labour begs the question (suggested by the Ricardian–Malthusian model) of why population does not respond to increasing real wages by increasing in quantity — and if labour expands *pari passu* with capital and land is not a limitational factor there will be constant marginal productivities of both factors, no long-run stationary state, and a rate of growth of output at any time determined by the rate at which capitalists choose to increase the stock of capital. Another form of this criticism, raised long ago by Frank Knight, is that if all factors can be increased by investment and there are constant returns in the production of each, and in the production of consumption and capital goods, the rate of return on investment of all kinds will be equal and constant, and again there will be no long-run stationary equilibrium state but instead an economy expanding indefinitely at a rate determined by the rate of increase of capital. This criticism gains extra point from the modern theory of human capital, according to which the effective supply of labour can be increased by investing in improving the educational level or 'quality' of the human population, not merely by increasing its numbers through some sort of Malthusian process.

It may be remarked in passing that this problem recurs in contemporary growth models. These models essentially recreate the classical and neo-classical long-run stationary state, but keep the economy growing by positing an exogenous growth force in the shape of an automatically expanding population and/or an automatically improving technology. Convergence on the equivalent of the classical–neo-classical stationary state is assured by assuming diminishing returns as capital, in whatever form (material, human, intellectual) is accumulated relative to the exogenously-growing natural human population. In the case of all three kinds of capital, the required assumption is that the depreciation on the capital stock grows in proportion to the existing stock, while the marginal productivity of the stock falls as it is accumulated relative to the limitational factor, the stock of raw labour given by the exogenous laws of population growth. (Note this point for future reference in connection with chapters 13 and 14.)

Time Preference
The classical and neo-classical models of the stationary state come into equilibrium at a positive rate of interest. For Ricardo and his contemporaries it was obvious that at some point the rate of return on additional capital would become too low for further accumulation to be worth the capitalists' while. For subsequent theorists basing their analysis on marginal utility or general equilibrium theory, the point was not so obvious, and required discussion. Marshall and Pigou in England (especially the latter) attributed the existence of time preference to short-sightedness or 'myopia' on the part of the average human being, i.e. to an underestimation of the value of future as compared with the value of present consumption. This view is puzzling, if we assume 'permanent' individuals who last forever and can always convert a small sacrifice of present consumption into a permanent, infinitely-lasting, higher stream of future consumption — in infinite time, it does not matter how long it takes them to reduce the marginal productivity of capital to zero. (Note, though this will not be discussed here, that there are logical difficulties in conceiving an infinitely-lived individual or society with absolutely zero time preference, because he or they would be indifferent between consumption streams that involved the same total consumption — due to zero interest on savings — distributed differently over time.) However, one can charitably interpret 'myopia' as a way of smuggling into the analysis the practical recognition that human life is finite, and that the chance of being physically present to enjoy the consumption possibilities one has created by one's own saving, instead of looking down from heaven or up from the other place as one's heirs squander them, is considerably less than unity even with the wisest financial planning. Both reasons — finiteness of life and uncertainty of age of death — would rationalize positive time preference. (One suspects that Marshall and Pigou, being good Victorian Englishmen, were implicitly criticizing their fellow citizens for paying insufficient regard to the assumed immortality of English society.)

Gustav Cassel of Sweden developed a theory of the minimum rate of time preference along the following lines: if the rate of interest fell too low, a saver would enjoy, in interest on his savings before his death, less cash income and consumption than he had paid in in savings during his life-time, and so would stop saving. This argument is logical, but only on the assumption that the saver plans to keep his capital intact and not use up the capital as well as the interest before he dies (e.g. by buying an annuity).

Joseph Schumpeter, as already mentioned, maintained that, in the static equilibria that would be interspersed with the periods of innovation that constituted the main element in his theory of economic development, the rate of interest would return to zero, interest being a monopoly rent extorted by the financiers from the innovators in return for the capital funds they needed for innovation. Schumpeter gave no satisfactory reason for this assertion, and he was unable to persuade his theoretician Harvard colleagues of its correctness.

Time preference remains an awkward legacy from our theoretical fore-fathers. It makes considerable human sense but not necessarily theoretical sense in the kind of non-human models our analytical tools enable us to construct most easily.

Final Note: Capital in the Production Function

In the Wicksellian tree model, the production function is basically $x = f(t)$, where x is output per period, t is the optimal life of a tree, and the production function assumes a balanced stock of capital. (Note that if we had only one tree of optimal age, we would have the same production function, *but for this period only*.) However the technical production process is specified, we could always write output for one period as a function of the inputs, and if we assumed a balanced stock of durable equipment producing inputs and a steady flow of immediate inputs we could write the production of ouput as a function of the (balanced) stocks of equipment and the flows of immediate inputs (labour services, raw materials). The difficulty comes when we have to aggregate over the economy and (ignoring the problem of measuring the outputs) we have to aggregate the inputs for simplicity. We could always, of course, write an aggregate production function for current output as a function of everything relevant to production, e.g.

$$f(x_1, x_2, x_3, \ldots, x_n; y_1, y_2, y_3, \ldots, y_m) = 0$$

where the x_i are everything we might want to produce and the y_i everything we have to hand to help produce it with. But that would not be informative; nor would assuming a balanced capital stock of everything relevant help much. We could instead write aggregate output (disregarding the aggregation problems involved on that side of the production process) as a function of, say, aggregated labour inputs (disregarding the aggregation problems involved there) and the aggregate stock of capital, expressed either in physical or value terms. The latter involves the problem of the Wicksell effect, specifically the need to write the marginal product of the value of capital as zero when only the Wicksell effect operates. The former requires us to develop a chain index of physical capital that cancels out the Wicksell effect. It is easy both to stress the great practical difficulties involved, and to find mathematically possible cases where these procedures break down. But one must remember that the problem is created by the classical tradition of economic theory, and that if there is a problem where a simple aggregate production function will not work it can be solved, if the problem is understood, by disaggregating the system.

A final point concerns the way in which capital participates in the production process. Much traditional theory assumes that capital contributes to production by being used up in the process of production. This is incorrect; the using up is an accident of production technology, and unfortunate — if capital equipment lasted forever, instead of wearing out, net production would be higher (no depreciation and replacement) and the capital stock would also be more valuable at any given rate of interest. The function of capital in the production process is to facilitate production by the immediately rendered services of less durable factors through the presence of capital as a stock rendering productive services. The fact that individual items in the stock wear out and have to be replaced renders the stock less helpful to production than if the opposite were true. To illustrate the point, consider an inventory of raw materials or finished goods. The contribution of an inventory to production comes from the presence of the stock, not from the fact that individual items in it are used up and have to be replaced by others. Further

— a point noted and explained by Böhm–Bawerk — the 'productivity' of capital in production comes not from its being used up in production, but from the fact that in the process it generates a surplus of productive contribution above its replacement cost.

12

CAPITAL AND INTEREST: THE FISHER MODEL

Introduction

In the dominant tradition of economic analysis, inherited from the English classical economists via the neo-classical writers of England and elsewhere, and, of course, much refined since, the economy is conceived of as using its available supplies of land, labour and capital equipment to produce a national income or net product (i.e. output reckoned net of depreciation of its stock of capital equipment). The national income is distributed among wages of labour, rent of land and interest on capital (and in later versions also profits from entrepreneurship); and it is allocated by its recipients between current consumption, and investment in increasing the stock of capital equipment. This approach puts capital equipment at the centre of the analytical picture: witness the use of the term 'capitalism' to distinguish contemporary western society from both previous historical epochs and communist ('socialist') regimes, despite the fact that all societies, no matter how primitive, use equipment of some kind, and the ability to use equipment is what distinguishes mankind from the other animals. And, as seen in the preceding chapter, it creates both unnecessarily controversial social-philosophical problems about the justification for the receipt of income from the mere ownership of material property, and ultimately theoretically unresolvable issues concerning the nature and productive function of capital, centring on the difference between the physical quantity and the value of capital and the validity and usefulness of the concept of an aggregate production function. Also, though this is a problem in macroeconomic theory rather than in distribution theory, it creates difficult problems in the analysis of the determination of the rate of investment in new capital equipment.

The Fisherian approach with which this chapter is concerned departs from the main-line tradition in two fundamental respect. First, it places the emphasis on consumption, rather than output, in defining the concept of 'income'; specifically, the production of capital goods is regarded as a means of providing for future consumption, and should not be counted in income both when the capital goods are produced and when they yield future consumption. (In the Fisher analysis, the use of capital goods, their form, longevity, etc., are left implicit in the choice of optimal time-profiles of consumption.) Second, capital is identified with the sources of the time-streams of consumption or 'income', and 'income' is simply the time-stream of output yielded by capital. Capital and income are related by the rate of interest, which enables anything yielding a stream of future output to be given a capital value, and anything that has a capital value to be translated into an equivalent expression in terms of a perpetual stream of income. 'Interest', therefore, is not an income share, as in the classical and many modern models (where it is generally described instead as 'profits') but a way of describing a particular income share that can be applied to any other income share.

For example, the rent on land could be regarded as interest on the capital value of the land, though in the case of land that capital value (on the simplifying Ricardian assumption that rent accrues to the 'original and indestructible properties of the soil') has to be determined by capitalizing the land's rental value. This is disguised in England by the traditional terminology of fixing the purchase price of land in terms of 'n years purchase' of the rental value, which in mathematical terms says $V_A = nR$, where V_A is the purchase price of land (A standing for acres) and R is annual rental value, assumed constant in perpetuity for simplicity; in fact, in a rational market, n can only be determined by reference to some relevant interest rate i on alternative investment opportunities, with

$$V_A = nR = \sum_{t=1}^{t=\infty} \frac{1}{(1 + i)^t} R \quad \text{and} \quad n = 1/i,$$

so that for example 'twenty years' purchase' implies a 5 per cent rate of interest and 'twenty-five years' purchase' a 4 per cent rate of interest. Similarly, the wages of labour could be translated into interest on the value of the worker's human capital, the capitalization in this case being the more complicated one

$$V_L = \sum_{t=1}^{t=r} \frac{(1 - u_t)(1 - m_t)\, w_t}{(1 + i)^t}$$

where r stands for number of years to retirement, w_t the expected annual wage of an employed worker of this type in year t, u_t the probable proportion of unemployment of this type of worker in year t, and m_t the probability that this particular worker will be physically incapacitated or dead in year t (the 'mortality factor'). Note, incidentally, in connection with the earlier discussion of chapter 10 and the later discussion of chapter 17, that this computed capital value will not necessarily be the one that guides workers' choices among careers, both because their expectations of the three probability factors — future earnings, unemployment, age of death — may not correspond to the objective facts of economics and mortality, and because their choices may be influenced importantly by their attitudes towards risk, and also by the non-pecuniary advantages and disadvantages of various occupations. (Similarly, purchasers and sellers of land may be influenced by the social prestige of being a landlord, a fact which would be reflected in land trading at prices above the capitalized value of future rents at the current interest rate on alternative investments.) Note also that the capitalization of an income stream into a capital value is an exercise of mostly mathematical significance where the supply of the relevant factor of production is fixed, as in the classical view of land, serving only to determine (or help to determine) the market price of the asset that produces a stream of rental values, and a purely formal exercise where not only is the supply of the asset fixed but there is no market in the asset, only in its services (as in the case of the classical view of labour, combined with a democratic political structure that precludes slavery).

The capital–interest–income relationship derives its economic interest from the possibility of investing in the creation of new capital or income-yielding assets (discovery of new land or improvement of existing land, education and training of labour skills, in the two cases discussed; the general problem also involves investment in more capital equipment or in the discovery of new productive knowledge). This possibility raises the question of the costs and benefits of creating new capital of any kind — in the present context, the capital value of the new asset in relation to its cost — and of the relative gains from investing in alternative types of capital, including both different forms of the same type of capital (material, human, environmental, intellectual) and different types of capital.

In this framework of analysis, originated by Fisher and followed by Knight and subsequently many other distinguished theorists (including in the monetary economics field D. H. Robertson and his theory of 'loanable funds' and Keynes and his theory of 'liquidity preference') the central problem is the determination of the rate of interest by means of which the capital value of existing sources of future income streams is determined. The answer has to lie in the interaction between the willingness of the community to 'trade off' present consumption possibilities against future consumption possibilities, and the opportunities they have for doing so by using present resources to produce future resources (resources here being the potentiality of producing consumption goods). Note that this formulation of the problem by-passes the question of the aggregate production function, the meaning of capital, and related theoretical problems: existing assets have been created by past history and earn rents determined by the relation between the demand for and the supply of them; the capital value of these rents depends on the rate of interest, determined as above; and we do not need a concept or measure of the existing stock of material capital in either physical or value terms to determine the rate of interest (though the existing stock of material and human capital will of course exert an important influence on the terms on which present consumption possibilities can be converted into future consumption possibilities).

The Fisher Approach: Pure Consumption Model
The central concept is that of time preference, defined as the percentage excess of the marginal want for one more unit of present goods over the present marginal want for one more unit of future goods. This expresses the interaction between the individual's preference or behaviour system, characterized by his 'impatience' over the deferral of consumption, and the characteristics of the consumption stream that confronts him for the present and future periods, in terms of size, time-profile, composition by commodities, and risk (the following exposition abstracts from composition and risk). Note the difference between this concept, which involves the interaction of preferences and opportunities, and that discussed in the previous chapter, which constrains the individual to a constant stream of consumption.

The individual has a preference system characterized by impatience, and a stream of present and future receipts of consumption goods. He faces a loan market in which the rate of interest is parametric for him. This market provides him with an intertemporal budget constraint, since he can borrow or

lend in the market in order to rearrange the time profile of his consumption
— and may do either at different times — subject to the condition that
whatever he does the present value of his actual consumption stream must
be equal to the present value of his consumption receipts stream. This may
be expressed algebraically in the following two alternative forms:

$$\sum_{t=0}^{t=n} \frac{y_t}{(1+i)^t} = \sum_{t=0}^{t=n} \frac{c_t}{(1+i)^t}$$

$$\sum_{t=0}^{t=n} \frac{y_t - c_t}{(1+i)^t} = 0$$

where y_t and c_t are respectively receipts and actual consumption in period
t, i is the market interest rate (assumed constant for simplicity — but see
chapter 13) and n is the number of years until his death (expected with
certainty). The two statements say that the present value of receipts must
equal the present value of actual consumption over the period, and that the
present value of loans and borrowings over the period must be zero. The
formulation suggests a hard-hearted individual who intends to die leaving
nothing to posterity, i.e. with nothing left of his income except possibly
enough to pay his funeral expenses and provide two pennies to cover his eyes;
but the desire to leave an inheritance to posterity can easily be included as a
constituent of his consumption in the final period. This is the budget constraint which is a 'wealth' rather than an 'income' constraint; the individual
is conceived of as having a utility function $U = U(C_0, C_1, C_2, \ldots, C_n)$ which
he maximizes subject to this constraint; and the maximization process
determines how much he will lend or borrow in each period (again assuming
that the interest rate is parametric — in fact the interest rate in each period
will be determined by a general equilibrium process equilibrating desired
total borrowing with desired total lending).

Both the individual desire to lend or borrow and the equilibration of the
economy in the determination of the interest rate can be analysed in terms of
a simple two-period system. Diagram I depicts the equilibrium (maximization) position of an individual who has consumption goods receipts of R_1
in period 1 and R_2 in period 2. His wealth, measured at the beginning of
period 1, is W_1, and measured at the end of period 2 is W_2, the slope of the line
through P_1 being $1 + i$, where i is the market interest rate (figured as a
fraction and not as a percentage). Given the wealth constraint, the individual
can transform his receipts in the two periods into any intertemporal consumption pattern he wishes; what he actually does will depend on his
preferences. Individual A, represented by his maximum attainable utility
level U_A, will choose consumption point C_A and hence be a lender in the
market of $R_1 - C_{1A}$ in the first period and a borrower (seller of loan assets)
in the market in period 2 of $C_{2A} - R_2$. Individual B, represented by his
maximum attainable utility level U_B, will be a borrower in the market of
$C_{1B} - R_1$ in period 1 and a lender (buyer of loan assets issued by himself) in
period 2. Alternatively, if individuals have the same preferences but different
time-profiles of receipts in the two periods, their behaviour will be different.
This is illustrated in Diagram II, where U is the maximum utility level
obtainable by both A and B given their common tastes and equal wealth

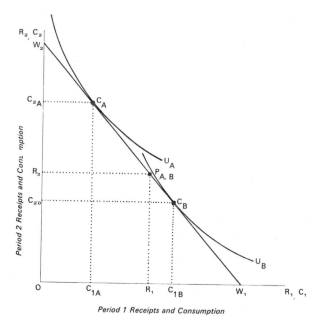

Period 1 Receipts and Consumption

DIAGRAM I: TWO-PERIOD INDIVIDUAL INTERTEMPORAL EQUILIBRIUM WITH DIFFERING PREFERENCES

W_1 or W_2; but A's receipt profile is R_A, making him a lender in period 1 and a borrower in period 2, while B's receipt profile is R_B, making him a borrower in period 1 and a lender in period 2.

Given the individual's preference pattern and receipts profile, the individual's borrowing or lending position in each period is a function of the market rate of interest confronting him. This permits the derivation of the individual's demand curve or supply curve of loans in the first period (and by the budget constraint also the second) as a function of the market rate of interest. If the individual is a net borrower, his demand curve for loans must show an increase in quantity demanded as the rate of interest falls, for the usual income and substitution effect reasons. If, on the contrary, he is a net lender, his supply curve of loans may be backward-bending — less lent at higher interest rates — because the income effect of higher interest rates on his total wealth may exert a wealth effect (the equivalent of an income effect) in increasing his current consumption.

To determine the general equilibrium position of the economy, it is necessary to find the interest rate at which the demand for loans equals the supply of loans in the first period (if there is equilibrium in the first period there must also be equilibrium in the second period). One way of doing this is to calculate the net excess demand for or excess supply of loans at each interest rate, equilibrium being achieved at the interest rate at which excess demand for (excess supply of) loans is zero. The equilibrating process is illustrated in Diagram III, where i_e is the equilibrium rate of interest deter-

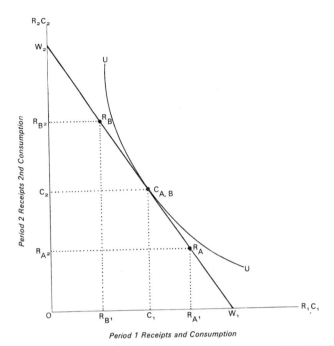

DIAGRAM II: TWO-PERIOD INDIVIDUAL INTERTEMPORAL EQUILIBRIUM WITH
DIFFERING RECEIPT PROFILES

mined in the market by the interactions of individuals with different preferences and different streams of receipts. In this equilibrium position, the
marginal rates of time preference of all the individuals in the economy have
been equated through lending or borrowing at the equilibrium market rate
of interest.

Equilibrium in this model requires that all the consumption goods available
in a particular period be consumed in that period, through the process of
lending and borrowing. This may involve a negative rate of interest on loans,
which may seem odd and uneconomic. If goods could be stored and carried
over from the present to the future period at no cost, the interest rate could
not fall below zero. But if there are storage costs on the carrying-over of
goods, the interest rate could be negative, up to the limit set by the proportion
of storage costs to the value of the goods stored. Thus a negative interest rate
is possible if there are storage costs of carrying goods over into the future
and the community has negative time preference (e.g. because future consumption goods availability is smaller relative to future demand than present
consumption goods availability relative to present demand). Note that the
availability of money, which presumably can be carried over into the future
without storage costs, makes no difference to this result. If money is hoarded
in the first period in order to be spent in the second, this merely implies that
money prices will fall in the first period, and rise in the second, to the extent

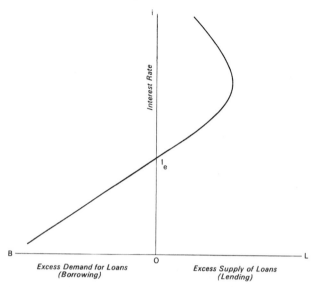

DIAGRAM III: LOAN MARKET EQUILIBRIUM IN A PURE CONSUMPTION ECONOMY

required to ensure that in each period actual consumption is equal to the quantity of consumption goods available (again assuming that storage is impossibly expensive; if it involves a cost equivalent to a negative rate of interest, the behaviour of prices will be such as to ensure that that negative rate of interest is earned on carry-overs of money holdings).

The Fisher Model: Investment Opportunities

The foregoing analysis assumed that the time-profile of consumption goods receipts was fixed, so that the individual's only choice problem was to rearrange the flow of actual consumption by lending and/or borrowing consumption goods in different periods. But the individual also has the choice between these opportunities provided by the capital market, and opportunities provided by the technology available to him to convert current consumption possibilities into future consumption possibilities through investment. Given the availability of the capital market, he can always convert any flow of consumption receipts made available by such investment into any flow of actual consumption he desires; hence his investment problem is to maximize the wealth value of his consumption receipts through investment, the larger the present value of these receipts the larger his wealth and the higher the level of utility he can achieve. In other words, the problem of maximization of utility over time can be decomposed into two parts: maximization of wealth (present value of future consumption receipts) and maximization of utility subject to the wealth constraint imposed by the wealth so maximized. In the context of the former problem, investment involves a choice among alternative time-profiles of consumption-goods receipts, and the problem is to choose the alternative with the maximum present value at the market rate of interest. This choice, in combination with the individual's choice of time-profile of consumption, determines his demand for or supply of loans in each period. And the aggregation of the net demands for or supply of loans determines, for the society, the equilibrium interest rates in each period. The central concept relating to investment choices is that of the marginal rate of return over cost, i.e. the proportional increase in the quantity of consumption goods available in future over the quantity available in the present period made possible by the investment of presently potentially available consumption goods in the production of consumption goods available in a future period.

To simplify the analysis, we again consider the two-period case, beginning with one in which the individual has a discrete choice between two alternative combinations of receipts in the two periods, represented by P_1 and P_2 in Diagram IV. P_2 as compared with P_1 can be regarded as an investment

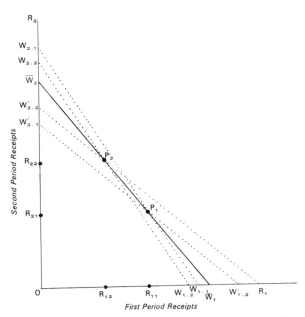

DIAGRAM IV: A DISCRETE INVESTMENT OPPORTUNITY

opportunity, since it involves a reduction of current consumption receipts in exchange for an increase in future consumption receipts. Whether this investment opportunity will be chosen or not depends on whether the choice of it increases the wealth of the individual. The criterion for choice can be expressed in two ways. First, the present value of each alternative can be calculated at the market rate of interest confronting the individual, the choice being determined by whichever alternative yields the higher present value or wealth. Thus, at the interest rate represented by the slopes of $W_{2,1}W_{1,1}$ and $W_{2,2}W_{1,2}$ alternative 1 yields a higher present value than alternative 2 and will therefore be chosen, whereas at the interest rate represented by the slopes of $W'_{2,2}W'_{1,2}$ and $W'_{2,1}W'_{1,1}$ alternative 2 yields a higher present value than alternative 1 and will therefore be chosen. (To avoid confusion, note that the latter two slopes visually imply a negative rate of interest but that this is only a matter of diagrammatic clarity, not economics.) Second, by drawing a line through P_1 and P_2 we determine implicitly the rate of interest in the market at which the two alternatives would be indifferent (yield equal present value). This rate of interest is the 'internal rate of return' on the investment opportunity. If it is higher than the actual market rate of interest (as reflected, say, in the slope of $W'_{2,1}W'_{1,1}$) the investment opportunity should be chosen because it increases present value, and vice versa. Note that whichever alternative is chosen, i.e. whether the individual chooses to invest or not in the opportunity, we do not know whether he will appear in the market as a lender or as a borrower. This will depend on the form of his indifference map as between present and future consumption; one of his indifference curves will be tangent to the highest budget line he can achieve, and whether this corresponds to P_1 or P_2 he may appear as a lender or as a borrower.

If, instead of a discrete choice between a limited number of alternatives, the individual is confronted by a possibility of continuous variation of combinations of present and future consumption receipts, this possibility can be represented by a transformation curve between present and future consumption receipts, shown by TT in Diagram V. His choice among these possibilities

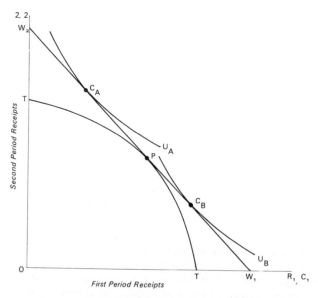

DIAGRAM V: CONTINUOUS INVESTMENT OPPORTUNITIES

can again be represented by two alternative approaches which lead to the same result. First, he chooses a point on the transformation curve that maximizes the present value of his wealth (the point P in Diagram V). Second, he carries investment, defined as the sacrifice of maximum possible potential production of consumption goods in the first period in exchange for production of consumption goods in the second period, up to the point where the marginal rate of return over cost is equal to the interest rate (the tangency point P: on the transformation curve to the right of P, the marginal rate of return over cost is greater than the interest rate). Again, note that the individual's investment decision does not tell us whether he appears in the first-period capital market as a borrower or as a lender. That depends on his preferences for consumption in the first and second periods. In the diagram, if his preferences indicate the optimal consumption point C_A, he will be a first-period lender, and if they indicate the optimal consumption point C_B, he will be a first-period borrower.

The analysis thus far determines only the equilibrium of an individual facing given investment opportunities and a parametric market interest rate. To determine what the interest rate will be, we must aggregate the net borrowing demands or lending supplies of the community, the interest rate being determined by the condition that net excess demand for or excess supply of loans should be zero. Refer back to Diagram III. Note that equilibrium in the loan market tells us nothing about the quantities of investment and saving. The reason is that, to define saving, we would need a definition of income from which to subtract the level of current consumption in order to arrive at saving as a residual. Two artificial and arbitrary constructs could serve this purpose. First, we could take the total consumption that the community could have in period 1 if it provided nothing for consumption in period 2. Second, we could define income as the amount of consumption that the community could have in period 1, subject to the restriction that consumption in period 2 must be exactly equal to consumption in period 1 (which is equivalent to the condition of maintaining capital intact). Standard national income accounting, by reckoning net investment at its value in terms of consumption goods, implicitly involves an approximation to the second alternative.

Applications of the Fisherian Approach to the Consumption Function
In *The General Theory*, at least as interpreted by his followers, Keynes made consumption expenditure a function of current income. The two major post-Keynesian theories of the consumption function — the Modigliani-Brumberg-Ando life-cycle hypothesis and the Friedman permanent-income hypothesis — have essentially reintroduced the Fisherian wealth approach into that theory.

The life-cycle hypothesis is illustrated in Diagram VI, where an individual is assumed to last two periods, during the first of which he works, earning the income $R_1 = W_1$, and during the second of which he is retired and living on his savings and the interest earned on them. He chooses the consumption point over the two periods C, involving consumption in the first period of $R_1 - C_1$ and in the second of $C_2 = (1 + i)(R_1 - C_1)$ where $R_1 - C_1 = K_2$ is the capital stock that the first-period savings make available to the community. Consumption per active worker is a fraction of labour income $c_w = C_1/R_1$; consumption per capitalist (retired worker) is a fraction (greater than one) of capitalist income $c_c = (1 + i)/i$, capitalist income being $i(R_1 - C_1)$; alternatively, capitalist consumption is equal to $(1 + i)$

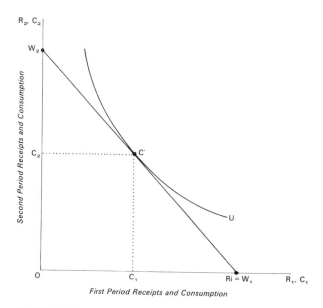

DIAGRAM VI: THE LIFE-CYCLE HYPOTHESIS OF SAVING

times the wealth of the capitalist $(K_2 = R_1 - C_1)$. If population is constant and technology is also constant, total consumption equals total production $[R_1 + i(R_1 - C_1)]$ and there is no net saving, though the economy has a capital stock which on a per capita basis is equal to $\frac{1}{2}(R_1 - C_1)$ — a half because every worker during his life counts as two people, one actively working and one retired.

Now suppose that the community is growing, in two senses: (i) workers each period are $(1 + n)$ times the workers last period; (ii) productivity increase makes wages each period $(1 + p)$ times wages last period. Then, for simplicity measuring aggregates per capitalist,

$$\text{total income} = (1 + n)(1 + p)W_1 + iK_2,$$

$$\text{total consumption} = (1 + n)(1 + p)(W_1 - K_2) + (1 + i)K_2$$

$$\text{net saving} = (n + p + np)K_2$$

and the ratio of consumption to income is

$$1 - \frac{(n + p + np)K_2}{(1 + n)(1 + p)W_1 + iK_2}$$

The general point is that a society, even though completely static, will have a stock of capital determined by the interaction between the life-time receipts stream of individuals and their life-time optimum consumption stream, that stock changing hands between generations as time passes; and that net savings in such a society depend on exogenous growth forces which make the savings of each generation exceed the dissavings of the previous generation.

The Friedman 'permanent income' savings hypothesis does not lend itself readily to exposition in terms of the Fisher two-period diagram, which represents the extreme of human impermanency. But it can be represented by a diagram due to Leontief. Diagram VII graphs current consumption on the horizontal axis and permanent consumption on the vertical axis. The 45° line represents equality of current and permanent consumption or the maintenance of capital intact. The indifference curves represent the trade-off in utility between current consumption and permanent consumption at

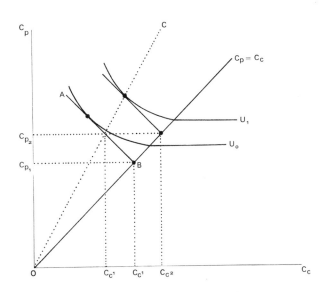

DIAGRAM VII: THE PERMANENT INCOME HYPOTHESIS OF SAVING

any point of time. They are assumed to be homothetic (i.e. the individual makes the same choice among current and permanent consumption regardless of the scale of his consumption possibilities) and to have the characteristic that the individual has zero time preference in the classical sense, i.e. that at a zero interest rate he will keep his capital intact and consume his permanent consumption level. (This is Friedman's symmetry assumption, expressed diagrammatically by the fact that the indifference curves are horizontal when they cross the 45° line.) Given a starting position C_{p1}, C_{c1} and the interest rate reflected in the slope of the budget line AB (the interest rate being the terms on which current saving can be translated into permanent income), the individual will sacrifice current consumption by $C_{c1}C'_{c1}$ in order to raise his permanent income and consumption possibilities to C_{p2}; and he will continue to make a sacrifice of current consumption for the sake of permanent consumption possibility increases so long as the interest rate is positive. Moreover, if the interest rate is constant, his savings ratio will be constant by the homotheticity assumption. In other words, the ratio of consumption to income will be constant so long as the interest rate is constant.

13

PROBLEMS IN INVESTMENT THEORY

Introduction
Fisher provided two alternative criteria for choice among investment opportunities:

1. Maximum present value at the market rate of interest;
2. Maximum rate of return over cost (in the case of continuous variation of investment opportunity, equate marginal rate of return over cost with the rate of interest).

In Fisher's two-period model, these come to the same thing so long as there is a perfect capital market.

The problems now to be dealt with are: (i) imperfect capital markets and capital rationing; (ii) mutually exclusive or interdependent investment opportunities; (iii) the meaning and relevance of the rate of return over cost or 'internal rate of return' criterion for investment opportunities extending over more than two periods.

Imperfect Capital Markets and Capital Rationing
Imperfect capital markets can be represented by assuming two market interest rates, a lending rate and a (higher) borrowing rate. For the pure consumption model, where the individual has a fixed pair of incomes for the two periods, the two interest rates divide the preference map into three regions (see Diagram I) where the slopes of $L'L$ and $B'B'$ represent the lending and borrowing rates, and OL and OB the loci of tangencies of these rates with the individual's indifference curves.

Regions:

I. The individual borrows at the borrowing rate and consumes at a point on OB;

II. He neither borrows nor lends; his marginal rate of time preference is between the two market rates;

III. He lends at the lending rate, consumes on OL.
   Where the individual finds equilibrium depends on which of the regions his initial income pair falls into.

Where the individual confronts an investment opportunity frontier, there are three possibilities of equilibrium, corresponding to the three regions shown on Diagram II:

I. with $T_I T_I$, the individual maximizes present value at the borrowing rate

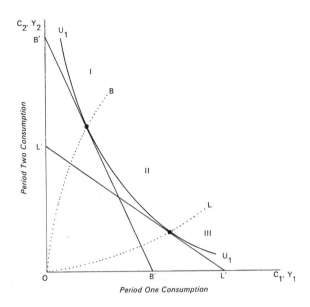

DIAGRAM I: IMPERFECT CAPITAL MARKETS: DIFFERENT BORROWING AND LENDING RATES

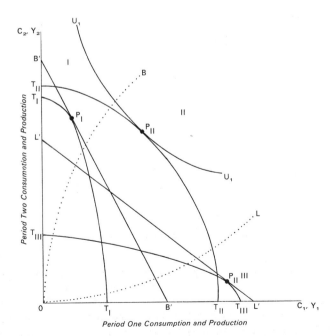

DIAGRAM II: IMPERFECT CAPITAL MARKETS: DIFFERENT BORROWING AND LENDING RATES, DIFFERING TRANSFORMATION CURVES

(point P_I), borrows and consumes on *OB* (equates marginal rate of return over cost to borrowing rate);

III, with $T_{III}T_{III}$ the individual maximizes present value at lending rate (equates *M.R.R.C.* to lending rate) at point P_{III} and consumes on *OL*;

II, with $T_{II}T_{II}$, the individual neither lends nor borrows, equates marginal rate of return over cost with marginal rate of time preference (point P_{II}) or maximizes present value at his marginal rate of time preference.

Either description is purely formal, however, as it is deduced from maximization and does not help to locate the equilibrium point. All that we know is that the marginal rate of return over cost and marginal rate of time preference lie between the borrowing and lending rates and are equal.

Rising Marginal Cost of Borrowing

This is an alternative specification of imperfect capital markets. (An extreme case fitting the notion of 'capital rationing' would be the ability to borrow at a fixed rate up to a maximum amount, nothing beyond.) In the general case (see Diagram III), the individual faces a budget line in the loan market

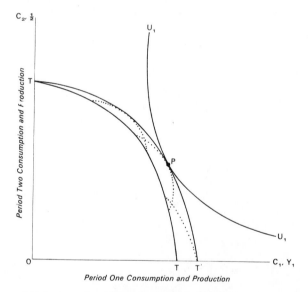

DIAGRAM III: RISING MARGINAL BORROWING COSTS

that is concave to the origin. By placing the origin of his budget line (curve) at successive points on the investment opportunity curve we trace out an opportunity envelope TT'; the individual maximizes utility when an indifference curve is tangent to the envelope at *P*. In equilibrium, the marginal rate of time preference equals the marginal rate of interest equals the marginal rate of return over cost. Again these conditions of marginal equality are purely formal and do not help us to locate the optimum decision point.

Non-Independent Investment Alternatives
The equivalence of the present value and marginal rate of return over cost criteria holds only if investment alternatives are independent (this permits ranking alternatives in order of decreasing rate of return over cost, to obtain the concave-to-origin investment opportunity curve employed so far).

In two sorts of cases the present value criterion continues to apply but the rate of return criterion is inadequate.

(1) *Mutually exclusive opportunities* The marginal rate of return (see Diagram IV) over cost equals the interest rate at P_1 and P_2 for opportunities

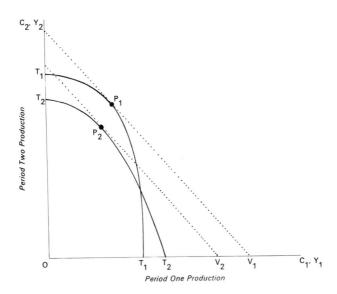

DIAGRAM IV: MUTUALLY EXCLUSIVE INVESTMENT ALTERNATIVES

$T_1 T_1$ and $T_2 T_2$ respectively. The criterion tells how best to use each opportunity, if it is selected, but not how to choose between them. According to the present value criterion, $T_1 T_1$ has a present value V_1 greater than V_2 the present value of $T_2 T_2$.

(2) *Interdependent investment opportunities* (see Diagram V) $T_2 T_2$ requires prior use of $T_1 T_1$ up to the level shown by the position of the lower end of $T_2 T_2$ on $T_1 T_1$. P_1 and P_2 indicate optimum choices with respect to $T_1 T_1$ only, and $T_1 T_1$ and $T_2 T_2$ together. The rate of return criterion does not permit decision between $T_1 T_1$ only and $T_1 T_1$ plus $T_2 T_2$. The present value criterion shows that the latter choice maximizes income. (Note: $T_1 T_2 T_2$ could be made a continuous curve representing the possibility that after a point some investment in $T_2 T_2$ yields a return equal to that on $T_1 T_1$, whereafter the return on $T_2 T_2$ rises for an interval.)

The rate of return criterion breaks down for multiple maxima cases, whereas the present value criterion does not. The present value criterion

F

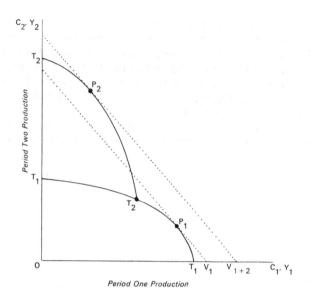

DIAGRAM V: INTERDEPENDENT INVESTMENT ALTERNATIVES

breaks down only if there are both multiple maxima and capital market imperfections.

Internal Rate of Return Problems
Generalization of Fisher approach to the n-period case We assume that continuous variation of outputs in the various periods is possible. 'Investment opportunities' can be summarized in the restriction

$$f(C_0, C_1, C_2, \ldots, C_n) = 0.$$

The present value of outputs in all periods is to be maximized. For this, it is necessary to assume a set of n one-period interest rates, not necessarily the same. Note that these are rates for separate single periods. All but the first are forward rates, i.e. rates for loans to start t periods ahead and be repaid $t + 1$ periods ahead.

Such forward rates are implicit in the term structure of rates ruling in the market at a point in time for loans of different maturities.

To illustrate, let r_1 be the rate for a one-period loan starting now, r_2 be the rate for a two-period loan starting now, i_1 be the one-period rate for period one ($i_1 = r_1$) and i_2 be the one-period rate for period 2. The present value of a two-period loan of one unit must be one:

$$\frac{r_2}{1 + i_1} + \frac{1 + r_2}{(1 + i_1)(1 + i_2)} = 1$$

This defines $i_2 = (2r_2 - r_1)/(1 + r_1 - r_2)$. Note: if $r_1 = r_2$, then $i_2 = i_1 = r_1 = r_2$.

The present value of outputs in all periods is

$$V = C_0 + \frac{C_1}{1 + i_1} + \frac{C_2}{(1 + i_1)(1 + i_2)} + \cdots + \frac{C_n}{(1 + i_1)(1 + i_2)\ldots(1 + i_n)}$$

This is to be maximized subject to $f(C_0, C_1, C_2, \ldots, C_n) = 0$.

Form the Lagrangean expression $V - \lambda f$ and differentiate with respect to $C_0, C_1, \ldots, C_n$, setting the partial derivatives equal to zero to obtain the first-order conditions for a maximum. (The second-order conditions are assumed satisfied by economic restrictions on the form of f.)

This yields

$$\frac{\partial V}{\partial C_0} = 1 \qquad -\lambda \frac{\partial f}{\partial C_0} = 0$$

$$\frac{\partial V}{\partial C_1} = \frac{1}{1 + i_1} \qquad -\lambda \frac{\partial f}{\partial C_1} = 0$$

$$\frac{\partial V}{\partial C_n} = \frac{1}{(1 + i_1)(1 + i_2)\ldots(1 + i_n)} - \lambda \frac{\partial f}{\partial C_n} = 0$$

For a pair of successive periods r, s, $(\partial f/\partial C_r)/(\partial f/\partial C_s) = 1 + i_s$. Holding $dC_i = 0$ for $i \neq r, s$, we obtain from f

$$\frac{\partial f}{\partial C_r} dC_r + \frac{\partial f}{\partial C_s} dC_s = 0$$

$$\frac{\partial f}{\partial C_r} \bigg/ \frac{\partial f}{\partial C_s} = -\frac{dC_s}{dC_r}$$

Hence

$$-\frac{dC_s}{dC_r} = 1 + i_s.$$

Define the left-hand side as $(1 + \rho_s)$, the (marginal) rate of return over cost from reducing C_r in order to increase C_s being ρ_s. Then maximization requires $\rho_s = i_s$. For non-adjacent periods, e.g. q and t, similarly

$$-\frac{dC_t}{dC_q} = (1 + i_r)(1 + i_s)(1 + i_t),$$

and we can similarly define a three-period marginal rate of return over cost and define the maximization condition in terms of it. The condition for optimal investment choice, in terms of marginal rate of return over cost, is that present value is maximized when, for each pair of successive periods, the marginal rate of return over cost is equal to the interest rate. A related proposition is that any 'investment opportunity' between a successive pair of periods should be chosen if $\rho > i$ for that pair of periods.

This proposition has been confused by some writers (partly due to some lack of clarity on Fisher's part) with a different and erroneous proposition. As a preliminary, consider an investment opportunity spread over several periods, involving a profile of consumption sacrifices and yields $x_0, x_1, \ldots, x_n$, where $x_t \geq 0$ and at least one $x_t < 0$.

$$\text{p.v.} = x_0 + \frac{x_1}{1+i} + \frac{x_2}{(1+i)^2} + \cdots + \frac{x_n}{(1+i)^n},$$

(assuming for simplicity a common one-period interest rate for all periods). The opportunity should be chosen if the present value exceeds zero. The proposition in question involves defining an internal rate of return as the rate of interest that would make p.v. = 0. That is, ρ is defined by

$$0 = x_0 + \frac{x_1}{1+\rho} + \frac{x_2}{(1+\rho)^2} + \cdots \frac{x_n}{(1+\rho)^n},$$

and asserting that the opportunity should be chosen if $\rho > i$. That is, if the internal rate of return exceeds the market rate of interest.

This approach encounters mathematical difficulties, does not necessarily yield the right results, and does not make economic sense. The mathematical problem can be illustrated with the three-period sequence $-1, x_1, x_2$; one or both of x_1, x_2 must be >0, but we allow the possibility $x_2 < 0$. An economic illustration is difficult to concoct, but our concern here is with the mathematics. (One economic illustration is the following: there is a piece of land under which there is a coal seam, and by buying the land one can mine the coal by 'open-cut' methods — digging away the top soil — but one is obliged by law to refill the hole and restore the top soil after the mining operation is finished.)

$$\rho \text{ is found from } 0 = -1 + \frac{x_1}{1+\rho} + \frac{x_2}{(1+\rho)^2}$$

$$\text{whence} \qquad \rho = \frac{x_1 - 2 \pm \sqrt{(x_1^2 + 4x_2)}}{2}$$

(a) if x_1, x_2 both >0, there is obviously one positive and one negative value for ρ, the economically relevant one being the positive one.

(b) if $x_1 > 0, x_2 < 0$, the solution may involve
  (i) two values of ρ, both positive, e.g. the sequence $-1, 5, -6$ yields $\rho = 1$ and $\rho = 2$.
  (ii) no real values of ρ, e.g. the sequence $-1, 3, -2\frac{1}{2}$ yields

$$\rho = \frac{-1 \pm \sqrt{-1}}{2}$$

On the question of correct results, the criterion assumes that present value varies inversely with i, hence that at interest rates below ρ the present value will be positive and the opportunity should be chosen.

$$\frac{d(\text{p.v.})}{di} = -\frac{x_1}{(1+i)^2} - \frac{2x_2}{(1+i)^3}$$

If $x_2 < 0$, present value does not necessarily rise as i falls; and it is not necessarily true that if $\rho > i$, the opportunity is profitable and should be chosen. For example, consider the sequence -1, 5, -6 above with $\rho = 1$ or 2; take $i = 0{\cdot}5$;

$$\text{p.v.} = \frac{-2{\cdot}25 + 7{\cdot}5 - 6}{2{\cdot}25} = \frac{-0{\cdot}75}{2{\cdot}25} = -\frac{1}{3}$$

In this particular case, the graph of present value against i looks like Diagram VI and the present value is positive only between $i = 1$ and $i = 2$.

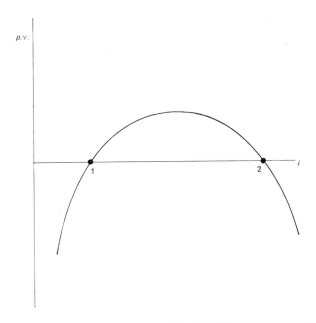

DIAGRAM VI: PRESENT VALUE AND THE INTEREST RATE

Further, if two options are being compared, it does not necessarily follow that the one with the higher ρ is the better investment; and this does not require $x_2 < 0$. Consider two options: -1, x_1, x_2 and -1, y_1, y_2

$$V_1 - V_2 = \frac{x_1 - y_1}{1 + i} + \frac{x_2 - y_2}{(1 + i)^2} = 0$$

when

$$x_2 - y_2 = -(1 + i)(x_1 - y_1).$$

Suppose $x_1 + x_2 > y_1 + y_2$; then $V_1 > V_2$ at $i = 0$. V_1 will be less than V_2 if $(1 + i)(x_1 - y_1) + (x_2 - y_2) < 0$. This must happen for some high enough i if $x_1 < y_1$ (implying $x_2 > y_2$). In other words, an option that delivers more output but delivers it later would always be better for a society with a zero interest rate, but would become inferior for a high enough interest rate.

ρ_1 will be less than ρ_2 if $x_1 + \sqrt{(x_1^2 + 4x_2)} < y_1 + \sqrt{(y_1^2 + 4y_2)}$ and conversely; but which option is the more attractive depends on the market interest rate.

The basic flaw in the internal rate of return concept is that the rate of return is not truly 'internal'. It assumes that excess receipts (over a regular flow of returns at the internal rate) can be reinvested at the internal rate, and that deficiencies of receipts can be borrowed (must be borrowed) at the internal rate. In fact, the relevant rate is the market rate, which leads to the present value approach.

Martin Bailey's Approach to Multi-Period Investment Opportunities
Bailey's approach to the theory of investment decisions is an extension of the Fisher approach. Consider a three-period sequence of costs and returns. This can be broken conceptually into an infinite number of pairs of one-period investment transactions. The opportunity is profitable if among these a pair can be found that yields a profit by comparison with the one-period market rates of interest.

(a) A 'normal' sequence $-1, 1, 1$ (see Diagram VII). Extremes: (1) Allocate the first-period unit return as the return on the cost, so that for the first period an investment of 1 yields an output of 1 and a zero rate of return; in the second period, we invest nothing and get a return of 1, i.e. an infinite rate of return (Diagram VIIa).
(2) Credit the cost with an infinite return in the first period, and regard the amount invested for the second period as infinity minus 1 for an output of 1, which in the limit is a rate of return of -1.

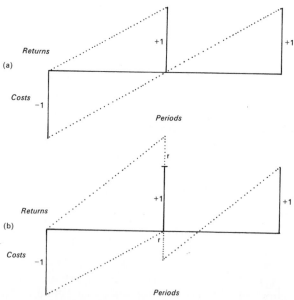

DIAGRAM VII: A 'NORMAL' INVESTMENT OPPORTUNITY: COSTS FOLLOWED BY RETURNS

In general, the proceeds of the cost of -1 at the start, in the first period are $1 + r_1$, where r_1 is chosen arbitrarily; the investment for the second period is r_1, and the return on this investment is 1, the rate of return in the second period implied by r_1 being $r_2 = (1/r_1) - 1$ (as $r_1 \approx \infty$, $r_2 \approx -1$) (see Diagram VIIb). The investment will be profitable if any pair r_1, r_2 can be found such that $r_1 = i_1, r_2 > i_2$ or $r_2 \approx i_2$, $r_1 > i_1$, or $r_1 > i_1, r_2 > i_2$, where i_1, i_2 are the one-period interest rates ruling in the market.

(b) An 'abnormal' sequence $-1, 3, -1$. In this case we conceptually divide the opportunity into a first-period investment and a second-period disinvestment by borrowing. In Diagram VIII an individual invests 1 unit for an output of 1 unit (zero rate of return on first-period investment) and borrows 2 for a repayment of 1 (negative borrowing rate of 50 per cent) in the second period.

In general, the individual can be conceived as obtaining an arbitrarily chosen rate of return r_1 on his first-period investment, and borrowing $3 - (1 + r_1)$ against a repayment of 1 in the second period, the rate of interest paid on the borrowing being

$$r_2 = \frac{1}{3 - (1 + r_1)} - 1 = \frac{r_1 - 1}{2 - r_1}$$

In practice, the relevant pairs will be those for which $r_1 \, r_2 > 0$.
The investment will be worthwhile if a pair r_1, r_2 can be found such that,

$$r_1 = i_1, r_2 < i_2$$

or

$$r_1 > i_1, r_2 = i_2, \quad \text{or } r_1 > i_1, r_2 < i_2,$$

where i_1, i_2 are the one-period interest rates for the two periods.

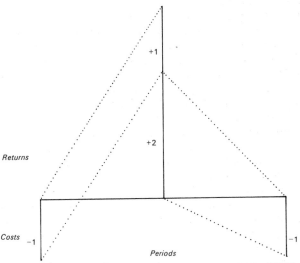

DIAGRAM VIII: AN 'ABNORMAL' INVESTMENT OPPORTUNITY: COSTS FOLLOWED BY RETURNS FOLLOWED BY COSTS.

14

MODELS OF ECONOMIC GROWTH: HARROD AND ONE-SECTOR NEOCLASSICAL

Introduction

The theory of economic growth is a topic that has been slighted by economists who, since the time of Ricardo, have been occupied with the problems of comparative statics. Contemporary interest is really a second phase of the Keynesian revolution, which was initially concerned with the determinants of aggregate output. In the Keynesian view, capital stock is fixed and investment equals saving. Investment is an addition to total demand which does not come out of income and fills the gap between current income and current expenditure created by saving. The problem of maintaining full employment is the problem of getting current investment equal to the full employment level of saving.

This, however, is a short-run analysis, and in the longer view, as Harrod realized, investment today will be increased productive capacity tomorrow. He developed an approach followed by many modern theorists based on a dynamic equation explaining how investment must behave in order to maintain full employment of the capital stock. Joan Robinson and Nicholas Kaldor also developed this line of thought but with a different emphasis. In the models, investment determines saving and not the other way around. This approach reflects the Keynesian tradition and focuses on investment as the key element in the system. Investment is held to be a function of entrepreneurial expectations and 'animal spirits'.

These models typically involve a 'knife-edge' instability of the system; if investment exceeds the equilibrium growth level, excess profits will lead to further increases in investment and vice versa. This characteristic led — starting in the 1950s — to interest in systems that were not so delicate. In particular, Swan and Solow questioned the assumption of the Harrod type model that there is a fixed capital–output ratio (K/Y) which had been defended by Harrod by arguments to the effect that fixed interest rates are set by liquidity preference. The question they raised was why the K/Y ratio did not adjust so that full employment could be maintained. In contrast to the Keynesian models, the neo-classical models view savings as determining investment, the absorption of capital accumulation consistent with a fully-employed labour force being ensured by changes in relative factor prices.

It should be pointed out that the growth models that have proliferated in recent years from this starting point are theoretical-mathematical *models* of growth, and not *theories* of growth. A *theory* of growth would be concerned with the *causes* of growth, not the *consequences* of growth assumed to be going on for some unexplained reason. The models in question are essentially static equilibrium models imposed on top of a mechanism of exogenous change — population growth and technical progress. New wrinkles include the accumulation of human as well as material capital, and technical progress as being the result of investment in the creation of new knowledge. Investment in human as well as material capital makes no essential difference to the results — the exogenous forces of population growth and technical change still determine the long-run equilibrium rate of growth. Investment in knowledge-production makes no essential difference either — the equilibrium rate of growth becomes a variable, instead of an exogenously-determined constant, but its value as determined by the equalization of returns on all forms of investment will be some parameter-determined multiple of the exogenously-determined basic growth rate. Essentially, these incorporations of recent theoretical developments merely embroider a basic principle of classical theory: if there are diminishing returns due to the fixity of quantity of one factor relative to the others, there is a limit to the increase in output achievable by increasing the relative quantity of the others, and this holds true whether the fixed factor is assumed to be absolutely fixed in quantity or growing along an exogenously-determined trend path.

To put the same point another way, if we assume (a) that saving is governed either by a fixed savings ratio or by a minimum acceptable rate of return; and (b) that capital of whatever kind is subject to diminishing returns when accumulated relative to labour, but carries a proportional depreciation requirement that has to be made good out of current (gross) saving, then the marginal return on the accumulation of capital relative to labour must fall as capital accumulates and either all saving must be absorbed in replacement of existing capital or the rate of return must fall to the point at which there is no incentive to increase capital relative to labour further. When this point is reached, the economy is in a state equivalent to static equilibrium; but if exogenous impulses to growth are postulated — such as population growth or the growth of the stock of basic knowledge exploitable by investment in either research and development or material capital — the economy will grow at an exogenously-determined rate. In the models, the exogenous growth forces constitute the equivalent of 'depreciation' of the existing stock of capital, which in effect shrinks in relation to the available labour force and/or technological opportunities for using it.

From the standpoint of the theory of distribution, the important point about the growth models is that, in general (but in certain cases requiring the imposition of empirical restrictions on the parameters), they converge on a steady-state growth-path with a constant cross-section structure of relations among the variables and a fixed distribution of income — exactly analogous to the classical stationary state discussed in the context of the Ricardian model. Analytical interest then centres on the influence of the interaction between savings behaviour and the exogeneous growth-determining factors on the distribution of income, though for the most part we shall be concerned with the models and their properties rather than with the distributional implications of parameter changes.

The Harrod Model

The crux of the Harrod model is that somehow liquidity preference determines the rate of interest and thus rules out changes in the marginal products of capital and labour. With fixed technology, this implies a fixed K/Y ratio.

In the simple model it is assumed that the economy saves a certain portion of income. If $\overline{Y}$ is the full employment level of output (capacity of capital), then: $s\overline{Y} = I = dK/dt$ is the requirement for achieving it. $d\overline{Y} = \alpha\,dK$, where $\alpha = Y/K$ is the output–capital coefficient; alternatively, $d\overline{Y} = (1/k)\,dK$, where k is the capital–output ratio. From this, $(1/\overline{Y})(d\overline{Y}/dt) = s/k = g_w$, then defines the condition for equilibrium with full capacity utilization, i.e. it is the rate of growth in which the entrepreneur will always find that past investment will pay a normal rate of profit and capacity will be fully utilized. This does not, however, ensure full employment of labour. The warranted rate of growth is not necessarily the actual rate of growth nor the rate of growth of potential output, as determined by population growth. In fact, if the actual rate falls on the warranted path, it is an unstable equilibrium since if I rises temporarily above its equilibrium level, there will be an excess demand for output and a shortage of capacity which will produce more investment cumulatively. Similarly, if I temporarily falls below its equilibrium level, demand for investment is decreased and excess supply results leading to a cumulative decline in investment. Thus the model yields an unstable knife-edge equilibrium path.

The warranted rate of growth may be either above or below the rate of effective population growth. The growth in the labour force may be divided into two parts: the natural rate (n), and the effective growth of the labour force due to technological improvements (t), i.e. $n + t$. The problem here is that with these conditions there is only one form of technological progress that will meet the conditions for a parametric warranted rate of growth and that is Harrod-neutral progress. Whereas with Hicks-neutral progress the marginal products of labour and capital rise in the same proportion as output (see Diagram I) with Harrod-neutral progress, capital accumulates until the rate of interest falls to that associated with the old level of productivity (see Diagram II) by assumption and maintains a constant capital-output ratio. Harrod-neutral progress thus raises the wages rate relative to the

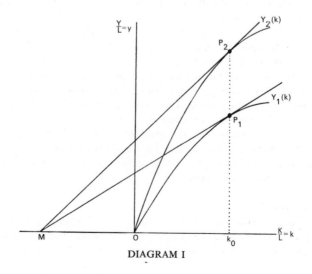

DIAGRAM I

rental rate on capital and is equivalent to a growth in the labour force with a corresponding growth in the capital stock, technology being unchanged.

Diagram I depicts a Hicks-neutral technical change; the capital–labour ratio is unchanged, and, as should be obvious from our earlier geometric analysis of distribution, the meeting of the two tangents to the two production function cross-sections $y_1(k)$ and $y_2(k)$ at the point M implies constant relative factor shares. Diagram II depicts Harrod-neutral technical change: capital

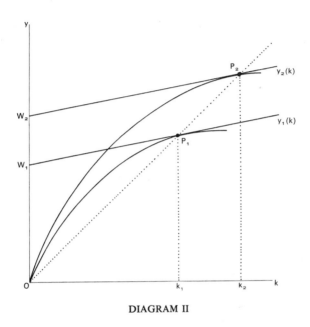

DIAGRAM II

accumulates (from k_1 to k_2) until its marginal product is reduced to its original level, and, as can be easily shown by similar triangles, relative factor shares are unchanged (labour's share is OW_1/k_1P_1 before and OW_2/k_2P_2 after the change). The two types of neutral technical change obviously need not be equivalent, since they relate to different points on the new production function. They will however be equivalent for Cobb–Douglas production functions, for which relative factor shares are constant.

The instability of the growth path led Harrod to a primitive theory of business cycles in which if $g_n > g_w$ there would be an increasing army of the unemployed although there could also be a prolonged business boom since unemployed labour permits a great deal of extra capital to be fully employed. (g_n is the rate of growth of 'effective' population.) If $g_n < g_w$, then stagnation is the result since the economy will run into a shortage of labour.

Others such as Kaldor and Robinson have tried to build more sophisticated growth models although they reject the notion of a production function. In Kaldor's approach, if the entrepreneur is constrained by the growth of the labour force, he has the ability to warp technological progress to enlarge the available effective labour supply.

162

The Neo-classical Model

The essential difference between the Keynesian and Neo-classical models is that in the Neo-classical model, what is saved is invested and the interest rate provides the adjusting mechanism. In contrast, the Keynesian approach assumed that what is invested is saved and that the adjustments of the two come through variations in output and employment. Thus in the neo classical world the assumptions are of one sector, full employment and (usually) savings as a constant proportion of income. (Alternative assumptions are: a minimum rate of time preference or a constant wealth-income ratio.) Using a cross-section of the production function (Diagram III) in per

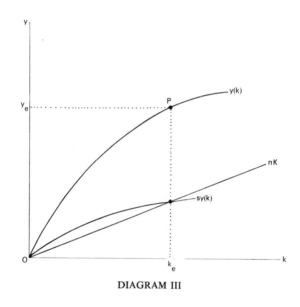

DIAGRAM III

capita terms, population growth is at a constant rate n and is equivalent to depreciation of capital at the rate nK — both require growth in the capital stock just to maintain capital per head constant — and the savings ratio s gives saving as $sy(k)$ (where k is the capital–labour ratio). Clearly the two curves must cross, and it is at this point that the steady state equilibrium occurs. To the left of this point, the amount of saving exceeds that needed to maintain the level of capital stock and so capital per head increases — capital deepening. To the right of the point, the amount of capital needed to maintain the capital stock is greater than saving and so capital per head is drawn down. Thus if the savings ratio is constant and there is a smooth diminishing marginal product of capital, the system will converge on this point and the rate of growth of the economy in the steady state will be the rate of growth of population. In short there is a unique cross-section equilibrium and the system must converge on it and on the exogenously-determined rate of growth. Interest has also focused on the maximization of consumption per head.

Additional capital per head adds its marginal product to output per head, but subtracts its replacement or depreciation requirement, which is fixed by the rate of growth of the 'effective' labour force, n, from consumption. Clearly there will be a net increase in consumption per head from additional capital per head only if the former exceeds the latter; and consumption per head will be maximized when the rate of return on capital is equated with the 'capital requirement', which is equal in the long run to the rate of growth of the 'effective' population. The point is illustrated on Diagram IV, where

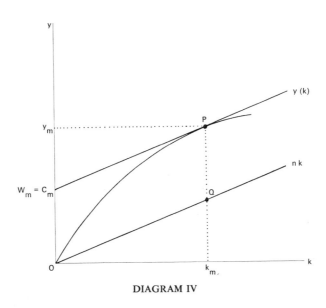

DIAGRAM IV

consumption per head is maximized when the slope of the production function cross-section is equal to the slope of the 'depreciation' function $O_1 kn$ (point P). When this occurs, the savings ratio has to be Qk_m/Pk_m; by similar triangles, savings have to equal the share of capital in total output $y_m . w_m/O . y_m$ and consumption has to equal wages. (Note that this position would be achieved automatically if, following Marxian theory, workers consumed all their wages and capitalists invested all their profits). The condition for maximization of consumption per head, which has come to be referred to as the 'golden rule' condition, can be expressed alternatively as equalization of the rate of interest (return on capital) with the rate of growth and equalization of the savings ratio with capital's share in output. In symbols, it is either

$$i = n \quad \text{or} \quad \frac{nK}{Y} = \frac{iK}{Y} = \frac{I}{Y} = \frac{S}{Y} = S$$

where K is the total capital stock ($K/Y = R$ in the diagram).

The 'golden rule' condition was initially interpreted as a welfare-maximization principle relevant to the prescription of economic policy to promote economic growth. This interpretation, however, is incorrect. It is more appropriately regarded as a technical condition specifying the maximum consumption per capita obtainable on a steady-state equilibrium growth path, in view of the fact that the 'technology' may be taken to include both the functional relationship between output and capital per head, and the rate of population growth regarded as an exogeneously-determined constraint on how much of the output is available for consumption under equilibrium growth conditions. It leads to a straightforward welfare recommendation ('move to the golden rule saving ratio') only in the economically uninteresting case of a society whose savings ratio exceeds the golden rule level; even in that case, the welfare conclusion follows only if society's welfare depends only on its consumption per head, and no utility attaches to the possession of wealth as such, regardless of its yield of consumption goods (this is the 'miser' case, which figured large in early Keynesian discussion of the possibility of long-run underemployment equilibrium). In the case of a savings ratio lower than the golden rule level, increasing the savings ratio to the golden rule level would entail a reduction of current consumption in the initial stages, followed by an eventual increase in consumption above the current level asymptotically approaching the golden rule level. This would be the equivalent of an investment problem: an initial cost in foregone consumption followed by a yield in terms of higher future consumption. But if, contrary to the assumption generally used in this exposition that saving is a fixed proportion of income, it is assumed that saving is governed by a minimum rate of time preference, society must be presumed to have chosen to forego the higher future consumption as not worth the cost in terms of lower present consumption. Hence the prescription that society should move towards the golden rule savings ratio must be based on a denial of the relevance of society's own chosen rate of time preference and the imposition of a zero rate of time preference by the economist making the prescription. (It should be noted that the rate of time preference in question is one that incorporates the assumption that capital per head should be maintained intact, i.e. it recognizes the 'depreciation requirement' of current investment to maintain the stock of capital per effective head of the population intact. If the rate of time preference were defined to be independent of this recognition, it is possible that the rate of time preference would, though positive, be lower than the rate of growth of the economy in steady-state equilibrium and that the economy would lie to the right of the golden rule capital-to-labour ratio.)

The two possibilities, of a savings ratio greater than and less than the golden rule level, are illustrated in Diagram V which depicts the time path of consumption immediately following a shift from the actual consumption level c_a achieved with the current savings ratio to the maximum possible consumption level c_m achievable with the golden rule savings ratio.

Some Applications to Development Economics

The one-sector model of economic growth can be used to illustrate two theories of the problem of economic development, though to do so is not meant to imply that these theories are correct.

The first is the theory of the 'take-off' or of the 'big push', or of the 'low-level equilibrium trap'. According to this species of theory, the economy is stuck in stable equilibrium at a low level of output and consumption per head. A small injection of savings or foreign aid will do no ultimate good. But there

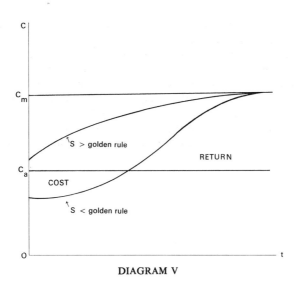

DIAGRAM V

are economies of scale available if the economy can only grow to a large enough size, and once these are obtained the economy will be capable of growing to a still higher level of income per head under its own steam. This theory is illustrated in Diagram VI, where P_1 represents the stable low-level equilibrium trap, P_2 the unstable equilibrium position through which the economy must be pushed by either a concerted effort to increase domestic savings by force or by foreign aid, and P_3 the equilibrium that the economy will attain by its own efforts once the 'big push' has been successful.

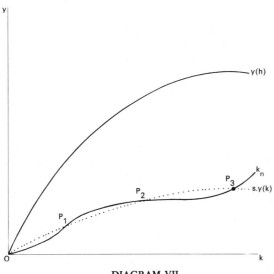

DIAGRAM VII

The other theory, very similar in logical structure, is that the rate of population growth, rather than being an exogenous variable as heretofore assumed, is itself a function of the level of income per head, and that any small effort at economic growth will be dissipated by an increase in the rate of population growth, whereas a sufficiently large effort will move the population into an income range in which the rate of population growth will be reduced by rational calculation on the part of the now-affluent population; and after that point, accumulation of capital will result in increased income per head and not merely more heads. This theory is illustrated in Diagram VII, where

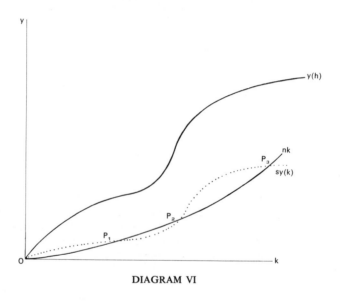

DIAGRAM VI

P_1 represents a low-level equilibrium with a low rate of population growth; the rate of population growth and hence the capital replacement requirement increase thereafter over a range as income and consumption per capita rise, but at a sufficiently high income per capita slow down, so that the economy passes through an unstable equilibrium point P_2 and can eventually reach a stable equilibrium point P_3 with a lower rate of population growth.

Depreciation
It has been assumed so far that capital equipment lasts forever, so that no problem of depreciation arises. But recognition of depreciation of the physical capital stock raises no problems for the analysis.

One point that is worth noting at the outset is that business practices and legal tax rules may lead firms to charge either more or less for depreciation than is required to replace the capital equipment that is actually wearing out and needs to be replaced. To the extent that they do, and this is not offset by a change in the real saving of their customers, the real rate of saving for the society as a whole is either increased or decreased by comparison with what the customers intend it to be. Moreover, the difference will be a function of the rate of growth of the economy, since this will determine the extent of the error relative to the current rate of investment.

Ignoring this point, and assuming that there is no difference between accounting and actual depreciation, we should note that there are two alternative assumptions about the way in which capital equipment wears out that can be used. One is the 'evaporation' assumption, according to which capital equipment becomes less productive each year by a given fraction of its initial productivity. The other is the 'one-hoss shay' assumption, according to which capital equipment remains equally productive throughout its life, but then suddenly collapses at the end of a given period of time.

In the case of the evaporation assumption, one has two alternatives which come to the same thing: either use the production function for gross output, and add dk (where d is the rate of evaporation) to nk to represent the gross capital replacement requirement, at the same time adding dk to the net saving prospensity function; or reckon output net of depreciation and continue to use the net savings ratio. The convergence property and the golden rule then emerge as before.

In the case of the 'one-hoss-shay' assumption, we have the capital stock at any point of time as

$$K_T = \int_0^T e^{gt}\, dt I_0$$

$$= \frac{1}{g}(e^{gT} - 1)I_0$$

and the replacement requirement as

$$I_T = I_0 = \frac{g}{e^{gT} - 1} K_T.$$

The replacement requirement therefore falls as the rate of growth of the economy rises. But we still have convergence and the golden rule condition.

Distribution Theory

As mentioned in the introduction, moving from a static equilibrium situation to a growth model merely alters the frame of reference for the application of traditional distribution theory.

In the Harrod growth model, the capital-to-output ratio and the rate of return on capital are both constant; hence the distribution of income is a constant, given these parameters, and will alter only if one or the other alters.

In the one-sector neo-classical model, the distribution of income is determined by savings behaviour in relation to the technology embodied in the aggregate production function; hence the distribution of income will depend on the savings ratio and the elasticity of the cross-section functional relationship between output and capital per head, or the elasticity of substitution, as has been discussed in previous analysis. This obviously is true also of the Harrod model.

The only difference between the growth models and the static model of distribution previously discussed, in fact, lies in the nature of the parameters taken to be exogeneous and therefore subject to exogeneous shifts.

Mathematical Appendix: The One-Sector Growth Model

The Cobb–Douglas Production Function

1. Assume an aggregate Cobb–Douglas production function

$$X = AL^\alpha K^{1-\alpha}\,e^{gt},$$

where X is aggregate output, L labour, K capital, g the rate of (neutral) technical progress. Capital is assumed to be identical with output and to last forever.

Using small letters to represent rate of change over time, we obtain

$$x = \alpha l + (1 - \alpha)k + g.$$

Assume that saving (investment) is a constant fraction of aggregate output, so that

$$k = \frac{sX}{K}.$$

Differentiating,

$$\frac{dk}{dt} = s\frac{X}{K}(x - k).$$

That is, if $x > k$, k rises over time, and vice versa. And since $\partial x/\partial k = 1 - \alpha < 1$, k will converge on x.

Substituting $k = x$ to obtain the long-run equilibrium growth rate, we obtain

$$x = l + g/\alpha.$$

2. We now want to obtain the rate of saving that maximizes consumption per head. Consumption per head is $C = (1 - s)X/L$. From the production function, we obtain

$$\left(\frac{X}{L}\right)^\alpha = \left(\frac{K}{X}\right)^{1-\alpha} A\,e^{gt}, \quad \text{or} \quad \frac{X}{L} = \left(\frac{K}{X}\right)^{(1-\alpha)/\alpha} (A\,e^{gt})^{1/\alpha}.$$

Whence, using the relation $sX/K = k = x$ to substitute for $K/X = s/x$, we obtain for consumption per head the expression

$$C = (1 - s)\left(\frac{s}{x}\right)^{(1-\alpha)/\alpha} (A\,e^{gt})^{1/\alpha}.$$

Differentiating with respect to s, we obtain

$$\frac{dC}{ds} = \left[\frac{1-\alpha}{\alpha}\left(\frac{1-s}{x}\right)\left(\frac{s}{x}\right)^{[(1-\alpha)/\alpha]-1} - \left(\frac{s}{x}\right)^{(1-\alpha)/\alpha}\right][A\,e^{gt}]^{1/\alpha}$$

$$= \left[\frac{1-\alpha}{\alpha}\,\frac{1-s}{s} - 1\right]\left(\frac{s}{x}\right)^{(1-\alpha)/\alpha} (A\,e^{gt})^{1/\alpha}.$$

Setting this equal to zero, we obtain the condition $1 - \alpha = s$ as the condition for maximizing consumption per head. This condition is that the savings ratio should equal capital's share in output.

3. The foreging development assumes that capital lasts forever. Now assume that capital depreciates by evaporation, a fraction δ of the existing capital stock disappearing each instant.

Then,

$$\frac{dK}{dt} = sX - \delta K$$

$$k = s\frac{X}{K} - \delta$$

$$\frac{dk}{dt} = s\frac{X}{K}(x - k).$$

So that k converges on x as before; and as before, $x = l + g/\alpha$ in long-run equilibrium.

In the analysis of the rate of saving that maximizes consumption per head, we now have

$$\frac{K}{X} = \frac{s}{x + \delta}.$$

Substitution of this in the expression for C, and differentiation with respect to s, yields the results,

$$\frac{dC}{ds} = \left[\frac{1 - \alpha}{\alpha} \cdot \frac{1 - s}{s} - 1\right]\left(\frac{s}{x + \delta}\right)^{(1 - \alpha)/\alpha} (A\, e^{gt})^{1/\alpha}$$

yielding the same condition $1 - \alpha = s$ as the condition for maximization of income per head. Again the savings ratio should equal capital's share in output; but this share is now gross profit, the sum of net profit and depreciation.

4. In long-run equilibrium, $x = k = s(X/K) - \delta$. If $s = 1 - \alpha$, as required for the maximization of consumption per head, $x = (1 - \alpha)(X/C) - \delta$. But $(1 - \alpha) X/C = \partial X/\partial C$, the marginal product of capital, and $(1 - \alpha) X/C - \delta = \partial X/\partial C - \delta$, the net marginal product of capital or (since output and capital are the same good), the own-rate of return or rate of interest on capital. Hence the condition for maximum consumption per head can be stated in an alternative form, $i = x$, equality of the rate of interest with the rate of growth.

The General Case

1. Here we employ the general linear homogeneous production function

$$X = Lf\left(\frac{K}{L}\right)e^{gt}$$

Using small letters for rates of change

$$x = l + g + \frac{Kf'}{Xf}(k - l) = \mu_L l + \mu_K k + g,$$

where the μ's are income shares,

$$k = \frac{sX}{K}; \quad \frac{dk}{dt} = s\frac{X}{K}(x - k) \quad \text{and} \quad \frac{\partial x}{\partial k} = \mu_K < 1.$$

Hence k converges on x, and $x = l + g/\mu_K$.

2. As regards the golden rule, we want to choose s to maximize consumption per head, $C = (1 - s) X/L$

First note that $\dfrac{X}{L} = f\left(\dfrac{K}{L}\right)$ can be written $\dfrac{X}{L} = f\left(\dfrac{K}{X} \cdot \dfrac{X}{L}\right)$

$$d\left(\frac{X}{L}\right) = f'\left[\frac{K}{X}d\left(\frac{X}{L}\right) + \frac{X}{L}d\left(\frac{K}{X}\right)\right]$$

$$= \frac{f'\dfrac{X}{L}d\left(\dfrac{K}{X}\right)}{1 - f'\dfrac{K}{X}} = \frac{f'\dfrac{X}{L}d\left(\dfrac{K}{X}\right)}{1 - \mu_K}$$

Also, treating x as constant, and using $sX/K = k = x$

$$\frac{d\left(\dfrac{K}{X}\right)}{ds} = \frac{K}{sX}$$

Differentiating

$$\frac{dC}{ds} = \frac{X}{L}\left(-1 + \frac{1 - s}{1 - \mu_K}\frac{f'K}{sX}\right)$$

$$= \frac{X}{L}\left(-1 + \frac{1 - s}{1 - \mu_K}\frac{\mu_K}{s}\right)$$

This vanishes when $s = \mu_K$, i.e. the savings ratio is equal to capital's share in total output.

Also, using

$$\frac{f'K}{X} = \mu_K = s = \frac{xK}{X}$$

and cancelling terms, $f' = x$, i.e. the marginal product of capital equals the rate of interest.

15

THE TWO-SECTOR MODEL OF ECONOMIC
GROWTH

Introduction
The one-sector neo-classical model of economic growth discussed in the preceding chapter has two characteristics: (i) convergence of the system on a unique equilibrium growth path, the uniqueness referring to the cross-section values of output, capital and consumption per head; (ii) a technical maximum to the consumption per head attainable, derived from the production technology in conjunction with the exogenously-given rate of population growth. The one-sector model however excludes most of the interesting problems of capital theory, in particular (i) changes in the relative prices of consumption and capital goods; (ii) the influence of changing income distribution in conjunction with demand differences (in this case, differences between factor owners in their demands for saving or for wealth) on the transitory equilibrium of the economy in its motion towards the steady-state growth path and on the cross-section characteristics of the growth path. The two-sector model, to which we now turn, introduces these problems.

It should be fairly obvious, to begin with, that the golden rule condition should continue to hold in the two-sector model (or indeed in a many-sector model). In a steady-state growth equilibrium, in which savings are just sufficient to keep capital per head intact, relative prices will be constant, and capital will have a clearly-defined marginal product in terms of itself, i.e. there will be a constant rate of interest. If that rate of interest is greater than the rate of population growth — the 'natural' rate of growth — the economy could obviously move to a steady-state path with a higher stock of capital per head, and gain the excess of the rate of interest over the rate of growth (which determines the 'depreciation' requirement) as higher consumption per head. Hence follows the golden rule that the rate of return on capital should be equal to the rate of growth for consumption per head to be maximized, or alternatively that the savings ratio should equal the share of capital in total output. Note again that the golden rule is a technical limitation on consumption per head attainable, and not a policy prescription for an economy whose savings ratio is below the golden rule level, because of the intertemporal utility-maximization problem or alternatively the investment problem involved in raising the savings ratio.

The variability of relative commodity prices therefore does not alter the golden rule analysis. But it does introduce problems concerning the uniqueness and stability of equilibrium (these are really the same problem, since according to well-known principles a unique equilibrium must be stable, whereas with instability there must be an odd number of equilibria with stable and unstable equilibria alternating and each unstable equilibrium flanked on either side by a stable equilibrium position). In fact, as will be seen, there are two separate types of multiple equilibrium problem.

1. There may be a unique equilibrium at any given level of capital per head, i.e. the short-run equilibrium of the economy is unique and stable, but there may be more than one equilibrium growth path, corresponding to different levels of capital per head, these paths being alternatively stable and unstable. This may occur even in the apparently very restricted case of a single savings ratio common to all factor owners and applied to all income (output), if capital goods are capital-intensive in production.

2. There may be a multiple-equilibrium possibility in the short-run with a given total stock of capital per head, if the owners of labour and capital have different savings ratios — specifically if the owners of capital save a higher proportion of their income than do the owners of labour — and if the production of capital goods is capital-intensive. (The parallel case of labour-intensive capital goods production and a higher savings ratio for labour than for capital can be ruled out as both generally considered implausible, and making a nonsense of the concept of a capitalist — since the 'workers' would eventually own more capital than the 'capitalists'.) More restrictive necessary conditions for the possibility of multiple equilibrium to arise will be specified later. It should be noted at this point, however, that the case is a special case of the possibility of multiple equilibrium discussed earlier in connection with the two-sector static equilibrium model, the special nature of the case being accounted for by the fact that the assumption of a constant savings ratio involves a unit income elasticity and a unit uncompensated (Hicksian) own-price elasticity of demand for investment goods by savers.

The Two-Sector Model: Assumptions

We proceed to construct a two-sector model of economic growth. For this purpose we use the static two-sector model of general equilibrium already developed, involving different factor-intensities of the two industries at any given factor or commodity price ratio, and constant returns to scale in production. Note that the assumption we shall make that an industry is always capital-intensive or labour-intensive relative to the other industry implicitly imposes a restriction either on the forms of the production functions, or on the range of factor-price variation that can occur over the relevant range of capital-to-labour ratios considered. The reason is that, if the elasticities of substitution of the production functions differ, a sufficient variation of relative factor prices will reverse the relative factor-intensities of the two industries. Hence either the elasticities of substitution must be the same or the reversals that could occur must be excluded by assumption. (This problem did not arise in the static two-sector model, because a factor-intensity reversal is only possible if there is a change in the overall ratio of labour to capital — which could not occur by assumption in that model but can occur in this one.)

To convert the static two-sector model into a growth model, we need merely change the two goods produced from two consumption goods to one consumption good and an investment good, and consider the implications of production of the investment good for the growth of the capital stock of the economy over time. To simplify matters, we assume that capital goods once produced last forever, although, as previously noted, depreciation can be easily handled by assuming one of the two standard models of depreciation: on the evaporation assumption, the rate of evaporation d is simply added to the natural rate of growth n to determine the overall 'depreciation' of the capital stock per head that has to be made good by new investment, the requirement being $(n + d)k$; on the 'one-hoss-shay' assumption, the rate of depreciation is a function of the natural rate of growth, but since that is given the functional relationship merely makes the formula more complicated.

To simplify further, we assume that the driving force in economic growth is an exogenously given rate of population increase, abstracting from technical progress. The model could easily handle Harrod-neutral technical progress occurring at the same rate in both industries, since such progress would merely increase the effective rate of growth of the labour force. Any other type of technical progress, either Harrod-neutral in one industry only or non-Harrod-neutral progress, would not lead to a constant rate of equilibrium growth.

As in the case of the one-sector model, it is simplest to tackle the problem in terms of the cross-section production-function relating output to capital per head. But in this case, instead of a single output per head, the fixed stock of capital per head provides a transformation curve between output of investment goods and output of consumption goods per capita attainable with that stock.

The Rybczynski Line

In analyzing the effects of capital accumulation, which has the general effect of shifting the transformation curve outwards throughout its length, it is necessary to distinguish between two cases: investment goods labour-intensive in production, and investment goods capital-intensive in production. The key analytical tool is the *Rybczynski line*, which is the locus of the points on successive transformation curves for which the commodity price ratio and hence the factor price ratio are constant. Note that the Rybczynski line is a reference line only, since it is not possible — except in the special case of one of the goods being inferior to exactly the right extent — to expand the capital stock consistently with constancy of relative commodity prices. As shown in previous analysis, expansion of the quantity of one factor, keeping the other unchanged in quantity, at constant commodity and factor prices, must lead to an absolute reduction in the output of the commodity that uses the other factor relatively intensively, and an expansion of the output of the commodity that uses the augmented factor relatively intensively by more than the increase in total output. The Rybczynski line merely represents this fact diagrammatically; it is a straight line sloping either downwards to the right or upwards to the left from the initial production point as capital per head increases.

The Rybczynski lines for the two cases of labour-intensive and capital-intensive investment goods production are shown in Diagram I. In the diagrams, TT, $T'T'$, and $T''T''$ are transformation curves representing successively higher stocks of capital per head, MN, $M'N'$, and $M''N''$ are

174

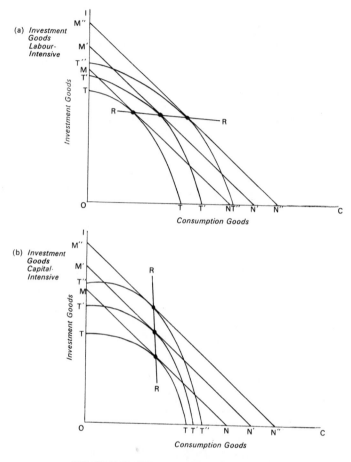

(a) *Investment Goods Labour-Intensive*

(b) *Investment Goods Capital-Intensive*

Consumption Goods

DIAGRAM I: THE RYBCZYNSKI LINE

the budget lines corresponding to the fixed commodity and factor price ratio assumed, and RR is the Rybczynski line. The Rybczynski line is a reference line to be used in the subsequent analysis, which involves bringing together the locus of combinations of consumption and investment goods production the economy will choose, given its fixed savings ratio and its current available transformation curve, and the combinations of consumption goods and investment goods it can produce consistently with maintaining its capital per head intact. We take up the latter problem first.

Investment Requirements

Continuing with the assumption of a fixed commodity and consequently factor price ratio, we can define a locus of points representing the amounts of investment required per capita to maintain constancy of the capital–labour ratio at successively higher capital-to-labour ratios represented by successively higher budget lines (tangents to the underlying transformation curves). Equi-distantly higher budget lines imply equal increases in the investment required to keep capital per head intact, hence the line is a straight line; but since, at constant factor prices, part of the output is contributed by the services of labour, and the marginal product of labour is constant, the line starts to the right of the origin on the horizontal axis. (On the assumption of constant factor prices, we can think of labour as renting capital from outside the economy in order to enable it to earn its marginal product; the more capital the economy possesses itself the higher its income from capital, but its wage income remains constant.) Note that the shape and position of the investment requirements line, derived on the assumption of a given commodity and factor price ratio, are not independent of that ratio (we have chosen the price ratio so that the marginal product of capital exceeds the natural rate of growth, so that an outward shift of the transformation curve in fact permits more consumption per head). However, the investment requirements line is only a reference line for the derivation of an investment requirements curve which shows the combinations of investment and consumption goods production that the economy can have, with successively greater levels of capital per head, consistently with constant capital per head, and which is independent of the actual price ratio that may chance to prevail in the economy. The point is that the investment requirements line by construction assumes that the economy can trade factors with an outside world, whereas in fact its production possibilities are constrained by its transformation curve.

The investment requirements line is shown in Diagram II, by the line *PQ*.

To derive the investment requirements curve, we project the amount of investment goods production shown on the investment requirements line

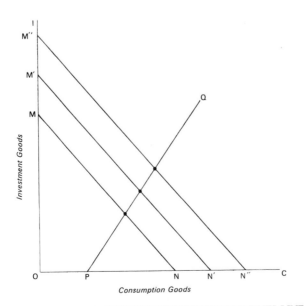

DIAGRAM II: THE INVESTMENT REQUIREMENTS LINE

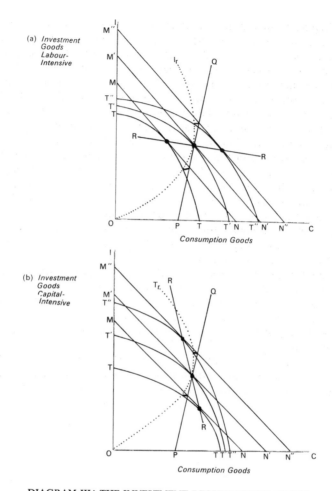

(a) *Investment Goods Labour-Intensive*

(b) *Investment Goods Capital-Intensive*

DIAGRAM III: THE INVESTMENT REQUIREMENTS CURVE

back on to the transformation curve that is tangent to that line. The procedure is shown in Diagrams IIIa and IIIb, which represent the two alternative cases of labour-intensive and capital-intensive investment goods production. It should be noted that the investment requirements curve OI_r will be tangent to the investment requirements line PQ at only one point — where the latter intersects the Rybczynski line. Otherwise, it must lie to the left of that line; and it must start at the origin, and eventually bend back on itself. The general shape is independent of whether the investment goods industry is labour-intensive or capital-intensive. Further, the point at which the investment requirements curve starts to bend back on itself towards the vertical axis is the 'golden rule' point, representing the maximum consumption per head that the economy can attain through the accumulation of capital. At that point, further capital accumulation adds as much to the investment requirement as it adds to output, leaving nothing over with which to increase consumption.

Investment Supply
In this neo-classical type of model, the supply of savings is also a supply of investment goods to the economy. We assume, following convention but not necessarily making economic sense in terms of the Fisherian approach to saving as a way of transferring consumption opportunities from the present to the future (since the assumption to be stated in effect treats saving as simply a 'commodity' that can be purchased out of present income as an alternative to current consumption), that the society saves according to a fixed savings ratio. The problem that then arises is to translate saving into a supply of investment goods, given that the value of income in terms of either of the two goods will depend on their (variable) relative price, and that a fixed quantity of saving in terms of consumption goods will have a variable value in terms of investment goods (one aspect of the central problem of neo-classical capital theory). To handle this problem, it is simplest to measure income in terms of investment goods. The diagrammatic construction necessary for our purposes is depicted in Diagram IV, where income in terms of

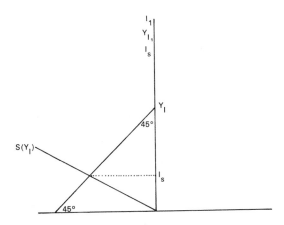

DIAGRAM IV: THE FIXED SAVINGS RATIO

investment goods (Y_I) is measured on the vertical axis. The line $s(Y_I)$ is a means of depicting the fixed savings ratio in such a fashion that actual saving measured in terms of the investment goods supply it represents can be projected back on to the vertical (I, Y_I) axis. To do this, draw a 45° line from Y_I to intersect the $s(Y_I)$ line. The horizontal projection of the intersection back on to the vertical axis gives the level of saving (supply of investment goods from saving) I_s corresponding to the initial level of income measured in consumption goods Y_I.

Having defined the technique of diagrammatic analysis, we move on to the determination of the level of investment in the short run, with a given stock of capital per head and corresponding transformation curve between investment and consumption goods production. In Diagram V, TT is the transformation curve defined by the given stock of capital. Arbitrarily choose a production point B, with a corresponding budget line MN. With income measured in investment goods OM, and the savings ratio shown by $s(Y_I)$, the economy would choose the levels of investment and consumption goods

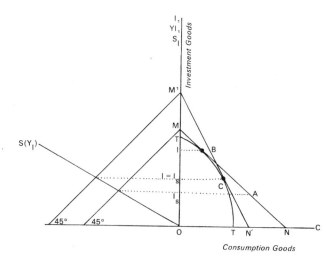

DIAGRAM V: SHORT-RUN SAVINGS EQUILIBRIUM

production represented by point A, on the budget line MN. This would obviously involve an excess supply of investment goods and excess demand for consumption goods, constituting a disequilibrium situation. To correct it, the price of investment goods in terms of consumption goods must fall. As it does so, production of investment goods falls (a shift down the transformation curve towards more production of consumption goods). This tends to eliminate the excess supply of investment goods by itself; but, in addition, the fall in the price of investment goods increases the value of current production of consumption goods in terms of investment goods, as does the increase in production of consumption goods induced by the relative price change. This increases the value of total income measured in investment goods, and thereby increases the absolute supply of investment goods provided by savings (more easily understood, the absolute quantity of investment goods demanded out of savings). Both influences tend to restore equilibrium, which will be reached at point C, where the demand for investment goods out of savings is equal to their supply out of current production. Point C represents a short-run equilibrium between savings and investment for a given stock of capital.

Point C, however, is only a short-run equilibrium. The next question is what happens to the location of point C if the stock of capital per head is increased. This is analysed in Diagram VI. If the commodity and factor price

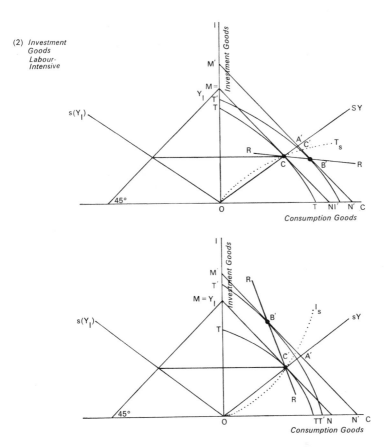

(2) *Investment Goods Labour- Intensive*

DIAGRAM VI: THE INVESTMENT SUPPLY CURVE

ratio were kept constant, the consumption-and-savings equilibrium of the economy would shift outwards along the fixed-savings-ratio line $O . sY$, to a point such as A'. The production point on the other hand would move along the Rybczynski line to the point B'. Because of the respectively down-ward-sloping and backward-sloping nature of the Rybczynski line in the two alternative cases, A' and B' cannot coincide; their respective locations must constitute in the first case an excess of demand for investment goods over the supply of them, and in the second case an excess of the supply of investment goods over the demand for them, requiring an appropriate price adjustment for investment goods relative to consumption goods. In each case, the resulting equilibrium position is represented by point C'. But in the first case of labour-intensive investment goods production, the relative price adjustment reduces the value of income in terms of investment goods below what it would be at constant commodity prices, and therefore the point C' lies below $O . sY$; whereas in the second case the value of income in terms of investment goods is increased above what it would be at constant commodity prices, so that the point C' lies above the line $O \cdot sY$. Hence in the case of labour-intensive investment goods production, the investment supply curve representing the relation between consumption goods and investment goods production must be concave to the horizontal axis, whereas in the case of capital-intensive investment goods production it must be concave to the vertical axis. This curve is represented in each part of Diagram VI by the curve $O \cdot I_s$.

Long-Run Growth Equilibrium

The two curves $O \cdot I_r$ and $O \cdot I_s$ representing the combination of investment goods and consumption goods production that are consistent with the maintenance of constant capital per head at any given level of consumption per head, and the combinations that the public would choose in the light of its fixed savings ratio and the various transformation curves confronting it, can be put together to determine the long-run growth equilibrium of the

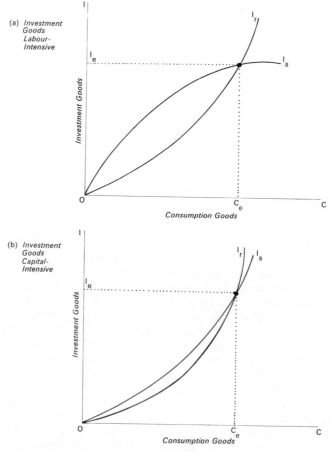

DIAGRAM VII: LONG-RUN GROWTH EQUILIBRIUM

economy, as shown in Diagram VII. This equilibrium occurs when the investment the public chooses to supply through its savings behaviour is just equal to the amount required to maintain capital per head intact in face of the exogenous growth-rate of the population.

In the case of labour-intensive production of investment goods, the long-run equilibrium must be unique and stable, because of the opposite concavities of the investment requirements and investment supply curves towards the two axes. In the case of capital-intensive investment goods production the long-run growth equilibrium may also be unique and stable (see Diagram VII for the two cases). But in the latter case it is also possible to have multiple equilibria, because the two curves are concave towards the same (vertical) axis and hence may, depending on the parameters, intersect each other more than once. This possibility is shown in Diagram VIII.

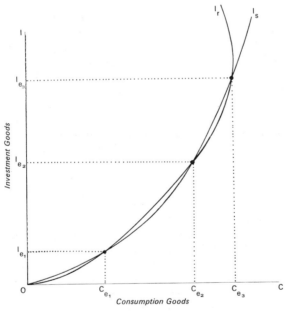

Investment Goods Capital-Intensive

DIAGRAM VIII: MULTIPLE GROWTH EQUILIBRIA

The possibility of multiple equilibria in this case has an obvious application to the theories of economic development discussed earlier: an economy might for one reason or another be trapped at the low level of consumption C_{e_1}, and be unable to escape without a 'big push' that would enable it to reach C_{e_3}. It also has relevance to the 'golden rule' analysis, in the sense that if C_{e_3} itself lies short of the golden rule position, and the economy is at C_{e_1}, government policy may, by dislodging it from that position, lead it to move voluntarily to equilibrium at C_{e_3}. (Note that it has been assumed, as a matter of realism, that economies are typically to the left of the golden rule position on the upward-right-sloping branch of the I_r curve.) But such a policy would still raise the question of intertemporal optimization of utility, even though the circumstances of multiple equilibrium would make the government's task of getting closer to the golden rule position easier than in the one-sector model.

Multiple Short-Run Equilibria

The possibility of multiple short-run disequilibria is a disturbing one for growth modellers, since it introduces not only the possibility of alternative cross-section growth paths but the possibility of discontinuous shifts from one such path to another in the course of growth. (Factor intensity reversals, which have not been discussed, raise similar problems for the analysis of the dynamic process of movement towards a steady-state equilibrium growth path.)

As already demonstrated (refer back to Diagram V), the short-run equilibrium of the economy must be unique and stable if there is a single savings ratio applying to the whole of income (output). The possibility of unstable short-run equilibrium depends on sectorizing the economy into two different groups of factor owners with differing savings ratios. More specifically, it depends on assuming that investment goods production is relatively capital-intensive, and that capitalists have a higher savings ratio than workers (the opposite set of assumptions has been dismissed earlier as unrealistic). On these assumptions, the shift of income distribution towards capitalists implicit in an increase in investment goods prices and production may increase the investment-goods equivalent of saving by more than it increases the production of investment goods, thereby giving rise to an excess demand for, rather than an excess supply of, investment goods and constituting instability of equilibrium in the neighbourhood of the initial production and consumption equilibrium point.

The possibility is illustrated in Diagram IX, which makes use of the concepts developed earlier on the relation between commodity prices and factor incomes. The initial incomes of capital and labour, associated with the production point on the total transformation curve indicated by the price ratio between the goods produced corresponding to the slopes of the relevant budget lines, are shown by the budget lines $M_c N_c$ and $M_L N_L$ respectively; on these budget lines, the fixed savings ratios of the two groups of factor owners determine the consumption-investment points represented by C_c and C_L respectively. A shift towards the production of investment goods alters the incomes to $M'_c N'_c$ and $M'_L N'_L$ respectively, with consumption-investment points C'_c and C'_L respectively. Vector addition of the consumption-investment points for the two production positions (see Diagram IX c) gives the original production-consumption equilibrium point P, C, and a new equilibrium consumption point C' for the economy as a whole, which may lie to the north-east of the new production point P', indicating an excess demand for investment goods with the new distribution of income. Note that the constant savings ratio assumption necessarily implies that the investment ratio of each group of factor owners is lower in the new than in the initial position — i.e. there is a sort of substitution effect resulting from the

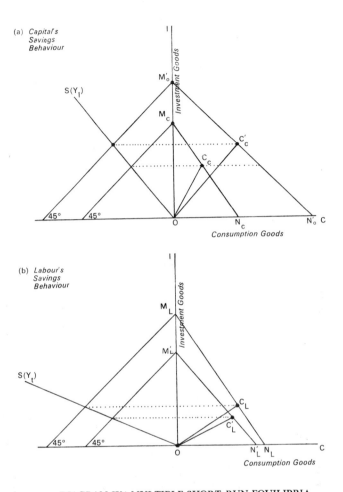

DIAGRAM IX: MULTIPLE SHORT-RUN EQUILIBRIA

higher price of investment goods in conjunction with the fixed savings ratio that reduces the ratio of investment goods to consumption goods purchased — and that this has to be outweighed by the effect of the redistribution of income in conjunction with the difference in the savings ratios. (Note also, from previous analysis, that the possibility of instability depends on the size of the income-redistribution effect, and that a necessary condition for it to be strong enough to outweigh the substitution effect is an average elasticity of substitution between the factors in the production functions that is less than one — a point to be re-demonstrated below.)

The Borts Technique
In the context of a growth model, the possibility of multiple equilibrium gives rise to trouble because if, as the economy accumulates capital, it somehow gets on a path of unstable equilibrium, further capital accumulation

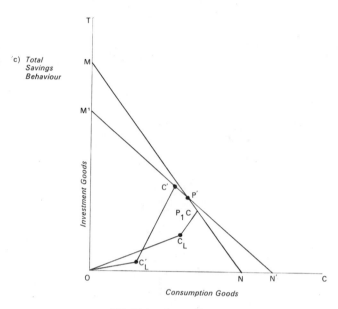

c) Total
Savings
Behaviour

DIAGRAM IX: CONTD.

may entail a rise in the rate of interest (rather than a fall as would normally be expected) in order to restore equilibrium. As a preliminary indication of the route ahead, the necessary conditions for this to occur may be successively narrowed down in three stages: (i) capital-intensive investment goods production on the assumption that capitalists save a higher proportion of their incomes than workers, (ii) elasticities of substitution in the production functions averaging less than unity, (iii) conditions on the elasticities of the saving and investment curves. The analysis follows but does not exactly conform to that of George Borts; it is couched in terms of comparative statics.

We assume to simplify the analysis that capitalists save a higher proportion of their incomes than workers. We then have two cases to consider: labour-intensive and capital-intensive investment goods production. In each case we construct two relationships, for a given stock of capital per head: one relating the rate of return on capital to the level of investment, and the other relating saving to the rate of return on capital. (The former, in the case of labour-intensive capital goods production, looks like the conventional downward-sloping relation between investment and the rate of interest, but it is not so: its downward slope embodies the Stolper–Samuelson relation between the allocation of production between the two industries and relative factor prices. The latter looks like a conventional upward-sloping curve for saving as a function of the rate of interest, but is not so: its shape reflects the redistribution of income from workers to capitalists as the rate of return on capital rises, and the effects of this on total saving due to the difference in savings ratios; and it may bend back on itself.)

See Diagrams X and XI. The existing fixed stock of capital sets a maximum and a minimum to the range of possible rates of interest. In the case of labour-

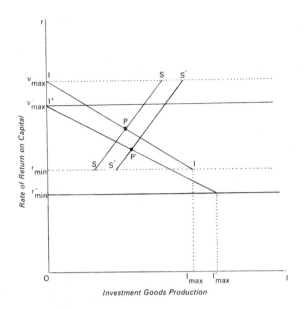

DIAGRAM X: GROWTH WITH LABOUR-INTENSIVE INVESTMENT GOODS PRODUCTION

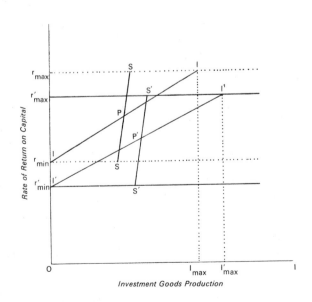

DIAGRAM XI: GROWTH WITH CAPITAL-INTENSIVE INVESTMENT GOODS PRODUCTION: NORMAL CASE

intensive investment goods production, the maximum occurs when zero production of investment goods occurs and the minimum occurs when maximum production of investment goods (zero production of consumption goods) occurs, and vice versa in the case of capital-intensive investment goods production. The curve *II* (drawn for simplicity as a straight line in these diagrams, as is the *SS* curve), is the relation between investment goods production and the rate of return on capital: it is downward-sloping for the case of labour-intensive investment goods production, and upward-sloping for the case of capital-intensive investment goods production. The curve *SS*, drawn for the range between the maximum and minimum rates of interest, reflects the effects of income-redistribution from labour to capital as the rate of return on capital rises. It must be upward-sloping in the case of labour-intensive investment goods production, because in this case the price of investment goods falls as the rate of return on capital rises, so that a given savings ratio buys a larger quantity of investment goods; it could be backward-sloping in the case of capital-intensive investment goods production, as in this case a higher average proportion of income saved could still mean a smaller quantity of investment goods purchased due to the rise in their price associated with the rise in the rate of return on capital. Assuming that neither group of factors-owners saves all of its income, the *SS* curve must start with a positive amount of investment goods demanded at the minimum interest rate, and end with less than the maximum amount of investment goods that the economy could produce being demanded at the maximum interest rate. This guarantees global stability of the system.

Our interest lies in the effects on the savings-investment equilibrium of an increase in the economy's capital stock — which must increase the maximum amount of investment goods that can be produced and reduce both the maximum and minimum interest rates attainable. At any given rate of return on capital, the *SS* curve must shift right by less than the *II* curve, as a consequence of the Rybczynski theorem. Hence, in all cases of labour-intensive investment goods production, shown in Diagram X, and in the 'normal' case of capital-intensive investment goods production shown in Diagram XI, the interest rate must fall as capital accumulates. (The volume of production of investment goods may, however, either rise or fall, depending on the parameters.)

The case of capital-intensive investment goods production, however, gives rise to the possibility of multiple equilibrium and of unstable equilibrium, the latter represented by point *B* in Diagram XIIa. If the economy were originally at point *B* (ignore the question of why its instability has not led the economy to points A or C), the accumulation of capital will require a rise and not a fall in the rate of interest, as shown in Diagram XIIb, to maintain equilibrium between savings and investment.

Our concern is the conditions under which this may occur. For this purpose we follow Bort's analysis. Diagram XIIIa depicts the familiar contract box, with production initially (with the original stock of capital) at point *P*. *P''* is the point on the new contract curve for the augmented stock of capital that maintains the same rate of return on capital. It cannot be an equilibrium position, because it involves a lower level of consumption goods production and a higher total output at the same relative prices, and this is

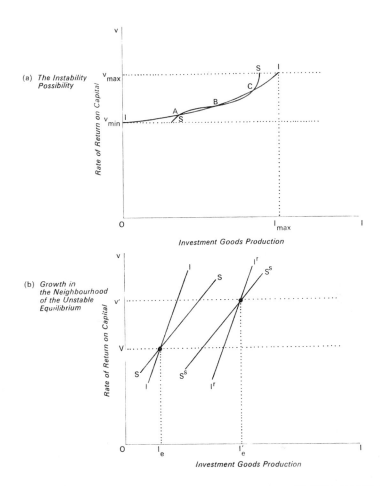

DIAGRAM XII: GROWTH WITH CAPITAL-INTENSIVE INVESTMENT GOODS PRO-
DUCTION: THE INSTABILITY CASE

inconsistent with the assumption that capital (which receives all of the increment of income) saves only a fraction of its income. For further analysis we
define the point P' as the allocation of production on the new contract curve
that would involve the same proportion of income being saved and invested
as was true at P. (Note that because the price of investment goods in terms of
consumption goods has fallen as compared with P and P'', investment goods
production increases more than proportionally to the increase in income as
measured between P and P'').

Now consider Diagram XIIIb, in which $I_0 I_0$ and $I_1 I_1$ represent the
initial and new relations between investment goods production and the rate
of return on capital and the three production points from the contract box
are marked in. We seek the location of the new SS curve. For the reason given
above, S'', the point corresponding to the savings ratio when the rate of

188

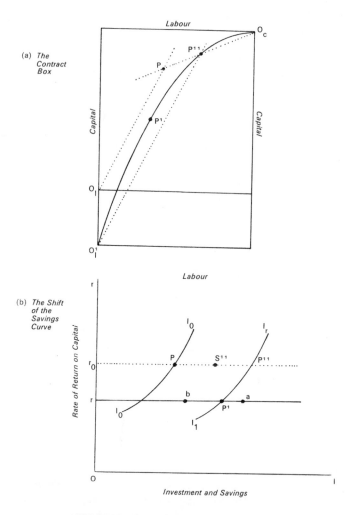

DIAGRAM XIII: THE BORTS ANALYSIS

return is kept constant, must lie between P and P''. Our concern is with the amount of saving that would be done at the lower interest rate corresponding to the point P', which is the production point at which the same proportion of income would be saved and invested as at P. To analyse this, we use the fact that the total share of capital in total output can be viewed as the sum of the share of capital in investment goods output multiplied by the share of investment goods output in total output, and the share of capital in consumption goods output multiplied by the share of consumption goods output in total output. By choosing P' as the point with the same division of the value of output between the two industries as occurred at P, we have pegged the second term of each element in the sum to constancy. We now consider the influence of the elasticities of substitution in the two industries on the change in capital's share in total output and therefore on the overall savings ratio.

If the elasticity of substitution in each industry is exactly unity, capital's share in each industry is unchanged, so that capital's share in income is unchanged, the overall savings ratio is unchanged, the point on the savings curve for the rate of return on capital r_1 coincides with P', equilibrium between saving and investment occurs at P' and the rate of interest falls from r_0 to r_1. If the elasticity of substitution in each industry exceeds unity, capital's share in the output of each industry rises as the rate of return falls, the overall savings ratio therefore rises, and the point on the new SS curve corresponding to r_1 must lie to the right of P', say at point a in the diagram. The new SS curve must run through S'' and a, hence cutting $I_1 I_1$ at an interest rate below r_0 and above r_1. Again the equilibrium interest rate falls as capital accumulates and all is well. But if the elasticity of substitution in each industry is less than unity, capital's share in the output of each industry falls as the rate of return falls, and the overall savings ratio falls, so that the point on the new SS curve corresponding to r_1 must lie left of P', say at point b. The new savings curve must pass through S'' and b; it may intersect $I_1 I_1$ either below r_1 (again all is well) or above r_0 (the awkward case) depending on the relative slopes or alternatively elasticities of the new SS and II curves.

This analysis ignores the possibility that one elasticity of substitution is less than unity and the other greater than unity; but clearly there must be some sort of weighted average of the two equivalent to the dividing line condition of unitary elasticity of substitution in both industries.

The crucial role of the elasticities of substitution can be demonstrated algebraically, as follows. Let

capital's saving $= S_K = s_K(Q_{IK}PI + Q_{CK}C)$

labour's saving $= S_L = s_L[(1 - Q_{IK})PI + (1 - Q_{CK})C]$

total saving $= S = s_L(PI + C) + (s_K - s_L)(Q_{IK}PI + Q_{CK}C$

where s_K, s_L are capital's and labour's savings ratios; Q_{IK} and Q_{CK} are capital's share in investment goods and consumption goods production; P is the price of investment goods in terms of consumption goods; and I and C are levels of investment goods and consumption goods production.

Now consider the effects on savings of a small increase in investment goods production.

$$\frac{dS}{dI} = (s_K - s_L) \cdot \left[(Q_{IK} - Q_{CK})P + IP\frac{\partial Q_{IK}}{\partial I} + C\frac{\partial Q_{CK}}{\partial I} \right],$$

if the value of total production remains constant, as it will for small changes in the neighbourhood of equilibrium,

$$\left[\frac{\partial s_L(PI + C)}{\partial I} \approx 0 \right].$$

But $(s_K - s_L)$ and Q_{IK} and Q_{CK} are necessarily fractions, so that if the latter two are constant dS/dI must be less than P, implying excess supply of the investment good as the quantity of it produced increases. (P is the value of the increase in investment goods production.)

For $\partial S/\partial I > P$,

$$\left[PI \frac{\partial Q_{IK}}{\partial I} + C \frac{\partial Q_{CK}}{\partial I} \right]$$

must be positive. Since our case involves an increase in investment goods production and therefore a rise in the price of capital in both industries, Q_{IK} will be positive only if the elasticity of substitution in the investment goods industry is less than unity, and similarly Q_{CK} will be positive only if the elasticity of substitution in the consumption goods industry is less than unity.

Summary on Instability Cases
We can make the two-sector growth model well behaved by accepting one of the following restrictions, which are of decreasing degree of severity (reminder: capital is assumed to save a higher proportion of its income than labour): (i) investment goods are labour-intensive in production; (ii) the elasticities of substitution between the factors in production are unity or greater, either individually or on some sort of weighted average, (iii) the SS curve is always more steeply sloped than the II curve.

16

FUNCTIONAL SHARES IN INCOME DISTRIBUTION

Introduction

We now return to the consideration of functional shares, and, in particular, the alleged problem of their presumed constancy over long periods of time in Western economies. Earlier, we dealt with a model of the determination of functional shares and changes in them in terms of a one-sector model in which income distribution depended on relative factor quantities and the elasticity of substitution between them in production. Technical progress as an influence on income distribution was introduced via the Hicksian concepts of neutral, labour-saving, and capital-saving innovation, though, as was there pointed out, one can alternatively regard technical progress as increasing the 'effective' quantities of factors within a given production function.

In a more general way, three types of parameters determine the distribution of income over time: changes in the quantities of factors; changes in technology; and the elasticity of substitution between factors. But even this is not a fully general system since technological progress might alter the elasticity of substitution as well as the optimal capital–labour ratio at given factor prices. Further, the ensuing analysis continues to assume a constant returns to scale production function although a more modern approach might want to assume one with increasing returns present. This is in sharp contrast to the classical notion of decreasing productivity although the classical notion really embodies the constancy of one factor, so regardless of the returns to scale assumption, as long as the scale factor was small, it was not important.

Before continuing, it is important to note that no theoretical apparatus will explain functional shares (the division of income between labour and property) in fundamental causal terms, but what can be done is to measure changes in observable inputs and then, in light of theoretical concepts, interpret the outcome. Indeed, in a full theory, it would be necessary to 'explain' many factors that usually lie outside the range of formal economics: the reasons for the changes in factor supplies and technical progress, and the reasons for changes in the elasticity of substitution, for example. In a sense all that has been done is to shift the need for explanation forward one step, and to account more logically for the causal relations running from exogenous to endogenous variables.

The focal point of the literature has been the observation, or the apparent observation, that historically relative shares have tended to be constant over time and that this has held for many countries as well. As is often the case, first observation suggests some puzzling regularity in the data and then, after the birth of theories to explain this regularity, it seems to vanish or diminish in importance. Whereas in the 1930s on the basis of statistical evidence available it appeared that shares had been roughly constant, subsequent statistical work indicated that they could change, or that the regularity was introduced by the nature of the statistical tests used to analyze the data.

Interest in the 1930s stemmed from two sources; Paul Douglas's extensive work at Chicago on aggregate production functions, historical and cross-country and cross-industry; and Keynes's seminar in economic theory at Cambridge.

Douglas's work involved fitting the new Cobb–Douglas production function, $X = AL^{\alpha}K^{1-\alpha}$. This necessarily gives constant shares, since for example $\partial X/\partial L = \alpha AL^{\alpha-1} K^{1-\alpha}$ and labour's share $L(\partial X/\partial L)/X = \alpha$. (This assumes that competition equates factor earnings with factor marginal productivities.) The function can be tested in two ways: by using the function as it stands and seeing how well it fits the data, or by giving K an unconstrained coefficient β, estimating α and β, and seeing whether $\alpha + \beta$ approximates to unity. Both tests seemed to perform well and validate the constancy of relative shares. Neither is a very good test really, and many of the statistical and economic reasons were understood by the end of the thirties. But it was not until the development of the 'C.E.S.' — constant elasticity of substitution — production function by Arrow, Solow, Chenery and Minhas at Stanford in the late 1950s (a function of which the Cobb–Douglas unitary elasticity of substitution is a special case) that the question could really be explored. (If $\alpha + \beta \neq 1$ in the Cobb–Douglas function, there are economies or diseconomies of scale uncomfortable for the 'adding-up' requirement of marginal productivity theory.) The use of the C.E.S. function in all sorts of contexts has amply demonstrated that there is no law of nature making elasticities of substitution normally unitary (actually, the measurements usually find them less than unitary), but it has also shown that, even so, the Cobb–Douglas usually gives an acceptable statistical fit — which suggests that the economists of the 1930s who were surprised at the goodness of Douglas's statistical fits and amazed at the apparent constancy of income shares were wrong to be so: the constancy was implicit in the mathematical form of the function, and the goodness of the statistical fits was not as persuasive as it was taken to be at the time, as to the appropriateness of the mathematical form.

The second and more important source of theoretical interest in the presumed constancy of relative shares developed from Keynes's seminar in Cambridge. In the background was the prediction of the analysis of the *General Theory* that, with the stock of capital assumed fixed in the short run, an increase in employment must lead to a reduction in the marginal product and real wage of labour; but empirical research by Tarshis and Dunlop contradicted this predicted cyclical variability of real wages. (Note that cyclical variability of real wages is quite consistent with constancy of relative shares, if the elasticity of substitution is unity.) In any case, Keynes opined that the constancy of relative shares was 'a bit of a miracle'; and in the climate of revolutionary zeal of the time, this was felt to constitute yet another proof of the uselessness of orthodox theory and the need for a new theory. Kalecki set out to construct one, to be described in more detail later, using the theory of imperfect competition in conjunction with the proposition that in the short run the firm's cost curve is flat up to capacity output (a notion consistent with Stigler's theory of built-in flexibility), contrary to Keynes's more classical assumption of continuously rising marginal cost of production. Subsequently, after the end of the Second World War, Kaldor produced a different kind of theory, also to be discussed later, to explain the same presumed fact of constant shares — a theory based on the Keynesian multiplier model.

Empirical Studies

Turning to specifics, D. G. Johnson found relative constancy in factor shares from 1850–1910, but between 1910 and 1952 labour's share rose from 68 per cent to 75 per cent. This would represent a substantial shift on the face of it but, Johnson argued, two types of statistical errors were responsible for it: (1) the substantial increase in government owned capital was ignored in accounting the National Income and so the earnings of capital were increasingly understated since the labour used by the government enters into the national income accounts but government capital does not; and (2) during this period there was a rapid shift of labour off the farm and into other activities. Much of the income that had been classified as property income on the farm was really entrepreneurial or farm labour and with the drift off the farm was then classified as labour income. The first of the above factors shifted the share from 75 per cent to 72 per cent and the second decreased the share still further.

Subsequent work by Kravis accepted the fact that there had been a shift from property to labour income and made attempts to account for it. Over the period, man hours increased by 50 per cent, the quantity of capital as measured increased by 200 per cent; this implied an increase in the capital–labour ratio of 100 per cent. Since the rate of return on capital remained relatively constant and real wages rose by 200 per cent, labour's share rose by roughly $\frac{1}{3}$. Kravis produced two major alternative lines of explanation of this phenomenon. The first employs the elasticity of substitution: an elasticity of substitution between labour and capital of around $\frac{2}{3}$ would account for the data. The second employs the concept of biased technical change. For this purpose Kravis employed a partitioning technique that was quite popular at that time but which, in my view, is to be avoided on general principle, for the same reason as the use of the quantity equation (NOT, it should be noted, the quantity theory) as a classificatory-descriptive device is to be avoided — because while it is easy enough to partition an aggregate into a sum (or difference) or a product (or dividend) of two or more components, it is not necessarily true that the components have the economic sense or relevance that is attributed to them. (Note that the Keynesian division of income into consumption and investment has been subjected to the same criticism by Milton Friedman.)

Specifically, we can write the share of capital relative to labour as $R/W = p_K Q_K / p_L Q_L$, where p's stand for prices and Q's stand for factor quantities. Multiplying and dividing through by total output Y, we obtain

$$\frac{R}{W} = \frac{Y/Q_L}{Y/Q_K} \cdot \frac{p_K}{p_L}$$

Then, taking the rise in p_K/p_L from 1 to 3 as a datum, capital's share would have fallen to one third of its initial value if the productivities per unit of factor had remained unchanged; the fact that capital's share did not fall by so much must be accounted for by a bias in technical progress such that labour's productivity rose more rapidly than capital's (the relevant figures being labour productivity up by 100 per cent, capital's up by 45 per cent). This difference in productivity changes, Kravis suggests, is accounted for by labour-saving innovations induced by the rise in the relative price of labour, the latter being attributable to the relative inelasticity of the supply of labour in the United States compared with the supply of capital. Note that use of this type of per-factor productivity statistic incorporates both the elasticity of substitution and the bias of technical change. Hence, while it is a commonly used and simply calculated type of statistic, we have to give it meaning by the interpretation we put on it, and that interpretation cannot be checked.

The basic problem in this kind of analysis, which has been recurring in subsequent, far more sophisticated work, is that there is no reliable way of separating historical data on factor quantities, prices, and income shares into the two components of substitution within a given production function and changes in the production function itself. Only if one can confidently (even if mistakenly) specify the influence of one component can one deduce the influence of the other. Consider Diagram I, where we have observations of two points on a map of p_K/p_L against Q_K/Q_L, with no outside information. We could assume (a) that technical progress has been either zero or Hicks-neutral; then (to fit the historical facts) the explanation of the change in relative shares has to be an appropriate elasticity of substitution, i.e. an elasticity of substitution of approximately $\frac{2}{3}$; (b) that the elasticity of substitution is unity; then the explanation has to be *capital-saving* innovation (since a lower Q_K/Q_L is required at any relative price of capital in terms of labour); (c) that the elasticity of substitution is zero (which requires explaining relative factor prices by some other consideration, such as the elasticity of supplies); then the explanation has to be labour-saving innovation, since the fixed ratio of labour to capital has been reduced between A and B. Only with outside information about one of the two components of the shift — substitution and technical change — could we partition the shift correctly between the two components.

In an article published in the 1950s, Robert Solow made the important point that one should not be surprised at the apparent constancy of factor shares unless one has some standard with respect to which these shares appear unexpectedly constant. (Many empirical observations on the economy easily seem surprising, until one asks oneself what should really have been expected.) Solow asked whether the aggregate share of labour fluctuated more or less than one should have expected given the fluctuations in labour's share in the individual industries of the economy, on the assumption that the latter are independent of one another. On the assumption of independent fluctuations, we have the statistical property

$$\sigma_s^2 = \sum_i^k w_i^2 \sigma_{s_i}^2$$

where the σ's are standard deviations of the subscripted share and w_i the weight of a particular industry in the aggregate. The evidence showed more,

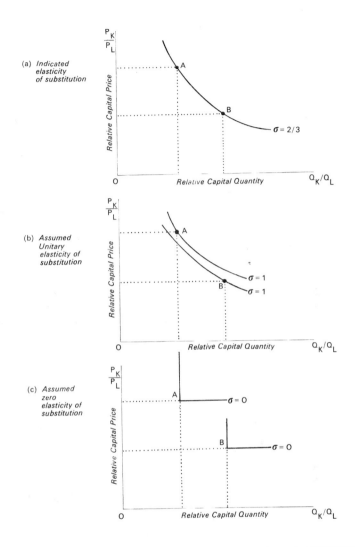

DIAGRAM I: CHANGES IN FUNCTIONAL SHARES AND THE ELASTICITY OF
SUBSTITUTION

and not less, variation in labour's aggregate share than would have been
predicted on the hypothesis of independent variations of labour's sectoral
shares in income.

Solow also remarked on the mildness of the trend towards a higher share
of labour, and asked whether it might have been predicted from the observed
rise in the capital–labour ratio. According to neo–classical production
function theory, the resulting trend of labour's share would depend on the

elasticity of substitution. The elasticity of labour's share with respect to the capital–labour ratio can be shown to be

$$-s_k\left(1 - \frac{1}{\sigma}\right)$$

where s_k is the share of capital and σ the elasticity of substitution. If σ were $\frac{2}{3}$, and s_k 0·3, the elasticity would be 0·15, and a rise in the capital–labour ratio of the observed order of magnitude of about 60 per cent would raise labour's share by about 4 per cent, in the same order of magnitude as the observed rise from about 70 per cent to 76·5 per cent. Solow also called attention to various data problems, to the possibility of technical change, and to the problem of increasing working force skill, which would appear as either rents for skilled labour or a larger-than-measured increase in actual labour available, as qualifications to the analysis.

In a parallel but more narrowly mathematical analysis, Bronfenbrenner produced essentially the same formula: the elasticity of labour's share with respect to the capital–labour ratio is

$$(1 - s)\left(\frac{\sigma - 1}{\sigma}\right)$$

where s is labour's initial share and σ is the elasticity of substitution. (Note the change of sign). He argued from the formula that in the nature of things labour's share will change very little, since labour's initial share is relatively large, so the first of the two terms will be small, unless the second term is large, which will occur only if the elasticity of substitution is substantially less than unity.

The apparent historical stability of relative shares, or the apparent mildness of the trend in them, is not all that clear. A change of 7/70 percentage points over more than half a century (10 per cent in all) seems mild; but measurement of the change in capital's share, 7/30 or 7/23 depending on which end point is taken (23 per cent or 30 per cent) might not seem so mild. In any case, stability or not of the share of labour constitutes no test of marginal productivity theory; rather, given the slowness of the historical processes of capital accumulation and population growth, it would require considerable instability of relative shares over time, and especially regular fluctuations not explainable by the business cycle, to produce an apparent contradiction of marginal productivity theory.

Finally, one should note Solow's point about the accumulation of human capital, the earnings of which are included in labour's share even though they are essentially a return on 'capital' rather than 'labour'. It could be that if the two classical factors were properly measured relative shares would be approximately constant over time and the elasticity of substitution unity. Alternatively, as already mentioned, technical progress of the right kind could explain what has happened to relative shares. (Also, one might note that the constancy or otherwise of relative shares has little obvious political significance: one would assume that the potentially revolutionary worker would have his eye on the behaviour of his own standard of living, not on the relative share of total output he shares with his fellow workers in proportion to their numbers.)

Unorthodox Theories of Distribution: Kalecki
The more unorthodox theories of distribution current at the present time arise from the two theoretical revolutions of the 1930s: the imperfect or monopolistic competition revolution, and the Keynesian Revolution. (The latter attribution is not strictly correct, since what is actually used in the Kaldor theory, specifically, is based more on the *Treatise on Money* than on the *General Theory*; but the *General Theory*, or that in combination with imperfect competition theory, may be fairly said to have been the inspiration of the work on distribution theory of a number of lesser writers.)

The Kalecki theory, as mentioned, was designed to explain the assumed constancy of relative shares. It starts from the basic equation of imperfect competition relating marginal to average revenue.

$$MR = AR\left(1 - \frac{1}{\eta}\right)$$

where η is the elasticity of demand for the product of the monopolistically competitive firm defined in Cambridge fashion with a positive sign. This can be rearranged into

$$\frac{AR - MR}{AR} = \frac{1}{\eta}$$

where the term on the right, which measures the ratio of the excess of average over marginal revenue to average revenue, can be defined following Kalecki and Lerner as 'the degree of monopoly'. It can be identified with the degree of monopolistic distortion of the market, though the welfare implications of such 'distortion' are not clear (pp. 33–34 above). Next, we substitute marginal cost for marginal revenue in the formula, using the profit-maximizing condition marginal costs equals marginal revenue. Marginal cost equals marginal variable cost (v) in the short run, and this consists of wages and raw materials. For a closed economy, which produces its own raw materials, aggregation would reduce raw materials to labour costs in the producing industries. Substituting unit values of products and raw materials in the previous equation, we obtain

$$\frac{p - v}{p} = \frac{1}{\eta}$$

or

$$v = p\left(1 - \frac{1}{\eta}\right).$$

Next we assume that in the short run variable costs are constant up to a capacity level of production (which we assume normally not to be reached). (Note the analogy to Stigler's theory of 'built-in flexibility' in the production function, arising from uncertainty, which makes the cost curve virtually flat in the neighbourhood of planned capacity production.) We can then interpret v in the formula as average variable cost, and

$$\frac{v}{p} = \left(1 - \frac{1}{\eta}\right)$$

as an equation determining the share of variable costs in total output. Finally, aggregating over the whole of the economy, and remembering that for a closed economy raw materials costs will be reducible to labour costs, we obtain a formula for labour's share in output,

$$w = \left(1 - \frac{1}{\bar{\eta}}\right)$$

where $\bar{\eta}$ is some sort of weighted average of the 'degree of monopoly' in the economy. Thus we get the result that labour's share is inversely related to the 'degree of monopoly'.

Unfortunately, for an open economy such as England, with which Kalecki was concerned, raw materials are imported and their price is determined in world markets; and an obvious fact of the 1930s was cyclical variations in their prices relative to wages. Hence while a constant degree of monopoly would ensure a constant share of wages plus raw materials' costs in total output, the fall of raw material prices in depressions and rise in booms would lead to a fall in labour's share in booms and rise in depressions; to overcome this theoretical flaw Kalecki was obliged to assume that the degree of monopoly rose in depressions and fell in booms.

The 'degree of monopoly' explanation of income distribution was and still is appealing to some people, because it carries the implication that distribution is a monopolistic phenomenon and determined by the behaviour of the capitalists. Reflection on the logical structure of the theory shows nothing of the sort, however; the elasticity of demand is not determined by the capitalists in a particular industry, since it is not a parameter of behaviour but a variable, and the precise value of it at the profit-maximizing point is determined by profit-maximization by entrepreneurs, while the underlying behaviour determining the demand expressed in the markets for products is a matter of consumer preferences, not of monopolistic firm behaviour. Further, while it may make some sense to regard the 'degree of monopoly' as a measure of the opportunities for profits confronting a firm in a particular industry, the notion of an aggregate community-wide degree of monopoly expressing the behaviour of capitalists in the aggregate makes no sense at all.

Contemporary theory along these lines has therefore dropped the concept of the degree of monopoly, and instead made use of the concept of determination of price by a standard mark-up on prime costs (in the process either assuming a closed economy or including imported raw materials in prime costs). This, it should be noted, does not really provide a theory of distribution — though with relatively constant raw material prices or prices fluctuating with the price of labour it does ensure constant shares — since there is no theory provided of the determination of the profit margin itself and usually no exploration of the consistency of a constant mark-up with the possibility of substitution between labour and capital and the need for equalization of the rates of return on capital among industries. It must therefore be regarded as a short-run descriptive theory of how businessmen behave in setting prices — and even in that context a great deal of empirical work on how businessmen actually behave in the short run contradicts their own explanations of their behaviour (e.g. discounts from list prices tend to vary with the short-run state of the market). The assumption that the capitalist class can arbitrarily determine the profit mark-up does much to confuse readers of Joan Robinson's *The Accumulation of Capital*; though it must be admitted that, in line with her analysis, insistence on excessively high profit margins may help to account for the stagnation usually alleged to be characteristic of the less developed countries. The assumption of a fixed profit margin is also characteristic of many contemporary models of inflation; but in that context it has the justification of representing an adjustment of money prices to money wage changes, presumably within a context of (simplified) marginal productivity determination of real wages and relative prices.

The important point to note about theories of distribution of this kind is that they represent an attempt to build a macro-economic distribution theory on micro-economic foundations without devoting adequate attention to the problems of aggregation. In particular, micro-economic analysis can assume availability of factors at a given price or according to a given money supply curve, whereas macro-economics has to recognize the overall constraints on available factor quantities.

Unorthodox Theories of Distribution: Kaldor

As already mentioned, the Kaldorian theory of distribution is based on the *Treatise* rather than the *General Theory*. The *General Theory* is strictly classical or neo-classical in its distribution theory, once allowance is made for the fact that in contrast to the neo-classical assumption of full employment of an existing labour force Keynesian theory assumes that the amount of employment provided for the existing labour force is determined by effective demand. But the mechanism is the same: employment varies relative to a fixed capital stock, the marginal productivity of labour in real terms falling as employment increases — though the assumption of a fixed money wage rate means that this influence appears as an increase in absolute money prices of goods with a fixed money wage level. As in the neo-classical theory of distribution previously discussed, whether labour's share rises or falls depends on the magnitude of the elasticity of substitution between labour and capital, or on the direction of change of the elasticity of total output with respect to labour input.

The Keynesian theory is based on the concept of the real output multiplier with respect to the amount of real investment. However, exactly the same mechanism can be used to produce a theory of the determination of income distribution rather than of output determination, on the same assumption that in equilibrium saving out of income must be equal to investment. What is required is the assumption that society is divided into two classes, 'workers' and 'capitalists', the latter having a higher marginal propensity to save than the former. Hence there is a monotonic relationship between the share of capital in national income; and the amount of investment relative to income fixes the distribution of income between the two income classes. This idea goes back to the *Treatise*'s concept of the 'widow's cruse' — the

more the capitalists invest, the more profits they receive to spend on investment, in the form of 'windfall' profits. It was picked up by Boulding in his
Reconstruction of Economics. But it was Kaldor who developed the use of it
in an attempt — very dubious, as I shall show — to explain the 'stylized fact'
of the constancy of the share of labour in national income.

The basic analysis is as follows:

$$Y = W + P$$

where Y is national income, W wages, and P profits,

$$I = S$$

(saving equals investment in equilibrium),

$$S = S_w + S_p$$

(total saving is the sum of saving by workers and saving by capitalists),

$$S_w = s_w . W$$

$$S_p = s_p . P$$

$$s_p > s_w$$

(savings for each income group are proportional to its income, and capitalists save a higher proportion of income than workers.) Substituting,

$$I = s_p P + s_w W$$

$$= s_p P + s_w (Y - P)$$

$$= (s_p - s_w) P + s_w Y$$

$$\frac{I}{Y} = (s_p - s_w) \frac{P}{Y} + s_w$$

$$\frac{P}{Y} = \frac{1}{s_p - s_w} \frac{I}{Y} - \frac{s_w}{s_p - s_w}$$

$$\frac{W}{Y} = 1 - \frac{P}{Y} = \frac{s_p}{s_p - s_w} - \frac{1}{s_p - s_w} \frac{I}{Y}$$

Assuming that investment is independent of savings, there is full employment
and flexible prices, that $s_p \neq s_w$, and that $s_p > s_w$, the distribution of income
depends on the ratio of investment to national income, determined by the
capitalists. (The condition for stability of the system, it should be noted, is
$s_p > s_w$; this is necessary for a rise in the price of goods due to excess demand
created by more investment to increase savings by redistributing income
towards the capitalists.)

Kaldor's distribution theory can be represented very simply diagrammatically. See Diagram II, where aggregate savings are graphed against profits
as profits increase from zero to the total of output. The intersection of the
exogenously given total investment curve *II* with the *SS* curve determines
total profits, wages, and, hence, the share of labour in national income.
(Minimum and maximum profit levels could easily be inserted to represent

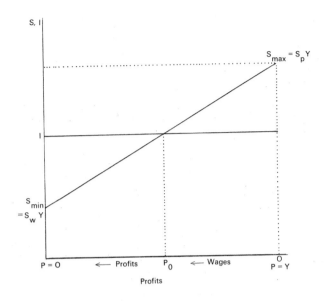

DIAGRAM II: KALDOR'S DISTRIBUTION THEORY

Kaldor's assumption, discussed below, that there are political limits on the acceptable range of income distribution determined by capitalists on the one hand and workers on the other.) Note the similarity of the diagram on the one hand to the familiar 'Keynesian cross' multiplier diagram, in which the intersection of a horizontal curve representing exogenous investment and an upward-sloping relation between saving and income determines the level of income, and on the other hand to the diagrams used previously in connection with the Borts analysis.

Note that

$$I/Y = \frac{dK}{dY}\frac{dY}{dt}\cdot\frac{1}{Y} = kG = s$$

where G is the growth rate, k is the marginal capital-output ratio, and s the total savings ratio, so that the Harrod–Domar equation is satisfied; but in the Kaldor model the warranted growth rate adjusts to the natural through the distribution of income.

This theory was used by Kaldor in a fashion conventional to the 1940s and 1950s, to examine the viability of capitalism. The theory involved was that capitalism must satisfy both the workers and the capitalists. To satisfy the former purpose, it has to provide something equal to or above a minimum acceptable wage rate ($\bar{w}$), i.e. we must have

$$\frac{P}{Y} \leqslant \frac{Y - \bar{w}L}{Y}.$$

To satisfy the latter purpose, we must have either a rate of profit equal to or above a minimum acceptable to the capitalists (a 'risk premium') ($\bar{r}$), i.e.

$P/kY \geqslant \bar{r}$; or a minimum rate of profit on turnover (profits mark-up) corresponding to the degree of monopoly $(\bar{m})$, i.e. $P/Y \geqslant \bar{m}$. This framework of analysis, it may be noted, though quite common at the time, represents a pretty naïve economic analysis of the political problem of socialism versus fascism in the 1930s. From a contemporary point of view, the problem then was that monetary mismanagement caused the system to fail to produce incomes for both capitalists and workers according to their expectations of continuing conditions of high employment. The political question was whether the capitalists could preserve the system by resorting to fascist methods of economic organization, or whether the workers would overthrow it in favour of socialists methods of economic organization. The political model referred to deals with the frustration of expectations about how the system should perform in quite a different context, of full employment and the levels of real wages and the rate of return on capital; and postwar experience shows that in a context of economic growth relative shares soon cease to be an important political consideration, though they can easily become so again when growth is interrupted by external events or the resort of policy to deflation as a means of stopping inflation.

The crucial weakness in the Kaldor theory is that the capital-output ratio is assumed not to be influenced by the rate of profit, as is reflected in the writing of the equation $s = Gk = I/Y$. As previous analysis has shown, the capital-output ratio should be dependent on the profit rate through two routes: the influence of the rate of profit on the value of capital goods in terms of consumption goods, and the influence of the profit rate (rate of interest) on the choice between relatively more and relatively less capital-intensive techniques. In order to defend his model against criticism based on the marginal productivity theory, Kaldor was forced to deny the aggregate production function, first on the grounds that marginal productivity determined only a maximum level for wages, then, more sweepingly, by the assertion that an aggregate production function does not exist, that relative shares are determined by his theory, and that entrepreneurs batter production technique into consistency with relative factor availabilities through their direction of research and development expenditure in the creation of technological progress.

As a theory intended to explain the assumed constancy of relative shares in national income, the Kaldor model is subject to the crucial objection that it generates much more instability of relative shares than does the neoclassical model to which it is intended to be superior. In the latter model, as shown earlier, relative shares will be constant if the elasticity of substitution in the aggregate is unity, and will be relatively constant if the elasticity of substitution does not depart too far from unity in the downward direction. In the Kaldor model,

$$\frac{d(W/Y)}{d(I/Y)} = -\frac{1}{s_p - s_w}$$

and

$$\frac{I/Y}{W/Y} \frac{d(W/Y)}{d(I/Y)} = -\frac{I/Y}{s_p - (I/Y)}$$

Hence, the absolute change in the wages share must be a multiple of the change in the share of investment in national income, except in the limiting case where all profits are saved and all wages consumed, in which case the two shares change in the same ratio; and the elasticity of the wages share with respect to the investment share must be a number significantly different from zero. This implication is not observed in reality; if it were it would be inconsistent with the Kaldor assumption of constancy of relative shares as the 'stylized fact' to be explained.

Secondly, the Kaldor theory begs all the interesting questions of capital theory, through its assumption of a constant capital-output ratio. In contrast to the Harrod model, where the rate of return on capital is assumed to be fixed by liquidity preference from somewhere outside the model, the rate of profit is itself a variable, and should influence choices of production techniques in the production and use of capital equipment. According to the model, the rate of profit is

$$
\frac{P}{kY} = \frac{1}{s_p - s_w} G - \frac{1}{k}\left(\frac{s_w}{s_p - s_w}\right)
$$
$$
= \frac{1}{s_p - s_w}\frac{1}{k}\frac{I}{Y} - \frac{1}{k}\left(\frac{s_w}{s_p - s_w}\right)
$$

(If, following Joan Robinson and the Marxian tradition, we assume that all profits are saved and all wages consumed, we obtained the result that the profit rate is equal to the rate of growth; as previously mentioned, this will ensure the fulfilment of the golden rule in a neo-classical growth model.)

Third, the Kaldor model is inconsistent with marginal productivity theory. A fixed ratio of investment goods production to consumption goods production implies a distribution of income between the factors which will not necessarily produce an aggregate savings ratio equal to the investment-consumption-goods production ratio. Kaldor's reply, effectively, is 'so much the worse for marginal productivity theory'; but marginal productivity theory has been demonstrated to work in all sorts of micro-economic contexts, and there is no a priori reason to assume that it is superseded at the macro-economic level by a contradictory theory. Kaldor also argues that marginal productivity theory only sets a maximum to what workers can earn, and that they could be paid less; but this is a one-way argument, since his theory applied on this assumption might require that workers be paid more than their marginal productivity in order to equate aggregate savings with aggregate investment.

Kaldor also argues that the crucial difference between micro- and macro-economic theory is that capitalists are not subject to a budget constraint in their investment expenditure decisions. But this can mean either that income distribution will adjust so as to provide the real savings needed to finance their investment, which raises the same problems of consistency with marginal productivity theory, or that they can finance their investment by monetary inflation, which puts us in a different ball-park of inflationary cheating of the workers out of their real marginal product — and that raises the question of whether the wage-determination process will be quiescent under such sustained cheating. It should be added that, in normal general equilibrium analysis, investors are not subject to a budget constraint either, in the sense that each can borrow as much as he wants at a parametric rate of interest; but the interest rate adjusts so that the aggregate amount of resources entrepreneurs desire to borrow is equal to the aggregate amount that savers desire to lend. Kaldor's model simply ignores this influence of the interest rate on desired investment; and it is this which creates the conflict between his theory and the marginal productivity theory of distribution.

A fourth, and fairly obvious, defect of the Kaldor model is that it breaks down as soon as there are more income groups than two (corresponding to different preferences for the two goods produced by the system, investment goods and capital goods) or in general more income groups than differentiated commodities produced. Re-working the algebra, we have, assuming a third group of income-receivers in the economy in the form of rentiers,

$$S = s_w W + s_p P + s_r R$$

$$\frac{W}{Y} = \frac{s_p}{s_p - s_w} - \frac{1}{s_p - s_w} \frac{I}{Y} + (s_r - s_p) \frac{R}{Y}$$

Hence the share of labour cannot be determined from the investment ratio or rate of growth of the system unless we know the income share of the rentier group, and will vary with the income of that group. To complete the model, we need a separate theory of the rentier share.

A fifth defect of the Kaldor model is that, once any income-recipient group understands the Kaldor model, it can appropriate all of the social income to itself by appropriate choice of its savings ratio. Thus, in the simple model of two goods and two income groups described above, labour could appropriate all the social income by setting its savings ratio equal to the investment-income ratio chosen by the capitalists (if $s_w = I/Y$, P must be zero in the equation $I = s_p P + s_w W$). This criticism was put rather humourously by James Tobin, who assumed n classes of income recipients and n goods, the amounts of the latter produced being fixed and the income groups dividing their expenditures in fixed proportions. Denoting the fixed quantities of goods produced by y_i, the proportions of expenditure on the goods out of income by the different income groups by b_{ij}, where the first subscript denotes the income group and the second the commodity, and s_i is the income share of the i'th group, we have the system

$$b_{11} s_1 + b_{21} s_2 + \ldots b_{n1} s_n = y_1$$
$$\vdots \qquad \vdots \qquad \vdots \qquad \vdots$$
$$b_{1n} s_1 + b_{2n} s_n + \ldots b_{nn} s_n = y_n$$

Any group of income recipients that chooses to divide its expenditure among goods in the same ratio as they are produced will receive all of the social income. (The mathematical reason is that if one substitutes $b_{1i} = y_i/s_i$ on the left-hand side, the determinant has two identical columns for any column other than the first, in the process of solution by Cramer's rule, and so becomes a zero in the numerator of the expression for the income share of any other income group.)

17

ASPECTS OF THE THEORY OF PERSONAL INCOME DISTRIBUTION

Introduction

Most of the theory of income distribution presented in this course has been concerned with the functional distribution of income, i.e. its distribution among the factors of production. However, the Ricardian identification of units of factors with individuals belonging to social classes is no longer valid (if it ever was more than a reasonable approximation to reality). The personal distribution of income is its distribution among persons or among families (which it is makes a considerable difference, both because in the Western world the family has been gradually narrowing down to the nuclear unit of husband, wife, and pre-adult children, while other societies differ from the West in the extent to which the family goes beyond the nuclear family to include either or both of grandparents and young adult children, and also cousins and other relatives). In the framework of analysis employed so far, the personal or family distribution of income will be determined by the distribution of ownership of factors of production of the various kinds among the human units considered: the person or family typically both provides labour services to the market and owns property of one kind or another — the relative importance of the different income sources varying over the life-cycle of the person or family. Thus functional distribution may have little to do with personal distribution, and constancy of functional distribution (if it is observed in fact) does not necessarily entail constancy of personal distribution. (Efforts to change the personal or family distribution by policies at the micro-economic level may, however, affect functional distribution at the macro-economic level by introducing factor market distortions or altering the relative supplies of factors.)

The distribution of factor ownership among persons or families is determined at any time by the combined result of two major forces: inheritance, and investment in factor accumulation. Inheritance is usually identified with the inheritance of material property; but it is much more complex than that. It includes also genetic inheritance — the inheritance of intelligence, strength, good health, etc. — and cultural inheritance — knowledge imparted informally by parents to children, attitudes to work and towards the accumulation of human and material capital, responsibility, determination — and all sorts of other imaginable differences in characteristics among individuals. The late Frank H. Knight used to be extremely scornful of policies designed to decrease personal inequality by taxation of inherited wealth, on the grounds that no tax system could really effectively get at inequalities in genetic and cultural inheritances; and it is important to remember in that context, that parents have a choice between leaving their children material property, and leaving them a cultural inheritance through informal and formal education.

Investment is also a complex phenomenon, since it includes both the accumulation of material property through saving and investment, and the accumulation of human capital through formal education and on-the-job training. It further includes investment in the capacity to enjoy income: with the same material income, one person can be happy and another miserable, because the former has developed his tastes and income-spending skill to make the most of his income, unlike the other.

Inheritance and investment are, moreover, closely interlinked: a person from an educated family is more likely to take a long view of his decisions as regards optimal level of education, choice of career, and management of personal finances and savings plans, than one from a family of low educational level. This is one reason why public policy to reduce inequality or relieve poverty tends to stress educational investment in the disadvantaged, at public expense. It is also a reason why differences in personal or family incomes tend to persist, and even to widen, over generations, hence giving rise to social concern that probably would not exist if every individual at birth had an equal random chance of ultimately enjoying either a high or a low income.

Just as in the case of the functional distribution of income, where the apparent constancy of the share of labour has been considered to be a paradox requiring explanation, so in the case of personal distribution an apparent constancy of the size-distribution of incomes has been observed, first by Pareto and described by him as a law of distribution represented by a simple statistical formula connecting the proportion of the population receiving incomes below a certain level to their share in total income. This law, like the constancy of the labour share, has been found by subsequent research to fit the data much less well than the original statistical results indicated. In any case, the social implications of both laws are not obvious.

The personal distribution of income has attracted considerable social concern from time to time, usually in periods of business cycle recession when people's expectations of jobs and rising incomes are frustrated, but also occasionally in periods of prosperity when people's consciences can be touched by concern for their less affluent fellow-citizens. Two kinds of concern need to be distinguished, though they are often confused in the minds of the people who express them. One is concern about inequality, i.e. the dispersion of incomes about the mean; the other is concern about poverty, i.e. the existence of people whose incomes are below some minimum level considered to represent a decent or socially acceptable standard of living. These concerns stem from different views about the nature of the good society. Concern about inequality stems from a definition of the good society as one in which all citizens should be economically equal (in terms of income), regardless of productive contribution or non-contribution. Concern about poverty reflects a definition of the good society as one in which income inequalities due to different inheritances or capacity for useful work are accepted, subject to the society guaranteeing every citizen a decent minimum of subsistence.

These concerns are frequently expressed in extremely naïve terms, from the point of view of economics, as evidenced by the types of statistics used to validate the demonstration of inequality or of poverty. First, there are income and wealth accounting problems: income is usually defined as current cash income, to the exclusion both of real income received in kind and the utilization of capital accumulated in the past for financing current consumption; and wealth is usually identified with material property yielding an explicit flow of income (an exception is the value of owner-occupied housing property), no account being taken either of human capital or of the wealth-equivalent value of access to 'public goods' which are equally accessible to all. The statistics are usually taken on a cross-section basis at a point of time, thereby, — in the case of income distribution — neglecting the life-cycle aspects of changes in the income of particular individuals and the influence of returns on educational investments in the creation of human capital; in the case of wealth, by neglecting human capital and the substitution of material for human capital as the life cycle progresses. Further, cross-section aggregative data fail to get at the real questions about inequality and poverty, which concern whether the same individuals or families figure at the same points in the income or wealth distribution (high or low) over the lifetime of the individual or of several generations of a family. In general, analysis of these questions so far has neglected three important concepts of the Fisher tradition of analysis: income and capital as concepts interrelated through the rate of interest; the distinction between cash receipts and consumption, the latter and not the former constituting 'income' in the true sense; and the concept of the life-cycle profile of cash income, consumption, and saving and dissaving. It has also neglected the roles of probability and of choice under uncertainty in determining personal income distribution.

A Simple Fisherian Model of Measured Inequality With Actual Equality
Assume a society with a static population, in which all babies born have exactly the same natural capacities, and all adults do exactly the same work. The minute a baby is born, it goes into an orphanage for rearing. The orphanage is a strictly commercial proposition, which debits the child with the costs of its upkeep until it reaches the age of fifteen, at which point it becomes a member of the labour force. Between fifteen and twenty five, for one reason or another (a pre-adult level of physical strength, or lack of training-on-the-job), it earns a standard wage; from twenty-five to forty-five it earns a premium wage for muscle-power or skill; thereafter it earns only the standard wage, until it retires at age sixty-five, and it dies precisely at the age of seventy-five. In the course of its working life (which means effectively its period of premium earnings) it must both repay its debt to the orphanage and accumulate savings on which to live during its period of retirement. For simplicity, we assume that the rate of interest is zero in this economy, and that individuals consume exactly the same amount at every age of life. (The zero interest rate assumption has the advantage of making labour income the only income in the economy, cf. earlier discussion of the Modigliani–Ando–Brumberg model.)

Diagram I(a) shows the lifetime income and consumption profile of the individual in the economy: every individual goes through the same income-consumption and childhood–working adult–senior citizen life history, and all are exactly equal. But if we take a cross-section of the income distribution, it appears as in Diagram I(b), which permits us to make such shocking observations as 'the top $26\frac{2}{3}$ per cent of income-earners receive 60 per cent of the total income', and 'one third of the population received no income whatsoever'—gross inequality in the first case, widespread and shameful poverty in the second.

Diagram I(c) shows the age profiles of material capital, human capital and net wealth. In net terms, the individual's wealth declines steadily from a maximum in the cradle to a zero in the grave. Initially, his human capital is constant (because he cannot yet work) but his material capital becomes increasingly negative as he borrows from the orphanage to finance his consumption. Once he reaches his peak earning period, he converts human capital into debt repayment and ultimately asset accumulation against his retirement. Cross-section statistics would show approximately half the population in debt and half having positive material capital, and that '$26\frac{2}{3}$ per cent of the population own 69 per cent of the economy's (positive) wealth'—a grossly unequitable state of affairs indeed!

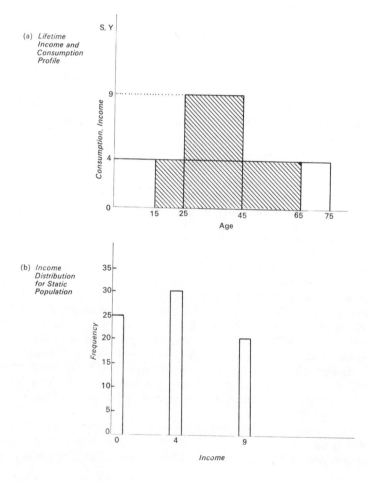

(a) Lifetime Income and Consumption Profile

(b) Income Distribution for Static Population

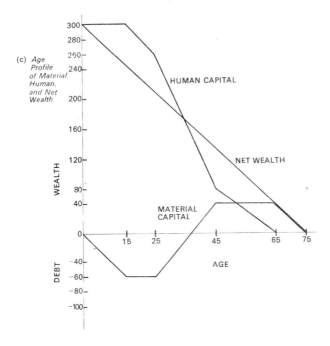

DIAGRAM I: HUMAN CAPITAL AND INCOME AND WEALTH DISTRIBUTION

Note that this model assumes that everyone is equal, and in contrast to many standard treatments, takes the whole present value of a worker's future earnings as a measure of his human capital (instead of the excess of those earnings over the wages of unskilled labour). If we were to introduce the assumption that production requires two kinds of workers, skilled and unskilled, and that skilled workers were trained up to the point where their extra contribution to output just paid for their training costs (consistently with the assumption of a zero interest rate), we would have still more inequality in the distribution of incomes as measured at a point of time. For example, consider a society of fifty unskilled workers who get 1000 credits a year each year between the ages of fifteen and sixty-five, and fifty skilled workers who get zero between the ages of fifteen and twenty-five (when they serve as apprentices), 1 500 credits per year between the ages of twenty-five and forty-five, and 1 000 credits per year between the ages of forty-five and sixty-five. At a zero interest rate, the unskilled and skilled jobs offer exactly the same life-time consumption possibilities; but the statistics will show the top 20 per cent of the working population receiving 30 per cent of the total income, and the bottom 10 per cent receiving no income at all.

Measures of Inequality
Studies of inequality of income distribution and changes in it over time typically use one or another standard statistic of dispersion. Usually a reduction in the statistic is taken to imply a reduction in inequality. Any such

statistic, however, incorporates implicitly a definition of the marginal social values of the incomes of individuals, and the implicit definition is frequently difficult to defend on rational economic grounds.

As an admittedly artificial example, consider a society consisting of three individuals of different incomes, such that two are below the average and one above (two 'poor', one 'rich'), and a measure of inequality by the average deviation of incomes from the mean (see Diagram II). Inequality can be

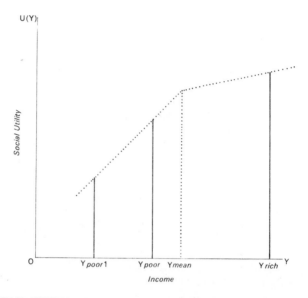

DIAGRAM II: INEQUALITY MEASURED BY AVERAGE DEVIATION FROM MEAN

reduced, on this measure, by taking money from the rich man and giving it to a poor man — but it does not matter which poor man gets it. Yet if it goes to the less poor man, so that the more poor man becomes relatively poorer in relation to him, it is by no means clear in any general sense that inequality has been reduced rather than increased. The measure, as shown in the diagram, involves attaching a lower social marginal utility to incomes above the mean than to incomes below the mean, but a constant marginal social utility to incomes on each side of the mean. If we postulated two rich men, one modestly rich and one filthy rich, a redistribution of income from the former to the latter would make no difference to the measure of inequality, though *a priori* most people would probably regard this as a socially undesirable redistribution.

Probability and Income Distribution
The observed apparent stability of personal distribution of income within society over considerable periods of time suggests a rigidity of the economic system in generating inequality and poverty, and also an inequity as among individual members of it. However, constancy of the observed distribution of income in cross-section is quite consistent both with individual persons

moving from one income group to another fairly frequently, and with individuals facing exactly the same income prospects. To demonstrate this simply, we assume that there are only three possible income groups in the economy; that between any two successive time periods an individual may either stay in the same income group or move to an adjacent one (restriction to only one step-wise move simply makes the algebra easier); and that his movement is determined by probabilities fixed by the economic system such that p_{ij} is the probability of his moving from i to j and $\sum_j p_{ij} = 1$.

Suppose that n_{it} is the number of individuals in group i at time t. Then we construct the dynamic system.

$$n_{1,t+1} = p_{11}n_{1,t} + p_{21}n_{2,t}$$

$$n_{2,t+1} = p_{12}n_{1,t} + p_{22}n_{2,t} + p_{32}n_{3,t}$$

$$n_{3,t+1} = p_{23}n_{2,t} + p_{33}n_{3,t}$$

It can be shown that this system will converge on an equilibrium set of the n_i's, which can be determined by inserting n_i without the t subscript into the equations. We obtain

$$n_3 = \frac{p_{23}}{p_{32}} n_2$$

$$n_1 = \frac{p_{21}}{p_{12}} n_2$$

$$n_2 = n \bigg/ \left(1 + \frac{p_{23}}{p_{32}} + \frac{p_{21}}{p_{12}}\right),$$

where $n = n_1 + n_2 + n_3$ is the total number of individuals.

(This involves the flows of people between adjacent groups being the same in both directions.) The point is that from a stochastic process in which anyone in an income group has the same chance as anyone else of moving to an adjacent group one can derive a determinate aggregate distribution of incomes by size classes. This is, of course, purely a statistical approach; it is quite conceivable that different individuals in the same size group have different probabilities of moving, some a zero probability, so that instead of everyone moving at random through the different income groups and having the same expectation of average income (in the very long run) of

$$\frac{n_3 w_3 + n_2 w_2 + n_1 w_1}{n_1 + n_2 + n_3},$$

where the w_i are the group incomes, each income group contains a 'hard core' of permanent inhabitants and there is genuine inequality.

Choice and the Income Distribution Under Certainty

One of the important aspects of personal income distribution frequently neglected by social critics is the influence on the distribution of income among persons of their own private choices among income-earning alternatives; a related aspect is the effects of taxation on these choices. The most important relevant factors have been discussed previously; here it is only necessary to recapitulate and bring out the implications of taxation.

The important thing about taxation is that if applied strictly proportionally to all income (and this may require 'loss offsets' where income is negative for some period) it will reduce income after tax in the same proportion, regardless of the shape of the age-income profile, so that two income streams with the same initial or gross present value will continue to have the same present value. If, however, not all income is subject to tax; or if the tax is proportional to income only above a certain exemption limit, some occupations carry income at times below the exemption level and there is no loss offset or equi-proportional 'negative income tax'; or if the tax rises progressively with income (proportional income taxation above an exemption limit being a special case of this), income taxation will discriminate in favour of choice of occupations yielding income streams either composed disproportionately of non-taxable constituents or less variable over time, and vice versa. If we disregard the possibility of peculiar income effects, a full treatment of which would also require analysis of the influence on work choices of benefits provided by government and financed by taxation — the analytical consequences are easy enough to work out — this will mean in long-run equilibrium that the occupations discriminated against will have to pay a relatively higher cash or expected cash income than those that tax discrimination favours. Hence, observed inequality among incomes measured at a point in time will increase. However, because the higher relative incomes in the disfavoured occupations will raise the relative costs of production of the goods they produce, the relative number of people in these occupations will tend to fall (again ignoring peculiar income effects) so that the effects on the standard statistical measures of inequality of income distribution will be uncertain.

(a) *Non-Pecuniary Advantages*
First, almost since the beginning of economics, it has been recognized that choices among occupations are determined by a balancing of pecuniary advantages (cash income) against non-pecuniary advantages and disadvantages. The individual choosing among occupations will choose that with the greatest total (in terms of utility) of pecuniary and non-pecuniary advantages; and competition among individuals will tend to equalize the marginal net advantages among occupations.

In this connection, we may contrast two types of society, one with very strong and homogeneous ideas about the relative desirabilities of different types of employment, and the other with strong but highly heterogeneous ideas on the same subject. We would expect that, in the first society, there would be very substantial differences among measured cash incomes, since the undesirable occupations would have to pay enough cash income above that paid by the desirable occupations to compensate those who adopted those occupations for the dissatisfaction they experienced from being in the occupation; whereas in the second society, people would allocate themselves among occupations according to their own tastes and, instead of wide differences among individual incomes correlated with social attitudes towards particular jobs, we would find a tendency towards equality of incomes, but also a segregation of the population into those who traditionally did one kind of job and those who traditionally did another (the tradition resting on personal tastes). This contrast between the two types of society provides a reason for expecting inequality in the distribution of personal incomes to fall as society becomes more democratic, more egalitarian, and more materialistic: the less cohesive society is in its ranking of occupations by social desirability, the more likely it is that incomes will be equalized (for the same skill level) but also the more likely it is that different categories of the population will be segregated among different types of jobs according to differences in their preferences among occupations. The student may speculate on whether equal incomes combined with segregation constitutes a more just society than one in which the high incomes go to those who violate the mores of society, and who are likely to be members of minority groups; turning the problem the other way around, the student may speculate on the effects on the cohesiveness of society of societal attitudes that result in above-normal rewards for those who are prepared to violate the society's standards of ethical behaviour. (In an earlier period the manufacturers and sellers of beer, and now the 'pushers' of marijuana, have provided a case in point. The Mafia is another example.)

We now turn to the effects of income taxation. It is clear that, in so far as income taxation is based on cash income only, to the neglect of non-pecuniary advantages or disadvantages of particular occupations, it will bias the choices of the population towards occupations that provide non-pecuniary advantages. This in turn means that those occupations that compensate through higher cash incomes for non-pecuniary disadvantages will have to raise the compensation offered relative to the compensation offered by those occupations with considerable non-pecuniary advantages. There will be a greater difference in measured incomes among occupations offering non-pecuniary advantages and non-pecuniary disadvantages respectively than previously; but whether the measured inequality of income distribution increases or decreases depends on the net balance of this effect and the effect of the higher cost of providing goods whose production involves non-pecuniary disadvantages in reducing the number of people employed in producing such goods.

(b) *Human Capital*
With a perfect capital market in borrowing and lending for the creation of human capital, competition would drive the earnings (net of interest payments on capital invested) of skilled or educated and unskilled or uneducated labour to equality (at least at the margin). Measured gross earnings taken in cross-section at a period of time would, however, show a pattern of inequality of incomes determined by the inequality of educational investment costs among occupations, inequality which would include the effects of differences both in tuition costs and in length of training period. Only if capital markets were imperfect, in the sense that individuals had to depend either on the possession of material wealth or on borrowing at interest rates above normal market rates for material investment, would there be a possibility of genuine inequality among individuals. In this case (see Chapter 13) the individual's decision between unskilled and skilled occupations, or

between careers requiring more and less educational attainment, would depend on his preference system as between present and future consumption; those with the lowest marginal rates of time preference (given their combination of directly available resources and their preference systems) would be the ones who opted for the more skilled or educationally-demanding jobs. However, the results might not be rents (above the value of the raw labour and the capital invested in educating it) for the more skilled or educated part of the population. Instead, there might result the analogue of the job segregation discussed above, in which those with inherited wealth or with high-income parents became the skilled or educated components of the working force and those without family resources remained the unskilled component, but the rate of return on educational investment was the same as — and might even be less than — that on investment in material capital. The empirical evidence provided by Becker and others strongly suggests that this is the case: the measured rate of return on education, both private and social (see below on this distinction), is more or less comparable to the rate of return on material capital; but skilled or educated people tend to come from high-education high-income families (the educational level achieved by the mother appears to be an important influence here), so that the educational system promotes the persistence of social but not (or at least not so much) economic inequality.

Turning to the influence of taxation, there are two sorts of problems. First, if we consider taxation simply as a means of raising revenue for the state, a progressive tax system will reduce the present value of careers requiring an education and a shorter earning life compensated for by higher earnings during working life, as compared with careers requiring less or no education and permitting an earlier start on a career yielding lower earnings per unit of calendar time. Hence, observed gross personal earnings at a cross-section of time should vary more widely among individuals in the presence than in the absence of a progressive income tax. What happens to measures of inequality of income distribution, however, will depend on the precise definition of the measure and on the conflicting effects of greater dispersion of individual incomes and a lower demand for educated labour due to the higher relative cost of its services. (Again, we ignore peculiar income effects.)

Second, assume (as is typically the case) that education is wholly or partially subsidized by the government out of general taxation of incomes imposed on one or the other progressive bases mentioned earlier (proportional tax above an exemption less than the average unskilled wage, or taxation at progressively higher rates as income rises), and that access to educational opportunities is rationed by some minimum level of academic performance. Then those who qualify for education will pay less than the full costs of their education (because of the tax contributions of the non-educated). The result at the micro-economic level will be an incentive to invest private resources in enabling student family-members to pass the educational qualification (thereby tending to perpetuate social inequality); and at the macro-economic level to lead to over-investment in education, since such investment will tend to be pushed to the point where the marginal private rate of return which, by assumption, exceeds the marginal social rate of return because of the public subsidy to education, is equal to the private rate of return on material capital investment.

This proposition, however, is subject to two qualifications. First, the total number of students may be rationed out by variation of the level of educational attainment required, and the numbers allowed to acquire educational qualifications may create a scarcity rent equal to or greater than the difference between marginal private and marginal social return. (However, if we recognize the possibility of private investment in obtaining educational qualifications, this investment at the margin will proceed to the point where net marginal private rate of return on educational investment is equalized with the private rate of return on other types of private investment, and we may have the worst of all possible worlds: under-allocation of resources to educational investment, produced by raising the resource costs of education above what is socially necessary by artificial restriction of educational opportunity, and the consequential private incentive to invest resources in acquiring access to that opportunity.)

Second, an educated person may convey 'externalities' on society not captured in his own private income. Whether such externalities exist in a society in which, as is typical of Western societies, almost all the population is required by law to finish high school and so acquire literacy, numeracy, and a good smattering of social culture, and the difference between the 'educated' and the 'uneducated' is a college and possibly a postgraduate degree, is a question currently being hotly debated in the literature. Three considerations arise in this context.

(1) Many college-level courses are fairly strictly vocational, and their graduates acquire little, if anything, that contributes to the well-being of their fellow-citizens other than through the market.

(2) It is not clear that the political and social activities of college students and graduates create a net social benefit, especially as a college education tends to endow them with a contempt for both the economic and social system into which they must fit upon graduation and for the practical experience of the formally un-college-educated people who have to take the decisions for a large part of the private sector of the economy. This point is particularly relevant to less developed countries, where the college graduate is trained in urban ways and tends to have a strong contempt for the illiterate farmer on whom basically he depends for his income. In addition, less developed countries tend to over-allocate resources to higher education, so that the higher-educated find their expectations of future cash income and social status frustrated in reality, and tend to take out their frustration in criticism of the society and in the organization and support of disruptive radical political movements.

(3) In so far as there are social externalities from the presence of higher-educated people in society, these may be captured within the utility functions of the educated people concerned, and constitute part of their expected return from the process of education. That is, a person may take pride in the fact that though his cash income is low, by comparison say with that of a business executive, he is more valuable to society as a teacher, doctor, lawyer, politician, or minister of religion than the business executive. This motivation is in fact recognized in our society by the concern of business men

H

with the 'social responsibility' of business — which involves the sacrifice of potential profit for the sake of a conception of the social good dictated by other members of society — and their efforts as individuals to take part in community and public activities requiring a great deal of time at the expense either of their leisure or of their obligations to their employers. The theory of the impact of income taxation applied only to measured cash income in the presence of non-pecuniary advantages and disadvantages of various occupations suggests, in fact, that society will tend to be relatively over-supplied with people anxious to do it good in one way or another, as con-trasted with people who are concerned only to maximize their monetary returns from economic activity. (My own long experience of British society suggests that an important causal factor in that society's low productivity and relatively slow rate of growth is the persistent draining of the most talented college graduates into the civil service, politics, and the communica-tions industries, together with the desire of the less talented people who go into industry to acquire knighthoods or other (higher or lower) public honours either by devoting themselves to part-time public service or by diserving their shareholders in order to serve some politically-dictated neces-sity for selling their products at a price below full cost including reasonable profits — the latter most noticeably in the case of export contracts under-taken at a loss in order to defend an overvalued exchange rate. The man who, quite honestly under the circumstances, signed the contract for aircraft engines that bankrupted Rolls Royce, because it contained no inflation escalation clause, was awarded a knighthood.)

Uncertainty of Income Prospects and Differing Attitudes Towards Risk
If different occupations involve differing degrees of uncertainty about income prospects, the distribution of income as measured on a cross-section basis will reflect both the effects of the riskiness of the outcomes of occupa-tional choices and the effects of the attitudes of the population towards the assumption of the risks of uncertain outcomes involved.

Here we should note Knight's distinction between risk and genuine uncertainty: risk is 'insurable', in the sense that the probabilities of various outcomes are known in advance and, by pooling enough risky opportunities, the actuarial value of the outcome can be reduced to a 'certainty equivalent'; true uncertainty permits no such calculation, the outcome of any choice or combination of choices being genuinely incalculable. This distinction is the foundation of Knight's theory of profits, which in his view result from the undertaking of genuinely uncertain opportunities (involving the hiring of factors at contractually agreed rates of payment) depend on the supply of people willing to take on uncertain prospects and the accuracy in direction of error of their 'hunches', and may turn out in the aggregate to yield net positive or net negative profits for society as a whole, depending on whether there is a relative undersupply of people who turn out to have correctly foreseen chances of excess of revenue over contractual factor payments or relative oversupply of people who have underestimated the likelihood of an excess of contractual factor payments over prospective revenues. (The latter case is exemplified by Adam Smith's proposition that there will tend to be an oversupply of lawyers, because prospective lawyers are attracted to the profession by the high earnings of a few successful practitioners; also by Knight's example of the restaurant business, to which many people are attracted by the belief that they are good cooks or experts in popular-appeal restaurant décor; and in contemporary times by the franchise business in specialist restaurants, motels, and dry-cleaning and other establishments, to which people are attracted by the belief that they have above-average managerial ability.)

Analysis of cases of genuine uncertainty in Knight's sense, in which rational calculation is by definition impossible, is a task for the social psychologist, anthropologist, or more broad-ranging economic historian, rather than for the economic theorist. Here we follow Friedman (whose work in this respect followed Friedman and Savage's explanation of why people are prepared both to gamble on actuarially disadvantageous terms and to buy insurance against risk at a net cost to themselves) in assuming that different occupations involve different risks with different but known probabilities of alternative possible outcomes (not uncertain outcomes in Knight's sense), and that individual choices among occupations differentiated in this way are based, not on the actuarial expectation of income from these occupations, but on the actuarial expectation of utility from them. (For this purpose, in contrast to the theory of choice under absolute certainty, it is necessary to assume that the relation between income and utility is a cardinal and not simply an ordinal relationship.) The choices made will therefore depend on the precise shape of the utility-cash income relationship, and specifically on whether the marginal utility of income diminishes as income rises (in which case people will be 'risk-averters') or whether it rises as income rises (in which case they will be 'risk-lovers'). Note that the original Friedman–Savage analysis explained the co-existence of gambling and the purchase of insurance by assuming a utility function such that the marginal utility of income increased in the immediate neighbourhood of current income, but decreased for large positive or negative changes in income from the current level.

For diagrammatic simplicity, we assume that an individual has only two choices among alternatives: a certain income of y_0, and a fifty–fifty chance of incomes of y_{-1} and y_{+1}, which income alternatives yield a mathematical expectation of income of $\frac{1}{2}y_{-1} + \frac{1}{2}y_{+1} = y_0$. The individual's choice among them, however, is based on his expected utility from the two alternative income possibilities; that is, he compares

$$U(y_0) \text{ with } \tfrac{1}{2}U(y_{-1}) + \tfrac{1}{2}U(y_{+1}),$$

and chooses the certainty income y_0 over the probability $\frac{1}{2}y_{-1} + \frac{1}{2}y_{+1}$ if the expected utility from the former exceeds that from the latter, and vice versa. The result obviously depends on the relation between utility and income. This is illustrated in Diagrams IIIa–c, which are drawn on the stated assumption of a choice between y_0 and a fifty–fifty chance of y_{-1} and y_{+1}.

Diagram IIIa illustrates the original Friedman–Savage explanation of the existence of gambling and insurance. With initial income y_0 and the availability of a gamble involving equal chances of an increase in income to y_{+1} and a decrease of income to y_{-1}, the individual will gamble, because the expected utility from the gamble (U_0^e) exceeds the expected (certain) utility

218

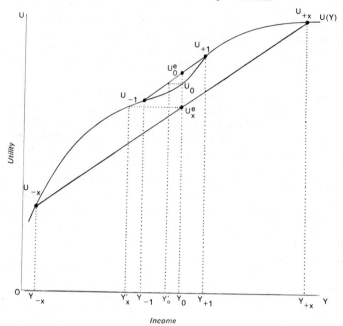

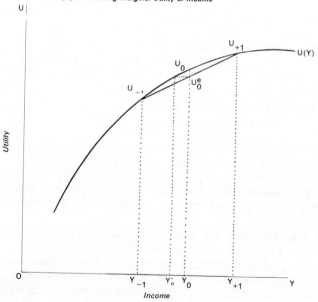

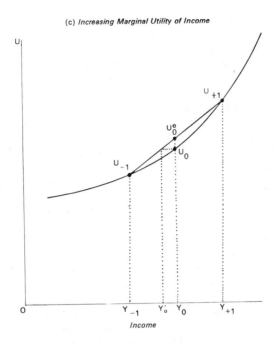

(c) *Increasing Marginal Utility of Income*

DIAGRAM III: CHOICE UNDER UNCERTAINTY

from not gambling (U_0). In these circumstances, the individual will be willing
to pay $y_0 - y'_0$ for the privilege of gambling, since this payment will make
his expected utility the same whether he gambles or not. These results follow
from the fact that over the range of income variation relevant to the gambling
opportunity his marginal utility of income is rising, so that a fair chance of
income variation yields a higher expected utility than its certainty equivalent.
However, for a large enough income gamble (y_{-x} versus y_{+x}) the expected
utility U_x^e is less than the certainty-equivalent utility expectation U_0, and
the individual will be willing to pay (buy insurance) at a cost $y_0 - y'_x$ in order
to avoid having to gamble. The reason is that over this range of income
variation the marginal utility of income (globally) is diminishing, so that
certainty yields a higher expected utility than risk. Diagrams IIIb and c
assume constant instead of varying curvature of the relationship between
utility and income, and contrast the effects of diminishing and increasing
marginal utility of income ('risk aversion' versus 'risk loving') on the choice
between certain and risky income prospects. Diagram IIIb shows that an
individual with a diminishing marginal utility of income (a 'risk-averse'
person) will always choose a certain income prospect over a risky one with
the same actuarial value (expected income), and will be willing to pay
$y_0 - y'_0$ in order to avoid taking risk. Diagram IIIc shows that an individual
with an increasing marginal utility of income (a 'risk-lover') will always
choose a risky over a certainty-equivalent alternative income opportunity
with the same actuarial value, and will be willing to pay a premium up to
$y'_0 - y'_0$ in order to undertake the risk.

The implications for income distribution (assuming that individuals are either risk-averters or risk-lovers, but do not change from one to the other as the size of the income gamble increases) are as follows. In a society composed of risk-averters, the average income earned in the more risky occupations must be higher than that earned in the certainty-income occupations. Hence there must be higher incomes earned by both the successful and the unsuccessful entrants to risky occupations than would occur in a risk-indifferent society, and the income distribution must be skewed to the right, there being a larger difference between the incomes actually received by the successful risky-occupation-undertakers, and a smaller difference between incomes earned by the unsuccessful risky-occupation undertakers, and the incomes received by the non-risky-occupation undertakers, than would occur in a risk-indifferent society. However, since the average income of risk-takers has to be higher than that of non-risk-takers, this will reduce the relative proportion of the total population that can be employed in risky occupations, and the two forces of biased dispersion of incomes and smaller numbers in risky occupations will work in opposite directions as regards the usual statistical measures of inequality of income distribution, so that the effects on these measures will be uncertain.

On the other hand, in a society composed of risk-lovers, there will be a smaller difference between the incomes of successful risk-takers, and a larger difference between the incomes of unsuccessful risk-takers, and the incomes of non-risk-takers, than would prevail in a risk-indifferent society. The income distribution would tend to be skewed to the left. However, such a society would have relatively more people engaged in risky occupations, and the effect of this fact combined with the larger difference between the incomes of unsuccessful risk-takers and non-risk-takers than between the incomes of successful risk-takers and non-risk-takers on the usual standard statistical measured of inequality of income distribution would again be problematical.

We now turn to the effects of income taxation. Clearly, if income tax is strictly proportional to income, the net expected returns from risky and certainty-of-income occupations will remain equal, and any effects of the tax have to depend on income effects on the willingness to assume risk. (If risk-aversion increases as income diminishes, income inequality as measured by dispersion of actual incomes will increase with the rate of income tax, and vice versa.) If we disregard income effects of this kind, and assume a progressive income tax system, the average gross-of-tax income from the more risky occupations will have to increase relative to the gross-of-tax income from the certain-income occupations, and the observed inequality of gross-of-income-tax incomes will increase, as measured by the dispersion between high and low gross incomes. But this will entail a relative decrease (on normal assumptions) in the number of people demanded in risky occupations, and the net effect of these two conflicting forces on the measured inequality of income distribution (gross or net, i.e. before or after tax) is problematical.

Concluding Remarks

The most important conclusion that emerges from the economic analysis of the personal or family distribution of income is that, in a very broad sense and subject to inequalities of initial circumstances (which may be very important, in spite of social efforts to remedy such inequalities through public policy, in the form especially of social transfers to poor families with children and through subsidies to education that disregard parental circumstances), the distribution of measured income at a point in time is to an important extent determined by individual choice among opportunities that yield both different combinations of cash income and non-pecuniary advantages, and different profiles of cash income over time. And this choice is influenced heavily by the prevailing system of income and property taxation, which may promote private choices undesirable from a social point of view. Individuals may be equal in their opportunities, but unequally treated by the tax system according to the choices they make; and their tax-influenced choices may be inimical to the social good, since the tax system discriminates in favour of leisure as against productive effort, or against educational attainment and in favour of an early start on a cash-income-earning career in the productive system of society, or against risk-taking. Probably the major problem in designing a just economic society is to design a tax and income reward system that will encourage people to maximize their contribution to the productive effort of society (including both physical production and the generation of cultural and other externalities) and forestall them from choosing to retire from productive contribution into a rentier capacity that gives them an income without obliging them or inducing them to invest further effort in work for society's benefit.

18

INEQUALITY OF INCOME DISTRIBUTION AND THE POVERTY PROBLEM

Introduction

In the previous chapter, it was mentioned that there are two possible sources of concern about the personal distribution of income, which do not amount to the same thing: concern about inequality in the personal distribution of income, which may exist even if no-one is actually poor by generally-accepted social standards, and concern about the prevalence of poverty, which may exist even if incomes are not very unequally distributed among individuals. These concerns reflect different philosophies of the 'good society' and indicate different types of social policies to move towards such a society, though the differences are often obscured by concentration of both philosophies on the low-income groups in society.

In the United States, beginning around 1963, there was a rise of concern about poverty in the population, leading to the announcement of a 'war on poverty' and to the Economic Opportunity Act of 1964. The emergence of this concern had certain striking economic similarities with the previous occasion of American concern about poverty under President Roosevelt in the 1930s. Roosevelt found one-third of the nation in poverty that should be remedied by social action; President Johnson found one-fifth. In each case, the finding of poverty of a nationally shameful kind followed a period of prolonged recession (much less serious in the case of President Johnson than in the case of President Roosevelt) during which real incomes may be assumed to have fallen well below the expected trend. This suggests that there is a causal relation between the downswing of a relatively severe depression and the upsurge of concern about poverty, the upsurge of concern being motivated less by Christian feeling on the part of the majority middle class for the poor who are always with us than by the uneasy feeling on their part that they are, through no fault of their own, poorer than they expected or deserve to be. (There is a well-documented relationship historic-ally between the downswing of the business cycle and the upswing of religious revival movements, the psychology of which is equally simple to explain.) Be that as it may, the mid-1960s concern about poverty as a national problem has led to considerable analysis of it with the aid of the techniques of the economic theory of income distribution.

To begin with, it is necessary to arrive at a definition of poverty. To the economist, such a definition is in principle simple: poverty consists in having insufficient spendable resources to maintain a standard of living deemed by some standard to be adequate for civilized survival. And it carries with it the simple policy recommendation, at variance with the recommendation of most social philosophers and poverty experts, 'don't come yourself, just

send money'. (The non-economists view poverty as a sociological phenomenon requiring the administrations of social workers rather than the mere
dispensing of cash.) But such a definition, while satisfactory in principle,
necessarily raises problems. First, there is the question of what is an adequate
standard of living, falling below which indicates poverty. The definitions are
set by social workers, and show a strong tendency to rise over historical
time more or less proportionally to the average income of society. In the
United States, over the past hundred years or so, the generally accepted
poverty standard as revised from time to time by social workers has been
approximately half the average income per head. In the United Kingdom,
researchers repeating Rowntree's famous work on poverty in the city of
York for the immediate postwar II period found that by Rowntree's pre-war
standards there were virtually no poor left in the city; so they hastily revised
his standard so as to create an adequate showing of poverty in the period
they studied. Apart from the definition of poverty, there is the question of
measuring it; this involves on the one hand the definition of the spending
unit whose poverty or otherwise is to be assessed, the general tendency
being that the larger the family unit is defined to be the smaller is poverty
as measured (because the typical nuclear family passes through a stage of
youthful struggle to make ends meet into a stage of middle-aged affluence
and then into a stage of penurious retirement, whereas if all generations of
the family — parents, young or middle-aged married couples, and children —
are lumped together in one reckoning the average will pass the test of non-
poverty). On the other hand it involves the measurement of spending
power: both young people and retired parents living independently tend
to receive subventions respectively from their parents and from their
children, and young people can borrow against their future income prospects
whereas old people can live on their accumulated savings, neither source of
spending power appearing in the usual statistical measurements of 'income'.
The question of actual family size to be supported from a given income is
also important, as is the question of dwelling location: the Council of
Economic Advisors made a big mistake in 1964 in defining the poverty
line at $3,000 per year per family, a definition which led it to overlook both
the influence of family size on the prevalence of poverty (and especially to
overlook the prevalence of poverty among unmarried female negro heads
of households) and the influence of high urban rents in causing poverty
among people who, had they lived in the country, would have been accounted
well off by comparison with their neighbours.

These questions apart, the fact that the definition of poverty is not a matter
of objective specification of minimum cost of physical survival but of subjective specification of what money it takes to lead a life considered socially
decent means that the definition of the poverty line keeps rising over time as
average income per head rises, so that one cannot rely on the general progress
of society to remedy poverty. Instead, the reduction or elimination of poverty
requires a reduction in the inequality of distribution of income, raising the
incomes of the lowest-income groups relative to those of the highest-income
groups. This in turn means that poverty so defined can only be reduced or
eliminated if general economic progress raises the share of productive
assets owned by the initially lower-income groups at the expense of the share

of the initially higher-income groups. There is nothing in the theory of economic growth to suggest that growth will be biased in this direction, though it does perhaps signify something that, whereas Roosevelt found a third of the American nation in poverty, Johnson found only a fifth—but a cynic might interpret these figures merely as showing that Roosevelt wanted to dramatize the problem to the electorate whereas Johnson wanted to prove that it was not too large to be manageable. Consequently, poverty will not cure itself through economic progress; there are only two broad ways to cure it: redistribution of income from the rich to the poor through the fiscal mechanism, and redistribution of property (the source of income) from the rich to the poor, either directly or, more acceptably, through public investment in increasing the human capital of the poor, e.g. by public education, retraining programmes, etc.

Growth Models and Poverty
Assuming that the poverty standard involves a fixed minimum of command over goods and services, the question arises as to how economic growth will affect the proportion of the population in poverty. Consider first the aggregative models of economic growth discussed in previous chapters. On the one hand, there is the Malthusian-Ricardian model. According to this model, population breeds to the level of subsistence, and there is no hope for growth to relieve poverty unless the poor can be persuaded to raise their minimum subsistence level to something above the poverty line. Malthus and his followers preached abstinence from marriage to begin with and from sex to follow. (It is an interesting reflection that the first birth control movement, in the early nineteenth century, was a movement to relieve the poverty of the working class; the second one, in the late nineteenth century and early twentieth, was a movement to relieve middle-class women from the dreary obligations of child-bearing and consequent second-rate-citizenship; it is interesting too, that the contemporary movement is again one designed to raise the subsistence level of the working class, both in the underdeveloped countries and in the ghettoes of the United States.)

On the other hand, there are the contemporary growth models. According to these models, which assume an exogenously given growth rate of the labour force, wages per worker tend to rise towards a level set by the accumulation of capital relative to labour and the equilibrium ratio of capital to labour on the equilibrium growth path, and to rise on a trend path per worker to the extent that there is Harrod-neutral technical progress. In terms of these models, poverty, if defined by a fixed level of consumption per head, should be eliminated eventually; but if poverty is defined in relation to average income per head, it will become a permanent feature of the economy, though the proportion of the poor may be larger or smaller depending on the characteristics of the growth model.

Turning to micro-economic approaches to the theory of economic growth, T. W. Schultz has stressed the question of the incentives that the economy offers to people to investment in the augmentation of their human capital and the acquisition of educational and other skills. A general characteristic of economic development in the twentieth century has been that human skills and education have accumulated without appreciably driving down the rates of return on human capital investment — in other words, technological progress has created a relatively expanding market for human capital, and permitted people to elevate themselves out of poverty by investing in such capital. This is a 'stylized fact' — there is no more fundamental explanation of it, though students may like to speculate on one, and some observers have raised the question whether the tendency will continue, or whether in future the education of more and more students to increasingly higher educational levels will simply result in a reduction in the rate of return in educational investment and a rise in the educational and gentility level of the poor.

A further point emphasized by Schultz, and worth mentioning, is that measured poverty is to some extent a consequence of voluntary choice, and that choices which make people better off in terms of utility may make them worse off in terms of measured income. A particular case in point is the 'undoubling' of families: if people are poor enough, unmarried sons and daughters have to live at home and make do with their share of the family accommodation and living space; similarly, widowed parents can only be supported by provision of a room in their married children's homes. As incomes rise, children prefer to set up independent establishments even before they are married, and retired parents prefer an independent room or apartment of their own to more luxurious but freedom-restricted accommodation with their married offspring. When peoples' incomes are measured on a per household basis, even allowing for the number of people supported by the family income, the multi-generational family unit appears to be affluent whereas the single-generation unit frequently appears to be poor by statistical standards. A further point in this connection is that the greater freedom of divorce in contemporary times, and the greater opportunities for women to earn an adequate income to support themselves and their children, albeit with financial stringency, have led to an increase in the relative number of households with female heads which by statistical standards fall below the poverty line. In a significant sense, statistical poverty may be the price of freedom, privacy, and independence, and hence its measured existence may represent an improvement and not a deterioration of the condition of mankind. Of course, this conclusion does not amount to a contention that poverty does not exist, only to a warning that measured poverty may not be a measure of the constraints of the economic system on human liberty.

A Classification of the Sources of Poverty

Poverty can be simply defined as inadequacy of income receipts to support a standard of life considered socially to be decent. This brings into the question the relation between the income earned by the family unit and the size of the family supported. The family can in this connection be conceived of as a utility factory selling productive services in the factor markets in order to earn income to spend on satisfying its wants for utility-yielding goods and services. This in turn suggests a broad classification of the sources of poverty into two sorts, corresponding to the size of the family relative to its income-earning opportunities on the one hand and the value of the services of its income-yielding assets in the market place on the other.

The first type of poverty is associated with an excessive number of people dependent on the earning capacity of the family unit for their sustenance and support. This type of poverty is due on the one hand to the system of free enterprise in the supply of labour, which makes the family's spending power a function of the productive services it can supply and not of its need for economic support, and on the other hand to various cultural restrictions on rational family planning and weaknesses in the legal system governing the economic claims of mothers on the fathers of their children. If there were a fully rational and adequately informed free enterprise system in the formation of families, supported by adequately enforced rules of contract between spouses, the size of the family would be an economic choice variable governed by preferences and the budget constraint. Large families living on relatively low incomes per head would be the result of rational choice between material and 'familial' welfare and no cause for social concern; and the result of decisions by spouses to separate would not, as it so frequently does now, consist in the imposition of poverty on the children, through the unwillingness or inability of the father to support his offspring and the inability of the mother to earn enough by her own labour to do so. (In this connection, economic irrationality in child-bearing interacts with the effects of discrimination against women in the labour market to enforce poverty on the children of unmarried, separated, divorced and widowed mothers — a type of poverty particularly prevalent among the black population of the United States, where the slavery tradition still makes the mother rather than the father the head of the household, but also prevalent in other countries.) An alternative social arrangement, which is partially but not wholly reflected in the social security and other arrangements of various countries, would be for society to regard the raising of children not as a family responsibility but as an activity in the social interest, providing population for the future, and to assume social responsibility for the economic costs through the provision of children's allowances, free education, etc. (The United States is exceptional among advanced countries in not having some sort of system of family allowances payable by right to the mother.)

The second type of poverty — inadequate income to support the individual or a normal-sized family — is attributable to several reasons. One is inadequate employment opportunities for workers of sufficient skill to support themselves and their families above the poverty line if they were normally employed. Inadequate employment nowadays has to be the result of deliberate choice by the macro-economic policy-makers, and while this choice may be necessitated by domestic or international difficulties (and the need to enforce unemployment for macro-economic disciplinary reasons cannot simply be denied on the grounds that unemployment is distasteful), it is arguably unfair that a subset of citizens should have to suffer poverty to discipline the others, and reasonable to argue that unemployment benefits should be generous enough to shield those made unemployed by national economic policy from being forced to descend into poverty. There are two further considerations pointing in this direction, both the result of research in the United States into the consequences of unemployment. First, crimes against property (robbery, etc.) tend to increase as unemployment rises; second, a transitory period of unemployment tends to lead to a permanent increase in poverty, for two reasons: elderly people get thrown out of work and cannot find their way back into the labour market at their customary wages; and youths entering the labour market cannot put their foot on the first rung of the ladder of promotion to a non-poverty life-time income stream via on-the-job training.

A second cause of poverty of this kind is inadequacy of the factors of production the individual or family can supply to command a non-poverty level of income. In a broad sense, this can be regarded as due to the immobility of the family's factors of production, either between occupations or between regions, the assumption being that the normal individual could earn a non-poverty income if either he were located in a prosperous instead of a declining region of the country or his native skills had been trained to the needs of expanding rather than contracting industries. One of the problems here is that indigent parents tend to produce and raise children who retrace their own poverty-stricken footsteps: if the children grow up in a poor environment, they tend to face opportunities and make choices that keep them condemned to poverty. This is a major reason why 'regional development policies', which have existed under one or another name for over a century, have tended to fail consistently to remedy regional poverty; by attempting to resuscitate industries declining in response to economic pressures they both doom themselves to failure and guarantee the preservation of a next generation of poor people who will have a legitimate claim for public help.

There are exceptions, however, to the implied anti-poverty policy of solving the problem by re-training or assisted migration. First, some individuals are physically or mentally incapable of rendering sufficient labour service to the productive system to be capable of supporting themselves, so that relief of their poverty would be more cheaply accomplished by direct cash payments. One suspects, however, that some of the prevalent unwillingness to employ physically or mentally handicapped people is due to discrimination against them on the part of the able-bodied and/or normal-minded, an indulgence in the avoidance of negative personal consumption externalities (who likes to be reminded of the risks of human existence by the daily sight of a one-armed, one-eyed, dwarfed, or otherwise disfigured elevator operator when for a somewhat higher wage one can obtain the services of a fully-able-bodied man or woman whose presence in the elevator daily reminds one that one's superior income is due to one's superior ability and not merely to one's physical health?). Second, the pay-off from public investment in assisting labour mobility depends on the remaining length of productive life of the assisted, in conjunction with the cost of the investment, and the pay-off may be too small — as probably in the case of the re-training of unemployed clerks in their late fifties — to justify such investment as contrasted with the award of a cash income stream. Even so, it may be socially profitable to make economically unprofitable investments of this kind, for the sake of providing a normal family life (father regularly employed in a respectable job, mother keeping house within a reliable budget constraint) for the children.

A third source of inadequate earnings from the individual's or the family's stock of productive assets is, in a broad sense, discrimination against the hiring of those assets. Modern society has more or less reduced discrimination on grounds of religion to negligibility; but it continues to discriminate for various (and usually philosophically very confused) reasons against the coloured, the aged, the uneducated, and the female. Colour discrimination, it should be noted, is not peculiar to predominantly white societies; it also exists in countries like India and Pakistan where variations in climatic conditions produce people of differing shades of brown-ness, and among American blacks, as well as in countries like Brazil which pride themselves on their lack of colour discrimination, but are still capable of discriminating between more and less acceptable shades of brown. Discrimination against the aged reflects a variety of forces: intergenerational rivalry; the tailoring of jobs to the assumption that the typical worker is young, muscular, adroit, and clear-sighted, even though the job may technically require none of these characteristics; and the fact, noted long ago by Jeremy Bentham in his *Book of Fallacies*, that in a changing society in which most people survive into adulthood it is youth and not age that has the widest and most flexible grasp of human experience. (This proposition obviously requires qualification; as a person matures he acquires more knowledge of the society he lives in but loses flexibility in adaptation to change, so that he is at his best somewhere between adolescence and middle age. However, Bentham was calling attention to the important point that in a literate society one can acquire knowledge of the past by reading about it rather than having lived through it, and the former is often more informative than the latter.) Discrimination against women reflects an archaic view of the function of the family in contemporary society. In primitive nomadic or settled agricultural societies, women's inferior strength and probably superior manual dexterity — themselves probably the result in part of cultural definitions of the desirable characteristics of female mates, since no culture that I am aware of has extolled size and muscularity as a criterion of desirable womanhood, matrilineal societies apart — provided a natural basis for a division of labour between men and women that was mutually satisfactory on the whole if not always mutually tolerable. In advanced industrial society, where reasonably good health and trained intelligence rather than muscular strength constitute the foundation of productive contribution, the traditional assignment of women to household management and child rearing is an anachronism, and discrimination against women in employment based on the view that this is either their preferred social role or the role to which society should assign them prevents them from realizing their full economic potential and condemns many of them — especially those who have essayed marriage and emerged at the other end as heads of households of children whom they must support largely by their own economic efforts — to unnecessary poverty. Discrimination against the uneducated reflects the desire of the educated to enjoy the consumption externalities of communication with others of the educated, and their instructed faith in the socially discriminatory value of educational qualifications. It is an interesting question whether a society which does not discriminate on grounds of race, colour, creed, religion, sex, or age, but does discriminate by educational attainment, will be a better society than one that regards educational differences as secondary to the others.

In any case, if society is concerned about the problem of poverty, one line of solution is to eliminate the various kinds of discrimination that help to create and preserve it; or else to recognize that the discrimination is based on a social philosophy which penalizes unjustly those who are discriminated against, and to award adequate compensation for this discrimination. Thus, in the case of the elderly, society should either re-design its work specification and hiring rules to give equal opportunity to the older in competition with the younger citizens, or if it wishes to push the elderly out of the labour market provide an adequately non-poverty system of pensions. In the case of the coloured, if they are accepted as citizens, they should have the same opportunities to earn income as other citizens (if the sight of their presence offends the white fellow-citizens, it should be possible to assign them to less visible jobs without jeopardizing their incomes — as Becker points out, colour prejudice may lead either to segregation of jobs among white and coloured, each earning the same wage, or to discrimination involving the coloured earning less than the white for the same job). Note that the easy way out for the whites — to deny the blacks the opportunity to immigrate and become citizens — has not been available to the United States because of its history of slavery but has been resorted to by other ex-imperial countries. This makes the United States easy game for criticism by the intellectuals of other countries whose governments have thoughtfully prevented them from having to think seriously about the manifold problems of racial integration; English intellectuals, whose contacts with coloured people have mostly consisted of meeting the prospective rulers of coloured colonies as fellow-students at Oxford and Cambridge, have a particularly easy task in telling the United States how to handle its racial problems. In the case of women, society has to face a difficult and unacknowledged choice: either women are really equal to men as citizens, discrimination has to be abolished, and the family has to be re-designed to eliminate the differential burden it imposes on women as compared with men; or society has to recognize explicitly that the woman's role in managing the household and rearing children is as exacting as that of the man's in earning the income to maintain the household, and deserves the support both of contractual arrangements specifying the financial obligations of the husband towards the partnership involved in marriage, and of public subvention of the costs of rearing the children that result. In the case of the uneducated, society should recognize that lack of education is a lack of human capital, brought about by the unwillingness of society itself to invest resources in individuals unpromising in their ability to accumulate such capital, and that such individuals should in equity be compensated by the transferral to them of material capital. (Eighteenth-century plays and nineteenth-century novels abound in individuals who have to be admitted to civilized society because they have a substantial property income, even though they lack the graces conveyed by education; contemporary society might well be better off if it had to allow for a lower degree of correlation between education and income than now prevails.)

Apart from these forms of social discrimination, contemporary society contains important forms of discrimination on other grounds, nominally economic, which help to create a poverty problem. One such is trade unionism, which by establishing a differential wage for union members over non-union members helps to keep the non-union members poor. Another is minimum wage laws, which benefit those fortunate enough to obtain employment in minimum-wage-law industries at the expense of those not so fortunate. (For a fuller analysis refer back to Chapter 10). A third is the practice of recruiting civil servants on the basis of educational attainment, which discriminates against those who lack the capacity for such attainment but may nevertheless have the capacity for arriving at intelligent public policy decisions. (Related to this is the practice of business firms of using educational attainment as a 'filter' for the selection of potential executive material; this particular filter may be both unnecessarily expensive socially, and inefficient in selecting effective business executives.) Finally, the legislation of 'equal pay for equal work' for the public sector only, when the private sector is characterized by discrimination against the employment of women, may contribute to poverty among women by creaming off the most talented and leaving the rest to serve as examples of the proposition that women are less efficient than men. Insistence on equal pay in one sector only, when discrimination in conjunction with relative supplies makes pay for women generally lower elsewhere, will result either in women taking over employment in that sector completely, or in the women who obtain employment in that sector being in fact considerably better qualified than the men employed in it.

Poverty Programmes: Promising and Unpromising
Assuming the existence of a social concern about poverty, there are a number of points at which the economist has questions to ask or suggestions to make and advice to offer.

First, there is the question obvious to the economist of what the effect of transfers of income to the poor will be on their incentives to work and to improve their economic position by their own efforts. In posing this question in modern times, however, economists frequently make the mistake of thinking themselves back into classical times, when life really was a hard struggle for survival and the blunting of incentives to work was a really serious matter, because it entailed a drain on the meagre resources of the responsible hard-working citizens for the benefit of the social drones, or else a tax on the god-given rightful income of the propertied classes for the benefit of those who should be grateful for the opportunity to find gainful employment in their service. In contemporary affluent times, there is both less obvious necessity for hard work on the part of everyone — as reflected in the increasing cultivation of leisure-time activities for the middle and lower-middle class — and less moral certainty about the rights of those who earn high incomes by virtue of possession of material or human capital to spend the income from it according to their own desires. In other words, the insistence on efficiency of the economic system at the cost of poverty for some is no longer a tenable starting point; and the classical concern about efficiency has to be modified into a weighing of costs and benefits of poverty relief against one another. This is not to say that efficiency and incentives are unimportant, only that one has to recognize that it is not only the poor that may be inefficient, and that a certain amount of inefficiency may be and probably should be tolerable if the overall outcome of such toleration is socially desirable. But there are still potentially important problems where the economist's concern with efficiency is relevant, notably the possibility that generosity in providing for the poor may result in a proliferation of their numbers as a result of both voluntary choice of poverty status rather than work, and natural increase through procreation.

Second, there is the question, assuming in general that poverty can be identified with insufficiency of income received or receivable through the market mechanism, of how best to arrange for the poor to receive sufficient incomes. (Note that to social and charity workers, poverty is often identified not with its market results in terms of income but with the social and personal characteristics of the poor, and its relief with a reformation of those characteristics; this corresponds to a long-standing social differentiation between the 'deserving' and the 'undeserving' poor, the former being regarded as poor through no fault of their own and entitled to the provision of work and opportunities, the latter being feckless and entitled only to what charitable gifts the conscience of the rich was prepared to offer.)

One way of attempting to transfer incomes towards the poor, which is obvious and appealing to the non-economist, is to allow or legislate tinkering with the market mechanism in order to provide prices more favourable to the poor. Previous analysis suggests that programmes of this kind are not likely to be promising. As shown above (especially pp. 97 to 109), neither trade unionism nor minimum wage legislation is likely to benefit the working class as a whole; on the contrary, both are likely to ensure adequate incomes for a favoured group at the expense of a large degree of poverty for the disfavoured group. This is particularly true of minimum wage laws, especially if as in the United States the minimum wage is set regardless of the age and position in the labour force of the workers covered. Similarly, a policy of farm price supports (above pp. 83–84) is likely to do little to raise the incomes of farm workers (as distinct from farm owners) and has the undesirable side-effect of raising the cost of food to the urban poor, a side-effect which it is difficult to counteract effectively and efficiently by food-stamp plans and other methods of subsidizing the food-consumption of the poor. To the economist, the most efficacious way of transferring incomes is to transfer incomes by direct fiscal means.

Benefits in Cash Versus Benefits in Kind

A standard controversy concerning measures to relieve poverty, which puts the economist in general conflict with the non-economist humanitarian, is over the issue of payment of subsidies to the poor in cash versus payments in kind — economists favouring the former and humanitarians and professional poverty-workers the latter. Standard economic theory leads to the conclusion that cash is always better than kind (because it permits individual utility maximization and preserves consumers' sovereignty) unless *either* benefits in kind amount to less than the poor recipients would have freely bought if they had received cash instead, *or* the recipients are free to sell the benefits in kind in the market and the transactions costs entailed are negligible — in which cases it makes no difference to the ultimate consumption pattern of the poor whether benefits are paid in cash or in kind. To this argument, the economist usually adds the observation that costs of administration and policing of benefits in kind absorb a large proportion of the budgetary allocations nominally destined to the relief of poverty — much of this in the form of salaries for middle-class people appropriately qualified by higher education. He is also inclined to feel that the bureaucratic control involved entails discriminatory interference with the civil liberties of the poor — discriminatory because the rich are allowed to waste their money and their lives as they like, and only if they want psychiatric treatment and financial discipline do they need to hire experts in these subjects to help them to live better; they are not obliged to accept a 'tied sale' of such help as the price of receiving their incomes.

It is such considerations that in the mid-1960s led economists such as Milton Friedman and James Tobin, otherwise strongly divided on almost every conceivable fundamental scientific issue, to concur both in recommending the 'negative income tax' (i.e. income subventions from the Treasury to people whose cash incomes put them below some socially-accepted 'poverty line') and in exploring the difficult technical question of reconciling this scheme with the existing income tax system. (The technical problem here is that most existing poverty relief systems impose a 100 per cent or near 100 per cent marginal income tax rate on the poor, in the sense that their benefit payments, whether in cash or in kind, are reduced more or less to the extent that their earned income rises, up to the point at which they cease to be classified as poor, receive no benefits, and become ordinary taxpayers. This feature obviously discourages the poor from attempting to earn income in the market place. On the other hand, it would obviously be inequitable — and expensive to government as well — for persons who once succeeded in getting themselves classified as poor to go on receiving their benefits as of right regardless of what they earned on top of their benefits, paying the same taxes on their earned incomes as the non-poor who earned all their cash receipts for themselves and paid the normal taxes on them. The technical problem is to devise a schedule of tax rates for the poor that will not have the disincentive effects of a 100 per cent marginal tax rate on the earnings of the still-poor, while restoring equality of tax treatment between the two groups at some non-poverty level of income.)

Nevertheless, there are various legitimate or at least plausible arguments for giving benefits in kind. One, which goes back at least as far as John Stuart Mill's arguments for public education as against private education, is that the poor, like children, do not know what is good for them and need, in both the social and their own true private interests, to have imposed on them the superior judgment of more intelligent and better-educated and more successful people. (The counter-arguments are that the preferences of such people are not necessarily superior to those of the poor; that under the guise of improving the poor they are really seeking to create a society more deferential to people like themselves; and that the poor will not learn to be self-reliantly independent if they are denied the opportunity to learn by making their own mistakes in the spending of money.) A second argument is that the competitive market, at least as it confronts the poor, is less efficient than centralized administration in providing the goods necessary to the relief of poverty. (The counter-arguments are that if a centralized administration and not the collectivity of the poor determines the spending of the funds allocated to the relief of poverty, the private market system will naturally cater to the tastes of the administration rather than attempt to determine and educate the tastes of the poor.) A third argument is that centralized administration and distribution of benefits in kind can offset market imperfections that would otherwise prevent or impede the poor from making choices in accord with true social costs and benefits. One example concerns 'food stamp' plans, which can be interpreted as devices for relieving the poor of the necessity of making consumption choices in face of artificially high food prices created by farm price support policies. Another, more complex, example is the imperfection of the market in human capital that makes it extremely difficult for the intelligent poor children to invest in their own human capital via education. (The counter-argument, a rather idealistic one, is that government should abandon economic policies such as farm price supports that involve regressive taxation of the consumer, and correct the imperfections of the markets in human capital, rather than pre-serve these policies and then seek to mitigate their impact on the poor.)

These arguments for benefits in kind stress questions of economic efficiency in the relief of poverty, considered as a programme of transferring resources in general to the poor. But it is quite conceivable that those who wish to relieve poverty do not conceive of it (as the economist does) as consisting of a general shortage of income or spendable resources, but instead are concerned about certain aspects of the condition of poverty that impinge on their consciousness as a species of negative consumption externality, and seek to eliminate such externalities by making transfers of specific benefits in kind. Thus James Buchanan has argued that the popularity of benefits in kind rather than in cash is attributable to the fact that the affluent do not like the thought of (say) starving people, especially children, of bright children whose parents cannot or will not give them a decent education, of shabbily-clothed people infesting the streets, and of crowded, littered, and dangerous neighbourhoods. Hence the public preference for benefits in kind in the form of cheap or free food, clothing, slum clearance and public housing, and subsidized education. The fact that the poor frequently resent and even refuse to take advantage of such benefits in kind implies that they are less willing to sell positive externalities than the affluent are eager to purchase them.

It should be noted in conclusion that benefits in kind may have the contrary effect to that intended, of improving the lot of the poor, because such bene-fits may carry side-costs with them. For example, efforts to relieve poverty in the long run by forcing the children of the poor to stay in school and acquire an education by the imposition of a minimum school-leaving age may impose considerable extra costs of child maintenance on the poor family during the extra years at school, without providing the child (if he or she is incapable of learning beyond a certain point) with additional education-based income-earning capacity, and even have the effect of inculcating irresponsible habits and antagonistic attitudes towards authority that reduce the child's employment prospects in the labour market. As another example, in the 1930s in England there was a widely told tale to the effect that it was useless to provide the poor with modern apartment-block housing containing all modern conveniences, because they simply used their bathtubs for storing their coal; the facts seem to have been that the architect put the coal-storage bins at the ground level, on the assumption either that the poor would have the time and the strength to carry coal upstairs in small lots as needed for fuel, or that they would have servants to do the job for them.

Income Transfers Versus Investment in Poverty Relief
As mentioned already, public concern about the relief of poverty tends, in

contrast to the economist's identification of poverty with inadequacy of money income or spending power, to see poverty as a problem of changing poor people's habits and relation to the economic system, and hence to favour investments — in education for poor children, in re-training of adults, and in the provision of capital to buy better equipment for poor farmers or self-employed workers — over the cash income transfers that appeal to the economist. This orientation is a mixture of prejudice and prescience. The prejudice involves the attitudes already referred to, which discriminate between the deserving and the undeserving poor and assume that, with some public help, the deserving can be given a place in the productive system that will enable them to be self-supporting at a non-poverty level. To the economist, two questions arise concerning this attitude. First, do the poor typically represent some sort of social disequilibrium situation, in which people who could participate effectively in the economic system at a non-poverty level of income are somehow disbarred from the opportunity to do so but could be restored to participation by a relatively small amount of social expenditure? Or do they represent an equilibrium situation, the result either of their own choices to disregard opportunities for higher incomes based either on myopia or on a strong preference for leisure and aversion to industrial discipline, or on their own limited talents and capacity for acquiring the education necessary for success in the industrial system? Economic analysis suggests that the equilibrium explanation is more reasonable than the disequilibrium explanation — see T. W. Schultz's book on *Transforming Traditional Agriculture* — and that, consequently, the rate of return on investments designed to overcome the presumed disequilibrium is likely to be low and not, as implied, incredibly high. A corollary is that it might be economically and socially more efficient to allocate to the poor a block of stock in General Motors, or even a chunk of Government debt (rigged as the rate of return on that is to give the owners less than a fair rate of return on their capital), rather than give them their benefits in the form of a specific investment in their human or material capital. Second, and related, is investment in the creation of human capital in the poor a better investment than a cash income subsidy? If the object is to give people adequate spending power to maintain a decent standard of living, rather than to transform them into a different type of person, a cash income subsidy may be far more economical than an investment in the formation of human capital, especially if the investment is chosen by the governmental bureaucracy in the light of the social circumstances of the poor person concerned. To put the point another way, it is not clear that a poor person is benefitted more, in terms of relieving his poverty, by an educational investment than by the gift of an equivalent allocation of government bonds.

The prescience of this point of view enters the picture when one considers (a) the externality aspect of poverty — if poverty is offensive, not because the poor have low standards of living, but because they behave in an offensive way affronting the middle-class belief in responsibility and hard work — giving the poor more money to spend as they like simply adds insult to injury, and the money should be used instead to bribe them into conformity with middle-class standards of good citizenship; (b) the inter-generational aspect of poverty — some (but not all) of the children of poor parents constitute a poverty problem for the next generation, either because they have acquired poverty-prone attitudes towards life from their parents or because their parents' choices for them have left them insufficiently equipped with productive capacities to achieve a non-poverty level of participation in economic society. In such cases, social investments in the transformation of the parents into worthy citizens may not pay off, in terms of the returns in parent income, but may be well worth while when the side-effects on the attitudes and educational attainments of the children (and of subsequent generations as well) are taken into account. An important implication for United States policy, in contrast to the policy expressed in the Economic Opportunity Act, is that instead of trying to relieve rural southern poverty by subsidizing loans to farmers to buy capital equipment, the government should retire farmers on pensions paid *ex gratia* to 'victims of economic progress', on condition that they move to California, or Florida, or if they can stand the climatic misery to one of the big northern cities, where their children will have the educational opportunity to fit themselves into industrial society at a non-poverty level of income. A rational economic attitude towards the poverty problem would probably accord consumers' sovereignty to the preferences of parents, pay income subsidies to those deemed poor and let them spend the subsidies on current consumption or investment as they saw fit, but intervene in one way or another to rescue the children from the psychological conditioning and the inappropriate choices that irresponsible parents impose on them. (Some social philosophers, including most of the utopian socialist philosophers, have so despaired of the family as an efficient agent for child-rearing that they have proposed that all children be reared communally.)

APPENDIX I: FINAL EXAMINATIONS, 1967–1972

Final Examination, 1967

Time: Two hours

All questions carry equal weight. Candidates are advised to read each question carefully, and to remember that they have on the average eight minutes per question.

Discuss critically the following propositions:

1. In the absence of technical progress, economic growth will raise both the absolute and the relative share of rent in total income.

2. Production functions must be homogeneous of the first degree if distribution according to marginal productivity is to exactly exhaust the product.

3. While unionization must have harmful affects on the wages of non-union labour, it necessarily raises the wages of union labour. Therefore, to evaluate unionization, it is necessary to weigh the losses to non-union labour against the gains to union labour.

4. The fact that employers frequently provide specific training to employees, recoupling the cost by subsequently paying wages less than the employee is worth to the firm, means that some labour is paid less than its marginal product is worth, and is therefore exploited.

5. Because an increase in the quantity of capital generally changes the value of the previously-existing capital stock, investment by private enterprise in response to the prevailing rate of interest will result in the accumulation of a non-optimal stock of capital.

6. Capital earns a rate of return, above the cost of replacing it, because the accumulation of capital permits the use of more roundabout methods of production, and more roundabout methods of production are more productive.

7. Rent differs from other income shares in being price-determined rather than price-determining.

8. Fisher's concept of time preference implies that people always have a preference for present over future goods, and therefore bases the theory of interest and capital on irrational behaviour.

9. The discounted present value criterion of investment decision always provides a clear and reliable indication of the best investment opportunity.

10. The maximization of the internal rate of return criterion for investment choice does not make economic sense in most cases.

11. The Harrod–Domar model demonstrates that a capitalist system will encounter great difficulty in maintaining full employment for any long stretch of time.

12. The 'golden rule' of accumulation establishes the conditions required for the long-run maximization of social welfare.

13. The observed constancy of the relative share of labour in national income discredits the marginal productivity theory and validates the alleged superiority of Kaldor's alternative Keynesian theory of income distribution.

14. The observed inequality of income distribution is consistent both with the view that individual incomes are determined entirely by luck (chance), and with the view that what the individual earns is determined by his own decisions and efforts.

15. An efficient 'war on poverty' should involve two key elements: (1) an increase in the minimum wage to a non-poverty level; (ii) a programme to educate and train 'poor' labour.

Final Examination, 1968

Time: Two Hours.
Notes: Question 1 carries double the weight of the others. Please read the questions carefully.

1. (One hour). Assume a perfectly competitive two-commodity, two-factor model in which one factor is labour and the other capital (assumed to be malleable and immortal), the owners of capital receive higher per capita incomes than the owners of the labour, and one of the commodities is a luxury good while the other is a necessary good. Use the model to analyze the following remedies for poverty, defined as prevailing wages falling below some socially defined minimum:

(i)   A legal minimum wage fixed at the social minimum and applicable to both industries;

(ii) A tax on the consumption of luxury goods, the proceeds of which are distributed proportionately to workers as income subsidies;

(iii) Assuming now that one industry is unionized and has wages above the social minimum, unionization of the other industry;

(iv) Propaganda for, and instruction in, birth control techniques.

(Note: candidates short of time will not be penalised for stating some conclusions without proof, providing that their answer overall shows understanding of the model.)

2. What is the function of capital in the production process? Discuss the problems that arise for the theorists in analyzing the accumulation of capital.

3. Write short notes on:

(i) The classical proposition that the share of rent will rise as population increases.

(ii) The relevance of Euler's Theorem to the theory of distribution.

(iii) The implications of the theory of on-the-job training for the problem of 'brain drain'.

(iv) F. H. Knight's theory of profit.

4. (Thirty minutes). Assume a one-sector economy, using two factors of production, labour and capital, production being subject to constant returns to scale. The labour force grows at the exponential rate n, a constant fraction s of output is saved, and output accumulated as capital lasts for ever.

(a) Prove that the economy's growth rate will converge in the long run on the rate n. Discuss the relation between the savings ratio s and consumption per capita in long-run growth equilibrium, and the implications of this relation for long-run social optimization.

(b) Assuming that the savings ratio s is an increasing function of the rate of population growth, and that the rate of population growth may be varied between a lower and an upper limit, develop a 'golden rule' of population growth.

Final Examination, 1969

Time: Two Hours.
All questions carry equal weight.

1. Examine the likely effect on the dispersion of measured income of the following changes:

(1) Emigration of the more adventurous citizens;
(2) Assumption by the state of the major part of the costs of tuition;
(3) An increase in the normal age of retirement;
(4) The Friedman negative income tax proposal;

(5) Moral revulsion against participation in military activities, under a volunteer army system.

2. Consider the following Fisherian investment opportunity: -10, $+8$, $+8$, -3. One-period interest rates are respectively 30 per cent, 20 per cent and 40 per cent.

(a) Is the opportunity profitable?
(b) What first-period interest rate would make an investor indifferent between investing and not investing?

(Explain the logic of your answers so that arithmetical errors will not count against you.)

3. Consider a two-sector model, constructed on the usual assumption of two factors of production and constant returns to scale. Assume that there is unionization in one sector, and that there is a minimum wage law for the other. Analyze the differences that will result, as compared with a purely competitive situation.

4. Write a paragraph on the following subjects:

(1) The Ricardo effect;
(2) The effects of economic progress on the share of rent in national income;
(3) Schumpeter's theory of profits;
(4) The economics of the apprenticeship system;
(5) The reasons why universities give fellowships to graduate students.

Final Examination, 1970

Time: Two Hours.
All questions carry equal weight.

1. Write brief notes on the following:

(a) The negative Wicksell effect;
(b) The intensive and extensive margins;
(c) Schumpeter's theory of profits;
(d) Neutral technical progress;
(e) The economics of pollution;
(f) Specific training.

2. Sketch a theory of the personal distribution of income. Discuss the implications of your theory for personal income taxation.

3. Employ a two-sector two-factor model with constant returns to scale in each sector. Assume that the labour-intensive good is a capital good that lasts for ever, and that the labour force grows at the rate n. Analyze the long-run growth equilibrium of the economy on the assumptions:

(a) That the economy saves a fixed proportion of its income.

(b) That the economy accumulates capital until the rate of return falls to its minimum rate of time preference.

BONUS: Bonus marks are offered to anyone who can explain why the assumption of labour-intensive capital goods production is convenient in case (a), and necessary in case (b).

4. The market rate of interest is 10 per cent for a one-period loan; and 14 per cent for a two-period loan, the first interest payment on the latter being compounded and the total of interest and principal being repaid at the end of the period. An investor has the following investment opportunities:

(1) Buy a swampy piece of land at a cost of $5000, contract for its use as a garbage dump for a price of $10 000 payable at the end of the first period, and cover it and resell it at a net loss of $5250 in the second period.

(2) Buy a swampy piece of land at a cost of $5000, develop it with clean fill at a cost of $10 000 payable at the end of the first period, and sell it to a realtor for a price of $17 450 at the end of the second period.

(a) What should he do? Explain carefully the theory you are using, so that arithmetical mistakes will not count against you. (In any calculations, two figures of decimals will be deemed sufficient.)

(b) What difference, if any, would it make if it cost him $100 payable at the end of the first period to make the transaction?

Final Examination, 1971

Time: Two Hours.

1. (40 minutes). Assume a two-sector model of general equilibrium and consider a government that wishes to redistribute income towards labour. Analyse the effects on the economy's equilibrium and the distribution of income of:

(i) A tax on the income of capital, the proceeds of which are redistributed towards labour;

(ii) An excise tax on one of the commodities, the proceeds of which are redistributed towards labour;

(iii) A tax on the use of capital in one sector only of the economy, the proceeds of which are redistributed towards labour;

(iv) A minimum wage law.

In each case, state whether or not labour can actually lose as a consequence of the redistribution policy.

How would your results be affected by the assumption that capital is in perfectly elastic supply at a fixed minimum rate of time preference?

2. (30 minutes). Write brief notes on:

   (i) The inefficiency of share-cropping;
   (ii) The principle of derived demand;
   (iii) The golden rule of accumulation;
   (iv) Inferior land as a cause of rent;
   (v) Knight's theory of profit;
   (vi) Inequality and poverty.

3. (20 minutes). (a) Is the constancy of relative shares a puzzle neo-classical economics cannot explain?

   (b) Discuss critically Kaldor's theory of distribution, in the light of your answer to part (a).

4. (30 minutes). Write brief essays on the following topics:

   (i) Euler's theorem and distribution theory;

   (ii) Risk and the personal distribution of income;

   (iii) Human capital and marginal productivity theory;

   (iv) Sufficient conditions for a unique equilibrium in the two-sector model.

Final Examination, 1972

Time: Two Hours.

I.   (60 minutes). State briefly the conditions under which:

   (1) Worker control of industrial enterprises will be efficient;
   (2) Profits aggregated over the economy will be negative;
   (3) Imperfect competition is welfare-efficient;
   (4) Workers in a particular industry can genuinely be said to be exploited;
   (5) The income share of land rent will fall with technical progress;
   (6) Conversion of a share-cropping system into a fixed rent system will be inefficient;
   (7) Pollution of the local environment should not be restricted by legislation;
   (8) A majority view that a certain type of job is socially undesirable will *not* lead to a premium wage for that job;

(9) Unionization reduces the welfare of labour in the unionized industry;

(10) Employers pay *all* the training costs of their workers;

(11) The Wicksell effect is negative;

(12) The marginal rate of time preference will be negative;

(13) The internal rate of return criterion for investment choices is reliable;

(14) The long-run equilibrium growth cross-section of the economy is unique;

(15) The short-run equilibrium of a two-sector growth model is unique;

(16) The 'golden rule' constitutes a welfare prescription;

(17) Inequality in the measured cross-section distribution of income does not indicate inequality among individuals (one reason);

(18) Inequality in the measured cross-section distribution of income does not indicate inequality among individuals (another reason);

(19) Benefits in kind are superior to income subsidies as a means of relieving poverty;

(20) Educational subsidies are superior to income subsidies as a means of relieving poverty.

II. (40 minutes altogether)

(a) (15 minutes). Consider a one-sector growth model in which capital has a different and higher savings-to-income ratio than labour. Show that the long-run growth equilibrium must be unique. (Hint: consider saving per unit of capital).

(b) (25 minutes altogether). Consider a one-sector model of economic growth, in which the initially-given capital stock grows at a constant rate determined by the capitalists and the labour force is perfectly elastic at a given subsistence wage.

(i) (10 minutes). Discuss convergence and the 'golden rule' in this context.

(ii) (5 minutes). What would happen in the model if the accumulation of capital were governed by a fixed minimum rate of time preference on the part of the capitalists?

(iii) (10 minutes). What would happen in the model if the subsistence wage were $w + cn$, where w is the cost of living of a man and his wife, c is the cost of supporting a child, and n is the number of children? (Admittedly this is a very crude approximation to the realities of family life.) Discuss the implications for the rate of growth of the capital stock which the capitalists should choose.

III. (20 minutes). In the standard Johnson–Mieszkowski analysis of unionization, unionization is treated, following Lewis, as introducing a fixed percentage differential between union and non-union wages. How would that analysis be affected by making the alternative assumption that the union acts as a monopolist of labour? (Be careful to consider what the union might be maximizing.)

APPENDIX II: NOTES ON ANSWERS TO QUESTIONS

Final Examination 1972 and Annotated University of Chicago Qualifying Examinations in Price Theory, 1970, 1971 and 1972 Summers

Theory of Distribution — Summer 1972 Examination

Notes on the answers

I. (60 *minutes*). *State briefly the conditions under which:*
   (1) *Worker control of industrial enterprises will be efficient.*
   The entrepreneurial function is to hire the other factors in hopes of making a profit on the difference between realized revenues and costs (contracted, or imputed in the case of a factor that both works in the enterprise and assumes the entrepreneurial function). Worker control should be as efficient as any other form of enterprise, provided workers seek to maximize profits and face competitive factor markets. (If, however, for example, the state subsidizes such enterprises through e.g. provision of capital at subsidized rates, they will naturally use an inefficiently large amount of capital.)

   (2) *Profits aggregated over the economy will be negative.*
   Knight's theory of profits: if a sufficiently large number of entrepreneurs consistently overestimate their prospects of profit. (Note that profits have to be defined in Knight's sense; accounted profits include returns on capital and labour provided by the owners, and are unlikely to be negative in the aggregate even though Knightian profits may be.)

   (3) *Imperfect competition is welfare-efficient.*
   If the value to consumers of the variety of goods provided outweighs the higher average cost of providing differentiated products.

   (4) *Workers in a particular industry can genuinely be said to be exploited.*
   If their wage is below their marginal value product, for example if there is monopsony in the labour market or there is some kind of slavery.

   (5) *The income share of land rent will fall with technical progress.*
   In a Hicksian one-sector model, if technical progress is land-saving. If technical progress is defined as augmenting effective supplies of factors used in a given production function, if progress is land-saving (effective-land-supply-augmenting) and the elasticity of substitution is less than unity or vice versa.

(6) *Conversion of a share-cropping system into a fixed rent system will be inefficient.*
Cheung showed that share-cropping is efficient under competitive conditions governing contracting. The fixed rent system is efficient under the same circumstances. Conversion will only be inefficient if the fixed rent system adopted is inefficient, as in the case of land reform coupled with compulsory rent reduction and/or assignment of standard sizes of land plots to tenants.

(7) *Pollution of the local environment should not be restricted by legislation.*
The Coase theorem: if property rights in the environment are clearly defined and the transaction costs of contracting (and if necessary of litigation) are small. Note that the proposition refers to restriction, not prohibition, of pollution; hence explanation that prohibition is a second-best to other forms of restriction is not germane.

(8) *A majority view that a certain type of job is socially undesirable will not lead to a premium wage for that job.*
If the minority that does not regard the job as socially undesirable is large enough to meet the demand for labour in it without commanding a premium wage. (Note, incidentally, that the fact that a garbage man is relative unskilled and earns less than a medical doctor does not prove that he commands no premium wage, when due allowance is made for returns on investment in human capital.)

(9) *Unionization reduces the welfare of labour in the unionized industry.*
Standard analysis: if the unionized industry is labour-intensive *and* demand for the unionized product is sufficiently elastic (in a sense including income redistribution effects) to depress the wages of non-unionized labour by more than the differential established by the union.

(10) *Employers pay all the training cost of their workers.*
Note the word '*all*': not only must the traning be completely specific to the firm, but the employer must have confidence that the worker will stay with the firm long enough for him to recoup his costs from the excess of the worker's marginal product over his wage, while the worker must have doubts about whether the firm will survive long enough for him to be able to recoup if he paid his own training costs and received the return on them in the form of higher wages. (If both had complete confidence on this score, both would be prepared to pay the costs or a share of them and the employer would not necessarily pay all. Note that if the employer had both some monopoly power in the product market and difficulty in recruiting workers willing to pay their own training costs, he could find it profitable to pay all the training costs and later pay the worker a premium wage to stay with the firm.)

(11) *The Wicksell effect is negative.*
The Wicksell effect will be negative in a model in which capital goods are not physically identical with consumption goods and a fall in the rate of interest reduces the value of the optimal capital stock in terms of consumption goods.

(12) *The marginal rate of time preference will be negative.*
If consumption goods cannot be carried forward through time without significant storage costs (or technology is such that the rate of return on investing current consumption in producing future consumption goods is negative) *and* people in general have a strong preference for future over present consumption, possibly because they expect a serious crop failure or, in more modern context, because they anticipate deterioration of the environment for future production as a consequence of pollution caused by present production.

(13) *The internal rate of return criterion for investment choices is reliable.*
Loosely, if the present value of an investment opportunity is a monotonically decreasing function of the market rate of interest; more accurately, if there is only one positive rate of interest at which the present value is exactly zero. Mathematically, this requires that the investment project under evaluation consists of a stream of negative returns followed by a stream of positive returns. (Other conditions can also be stipulated, but this is the one appropriate for the scope of this answer.)

(14) *The long-run equilibrium growth cross-section of the economy is unique.*
Always in a one-sector growth model with a constant-returns-to-scale production function. In a two-sector model, if the savings ratio of capital is higher than that of labour and the investment good is labour-intensive in production.

(15) *The short-run equilibrium of a two-sector growth model is unique.*
Assuming that the savings ratio of capital is higher than that of labour, if the investment good is labour-intensive in production, or if the investment good is capital-intensive in production and the average elasticity of substitution in the two production functions exceeds unity, or failing the latter some more complex conditions are fulfilled.

(16) *The 'golden rule' constitutes a welfare prescription.*
If capital per head is above the 'golden rule' level, consumption at all points of time starting from now can be increased by reducing the savings ratio towards the golden rule level. (Note, however, that this assumes that welfare depends only on consumption, and that no utility attaches to the ownership of wealth as such.)

(17) *Inequality in the measured cross-section distribution of income does not indicate inequality among individuals (one reason).*

(18) *Inequality in the measured cross-section distribution of income does not indicate inequality among individuals (another reason).*
Individuals may have exactly the same life-time income profiles, but a cross-section catches them at different ages.

Individuals may have exactly the same opportunities of investing in their human capital through training, but some choose higher income in youth over higher income at a later age and vice versa. A cross-section catches individuals of the same age with different current incomes, though they have had equal opportunities.

Individuals confront exactly the same risky income stream, but some are lucky and some are not. Both have the same mathematical expectation of income at the start, but the measured outcomes are unequal.

Individuals confront the same choice among riskier and less risky occupations, the differences in risk themselves produce inequality in measured outcomes; this is compounded by differing attitudes towards risk.

Different occupations offer different combinations of pecuniary and non-pecuniary advantages. This will show up in measured cross-section inequality, which measures only the pecuniary rewards to work.

A particular case of the last point is differences among occupations in the ratio of income in cash to income in kind, only the former usually being measured in cross-section data.

(19) *Benefits in kind are superior to income subsidies as a means of relieving poverty.*
If the costs of direct distribution of benefits in kind are lower than the costs of relying on the market to supply goods against expenditure of cash benefits, if the preferences of the benefit-donors are deemed superior to those of the benefit-recipients, if the process of distribution in kind is deemed to have educational externalities, or if 'relief of poverty' is identified, not with the raising of consumption possibilities *per se*, but with the removal of negative externalities for the non-poor achievable by increasing the poor's consumption of certain specific goods, e.g. better housing, more food, more presentable clothes.

(20) *Educational subsidies are superior to income subsidies as a means of relieving poverty.*
If the poor do not adequately evaluate the returns from education, or if imperfections of markets for human capital prevent them from turning an income subsidy into an educational investment.

II. (40 *minutes altogether*)
(a) (15 *minutes*). *Consider a one-sector growth model in which capital has a different and higher savings-to-income ratio than labour. Show that*

the long-run growth equilibrium must be unique. (Hint: consider saving per unit of capital.)

In per capita terms, $y = y(k)$

capital's income $y_k = ky'(k)$

labour's income $y_L = y - ky'(k)$

total saving $S = s_k y_k + s_L y_L$

saving per unit of capital $s/k = \dfrac{s_k k\, y'(k) + s_L y - s_L k\, y'(k)}{k}$

$$= (s_k - s_L)\, y'(k) + s_L y/k$$

$$\frac{d(s/k)}{dk} = (s_k - s_L)\, y''(k) + s_L \frac{ky'(k) - y(k)}{k^2}$$

The first term is negative due to diminishing marginal productivity, the second is negative since capital's income is less than total output. Thus saving per unit of capital falls as capital accumulates, whereas the capital replacement requirement is strictly proportional to the capital stock. This proves convergence.

A less mathematical, more intuitive, proof can be provided along lines based on the Kaldorian theory of distribution (though only so far as the algebra is concerned.)

$$Y = W + P$$

$$s_A Y = s_w W + s_p P = s_w Y + (s_p - s_w)P$$

$$\frac{s_A Y}{K} = s_w \frac{Y}{K} + (s_p - s_w)\frac{P}{K}$$

As capital per head accumulates, Y/K, output per unit of capital, must fall due to diminishing marginal productivity; so must P/K, the rate of return on capital or earnings of capital per unit; hence saving per unit of capital must fall, but the replacement requirement (investment necessary to keep capital per head intact) is constant per unit of capital. Hence there must be a unique equilibrium stock of capital per head at which the two are equal.

(b) (25 *minutes altogether.*) *Consider a one-sector model of economic growth, in which the initially-given capital stock grows at a constant rate determined by the capitalists and the labour force is perfectly elastic at a given subsistence wage.*
Comment: any growth model of the contemporary type has to replace the Ricardian assumption of a given stock of land subject to diminishing marginal productivity of other factors applied to it in increasing quantities, by an equivalent factor which grows at an exogenously given rate in relation to which other factors can be increased only subject to diminishing marginal productivity as their relative quantity increases. In contemporary growth models it is

I

conventionally assumed that labour is the limitational factor, growing at an exogenously-determined rate (the more sophisticated models allow for investment in human capital and/or in improvement of technology, but they have to assume diminishing returns, or depreciation of the stock so created, to produce convergence on a stable growth path with a constant cross-section of relationships). A simple modification of assumptions in the one-sector growth model is to assume. instead of a constant aggregate savings ratio or constant but different savings ratios for capital and labour, a minimum rate of time preference for the society as a whole. The model specified here simply switches the assumptions of the standard model presented in the lectures from exogenous growth rate of labour supply and minimum rate of time preference on the part of the capitalists to exogenous growth rate of capital supply and subsistence wage at which labour is in perfectly elastic supply. In both cases, the 'golden rule' has to be modified to fit the changed specification of the choice variable — the minimum rate of time preference, or the subsistence wage. However, there is an alternative specification of the choice variable, the rate of growth of population chosen by the labour force or the rate of capital accumulation chosen by the capitalists. Recognition and discussion of the possibility and consequences of switching the assumptions of the standard model is what this question calls for.

(i) (10 *minutes*). *Discuss convergence and the 'golden rule' in this context.* The economy will converge on a steady-state growth path, with the rate of growth of the labour supply equal to the rate of growth of the capital stock determined by the capitalists. If the labour supply grows faster than this, real wages will fall below subsistence, and vice versa, so that such divergences will be corrected by changes in the labour supply and the system will be stable. The cross-section equilibrium of the economy must be such that capital per head is exactly sufficient to make the marginal product of labour equal to the subsistence wage. This will be true whatever the rate of growth chosen by the capitalists. Consumption per worker will be constant. Capitalist income per head will be output per head minus the subsistence wage (all these models implicitly assume that capitalists have no physical existence, or perhaps merely no heads). Capitalist consumption will be capitalist income less the capital replacement requirement, which will be the stock of capital per head multiplied by the rate of growth chosen by the capitalists.

It follows that, if the subsistence wage is taken as given exogenously, consumption per head will be maximized if the capitalists choose a zero growth rate. So will the consumption of the owners of capital. If, on the other hand, the growth rate chosen by the capitalists is taken as given exogenously, the workers can maximize consumption per head by choosing a subsistence wage such that the rate of return on capital which it implies is just equal to the rate of growth chosen by the capitalists.

The argument can be illustrated by the accompanying diagram. For the subsistence wage $\overline{w}_0$, the optimal capital stock per head is k_0 and total output $\overline{y}_0$; with the chosen growth rate g, consumption per head is $P_0 I_0$, $\overline{k}_0 I_0$ representing the capital requirement for maintaining capital per head intact. If the subsistence wage is

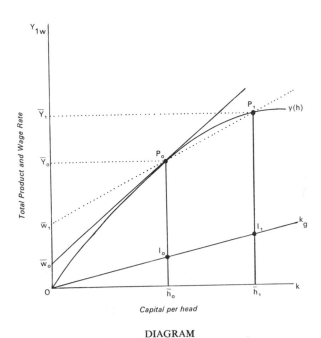

DIAGRAM

fixed, consumption per head will be maximized if the capital requirement is reduced to zero, and the $O . kg$ line made coincidental with the horizontal axis, by the capitalist choice of a zero rate of growth of capital stock. If on the other hand the chosen growth rate is regarded as exogeneously given, consumption per head will be maximized if workers raise $\overline{w}_0$ to $\overline{w}_1$, which will maximize the excess of total output over the capital replacement requirement. (Conversely, $\overline{w}_0$ would have to be lowered if k_0 lay to the right of the golden rule position.)

Note for future thought that maximization of consumption per head only makes sense if we assume implicitly that all workers have a proportionate share in the ownership of the capital stock. If there were a fixed number of capitalists, they would not necessarily, or even probably, settle for a zero growth rate of the capital stock. They would instead have a sort of investment opportunity: by accumulating capital they reduce their consumption at any point of time below what it could be, but increase their future consumption above what it would be with a constant stock of capital and labour.

(ii) (5 minutes). *What would happen in the model if the accumulation of capital were governed by a fixed minimum rate of time preference on the part of the capitalists?*

The subsistence wage fixes the rate of return on capital. If this exceeds the minimum rate of time preference of capitalists the economy explodes; if it falls short of the minimum rate of time preference, the economy implodes and eventually vanishes. If the minimum rate of time preference and the rate of return on capital fixed by the subsistence wage are equal, the economy will be in meta-stable equilibrium at any rate of growth, i.e. the growth rate could be anything at all.

(iii) (10 minutes). *What would happen in the model if the subsistence wage were w + cn, where w is the cost of living of a man and his wife, c is the cost of supporting a child, and n is the number of children? (Admittedly this is a very crude approximation to the realities of family life.) Discuss the implications for the rate of growth of the capital stock which the capitalists should choose.*

This part of the question appears in the light of hindsight to have been even less carefully framed than it admits. The general idea was to make the subsistence wage an increasing function of the rate of growth chosen by the capitalists. Thus with a given subsistence wage function, the capitalists would have a dual incentive to reduce the chosen rate of growth to zero: to increase the marginal product of capital and to reduce the capital replacement requirement. Given the rate of growth chosen by the capitalists, the application of golden rule logic to the choice of the constant in the subsistence wage function would be the same as in part II(i).

III. (20 minutes). *In the standard Johnson–Mieszkowski analysis of unionization, unionization is treated, following Lewis, as introducing a fixed percentage differential between union and non-union wages. How would that analysis be affected by making the alternative assumption that the union acts as a monopolist of labour? (Be careful to consider what the union might be maximizing.)*

Since monopoly can always be thought of as fixing a profit margin between price and cost, the Johnson–Mieszkowski analysis can be reconciled with monopoly behaviour by unions by interpreting the union-non-union differential as that established by the optimizing behaviour of the union. But then the Johnson–Mieszkowski findings of possible adverse effects on the welfare of union members would be inconsistent with the idea that the union seeks to exploit monopoly power, unless its efforts in this direction are based on ignorance of the general equilibrium repercussions of its actions on the welfare of its members. In general, one would expect the union to recognize these repercussions; the question then becomes, what the union is seeking to maximize.

The simplest procedure is probably to adopt the Johnson–Mieszkowski finding that if unionization occurs in the capital-intensive industry its general equilibrium repercussions are favourable to workers remaining in the unionized sector, and vice versa, and that this will reinforce union exploitation of monopoly power in the one case and modify it in the other; and then to discuss the problem in partial equilibrium terms.

In the partial equilibrium context, it is nonsense to say that the union will attempt to maximize income per employed worker, because this would entail raising the wage rate to a level at which only one worker was employed. For maximization, there must be a trade-off of some sort between quantity and price per unit.

It is necessary to distinguish between the case in which the union can be taken simply as a collective representative of its members, and that in which it is a separate governmental unit distinct from its members; also between cases in which the union takes account of the interests of members who become unemployed as a result of union-obtained increases in wages, and those in which it does not.

If the union takes account only of the interests of its employed members, it should seek to maximize their total income. This will be so if the union obtains a fixed proportion of members' wages as dues; and also if unemployed members receive income supplements from union dues. Qualifications: if unemployed members derive utility from leisure time, the union should push wages above the cash-income-maximizing level; and if the employed members dominate the union they will not push wages up so far because to do so creates more unemployment of members and the support of the unemployed members is a rising tax on their net incomes (unless dues are a fixed proportion of employed unionists' wages and are divided pro rata among the unemployed).

If the union is regarded as a separate entity having a monopoly position in the sale of unionized labour services and a monopsonistic position in the acquisition of such labour, it will maximize its own profits by equating marginal revenue from the sale of labour services with the marginal cost of acquiring them. A standard proposition in the theory of international trade shows that in this case the union will raise wages above the level that would maximize members' incomes, since by restricting the supply of labour services below that point it can increase its own profits via the induced reduction in the net wage (net of union dues) acceptable to the marginal union member. To be able to pursue a policy of this kind, however, the union must be able effectively to control entry to the union. Also, to the extent that this control requires the use of real resources, e.g. in excessively long apprenticeship or training periods, there is a waste of social resources over and above that due to the union differential *per se*.

University of Chicago Qualifying Examination in Price Theory, Summer 1970

All questions are compulsory. Total time allowed is three hours. The maximum score is one point per minute. Unless otherwise indicated, sub-sections of questions carry equal weight.

A. (70 *points*). *Indicate whether you believe each of the following statements to be true, false or uncertain. In each case write a few sentences explaining your answer. Your grade will be determined by your explanation.*

   1. *If the market real rate of return is r, and the individual expects this real rate to jump to 2r five periods from now, his current real consumption will fall.*

   Various answers are possible, depending on the theory of saving used and the assumptions made. If the individual is viewed as having no assets at the beginning, and as planning to provide for consumption over a period running past period five, we get an income effect favoring saving *and a substitution effect discouraging it*, in the present period. If the individual is viewed as possessing wealth in the form of assets with lives extending over more than the fifth period, the rise in the real rate of interest expected five periods from now will reduce the value of his wealth at the present time and thus may be argued to reduce his current consumption. At this point we run into the tricky question of whether he originally planned to dispose of his assets before they matured, or not. If his portfolio is exactly tailored to mature when he needs cash, the current capital loss due to the rise in the interest rate expected in the fifth period may make him wish he had indulged himself in liquidity preference but won't affect his consumption behaviour.

   Notes on illegitimate arguments:
   A. The question specifies that the real rate *is r*, and will jump to 2r five periods from now; it is not legitimate to argue that we do not know what the rate of interest will be between now and five periods from now and hence cannot answer the question.
   B. While the verb 'expects' is a bit ambiguous, clearly the question makes no sense if the individual is assumed to have already adjusted his portfolio to the expected rise in the real rate; his expectations must be assumed to have changed.

   2. *For normal goods, Marshallian consumer's surplus must be greater than the compensating variation and less than the equivalent variation.*

   Marshallian consumer's surplus (MCS) is the extra amount that the consumer could be made to pay for the quantity he consumes, above the price he actually pays; the compensating variation (CV) is the amount of money that could be extracted from him for the privilege of buying the good at the fixed price he actually pays; the equivalent variation (EV) is the amount by which he would have to be bribed to forego the opportunity to purchase the good at the market price. Clearly, more money can be extracted from him if he is free to adjust his consumption pattern as his income falls than if he is constrained to consume his original quantity of the good.

Hence CV exceeds MCS. Also, for the same level of utility, the marginal utility of money must be lower if he cannot spend it on the good than if he can; hence more money is required to compensate him for not being able to trade than can be extracted from him when he is able to trade. So EV must be greater than CV.

An alternative answer to this question is to use the Hicksian bounds for compensating and equivalent variation. For a price decrease, the answer becomes

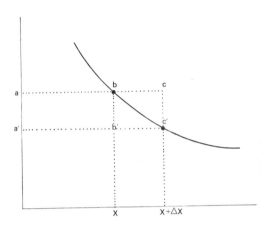

$$CV \geqslant abb'a'$$

$$EV \leqslant acc'a'$$

Marshallian Consumers Surplus $= abc'a'$.

Thus CV < Marshallian CS < EV.

3. *If a firm has monopoly power in selling commodity X, and the firm's management maximizes sales subject only to non-negative total profits, the firm's debt-to-equity ratio will be higher than the average for profit maximizing firms.*
The value of stock in a firm that makes no profits ought to be zero. Such a firm could only finance itself by debt-issuance, and its debt-equity ratio should be infinite. Profit-maximizing firms will have positive profits and positive equity value. Q.E.D.

4. *Engel's Law states that people spend approximately 25 per cent of their income on housing regardless of their level of income.*
It is necessary to distinguish between the Engel curve or income-expansion line, which is a theoretical technique, and Engel's Law, which is the empirical finding that as income rises expenditure on food (or more generally perhaps 'necessaries') falls as a proportion of total income. Engel's Law should not be confused with the 'safe

rule' proposed by many financial experts (household finance, that is, including mortgage companies) that expenditure on housing should not exceed 25 per cent of total income.

5. *A competitive firm is less likely to practice racial discrimination in hiring than is a non-competitive firm, and any kind of firm is less likely to practice racial discrimination for high-skilled jobs than for low-skilled jobs.*
There is no obvious reason why discrimination should apply more to low-skilled than to high-skilled jobs. As regards the influence of competition, if discrimination results from employer prejudice it can be financed out of potential monopoly profits but not out of profits in a competitive industry unless all the capital is owned by the discriminating entrepreneur (all the capital of his own enterprise, that is). Where discrimination is insisted on by white workers, the situation is more complicated, but the likely result is not discrimination but segregation of white and black workers in different firms without a wage differential.

6. *If A is a substitute for B, B is a complement of C, and C is a substitute for D, then A and D must be complements.*
One might assume that if they are defined for a constant level of utility, substitutability and complementarity must be transitive; and that therefore the statement must be true. An argument on these lines would be acceptable. However, the answer is questionable. Since the substitution matrix is symmetric, one needs $n\left(\dfrac{n-1}{2}\right)$ pieces of information to determine fully a $n \times n$ matrix. Thus in a 4×4 matrix we need six pieces of information, yet we have only three.

7. *If all the firms in an industry quote the same price to all consumers then the industry must be competitive.*
Obviously the same price need not be the competitive price.

8. *If an educational loan programme were introduced and if the expected return to the borrower exceeded the cost of the loan an individual would be irrational if he did not accept the loan.*
The statement is a little ambiguous, since there may be both costs not covered by the loan, and psychological satisfactions or dissatisfactions from the educational process itself. But the main point is that a risk-averter will take into account the variance as well as the expected return of his investment and may rationally not take the loan even though the expected net return is positive.

9. *On Friedman's interpretation of it the Marshallian demand curve must always be less elastic than the Hicksian demand curve.*
The Hicksian demand curve keeps money income constant, and

hence incorporates an income as well as a substitution effect. The Marshallian demand curve on Friedman's interpretation (and ignoring some complexities about whether compensation for price changes is exact in terms of maintaining constant utility or overcompensates by maintaining the capacity to purchase the original quantities of goods) contains only the substitution effect. Hence which curve is more elastic depends on whether the income effect is positive or negative, i.e. on whether the good in question is normal or inferior.

10. *If two individuals with identical preferences and incomes choose different mixes of goods, one of them must be irrational.*
There are two possibilities of both individuals being rational: either they confront different prices in the market, or there is a linear segment (with slope equal to the price ratio) in their indifference curve. Appeal to differences in attitudes towards risk, etc., violates the 'identical preferences' assumption.

11. *If the rate of return on capital is higher than the natural rate of growth society should increase its savings ratio; if the natural rate of growth exceeds the rate of return on capital one requires an intertemporal utility function to determine whether society should increase its consumption ratio.*
Both halves of the statement are the exact opposite of the correct proposition.

12. *The theory of common property resources suggests the conclusion that California is overpopulated relative to the rest of the United States.*
The theory of common property resources applies not only to fisheries, as some assume from the literature, but to any aspect of the natural environment that contributes to production or utility and yet for which no rent is charged. If people are attracted to California by sea, sun, mountains etc. for which they do not pay, they will come until the average amenity value of these goodies plus their wages equals amenity values plus wages elsewhere in the USA. Hence California would be overpopulated relative to the rest of the USA if the assumptions of the argument hold. But (i) the amenities of California may not be greater than those available elsewhere (ask any State tourist office!); (ii) rent for the amenities may be absorbed into the values of California land properties; (iii — a lesser point) since wages in California tend to be higher than those elsewhere one might argue that California has not yet reached the theoretically predictable point of overpopulation.

13. *Except in long-run stationary equilibrium the net marginal product of capital, the rate of interest, and the rate of time preference will not be equal to one another.*

If one uses the Fisher model, the rate of interest, rate of return over cost on investment, and marginal rate of time preference are equal. If, on the other hand, one distinguished between the marginal product of capital as the rate of return in long-run stationary equilibrium, the rate of time preference as reflecting the marginal rate of substitution between present and future consumption in the same stationary conditions, and the rate of interest as reflecting the balancing of the desires to save and to invest whether the economy is in long-run stationary equilibrium or not, the statement is true.

14. *If a sample of prices in the Chicago area shows that the price of $X(P_x)$ varies from 50 per cent to 150 per cent of its average, while the price of $Y(P_y)$ varies only from 90 per cent to 110 per cent of its average, then you can be relatively certain that $XP_x/YP_y < 1$.*
This is a cross-section sample of prices at a given point of time; hence all references to demand and supply elasticities, cyclical variations, etc., are completely irrelevant. The question refers to the extent to which the 'law of indifference' according to which prices should be equalized throughout the market area is not fulfilled. The answer lies in the costs of search, and the Stigler proposition that consumers will invest more in market search the larger their total expenditure on the relevant goods (note that the absolute price of the commodity has nothing to do with this proposition: price per unit may be high or low in nominal terms without telling us anything about expenditures). The proposition is a probability, not a certainty, hence 'you can be relatively certain'.

B. *(20 points). In February 1971 Britain will convert its currency system from pounds, shillings and pence to a decimal system. A penny in the new system will correspond to 2·4 pence in the old system; there will also be a new half-penny worth 1·2 old pence. Some economists have argued that decimalization will be inflationary (i.e. raise the price level and the cost of living) because merchants and shop keepers will, for convenience in book-keeping and making transactions, 'round up' their quoted prices into the nearest equivalent in new currency units. Discuss this argument.*
Contrary to what many students assumed, this a price theory and not a monetary theory question. The essential point in the answer is that sellers fix not only a price but a quantity to which that price applies. If you get one ounce of something for an old penny and 1·2 onces of it for a new half-penny, prices in the economic sense have not risen. Further, price-cum-quantity adjustments of this kind are the only rational ones for sellers, if initially their prices were equilibrium prices. This has two implications: (a) The argument of some candidates that some prices would be rounded up and others rounded down, with no net inflationary effect, assumes initial disequilibrium (although some were clever enough to introduce differential transactions costs with the new currency as an influence on the decision); (b) If there is an inflation going on, and sellers are reluctant to raise posted prices overtly for fear of loss

of goodwill, decimalization may enable them to make more covertly and hence faster price adjustments they would have made anyway. Candidates who placed their faith on MV = PT might nore that if prices are rounded up and then forced down in nominal terms by the inexorable operation of the honorable equation, there could still have been a redistribution of income from consumers to merchants and hence in a relevant sense an 'inflation'.

Some candidates, confident of their grasp of economic theory, especially monetary theory, wondered why any 'economists' could be silly enough to consider this a real problem. They may be interested to know that the Social Science Research Council of Great Britain is spending quite a lot of public money to find out the answer. It is a reasonable question if one believes in cost-push inflation, which some people outside Chicago do.

C. (20 *points*). *Walter Heller, Arthur Burns, and other eminent economists have argued for selective controls on prices as a means of reducing the current rate of inflation. Discuss the theory underlying this proposal in terms of a standard model of general equilibrium containing two goods and money.*
The sum of the excess demands in all markets must be zero. Inflation involves excess supply of money and excess demands for goods. In this framework, selective price control must depend on the proposition that holding down the relative prices of the selected goods reduces the excess supply of money by inducing people to substitute money rather than the uncontrolled good for the price-controlled good. Some candidates took the line, which at a stretch fits into this frame of reference, that the public's expectations of continued inflation were unrealistic and likely to produce 'overshooting' and a cyclical movement of prices, and that price controls on key items would fix prices at the levels at which they ought to be, given the government's deflationary policies.

D. (15 *points*). *An economist went into a bar where beers and whiskies cost $1·00 each and drank six beers and four whiskies. The next night he went into another bar where beers cost 50c and whiskies $1·50. He drank six whiskies and two beers. Was he rational enough to pass the Core the next day?*
This is a straight exercise in the weak axiom of revealed preference. The student's first-night consumption could have been bought by the second night's at a saving of one dollar on the amount actually spent, and his second-night consumption could have been bought by the first night's at a saving of two dollars on the amount actually spent. Hence his preferences on the two nights were inconsistent. Efforts to conjure up a greater need for alcohol as the writing of the Core approached, or the presence of companions unnoticed by the composers of the question, who for sociological reasons (externalities) affected the utility-maximizing choices of the student, evoked amusement but no credit.

E. (25 *points*) (1) *What, if any, economic reasons are there for the contemporary concern about pollution?*

(2) *Under what arrangement would the amount of air pollution be socially optimal?*

(3) *What are the main obstacles to the establishment of such arrangements?* This was a straightforward application of the Coase Theorem and surrounding argument, though the first part allowed the alternatives of explaining why pollution poses a real economic problem, and explaining (in terms of population growth and urbanization, rising income and income-elastic demand for amenities, the horrors of modern chemical technology, etc.) why concern about it has been mounting.

F. (30 *points*). *Consider an economy producing two goods, X and Y, using two factors of production, K and L, under conditions of constant returns to scale. X is K-intensive and Y L-intensive at all factor price ratios.*

(1) *Analyse the effect of an increase in K on the production of X and Y and the distribution of income on the assumption that the relative price of X in terms of Y is constant.*

(2) *Repeat the analysis on the assumption that the economy divides its expenditure in a constant ratio between the two commodities. What conclusions can you establish on the assumption that the production functions are of Cobb–Douglas form which would not hold in the general case?*

(3) *Assume that Y is a permanently-lasting capital good, that a constant fraction of income is saved, and that labour grows at a fixed exponential rate. What would happen to the economy?*

(4) *On the assumptions of (3) what will be the effects of a once-over labour-saving technical improvement in the production function for Y?*

Part 1 is straight Rybcynski theorem: production of X expands and of Y contracts, and all the additional income goes to the owners of capital. A number of candidates confused themselves with the idea that the production changes required factor price changes, though these are ruled out by the assumption of the model; others ignored the given assumption that factor prices are fixed (via the fixity of commodity prices) and plunged into the discussion of the price changes required to preserve equilibrium in a closed economy, a problem deferred until Part 2.

Part 2, properly executed, would have led into the diagrammatics of Part 3, particularly the finding that with expenditure divided in a constant proportion between the goods, and with the price of X having to fall, production of X must expand proportionally more than that of Y. In general one can only show that the absolute income of labour must increase; what happens to the absolute and relative shares of capital depends on the parameters. But with Cobb–Douglas functions in each industry, factor shares in the amount spent on each industry must be constant; and with expenditure equally divided between the industries, constant industry shares necessarily impy constant overall factor shares in total income. This in turn implies an increase in the absolute share of capital. Note that both the Cobb–Douglas and the equal expenditure (or any other fixed expenditure ratio) assumption are necessary to this result. Some candidates reverted to a one-sector model and assumed that

Cobb–Douglas production functions (or a C–D function for the whole economy, which there is not) would be sufficient for the result.

On Part 3, again, many candidates reverted to the single-sector assumption, which is not the model of the question. Some did note that with the capital good labour-intensive, the possibility of multiple equilibria is ruled out, though few if any really understood why; and that therefore the two-sector model specified would behave like the one-sector model, and converge on an equilibrium growth path given by the exogeneous exponential rate of population increase. Only a few used the Ramaswami–Johnson diagrammatic technique to expound the results.

Part 4 is easily answered with the above-mentioned technique, though it can be answered without it. Start from the long-run equilibrium growth path, and introduce the labour-saving technical improvement in capital goods production, keeping relative prices initially constant. Income at those prices must increase, implying that the economy can have more consumption per head while maintaining its capital stock per head intact. Increased income implies more saving and more investment, at those prices, hence the capital per head must grow. Moreover, this effect is reinforced by the fact that at constant relative prices with a labour-saving invention in the labour-intense industry production of consumption goods must fall and of capital goods (the labour-intensive goods) must increase by more than the value of the increased income. Hence there will be an excessive supply, of, and consequently fall in the price of, the capital goods; hence, the relative price of capital goods falling, saving buys more capital. Hence both capital per head and consumption per head must increase by comparison with the pre-technical change situation.

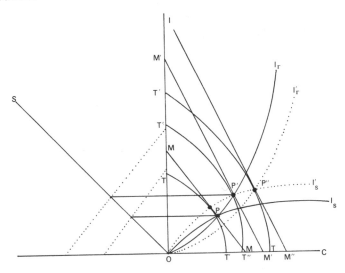

TT	initial transformation curve
P	initial equilibrium
S	savings relation

I_r investment requirement curve—to keep capital per head constant

I_s investment supply with fixed savings ratio

MM initial budget line

$M'M'$ new budget line at old prices; $P' =$ production point

I'_r new investment requirement curve

I'_s new savings supply curve

P'' new long-run equilibrium growth position

University of Chicago Qualifying Examination in Price Theory, Summer 1971

All questions are compulsory. Total time allowed is three hours. The maximum score is one point per minute. Unless otherwise indicated, sub-sections of questions carry equal weight.

  I. (*60 points*). *Indicate whether you believe each of the following statements to be TRUE, FALSE, or UNCERTAIN. In each case write a few sentences explaining your answer. Your grade will be determined by your explanation.*

    1. *In a society of risk-averters, the distribution of personal income would skewed to the right.*

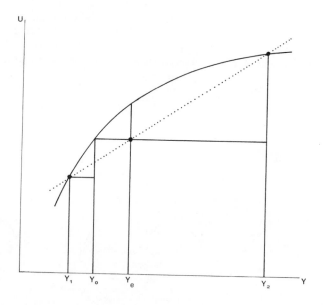

The statement is true. Consider for simplicity an economy with only two careers open, one offering a certain income Y_c and the other a fifty-fifty chance of Y_1 and Y_2, the mathematically expected income being $Y_e = \frac{1}{2}Y_1 + \frac{1}{2}Y_2$. The allocation of people to careers must adjust so that the incomes, Y_c, Y_1 and Y_2 are such that $U(Y_c)$ is equal to $\frac{1}{2}U(Y_1) + \frac{1}{2}U(Y_2)$. Risk aversion means that Y_e must exceed

Y_c to an extent depending on the degree of risk aversion, i.e. $Y_2 - Y_c$ must exceed $Y_c - Y_1$. In equilibrium a certain number will receive Y_c, and each half of the rest will receive respectively Y_1 and Y_2; hence the distribution will be skewed to the right.

2. *A competitive firm that has a Cobb–Douglas production function will have a wage bill which is independent of both factor prices and the price of its output.*
False. The share of wages in total cost is a constant, but total cost will depend on the price and the firm's output, the latter being indeterminate for a competitive firm with a Cobb–Douglas production function.

3. *If capitalists demand a premium rate of return for investing in certain socially unpopular activities such as illegal gambling, drug-peddling, and prostitution, the result will be that all capitalists will earn a lower rate of return on their capital than they otherwise would.*
Uncertain. Those in the unpopular activities earn a premium rate of return over the rest. This is like a tax on the use of capital in the unpopular activities and reduces the scale of those activities. If they are capital-intensive, the rate of return elsewhere is lower than it would be without the premium and may be so low that the return including the premium in the unpopular activities is lower than it otherwise would be. Conversely, if the unpopular activities are labour-intensive, the rate of return in them must be higher than it would be otherwise and the rate of return in ordinary activities may also be higher.

   If capital is supplied according to a minimum rate of time preference, no capitalist will earn less than he otherwise would and those in the unpopular activities will earn a higher rate of return (this return being necessary to compensate for the disutility of being unpopular and therefore not prompting more saving).

4. *It will never pay an employer to bear the costs of training his workers, if after completing training the worker can move to another job with another employer.*
The question is not whether the worker can move but whether he will have an inducement to do so. If the training paid for by the employer is general training, he will, so the employer will not undertake the cost. If the training is specific to the employer, the worker cannot gain by moving and it may be worth the employer's while to pay the cost of training. The statement is false.

5. *One of the major difficulties in measuring the economic benefits of scientific research is due to the conventions of national income accounting according to which government expenditures are treated.*
Note that the question says one of the major difficulties; assertions that some other difficulty such as externalities is more important cut no ice. The problem is to attach a cash value to the benefits, i.e. a

return to expenditure. But government activities are entered in the social accounts at cost (it is not true that they are reckoned as consumption and not investment, since one has the breakdowns) hence there is no income flow for the benefits of government R & D in the accounts. The statement is true.

6. *An individual with wealth of $1000 is willing to wager anything from $1 to $1000 in a coin-tossing game so long as he will gain twice as much on heads as he will lose on tails. Over this region his utility of wealth curve is linear.*

An individual with a linear utility of wealth curve will bet any amount on a fair coin-toss provided he gains the same amount on a head as he loses on a tail. This individual requires double as much on a head in gain as he loses on a tail; hence his marginal utility of income must be decreasing. Note that either a risk-lover or a risk-indifferent individual would bet the whole $1000 on a bet like this, not be indifferent about the amount he is willing to bet, so that it is incorrect to argue that the individual in question might be one of these as well as a risk-averter. The statement is false.

A further note on TFU no. 6:
The foregoing notes follow the approach adopted by all candidates in tackling the question. However, the information given implies the following specific form of the individual's utility function, depicted in the accompanying graph.

$$U = a\,Y, \qquad \text{where} \qquad Y \leqslant \$1000$$
$$U = \tfrac{1}{2}\,a\,Y, \qquad \text{where} \qquad Y \geqslant \$1000$$

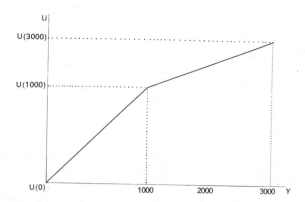

(Note that addition of a constant would not alter anything.) His utility of wealth curve is therefore linear over the range from zero to one thousand dollars, and also linear over the range from one thousand dollars up to three thousand dollars (the maximum amount he can gain if he bets his whole wealth). The statement is therefore either true or false, depending on whether the phrase 'over this region' is interpreted as pertaining only to the range of possible outcomes if he loses or if he wins, or the whole range of possible outcomes from gambling.

Another interpretation of the statement is permitted by its wording, though this one is rather far-fetched. Assume the individual pays X for a ticket on the toss, and if it comes up tails he gets nothing back whereas if it comes up heads he gets back $2X$. He gains gross twice as much as he loses gross. This is a fair bet and his utility of wealth curve will on this interpretation be linear.

7. *The accumulation of capital in a long-run Ricardian model must increase both the relative share of labour and the relative share of land.*

The accumulation of capital in a long-run Ricardian model must increase the relative share of labour, because the wage is set at subsistence and the average product of labour is falling. But while the absolute share of land must rise, the relative share of land will rise only if the elasticity of substitution between labour and land is less than unity. (Remember that in a Ricardian model, capital is the subsistence of the workers and does not enter into the production function directly.) The statement is therefore false.

8. *A patent usually entitles the owner of an invention to charge as much as he wants for the right to use his invention. Hence a patented cost reduction will not affect the price of the product because the optimal royalty rate will just equal the cost reduction.*

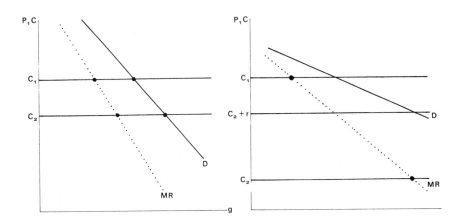

Note first that for theoretical purposes we assume that the patentor can charge a price that leaves the purchaser on the margin of indifference; hence it is no answer to say that he must charge less to induce use of his invention. (Anyway, under competition the user will have to pass the benefit on to the consumer of the product, retaining no profit for himself.) Under competition in the using industry we have two possibilities, shown in the diagrams. In each case an implicit demand curve for the use of the invention is given by the current cost curve up to the current level of output, then by the marginal revenue curve beyond that point, with a discontinuity between. If the new cost curve cuts through the discontinuity, the statement would be correct; if the new cost curve cuts the marginal revenue curve below the discontinuity, the inventory will charge less than the cost difference. Note that it makes no difference whether the inventor charges a price per unit of output with his process, or a flat sum with the user free to decide how far to use it, provided he fixes the flat sum to yield the same revenue, because users will have to cover their costs. In the case of a monopolized user industry, there is an obvious problem of bilateral bargaining. Ignoring that possibility, and assuming that the inventor sets a price for his invention which the monopolist either takes or leaves, the monopolist's marginal revenue curve is the demand curve for the invention, and the same two cases arrive as in the case of a competitive industry. It is not correct to treat the potentialities as without limit. The inventor could charge the amount of the cost saving to the monopolist; or he could charge less in order to make it possible for the monopolist to lower his profit-maximizing price and increase his sales.

The statement is therefore either false or uncertain.

9. *The following consumer behavior is irrational:*

	p_1	q_1	p_2	q_2
Period one	1·00	75	1·00	25
Period two	0·90	70	1·50	30

$$\text{Calculation 1} \begin{cases} \Sigma\, p_0 q_0 = 100 \\ \Sigma\, p_0 q_1 = 100 \end{cases}$$

$$\text{Calculation 2} \begin{cases} \Sigma\, p_1 q_1 = 108 \\ \Sigma\, p_1 q_0 = 105 \end{cases}$$

The statement is true, though some candidates' arithmetic was not reliable enough to enable them to prove or determine it. It depends on the use of the weak axiom of revealed preference. According to the first pair of calculations, the individual bought collection number one when he could have bought collection number two at the same price; hence he either preferred collection 1 to collection 2 or was indifferent between them. Calculation two shows that in period 2 he bought collection 2 when he could have bought collection 1 for a smaller expenditure; hence collection 2 was preferred to collection 1 in that period. The individual's behavior was therefore inconsistent between the two periods. He can be described as irrational. Hence the statement is true. Of course, one could also say that his tastes changed between the two periods, but there is no reason why that should have happened.

10. *The elasticity of demand for a factor by a competitive industry must be lower when the quantities of other factors are held constant than when the prices of other factors are held constant.*

    This is necessarily true, regardless of any relations of substitution and complementarity among the various factors of production. With fixed quantities of the other factors, a fall in the price of the one factor can only lead to usage of additional amounts of that factor along with the fixed quantities of the other factors. With fixed prices of the other factors, it is possible both to substitute more of this factor for less of its substitutes, and to hire more of its complements to work with it. The proposition is one of the standard propositions of Samuelson's *Foundations*.

11. *The construction of a rapid-transit system should decrease rents at the urban center and increase rents in the suburbs.*

    In so far as the choice of central versus suburban location involves equalization of total cost of residence, i.e. rent plus cash and time cost of travel to and from work, a rapid transit system will increase the relative attractiveness of suburban versus central residence. It is obviously nonsensical to appeal to the exceptional possibility that the rapid transit system costs enough more than previous transport modes to offset the saving of time involved, since then the building of the system would be uneconomic. The only valid exceptional possibility is that the system attracts enough extra people into the metropolitan area to raise the demand for housing at the centre sufficiently to offset the induced exodus from the centre to the suburbs on the part of the existing population. (It cannot raise rents more, if we assume that people outside the city were previously on the margin of indifference between city (central or suburban) residence and rural residence.) The answer should be 'true', because the exception is a limiting case.

12. *The short-run equilibrium of a two-sector model will be unique if either each factor has a marginal preference for consumption of the commodity that uses it intensively, or the average elasticity of substitution between factors of production exceeds unity. Otherwise, there will be multiple equilibria.*

    The answer should be false, but the explanation should point out that only two of the three parts are false. There are two sufficient conditions for uniqueness, either each factor has a marginal preference for consumption of the good that employs it *unintensively,* or the reverse condition holds and the average elasticity of substitution between factors of production in the production functions exceeds unity. Even if neither of these conditions is fulfilled, multiple equilibrium may still not result, because under the second alternative possibility of elasticities of substitution averaging less than unity with a marginal preference of each factor for the good that uses it intensively, the redistribution effect may not be large enough to outweigh the production and consumption–substitution effects.

II. (30 *points*). *Production of a certain good can take place only in a plant of unique size, for which the daily fixed cost is $40 and the absolute capacity is* 20 *units of output per day. Variable cost is* 3 *per unit of output. These data are the same irrespective of the number of plants a firm may operate.* This is a trickier question than it looks, and needs to be read carefully. A number of candidates overlooked the 'both short and long run' in (a), and the information that a firm may operate more than one plant, and simply drew the cost curve for one plant. In (b) many did not realize that '(iii) no plant' did not mean 'no production'; it means a 'full capacity use of . . . (iii) no plant', as the sentence plainly says. In both (a) and (c), some assumed wrongly that the $40 fixed cost disappears in the long run, because 'in the long run there are no fixed costs'; what that phrase means is that the firm does not have to incur the $40 fixed cost of a marginal plant if it is not profitable to do so. In (c), many assumed that competition means firms have to charge marginal cost, and put this at $3; in fact competition means firms have to charge minimum average cost, which *is* 5. (This is, of course, the marginal cost of another firm to society under competitive conditions, per unit of its output.)

(a) *Describe, either geometrically or algebraically, the firm's total, average, and marginal cost curves, both long and short run.*

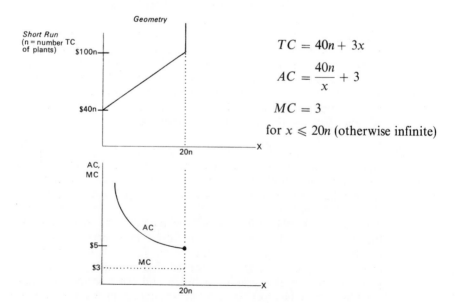

Geometry

Short Run
(n = number of plants)

$$TC = 40n + 3x$$

$$AC = \frac{40n}{x} + 3$$

$$MC = 3$$

for $x \leqslant 20n$ (otherwise infinite)

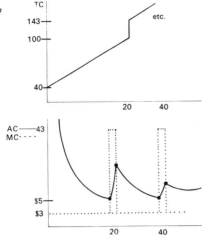

$$TC = 40\delta + 3x$$

$$AC = \frac{40\delta}{x} + 3$$

where $\delta = 1$ for $x \leqslant 20$

$\qquad = 2$ for $20 < X \leqslant 40$

etc.

$MC = 43$ for $x = 1, 21, 41 \ldots$

3 for other values

(b) *If the firm is a monopolist, show graphically the determinants of its long-run output. Illustrate possible equilibria with a full capacity use of (i) all plants (ii) some but not all plants (iii) no plant.*

The problem here comes from the discontinuity of the marginal cost curve. Consider the choice of whether to add a marginal plant, assuming as is necessary that marginal revenue exceeds $3 for the first unit it produces.

The marginal cost of the first unit produced with the new plant is $43, the next units have a marginal cost of $3 each. If y units are produced, total marginal cost is $40 + 3y$. The total marginal revenue is $\sum_1^y$ M.R.(y), and the plant will only be worth having if this sum exceeds total marginal cost. All plants will be fully utilized if *either* marginal cost exceeds marginal revenue in this plant, in which case the plant would not be built, *or* if the reverse were true *and* the marginal revenue from $y = 20$ just happened to be $3 (or the marginal revenue from $y = 21$ were $3 or less).

Note for (ii) that so long as one plant would not be fully used, it would be a matter of indifference how many plants were underutilized, since marginal cost is the same in all of them. The extreme case would be 19 plants producing 19 units each.

Note for (iii) that the marginal plant that is just worth building may be the first one (if it is unprofitable, there is no monopolist).

(c) *Suppose no firm is allowed to operate more than one plant but there is free entry (all firms having the same cost curves). What will the equilibrium price be if*

(i) *The nature of demand is such that there are several hundred firms in the industry*

(ii) *There are only two or three firms (but still free entry) in the industry?*

If each firm can have only one plant and there is free entry, entry will go on until it is unprofitable.
(i) With hundreds of firms, the marginal entrant will make no difference to the price; price will be driven down to minimum average cost, which will be $5.
(ii) With only two or three firms, the firms will collude to set a price, and an equal production quantity for each, such that an entrant who comes in would find that optimal collusion would involve losses all round, hence will refrain from entry. The collusion price could be above minimum average cost under competition.

III. (10 *points*). *In cities where apartments have been overbuilt, so that vacancy rates rise to abnormal levels, landlords typically do not reduce their rents, but instead offer concessions in the form of either one or more months of rent-free tenancy, or expenditure on redecorating to suit the prospective tenant's taste. Are these procedures rational? And is one more rational than the other?*
There are two questions here. The first is why landlords do not cut the rental rate per month instead of offering once-for-all transitory bonuses. The answer to this has to be a combination of the expectation that the apartment glut will disappear and the nominal rent prove appropriate later on, and costs of adjusting rents upwards (e.g. rent control or tenant ill-will). Comparing the two types of concession, a temporary rent reduction should be more attractive to the tenant than decoration at the same cost; but, from the landlord's viewpoint, temporary rent reduction encourages fly-by-nights who move out once the rent-concession terminates, breaking their lease, while redecoration encourages the tenant to stay. Also redecoration may cost the landlord less than it would cost the tenant. Finally, either type of concession permits discrimination in favour of new tenants as against existing tenants, in a form that makes it hard for the latter to see.

IV. (10 *points*). *Comment on the following statement: 'Although much has been made of the Coase Theorem in connection with pollution, it is not of much relevance to the important issue of determining the socially optimal amount of pollution, since the environment is a public good.'*
The Coase theorem is about externalities and the resolution of associated problems under a system of contract. Pollution involves such externalities. The environment is a common property resource, since it is not usually charged for; but it is not a public good, since when I pollute it I reduce the enjoyment you can get from it. The real problems with the environment are that the property rights in it are not clearly defined legally, so that the Coase type of contract solution is hard to arrange, and that the claimants are so many that transactions costs of settling compensation for externalities are extremely high and resort to the state's powers of legislation is more feasible.

V. (30 *points*). *The utility function of a society is* $U = X^{1/3}Y^{2/3}$, *where X and Y are the two goods produced. Their production functions are*

$$X = L^{3/4}K^{1/4}$$

$$Y = L^{1/4}K^{3/4}$$

where $L_x + L_y = \bar{L}$ and $K_x + K_y = \bar{K}$. *Which will produce the greater welfare lost, a tax on X at the rate of* 10 *per cent or a tax on labour used in producing X at the rate of* 20 *per cent? Explain your answer.*

A genius might have answered this one with a moment's thought and no algebra, owing to an oversight by the examiners. Given the specific coefficients of the production functions, a 20 per cent tax on the use of labour in X is a 15 per cent tax on the price of X, and in addition distorts the factor markets and causes inefficiency in production. Thus it must be worse for welfare than a 10 per cent tax on the price of X, which is at a lower rate and introduces no distortions.

For the ordinary economist, including the examiners who set the question, this is an exercise in indirect utility functions. The following notes set out the algebra for both the general case, and the specific case set in the question. Adepts should be able to solve the problem in much less space; in any case, candidates were given credit for incomplete answers provided they had started on the right lines.

THE GENERAL CASE

$$U = X^{\alpha}Y^{1-\alpha}$$

$$X = L_x^{\beta}K_x^{1-\beta}$$

$$Y = L_y^{\gamma}K_y^{1-\gamma}$$

$$L_x + L_y = \bar{L}$$

$$K_x + K_y = \bar{K}.$$

Hence U can be written as

$$U = L_x^{\alpha\beta}K_x^{\alpha(1-\beta)}L_y^{(1-\alpha)\gamma}K_y^{(1-\alpha)(1-\gamma)}$$

$$\frac{\partial U}{\partial X} = \alpha\frac{U}{X}, \qquad \frac{\partial U}{\partial Y} = (1-\alpha)\frac{U}{Y}.$$

Hence

$$\frac{\dfrac{\partial U}{\partial X}}{\dfrac{\partial U}{\partial Y}} = \frac{\alpha}{1-\alpha}\frac{Y}{X} = p_x = \tau c_x$$

where p_x is the price of X in terms of Y, c_x is the relative cost of X in terms of Y, and $\tau = 1 + t_x$ represents the distortion of market price from production cost due to the commodity tax.

$$\frac{\partial X}{\partial L_x} = \beta \frac{X}{L_x} \qquad \frac{\partial Y}{\partial L_y} = \gamma \frac{Y}{L_y}$$

$$\frac{\partial X}{\partial K_x} = (1 - \beta)\frac{X}{K_x} \qquad \frac{\partial Y}{\partial K_y} = (1 - \gamma)\frac{Y}{K_y}.$$

Using the conditions for competitive factor market equilibrium, with $\delta = 1 + t_{x1}$ to represent the tax on labour used in producing X

$$c_x \frac{\partial X}{\partial L_x} = \delta \frac{\partial Y}{\partial L_y} \qquad\qquad c_x \frac{\partial X}{\partial K_x} = \frac{\partial Y}{\partial K_y}$$

$$c_x \beta \frac{X}{L_x} = \delta \gamma \frac{Y}{L_y} \qquad\qquad c_x(1 - \beta)\frac{X}{K_x} = (1 - \gamma)\frac{Y}{K_y}$$

Substituting for Y/X in terms of c_x from above

$$c_x\beta \frac{L_y}{L_x} = \delta\gamma \frac{1 - \alpha}{\alpha} \tau c_x \qquad\qquad c_x(1 - \beta)\frac{K_y}{K_x} = (1 - \gamma)\frac{1 - \alpha}{\alpha}\tau c_x$$

$$\frac{L_y}{L_x} = \frac{\delta\gamma(1 - \alpha)\tau}{\alpha\beta} \qquad\qquad \frac{K_y}{K_x} = \frac{(1 - \gamma)(1 - \alpha)\tau}{\alpha(1 - \beta)}.$$

Using the factor endowment constraints and simplifying,

$$L_x = \frac{\alpha\beta}{\alpha\beta + (1 - \alpha)\delta\gamma\tau}\ \bar{L} \qquad K_x = \frac{\alpha(1 - \beta)}{\alpha(1 - \beta) + (1 - \alpha)(1 - \gamma)\tau}\ \bar{K}$$

$$L_y = \frac{(1 - \alpha)\delta\gamma\tau}{\alpha\beta + (1 - \alpha)\delta\gamma\tau}\ \bar{L} \qquad K_y = \frac{(1 - \alpha)(1 - \gamma)\tau}{\alpha(1 - \beta) + (1 - \alpha)(1 - \gamma)\tau}\ \bar{K}.$$

Substituting in the utility function,

$$U = \left[\frac{\alpha\beta}{\alpha\beta + (1 - \alpha)\delta\gamma\tau}\right]^{\alpha\beta}\left[\frac{(1 - \alpha)\delta\gamma\tau}{\alpha\beta + (1 - \alpha)\delta\gamma\tau}\right]^{(1 - \alpha)\gamma}$$

$$\times\ \bar{L}^{\alpha\beta + (1 - \alpha)\gamma}\left[\frac{\alpha(1 - \beta)}{\alpha(1 - \beta) + (1 - \alpha)(1 - \gamma)\tau}\right]^{\alpha(1 - \beta)}$$

$$\times\left[\frac{(1 - \alpha)(1 - \gamma)\tau}{\alpha(1 - \beta) + (1 - \alpha)(1 - \gamma)\tau}\right]^{(1 - \alpha)(1 - \gamma)}\ \bar{K}^{\alpha(1 - \beta) + (1 - \alpha)(1 - \gamma)}$$

Eliminating constant terms

$$\frac{U}{\text{constant}} =$$

$$\frac{(\delta\tau)^{(1 - \alpha)\alpha}\tau^{(1 - \alpha)(1 - \gamma)}}{(\alpha\beta + (1 - \alpha)\delta\gamma\tau)^{\alpha\beta + (1 - \alpha)\gamma}(\alpha(1 - \beta) + (1 - \alpha)(1 - \gamma)\tau)^{\alpha(1 - \beta) + (1 - \alpha)(1 - \gamma)}}$$

$$[\delta = 1]$$

$$\frac{U(\tau)}{\text{constant}} = \frac{\tau^{(1-\alpha)}}{(\alpha\beta + (1-\alpha)\gamma\tau)^{\gamma+\alpha(\beta-\gamma)}(\alpha(1-\beta) + (1-\alpha)(1-\gamma)\tau)^{1-\gamma+\alpha(\gamma-\beta)}}$$

$$[\tau = 1]$$

$$= \frac{\delta^{(1-\alpha)\gamma}}{(\alpha\beta + (1-\alpha)\gamma\delta)^{\gamma+\alpha(\beta-\gamma)}(\alpha(1-\beta) + (1-\alpha)(1-\gamma))^{1-\gamma+\alpha(\gamma-\beta)}}$$

Let $\gamma + \alpha(\beta - \gamma) = A$

$$\frac{U(\tau)}{U(\delta)} = \frac{\tau^{(1-\alpha)}}{\delta^{(1-\alpha)\gamma}} \frac{(\alpha\beta + (1-\alpha)\gamma\delta)^A(\alpha(1-\beta) + (1-\alpha)(1-\gamma))^{1-A}}{(\alpha\beta + (1-\alpha)\gamma\tau)^A(\alpha(1-\beta) + (1-\alpha)(1-\gamma)\tau)^{1-A}}$$

Using the specific values given in the question,

$$\alpha = 1/3, \beta = 3/4, \gamma = 1/4, \tau = 1\cdot1, \delta = 1\cdot2$$

$$A = \gamma + \alpha(\beta - \gamma) = 5/12, \ 1 - A = 7/12$$

$$\alpha\beta + (1-\alpha)\gamma\delta \qquad = 9/12$$

$$\alpha(1-\beta) + (1-\alpha)(1-\gamma) \ = 7/12$$

$$\alpha\beta + (1-\alpha)\gamma\tau \ . \qquad = 13/30$$

$$\alpha(1-\beta) + (1-\alpha)(1-\gamma)\tau = 19/30$$

$$\frac{U(\tau)}{U(\delta)} = \frac{(1\cdot1)^{2/3}(9/20)^{5/12}(7/12)^{7/12}}{(1\cdot2)^{1/6}(13/30)^{5/12}(19/30)^{7/12}}$$

$$\left(\frac{U(\tau)}{U(\delta)}\right)^{12} = \frac{(1\cdot1)^8}{(1\cdot2)^2}\left(\frac{27}{26}\right)^5\left(\frac{35}{38}\right)^7$$

$$= \frac{(1\cdot1)^8}{(1\cdot2)^2}(1\cdot03846)^5 (0\cdot92105)^7$$

For further working of the particular case see below.

THE SPECIFIC CASE

$$U = X^{1/3}Y^{2/3} \qquad L_x + L_y = \overline{L}$$

$$X = L^{3/4}K^{1/4} \qquad K_x + K_y = \overline{K}$$

$$Y = L^{1/4}K^{3/4} \qquad U = L_x^{1/4}L_y^{1/6}K_x^{1/12}K_y^{1/2}$$

$$\frac{U_x}{U_y} = \frac{1}{2}\frac{Y}{X} = (1 + t_x)c_x \qquad c_x = \frac{1}{2(1 + t_x)}\frac{Y}{X}$$

$$c_x\frac{3}{4}\frac{X}{L_x} = (1 + t_x)\frac{1}{4}\frac{Y}{L_y} \qquad c_x\frac{1}{4}\frac{Y}{K_x} = \frac{3}{4}\frac{Y}{K_y}$$

$$\frac{L_y}{L_x} = \frac{2}{3}(1 + t_x)(1 + t_L) \qquad \frac{K_y}{K_x} = 6(1 + t_x)$$

$$L_x = \frac{3}{3 + 2(1 + t_x)(1 + t_L)} \bar{L} \qquad K_x = \frac{1}{1 + 6(1 + t_x)} \bar{K}$$

$$L_y = \frac{2(1 + t_x)(1 + t_L)}{3 + 2(1 + t_x)(1 + t_L)} \bar{L} \qquad K_y = \frac{6(1 + t_x)}{1 + 6(1 + t_x)} \bar{K}$$

$$U = \frac{3^{1/4} 2^{1/6} [(1 + t_x)(1 + t_L)]^{1/6} 6^{1/2} (1 + t_x)^{1/2}}{(3 + 2(1 + t_x)(1 + t_L))^{5/12} (1 + 6(1 + t_x))^{7/12}}$$

$$\frac{U(t_x)}{U(t_L)} = \frac{(1 \cdot 1)^{2/3} (5 \cdot 4)^{5/12} 7^{7/12}}{(1 \cdot 2)^{1/6} (5 \cdot 2)^{5/12} (7 \cdot 6)^{7/12}}$$

$$\left[\frac{U(t_x)}{U(t_L)} \right]^{12} = \frac{(1 \cdot 1)^8}{(1 \cdot 2)^2} \left(\frac{27}{26} \right)^5 \left(\frac{35}{38} \right)^7 = \frac{(1 \cdot 4641)^2}{(1 \cdot 2)^2} \frac{26}{27} \frac{35}{38} \bigg/ \left(\frac{26}{27} \frac{38}{35} \right)^6$$

$$= \frac{2 \cdot 1435881}{1 \cdot 44} \frac{910}{1026} \bigg/ \left(\frac{988}{945} \right)^6$$

$$= \frac{1950 \cdot 665171}{1477 \cdot 44} \bigg/ (1 \cdot 0455)^6 = 1 \cdot 3203 / (1 \cdot 0455)^6$$

$$[(1 \cdot 0455)^2 = 1 \cdot 093; \quad (1 \cdot 093)^3 = 1 \cdot 30575]$$

$$= \frac{1 \cdot 3203}{1 \cdot 3058} > 1.$$

NOTES ON SHORT CUTS

Warning: with such small numbers, use of Taylor expansions may be dangerous in giving the wrong results.

(a) The numerator in line 3 is approximately $\dfrac{3}{2} \dfrac{9}{10} = 1 \cdot 35$

By Taylor expansion, $(1 \cdot 0455)^6 \approx 1 \cdot 273$

(b) $\dfrac{27}{26} \approx 1 \cdot 03856$, $\dfrac{38}{35} \approx 1 \cdot 0857$

Taylor expansions should obviously not be used for $\dfrac{(1 \cdot 1)^8}{(1 \cdot 2)^2} = 1 \cdot 4886$

Using them for the other two terms yields

$$\left[\frac{U(t_x)}{U(t_L)} \right]^{12} = \frac{(1 \cdot 4886)(1 \cdot 1928)}{1 \cdot 5999} = \frac{1 \cdot 7756}{1 \cdot 5999} > 1$$

FURTHER NOTES

Many candidates attempted to answer the question with the geometry of commodity and factor market distortions. There are two points to note here:

1. A commodity tax shifts consumption to a welfare-inferior point on the transformation curve, since production remains efficient but consumption is made inefficient by a divergence between private and social relative costs of commodities.
2. A factor use tax in one industry has two effects: (i) it distorts production efficiency, putting the economy on a lower (more contracted) transformation curve; (ii) it distorts consumption choices because the price of the commodity includes the tax on the factor, which is not a social cost.

Note also that one cannot say, because it is not true, that two distortions must worsen welfare more than one distortion.

GENERAL ADVICE

Think about the economics before you tackle the algebra.

VI. (20 *points*). *A foreign government proposes to impose a special flat-rate percentage tax on the profits of foreign-owned subsidiaries operating in that country. Analyse the effects of such a tax on total output and the distribution of income in the country imposing the tax. What would be the consequences if, instead of a percentage tax on profits, the government charged a non-negligible licence fee for the establishment of foreign subsidiaries in the country?*

There are two initial possibilities: (a) there is a double taxation agreement whereby local taxes are offset against parent country taxes on profits; in this case nothing happens unless the local tax rate exceeds the parent country tax rate, in which case the excess tax constitutes the basis for the other and more interesting case; (b) the tax is a net tax. (Candidates were not expected to mention case (a).) In case (b), presumably the supply of foreign capital is perfectly elastic at a world market rate of return, and in the long run the foreigners will disinvest until the local gross-of-tax rate of return is above the world market rate in proportion to the local profits tax. (In the short run, one might expect foreigners to sell out to residents at a price somewhere between the pre-tax price of the assets and the discounted present value of the prospective stream of net-of-tax profits from them.) Disinvestment in physical terms by foreigners must reduce total output, and redistribute income from local labour to local capital, if we assume that local capital is in fixed supply. If local capital is in perfectly elastic supply at the world rate of return, on the contrary, local capital will simply replace domestic capital and output and distribution will remain as before except that the total income of local capitalists will now be all instead of only part of the share of capital in domestic output. If the government charges a non-negligible licence fee instead of a flat-rate tax, this is the equivalent of a lump-sum tax. If foreigners remain invested in the country, the rate of return will have to rise (and production fall and income distribution shift towards local capitalists) to the extent required to permit the licence fee to be paid. The lump-sum tax will tend to confine foreign enterprises to the larger-scale ones, for which the flat-rate equivalent of the tax is lower.

Note that this question should *not* be tackled on Econ. 302 lines, as if the foreign capital sector were one part of a two-sector model. That approach assumes that if foreign capital moves to the other sector it ceases to be taxed, and if domestic capital moves to the foreign capital sector it becomes subject to tax. A more sophisticated answer would assume that the foreign firms could either invest in or export to the local market. In this case output would fall but income distribution remain unchanged, as foreigners liquidated their investments and replaced local production by imports.

Note that, if we assume that foreign capital cannot shift out of the country, both the profits tax and the licence fee simply reduce net profits without altering production, unless the licence fee exceeds total profits. The same results would follow if one assumed initial monopoly profits on foreign investments, providing the tax did not reduce net profits below the returns available elsewhere.

VII. (20 *points*) *Assume a one-sector model with a production function* $X = L^\alpha K^{1-\alpha}$, *where* $L_t = L_0 e^{\gamma t}$ *and* K *lasts forever. The economy's saving behaviour is governed by the desire to hold a given ratio k of capital to output. This ratio is defined in two alternative ways: (i) as a ratio* (k_1) *of material capital to output, (ii) as a ratio* (k_2) *of total wealth, including the capitalized value of labour, to output.*

(a) *Prove that in both cases the economy will converge to an equilibrium growth path with constant output per head.*

(b) *Derive expressions for both* k_1 *and* k_2 *that will maximize consumption per head along the equilibrium growth path.*

(a) By assumption, the economy raises or lowers capital stock until the capital–output ratio equals the given constant; hence convergence is given by assumption, and the problem is simply whether constancy of the capital–output ratio entails constancy of output per head.

(i) This is obvious for a fixed material capital to output ratio:

$$X_t = L_t^\alpha (k_1 X_t)^{1-\alpha}; \quad \text{hence} \quad \frac{X_t}{L_t} = (k_1)^{(1-\alpha)/\alpha}$$

(ii) The capitalized value of labour is

$$L_t = \frac{\partial X_t / \partial L_t}{\partial X_t / \partial K_t} = K_t \frac{\alpha}{1-\alpha}.$$

Total wealth is therefore

$$W_t = K_t \left(1 + \frac{\alpha}{1-\alpha} \right) = K_t \frac{1}{1-\alpha}.$$

(This is obvious from the fact that capital's share in income from total wealth is $1 - \alpha$)

$$k_2 = \frac{W_t}{X_t} = \frac{1}{1-\alpha} \frac{K_t}{X_t}$$

$$\frac{K_t}{X_t} = (1 - \alpha)k_2$$

Hence by previous reasoning

$$\frac{X_t}{L_t} = [(1 - \alpha)k_2]^{(1-\alpha)/\alpha}.$$

Note that the phrase 'saving is governed by the desire to hold a given ratio k of capital to output' is a tricky one. To get to equilibrium we must assume that the economy normally saves enough to keep capital per head intact, and increases or decreases its savings in relation to this level according to whether desired capital per head is less than or greater than this.

(b) Let $X_t/L_t = x = k_1^{(1-\alpha)/\alpha} =$ output per head. The replacement requirement is $\gamma k_1 x$ (note that k is per unit of output, not per unit of labour), so that consumption per head is $C = k_1^{(1-\alpha/\alpha)} - \gamma k_1^{1/\alpha} = k_1^{(1-\alpha/\alpha)}(1 - \gamma k_1)$

$$\frac{\partial C}{\partial k} = \frac{1-\alpha}{\alpha} k_1^{(1-2\alpha)/\alpha} - \frac{\gamma}{\alpha} k_1^{(1-\alpha)/\alpha} = \frac{1}{\alpha} k_1^{(1-2\alpha)/\alpha}(1 - \alpha - \gamma k_1).$$

This is zero when $k_1 = \dfrac{1-\alpha}{\gamma}$ or when $k_2 = \dfrac{1}{\gamma}$.

That is, consumption per head is maximized when the ratio of material capital to output is the ratio of capital's share to the rate of population growth, or when the ratio of total wealth to output is the reciprocal of the rate of growth of population.

(i)

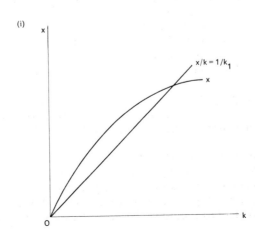

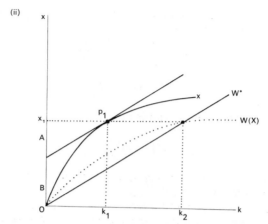

VII. A GEOMETRICAL APPROACH, USING THE STANDARD PER CAPITA DIAGRAM

For any point p_1, A is the income of capital and B the income of labour, k_1 is material capital and $k_1 k_2$ the capitalized value of labour, hence Ok_2 is total wealth per capita. $OW(X)$ is the function relating total wealth to output. The intersection of a vector OW^*, with slope equal to the reciprocal of k_2, with $OW(X)$ gives the economy's long-run equilibrium output per head.

University of Chicago Qualifying Examination in Price Theory, Summer 1972

Answer all questions. Time: three hours. Maximum score: one point per minute.

I. *(60 minutes, 4 per item) Indicate whether you believe each of the following statements to be TRUE, FALSE, or UNCERTAIN. In each case write a few sentences explaining your answer. Your grade will be determined by your explanation.*

1. *If all individuals had identical utility functions, a redistribution of income among individuals would not alter relative prices.*
   False. Invariability of relative prices to income redistribution requires not only identical but homothetic utility functions. If indifference curves are identical but not homothetic, marginal propensities to spend on various goods will differ with income levels, and income redistribution will create excess demands and excess supplies at current prices. (Note that it is marginal propensities to spend, not income elasticities of demand, that count; but specifying unitary income elasticities over the whole range of possible consumption guarantees homotheticity.)

2. *If commodities are properly defined as bundles of want-satisfying characteristics, there can be no such thing as imperfect competition.*
   The statement is *true* if 'want-satisfying characteristics' can be produced at equal cost by all producers, since then even though a particular producer's product has a unique characteristic differentiating it from other

producers' products he can only charge the competitive cost of production for it (because of the absence of barriers to potential entry). But if any producer has a monopoly of supply of a particular characteristic (which may include a brand name) he becomes an imperfect competitor.

3. *Suppose that a consumer's utility function were of the form:*

$$U = X^\alpha L^\beta$$

where X is the consumption of goods and L is non-working time. In the absence of property income, his compensated elasticity of supply of labour would be constant.

Let $\bar{L}$ be total labour time available, and w be the wage rate in terms of goods, so that $X = w(\bar{L} - L)$ and $U = w^\alpha(\bar{L} - L)^\alpha L^\beta$.

For a given wage rate, utility is maximized when

$$\frac{dU}{dL} = 0 = -\alpha \frac{U}{\bar{L} - L} + \beta \frac{U}{L}$$

and

$$\frac{L}{\bar{L} - L} = \frac{\beta}{\alpha}, L = \frac{\beta}{\alpha + \beta} \bar{L}, \bar{L} - L = \frac{\alpha}{\alpha + \beta} \bar{L},$$

and

$$U = w^\alpha \left(\frac{\alpha}{\alpha + \beta}\right)^\alpha \left(\frac{\beta}{\alpha + \beta}\right)^\beta \bar{L}^{\alpha + \beta}.$$

This involves a constant ratio of working and non-working time to available time, so that the *uncompensated* elasticity of supply of labour is zero (a constant).

The problem, however, is the compensated elasticity of supply of labour. The compensation process can be thought of as keeping $U = \bar{U}$ by changing $\bar{L}$ through taxation or subsidies so as to offset the effects of changes in w.

By appropriate choice of units,

$$\bar{L} = \bar{L}_0/w^{\alpha/(\alpha + \beta)}$$

where $\bar{L}_0$ is the total amount of labour time available in the absence of compensation and the corresponding $w_0 = 1$. Employing the relationship between leisure time and working time producing consumption goods derived above,

$$\bar{L}_0 - L = \bar{L}_0(1 - \beta/(\alpha + \beta)/w^{\alpha/(\alpha + \beta)}).$$

It can easily be verified that the elasticity of this expression with respect to w depends on the magnitude of w, and hence that the statement is *false*.

Another way to arrive at the same conclusion is to note that $L = K/w^{\alpha/(\alpha + \beta)}$, where K is a constant. If one part of a sum has a constant elasticity, the other cannot.

4. *If a tax of $1,000 leads a firm to withdraw from an industry, it must alter marginal cost, properly defined.*

True. The tax is an overhead cost to the individual firm, and does not alter its marginal cost of production *if it remains in production*; in this case it alters profits but not production. However, if the effect of the tax on profits leads the firm to withdraw from production, this means that the marginal cost properly defined—as the cost of keeping the marginal firms in the industry—must have risen.

5. *If individuals' utility functions were of the form:*

$$U = (AX^{-\beta} + BY^{-\beta})^{-(1/\beta)}$$

where X is food and Y other commodities, A and B weighting coefficients, and $1/(\beta + 1)$ the elasticity of substitution, and if 'death' means falling below a minimum level of utility, a rich enough man would never die even in a total famine.

False. An obvious and apparently valid short-cut that suggests the contrary is to assume that if $X = 0$ the utility function reduces to $U = B^{-1/\beta}Y$ and argue accordingly that a rich enough man could buy sufficient Y to make $U = B^{-1/\beta}Y > \overline{U}$, where $\overline{U}$ is the minimum death-survival utility level. But this short-cut is invalid. One must in generality tackle the problem by taking the limit of U, given Y, as X approaches zero. This limit turns out to depend on the elasticity of substitution. If $\sigma > 1$, the limit is that obtained by the above short-cut, and the proposition would be true; but if $\sigma \leqslant 1$, which may be presumed to be an empirical fact from the role of food in human life, no amount of income would prevent a man from falling below U and dying in a total famine.

The simplest way of demonstrating the falsity of the statement is to make use of the fact that when $\sigma = 1$, the utility function reduces to the Cobb–Douglas form:

$$U = X^{\alpha}Y^{1-\alpha}$$

where $\alpha = A/A + B$. With $X = 0$, $U = 0$.

More generally, substitute

$$-B = (\sigma - 1)/\sigma, \quad -1/B = \sigma/(\sigma - 1),$$

to obtain

$$U = (AX^{(\sigma - 1)/\sigma} + BY^{(\sigma - 1)/\sigma})^{\sigma/(\sigma - 1)}$$
$$= [A(X/Y)^{(\sigma - 1)/\sigma} + B]^{\sigma/(\sigma - 1)}Y$$

If $\sigma > 1$, the first term in the square brackets approaches zero as X approaches zero, and U approaches $B^{\sigma/(\sigma - 1)}Y$. But if $\sigma < 1$, the first term approaches infinity (because of the negative exponent) and U approaches $A^{\sigma/(\sigma - 1)}X$, so that if $X = 0$, $U = 0$.

6. *A rise in the price of TV dinners accompanied by a fall in the price of TV sets, so arranged as to hold real income constant, would result in an increase*

in the quantity of TV dinners demanded if TV sets and TV dinners were sufficiently complementary.

True. It would be false in a two-good case, because then one good must substitute for the other along an isoquant. It would appear to be false in the general case, on the short-cut argument that if the two goods are strict complements they constitute a 'Hicksian' composite good and consumption of each would be constant with constant real income because to keep real income constant the two price changes have to keep the price of the composite good constant. But this short-cut neglects the fact that in the general case, even though by assumption income effects are ruled out, these substitution effects may have either positive or negative signs and be as large-negative as one pleases, subject to an overall constraint imposed by the homogeneity conditions. Thus, even with real income held constant, the price-fall-induced substitution of TV sets for other goods in general may have a strong enough effect on the demand for TV dinners via complementarity (negative cross-substitution effect) to more than off-set the price-increase-induced substitution of other goods for TV dinners.

7. *The market price of a commodity falls equally when a firm expands its output by a given amount, whether the firm is a monopoly or one of a thousand competitive firms.*

False. The statement would be true if the initial price and the increase in total supply, therefore the final position on the demand curve, were the same in the two cases. But (a) if a monopolist increases his output by ΔX total supply increases by ΔX, whereas if a competitive firm increases its output by ΔX_i its rivals are unlikely to keep their outputs constant — in which case $\Delta X = \Delta X_i$ — but instead to contract their output in response to the resulting fall in price so that $\Delta X < \Delta X_i$; (b) a monopolist is likely to be charging a higher price than competitive price — not necessarily, because monopoly is usually associated with a lower-cost advantage over potential rivals — but in any case a different price. Hence, even if ΔX is the same in the two cases, the price fall will be the same only if the demand curve has a constant slope (i.e. is a straight-line demand curve).

8. *Competition under the patent system will cause innovations to be introduced before the socially optimum date.*

(This draws on an article by Yoram Barzel.) The optimal time for introducing an innovation is when its net present value is maximized. This present value may be assumed first to rise and then to fall with delay of introduction. Competition under the patent system will tend to lead to introduction as soon as net present value becomes positive, hence to introduction before the optimal date. The statement is *true*. Barzel points out that if the basic knowledge on which innovations draw were owned and priced, the timing would be optimal.

9. *The compulsory introduction of safety devices on automobiles raises the real income of automobile owners, if 'real income' is properly defined.*

This involve both externalities and the theory of voting. If the safety features of an automobile make a difference only to the welfare of the driver, and not to other drivers, each driver would choose the combination of safety features and cost optimal for his circumstances (that is, low-wage drivers would rely more on their driving skill and less on the safety features of their cars to reduce death risk, and vice versa for high-wage drivers, since money is more valuable and time less valuable to the former than to the latter). Compulsion to introduce more stringent safety requirements would constitute a tax on driving, raising the cost of the car above what owners previously were willing to pay and reducing their welfare. But if the driver's safety depends in part on the safety features of other cars, and transactions costs and/or poor definition of property rights prevent arrival at minimum safety standards for all cars by private negotiation and transfers, legislation may improve the welfare of drivers (automobile owners). It will do so if the legislation is introduced by public approval by the automobile owners; however, those who are no longer permitted to drive 'unsafe' cars at their own and other's risk will suffer a welfare loss — which is why the statement refers to automobile owners and not potential owners and drivers.

Another argument would be that drivers do not correctly evaluate their own welfare, being ignorant of the true risks that they incur by driving unsafe cars, and that the state evaluates these risks correctly. Hence in imposing the legislation the state is increasing the welfare, properly defined, of the automobile owners.

10. *If the imposition of a per unit tax on a commodity does not change the output of it, the industry could not have been in equilibrium initially.*
This is *true* except for two extreme cases: the completely vertical demand curve and the completely vertical supply curve. In the usual case of the downward-sloping demand curve and the upward-sloping supply curve, a per unit tax imposed on an equilibrium situation must reduce the industry's output, and output will be unchanged only if the industry were initially out of equilibrium.

11. *Garbage men earn less than industrial engineers because their work is dirty and disgusting.*
False. Garbage men earn less than engineers in spite of the fact that their work is dirty and disgusting. The reason is that engineers require more training, hence must earn more, than unskilled labour. Either garbage men get a premium over unskilled labour because the work is dirty and disgusting, but this premium is less than the premium commanded by the superior human capital of engineers, or there are enough unskilled workers who do not find garbage work dirty and disgusting (i.e. involving disutility) for garbage men to earn no more than comparably unskilled labour.

12. *Married couples with children are likely to patronize high-quality restaurants more frequently than couples without children.*
The phrase 'more frequently' is ambiguous as between 'absolutely more frequently' and 'relatively more frequently' (i.e., dining in high-quality

restaurants as contrasted with dining in cheap restaurants). If one hypothesized that children are a luxury good, those who had them would be able also to afford indulgence in high-quality dining more frequently (absolutely) than those who did not. because their incomes by assumption would be higher. If on the other hand one considers the relative frequency question, there are two alternatives for those with children — to take the children out too, or to have them baby-sat. In the former case, the tendency would be to patronize cheaper restaurants, since the children may be expected neither to be gourmets nor to appreciate elegant decor; hence childless couples would be expected to patronize high-quality restaurants relatively more frequently than couples with children, and the statement woulf be *false*. In the latter case, baby-sitting is a fixed cost of dining out, so that the relative cost of a meal in a high-quality restaurant is lower for the couple with children than for the childless couple, and one would expect those with children to dine out relatively more frequently at high-quality restaurants. so that on this assumption the statement would be *true*.

13. *In an economy with fixed supplies of productive factors, and fixed proportions in both production and consumption, some factors of production will be free goods.*
    With fixed supplies of productive factors and fixed coefficients in production, the transformation curve for a two-sector economy would be as shown in Diagram I; i.e., consist of two straight-line segments. At the point P both factors would be fully employed and have non-zero prices (with obvious and extreme exceptions where the consumer price ratio corresponds to the slope of $\overline{Y}P$ or $P\overline{X}$). In the range $\overline{Y}P$, the factor used intensively in X will have a zero price and be a free good; in the range

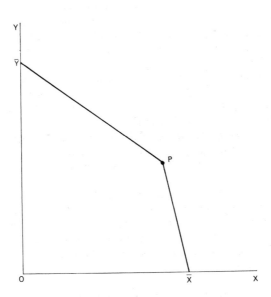

DIAGRAM I: PRODUCTION FRONTIER WITH FIXED FACTOR PROPORTIONS

$P\overline{X}$, the factor used intensively in Y will be a free good. If proportions in aggregated consumption were fixed, and the ratio happened to coincide with OP, factor prices would be indeterminate. Any other ratio would make one factor a free good. (Note: a fixed consumption ratio implies an L-shaped indifference curve.)

It is true but irrelevant to the question that if different producers of each good had different fixed factor ratios, and different income-receivers had different fixed consumption ratios between the commodities, we would restore normal-shaped transformation and indifference curves and attain an equilibrium with positive prices for both factors.

14. *Complete legal prohibition of environment-polluting activities is never rational; but legal restriction of such activities normally is rational.*
Since environment-pollution is normally a joint product with the production of useful goods, complete prohibition of one implies either complete prohibition of the other or a substantial increase in its cost (to eliminate pollution) and neither of these is likely to be rational as compared with some restriction of pollution. On the other hand the Coase theorem says that non-regulation would result in the social optimum if property rights were clearly defined and transactions costless. Since neither is the case, legal restriction is likely to be the lowest-cost way of moving towards the social optimum in a large number of cases. The statement is uncertain, but probably *true*.

15. *Some stores offer 'free delivery' to their customers. This implies that they are engaging in price discrimination and, therefore, that they have some monopoly power.*
True. Insofar as delivery costs vary among customers and some do not take advantage of the free delivery, customers shopping at the same nominal prices for goods are paying different prices for the same commodity (exclusive of delivery service) and are being discriminated amongst. The store can discriminate because near-by customers prefer to pay the higher price rather than go elsewhere. The free-delivery firm is exploiting the monopoly power it has by virtue of greater proximity to these customers than other firms enjoy, and using the profits to subsidize customers coming from greater distances.

Note that to describe free delivery as merely 'advertising' tells us nothing; also that the fact that delivery is available to all customers who want it does not mean there is no discrimination.

II. *(30 minutes, 10 per sub-section) Suppose that an individual's utility depends on two activities: an own consumption activity Z_1, and an aggregate consumption activity of other individuals Z_2. Z_1 is produced with goods and own time; Z_2 is produced by other individuals with goods, their own time, and a time contribution from the individual under consideration (the time contributor).*

1. *What would be the effect on his time contribution of :*
   a. *A rise in the own wage rate;*

b. *a rise in other people's wage rate;*
c. *a factor neutral improvement in the production of* Z_1;
d. *a factor neutral improvement in the production of* Z_2.

2. *If you estimated the elasticity of the time contribution with respect to the own wage rate, first in a cross section, then in a time series, which estimate would be larger?*
3. *If you supposed that education raised nonmarket productivity in a factor neutral manner, and if you estimated the elasticity of the time contribution with respect to own education, would the estimated effect be larger in a cross section or in a time series analysis?*

(Answer supplied by Gilbert Ghez.)

The time contributor's utility function depends on an own consumption activity Z_1 and an aggregate consumption activity of other individuals Z_2:

$$U^{(1)} = U^{(1)}(Z_1, Z_2)$$

Z_1 is produced with goods X_1, and own time T_1; Z_2 is produced with goods X_2, other individuals' time T_2, and a time contribution T_c:

$$Z_1 = F_1(X_1, T_1)$$
$$Z_2 = F_2(X_2, T_2, T_c)$$

The time contributor has a budget constraint:

$$X_1 + w_1 T_1 + w_1 T_c = M_1$$

where M_1 is his full income and w_1 is his wage rate (using goods as the numéraire).

He maximizes utility, giving the following equilibrium conditions:

$$U_1^{(1)} = \lambda_1 \pi_1$$
$$U_2^{(1)} = \lambda_1 \pi_2$$

where π_1 and π_2 are the marginal cost of Z_1 and Z_2

$$\pi_1 = \frac{w_1}{MPT_1} = \frac{1}{MPX_1}$$

$$\pi_2 = \frac{w_1}{MPT_c}$$

and where $U_1^{(1)}$ and $U_2^{(1)}$ are his marginal utility of Z_1 and Z_2.

Notice that X_2 and T_2 are taken as given: the time contributor has no *direct* influence over these variables.

The equilibrium conditions (which include the budget constraint) enable one to solve for T_c as a function of M_1 (which depends on w_1 and property income), w_1, X_2 and T_2:

$$T_c = T_c(M_1, w_1, X_2, T_2) \tag{1}$$

On the other hand, the 'time recipient' maximizes his utility function $U^{(2)}(Z_2)$ subject to his budget constraint:

$$X_2 + w_2 T_2 = M_2$$

where M_2 is his full income and w_2 his wage rate. His equilibrium conditions include:

$$MPX_2 = \lambda_2$$

$$MPT_2 = \lambda_2 w_2$$

Notice that T_c is taken as given: the time recipient has no direct influence over T_c.

These equilibrium conditions, together with his budget constraint, enable one to solve for Z_2, X_2 and T_2 as functions of M_2, w_2 and T_c:

$$Z_2 = Z_2(M_2, w_2, T_c) \tag{2}$$

$$X_2 = X_2(M_2, w_2, T_c) \tag{3}$$

$$T_2 = T_2(M_2, w_2, T_c) \tag{4}$$

Substituting (3) and (4) into (1) gives T_c as a function of M_1, w_1, M_2 and w_2. A direct inspection of the equilibrium conditions gives more insight, however, than this general solution.

In order to simplify the analysis, it is convenient to begin with the assumption that X_2 and T_2 do not affect the marginal product of T_c. It then follows that (i) a rise in X_2 or T_2 affect T_c only in so far as they raise the amount of Z_2 producible by 2 with given T_c. This raises the time contributor's level of real income, and therefore in (1) we would necessarily have

$$\frac{\partial T_c}{\partial X_2} < 0$$

$$\frac{\partial T_c}{\partial T_2} < 0$$

as long as the income elasticity of demand for Z_1 is positive. (ii) a rise in T_c has no effect on X_2 and T_2 since it does not alter their marginal products, i.e., in (3) and (4)

$$\frac{\partial X_2}{\partial T_c} = 0$$

$$\frac{\partial T_2}{\partial T_c} = 0$$

[even though $\partial Z_2 / \partial T_c > 0$ in (2)].

1-a. *Effect on T_c of a rise in w_1*

A rise in w_1 raises the marginal cost of Z_2 relative to Z_1, inducing substitution toward Z_1, thereby decreasing T_c. It also raises the contributor's real income. In total, therefore, assuming that Z_2 is normal in

1's consumption basket, he will contribute more (or less) if the income effect is stronger (is weaker) than the substitution effect.

1-b. *Effect on T_c of a rise in w_2*

A rise in w_2 raises 2's real income, therefore he can increase Z_2 with a given T_c. It also raises the cost of T_2 relative to X_2 inducing substitution in production toward X_2.

The rise in Z_2 producible at fixed T_c is a rise in 1's real income. He therefore reduces T_c since the income elasticity of demand for Z_1 can be assumed to be positive and relative prices have not changed (given the assumption about the marginal product of T_c).

1-c. *Effect on T_c of a factor neutral improvement in Z_1*

An improvement in efficiency in Z_1 implies a fall in its price, thereby inducing substitution toward Z_1 and hence discouraging time contributions. It also raises 1's real income. Therefore, assuming that Z_2 is normal in 1's consumption basket, T_c will increase or decrease as the income effect is stronger or weaker than the substitution effect.

1-d. *Effect on T_c of a factor neutral improvement in Z_2*

A rise in the marginal product of T_c implies a reduction in the number of units of T_c required per unit of Z_2, so that T_c would fall if Z_2 were held constant. The rise in MPT_c also implies a lowering of the marginal cost of Z_2, inducing substitution toward Z_2 and therefore greater time contributions. Finally, it implies a rise in real income and hence in T_c if Z_2 is normal in 1's consumption basket. The first effect works against T_c, while the latter two work in favor of T_c.

In addition, the marginal products of X_2 and T_2 are increased (by the same proportion). Hence the 'time recipient' can increase his production Z_2. X_2 and T_2 will not change since the income elasticity of demand for Z_2 by the 'time recipient' is equal to unity.

This rise in the amount of Z_2 producible by 2 is a rise in 1's real income. From this effect, T_c would fall as long as Z_1 is normal.

The assumption that MPT_c is independent of X_2 and T_2 is convenient because it enables one to neglect feedback effects. In the general case, we have (1), (3) and (4)

$$T_c = \tilde{T}_c(V_1, w_1, X_2, T_2)$$
$$X_2 = \tilde{X}_2(V_2, w_2, T_c)$$
$$T_2 = \tilde{T}_2(V_2, w_2, T_c)$$

where V_1 and V_2 are property income of 1 and 2. Differentiating the equations yields:

$$dT_c = \frac{\partial \tilde{T}_c}{\partial w_1} dw_1 + \frac{\partial \tilde{T}_c}{\partial X_2} dX_2 + \frac{\partial \tilde{T}_c}{\partial T_2} dT_2$$

$$dX_2 = \frac{\partial \tilde{X}_2}{\partial w_2} dw_2 + \frac{\partial \tilde{X}_2}{\partial T_c} dT_c$$

$$dT_2 = \frac{\partial \tilde{T}_2}{\partial w_2} dw_2 + \frac{\partial \tilde{T}_2}{\partial T_c} dT_c$$

and solving for dT_c gives

$$dT_c = \frac{\partial \tilde{T}_c/\partial w_1}{D} dw_1$$

$$+ \frac{[(\partial \tilde{T}_c/\partial X_2)(\partial \tilde{X}_2/\partial w_2) + (\partial \tilde{T}_c/\partial T_2)(\partial \tilde{T}_2/\partial w_2)]}{D} dw_2 \qquad (5)$$

where

$$D = 1 - (\partial \tilde{T}_c/\partial X_2)(\partial \tilde{X}_2/\partial T_c) - (\partial \tilde{T}_c/\partial T_2)(\partial \tilde{T}_2/\partial T_c)$$

First investigate D. If a rise in T_c raises (or lowers) the marginal products of X_2 and T_2 by the same proportion and if the production function for Z_2 is homothetic in X_2 and T_2, then clearly

$$\frac{\partial \tilde{X}}{\partial T_c} = \frac{\partial \tilde{T}_2}{\partial T_c} = 0$$

and therefore

$$D = 1 > 0$$

Clearly, as long as $D > 0$, a rise in w_1 raises T_c (assuming that Z_2 is not very inferior for 1).

---

[1] The assumption that MPT_c is independent of X_2 and T_2 implies that

$$\frac{\partial \tilde{T}_c}{\partial X_2} = \left. \frac{\partial T_c}{\partial Z_2} \right|_{X_2, T_2} \cdot MPX_2$$

$$\frac{\partial \tilde{T}_c}{\partial T_2} = \left. \frac{\partial T_c}{\partial Z_2} \right|_{X_2, T_c} \cdot MPT_2$$

so that in (5) we have

$$\frac{\partial \tilde{T}_c}{\partial X_2} \frac{\partial \tilde{X}_2}{\partial w_2} + \frac{\partial \tilde{T}_c}{\partial T_2} \frac{\partial \tilde{T}_2}{\partial w_2} = \left. \frac{\partial T_c}{\partial Z_2} \right|_{X_2, T_2} \left[MPX_2 \frac{\partial \tilde{X}_2}{\partial w_2} + MPT_2 \frac{\partial \tilde{T}_2}{\partial w_2} \right]$$

$$= \left. \frac{\partial T_c}{\partial Z_2} \right|_{X_2, T_2} \lambda_2 N_2$$

which is negative under the assumption that the income elasticity of demand for Z_1 is positive, and that working time of the 'time recipient', N_2, is positive.

Next consider the effect of a rise in w_2. This generates two effects. First it raises the amount of Z_2 producible with fixed T_c. This is the real income effect analyzed above, which tends to reduce T_c. But now, in addition, we get a change in relative prices confronting the time contributor, but the direction of change is not unambiguous. We know that for given T_c, X_2 rises with w_2, and T_2 could rise or fall. If the combined effect is to raise MPT_c then you get substitution toward Z_2 and greater T_c. If the combined effect is to lower MPT_c then you get substitution away from Z_2. The net effect of the rise in w_2 depends on the income and substitution effects.

2. *Comparison of the elasticity of T_c with respect to w in a cross section and in a time series.*

If we make the reasonable assumption that MPT_c is independent of X_2 and T_2, then a rise in w_1 could raise or lower T_c, while a rise in w_2 unambiguously reduces T_c. In a cross section w_2 is fixed, while in a time series w_1 and w_2 move in the same direction. Hence one predicts that the effect in the time series is likely to be smaller in algebraic value than in the cross section.

3. *Comparison of the elasticity of T_c with respect to education in a cross section and a time series.*

Consider the non-market effects of education alone. A technological improvement in Z_1 alone and in Z_2 alone produce ambiguous effects. In general, time series and cross section don't admit of a simple prediction on the ranking of the estimates.

III. (*15 minutes*) '*The Coase proposition is that. in the absence of transaction costs, assignment of property rights does not affect the allocation of resources (except through income redistribution). The converse is also true: in the presence of transactions costs, the assignment of property rights always influences the allocation of resources (even if there are no effects through income redistribution). Discuss this statement.*

In an obvious but trivial sense the proposition must be true, because if transactions require real resources and any transactions take place, the allocation of resources must be different than if transactions cost no real resources. Apart from that we have two cases. (1) Transactions costs are an overhead cost. If the overhead cost of transactions is less than the total benefit to the transactors in all cases, the same transactions would occur as in the absence of transactions costs, and—aside from the resource-allocation effects of the transactions themselves—the results on allocation would influence resource allocation only through income effects (any resource-allocation effects of transactions costs could be regarded theoretically as an income-effect due to the transfer of income from the transactions to the transactions-cost sector). (2) Transactions costs are proportional, in part at least, to the amount of transactions. They therefore constitute a tax on transactions; and since the direction of the desired transactions will be influenced by the distribution of property rights, the tax will cause transactions to fall short on one side or the other of the amount that would be socially optimal in the absence of transactions costs. Hence the distribution of property rights will influence the amount of transactions and the allocation of resources.

IV. (*15 minutes*) *The lowest price of gasoline among the dealers in a city fluctuates more widely over time than the highest price. What, if any, connection has this fact with:*
  i. *the incomes of consumers;*
  ii. *the extent of collusion among sellers;*
  iii. *the optimum search for information?*

The phrasing of the question obviously treats 'gasoline' as a single commodity. Hence answers that distinguish between 'premium' and 'regular' gas, identify low variability with the former and high variability with the latter, and attempt to explain the difference by income elasticities and search costs, misunderstand the question and are wide of the mark.

One might explain the facts along the following lines. (i) Consumers' incomes differ. The majority are indifferent among the stations they normally come across, if the posted price is the same, or are influenced by non-price factors if they attach themselves to a particular station (but will not stay with that station if its price is consistently higher that prices at nearby stations). For them search costs are too high (time-wise) to go looking in far-away or unaccustomed places for a lower gas price. Low-income consumers, on the other hand (and possibly some high-income consumers with a taste for bargains to brag about) are willing to search for lower-priced gas. In short, the income differences make some but not most consumers willing to search for cheap gas, hence provide sufficient elasticity of demand for gas at the cut-price stations to make it worth their while to cut prices, either permanently or temporarily, to attract more sales.

(ii) There may or may not be collusion. If stations offer a joint product of gasoline selling plus comfort stations plus availability of repair services, the latter two supported in whole or part by the price charged for gasoline, prices of gasoline could vary quite consistently with perfect competition, and one would also expect less variance among high-price than among low-price stations, as there is a limit to how much people will pay for the availability of convenience. However, the evidence is also consistent with collusion; the main suppliers fix a posted price for gasoline higher than is required to pay the costs of the most luxurious stations, or sufficient for this but higher than is necessary for the less luxurious stations, and some stations see a chance to cheat on the collusive agreement to their own profit, either temporarily or permanently

(iii) For price-cutting in relation to the standard price to be profitable to those doing it, demand must be elastic. This implies that incomes and search costs be such that a significant number of customers are willing to search for and buy lower-priced gas if there is some evidence that it is available somewhere.

V. (*30 minutes, 10 per section*) *A portion of American petroleum comes from abroad under a quota system whereby refiners are allotted specific amounts they may import. The foreign price of oil is $1.25 cheaper than the domestic* *price, after allowing for transport costs. The remainder of US consumption of petroleum comes from domestic oil wells, which are allotted given outputs per month. These domestic allotments are not transferable among wells.*

1. *If domestic allotments were made transferable (saleable), what would happen to domestic output and to the profits of oil well owners?*
2. *If import quotas were replaced by a $1.25 tariff, what would be the effect upon domestic price and upon refiner's profits?*
3. *If ALL allotments (domestic and foreign) were made interchangeable, what would be the effects upon*
   - i. *total domestic consumption;*
   - ii. *total domestic production;*
   - iii. *the profits of refiners;*
   - iv. *the profits of owners of domestic wells.*

This question contains some ambiguity, since no relation between domestic and foreign quotas is given. This means that there are two sets of alternative possibilities: (1) some domestic production quotas are not used, because marginal cost exceeds domestic price; or alternatively all domestic quotas are used; (2) marginal cost of domestic oil uniformly exceeds the price of oil imports; or alternatively it does not. (The logical assumption, given the quota system. is that foreign oil is generally cheaper than domestic oil.)

1. Transferability of domestic quotas will not change domestic output if all quotas were previously used; it will simply transfer production from higher to lower cost domestic wells, thus increasing the profits of well-owners as a group. If some quotas previously were not used, domestic production and profits will both increase.
2. Assuming no connection between domestic oil purchases and import quotas, replacement of import quotas by an equivalent tariff will transfer the profits from the right to import cheap foreign oil from the refiners to the government, without changing domestic consumption or production. (Note: if import quotas were related to domestic oil purchases, the quotas would have the effect of subsidizing domestic purchases, and replacement of quotas by a tariff would reduce domestic purchases and increase imports.)
3. Unless there were increased domestic quotas which now come to be used due to transferability, the domestic price and domestic consumption would remain the same. Domestic production would contract in wells whose marginal production cost exceeded the world price, and expand in those wells whose marginal production cost fell short of the world price. The empirical assumption would be that marginal production cost is higher from domestic than from foreign sources, so that domestic production would contract. Whatever the empirical assumption, refiners would get the same domestic price for their product but be able to choose freely among sources of oil supply, and choose the lowest-cost (domestic or foreign) source. Hence their profits would rise if they could sell their import rights to domestic well-owners who could produce more cheaply

than the foreign oil price, and remain unchanged (or possibly increase, depending on the balance of bargaining power) if they had to buy domestic quotas in order to import more cheap foreign oil — on the whole, one would expect their profits to increase, since at worst they would maintain the pre-existing quantities of domestic and foreign oil imports. The profits of domestic oil-well owners should increase, since they can sell production rights either to each other or to refiners who will import at lower cost instead.

The phrase 'made interchangeable' is however an ambiguous one, since it does not specify who has the property rights in the allotments. If the refiners can change import rights into domestic purchase rights at will, they cannot lose, though they may not gain; nor can domestic producers lose. If refiners could change domestic quotas into import quotas, they must gain, but domestic producers would lose. If domestic producers could change their production quotas into import quotas, they would gain (since they would only do so if foreign oil cost less than the production cost of domestic oil), but refiners might be no better off, since all the gain would be absorbed by domestic well-owners.

VI. *(30 minutes, 10 per sub-section) Consider the following model, in which aggregate production is a function of labour and capital used in the production process directly, and of a third factor (technology, or possibly the environment) the stock of which is determined by the amount of labour and capital currently used in the production or maintenance of it:*

$$X = A^\alpha L_p^\beta K_p^{1-\alpha-\beta}$$

$$A = L_a^\gamma K_a^{1-\gamma}$$

$$L = L_a + L_p$$

$$K = K_a + K_p$$

a. *Derive conditions for the maximization of output at any point of time, and express output as a function of total labour and capital only.*
b. *Assume that*

$$L_t = L_o e^{\ell t}, \qquad \frac{dK}{dt} = sX.$$

i. *Show that the system will converge on the rate of growth ℓ;*
ii. *derive conditions for the maximization of consumption per head at all points on the steady-state growth path.*
c. *Discuss the implications of the assumption that*

$$\frac{1}{A}\frac{dA}{dt} = L_{at}^\alpha K_{at}^{1-\alpha}.$$

(a) $X = A^\alpha L_p^\beta K_p^{1-\alpha-\beta}$

$A = L_a^\gamma K_a^{1-\gamma}$

$L = L_a + L_p$

$$K = K_a + K_p$$

$$X = L_a^{\alpha\gamma} K_a^{\alpha(1-\gamma)} L_p^\beta K_p^{1-\alpha-\beta}$$

$$\frac{\partial X}{\partial L_a} = \alpha\gamma \frac{X}{L_a} = \frac{\partial X}{\partial L_p} = \beta \frac{X}{L_p}$$

$$\frac{L_a}{L_p} = \frac{\alpha\gamma}{\beta}, \qquad L_p = \frac{\beta}{\alpha\gamma + \beta} \cdot L, \qquad L_a = \frac{\alpha\gamma}{\alpha\gamma + \beta} L$$

Similarly,

$$\frac{K_a}{K_p} = \frac{\alpha(1-\gamma)}{1-\alpha-\beta}, \qquad K_p = \frac{1-\alpha-\beta}{1-\beta-\gamma\alpha} K, \qquad K_a = \frac{\alpha(1-\gamma)}{1-\beta-\alpha\gamma} K$$

$$X = \left(\frac{\alpha\gamma}{\alpha\gamma+\beta}\right)^{\alpha\gamma} L^{\alpha\gamma} \cdot \left(\frac{\alpha(1-\gamma)}{1-\beta-\alpha\gamma}\right)^{\alpha(1-\gamma)} K^{\alpha(1-\gamma)}$$

$$\times \left(\frac{\beta}{\alpha\gamma+\beta}\right)^\beta L^\beta \left(\frac{1-\alpha-\beta}{1-\beta-\alpha\gamma}\right)^{1-\alpha-\beta} K^{1-\alpha-\beta}$$

$$= \left(\frac{\alpha\gamma}{\alpha\gamma+\beta}\right)^{\alpha\gamma} \left(\frac{\beta}{\alpha\gamma+\beta}\right)^\beta \left(\frac{\alpha(1-\gamma)}{1-\beta-\alpha\gamma}\right)^{\alpha(1-\gamma)} \left(\frac{1-\alpha-\beta}{1-\beta-\alpha\gamma}\right)^{1-\alpha-\beta}$$

$$L^{\alpha\gamma+\beta} K^{1-\beta-\alpha\gamma}$$

$$= HL^z K^{1-z}$$

where H and z are defined by the preceding formula. Note: many students confused themselves by using Langrange multipliers, or by using $L_a = L - L_p$.

(b)

(i)
$$x = \frac{1}{X}\frac{dX}{dt} = z \cdot \ell + (1-z)k$$

$$\left(\text{where } \ell = \frac{1}{L}\frac{dL}{dt}, \quad k = \frac{1}{K}\frac{dK}{dt}\right)$$

$$k = s\frac{X}{K}$$

$$\frac{dk}{dt} = s\frac{X}{K}(x-k)$$

k rises when $k < x$, falls when $k > x$, hence must converge on $k = x = l$.

(ii) From (i)
$$k = l = s\frac{X}{K}, \qquad K = \frac{s}{l}X$$

$$X = L^z K^{1-z} = L^z \left(\frac{s}{l}\right)^{1-z} X^{1-z}$$

$$\frac{X}{L} = \left(\frac{s}{l}\right)^{\frac{z}{1-z}}$$

Consumption per head is $c = (1 - s)(X/L) = (1 - s)(s/l) z/(1 - z)$

$$\frac{\partial c}{\partial s} = s \frac{z}{1 - z}\left(-1 + \frac{1 - s}{s} \frac{z}{1 - z}\right)$$

This is maximized when $s/(1 - s) = z/(1 - z)$ or $s = z$, i.e. the savings ratio equals the share of capital in total output. Since capital's share is iK/X (i being the rate of interest), and the savings ratio is $s = l(K/X)$ in long-rung equilibrium, an alternative condition is $i = p$.

A simpler proof is

$$C = \frac{C}{L} = \frac{X}{L} - l\frac{K}{L}$$

$$\frac{\partial C}{\partial K} = \frac{1}{L}\left(\frac{\partial X}{\partial K} - l\right) = \frac{1}{L}(i - l)$$

which is maximized when $i = l$ and $(iK/X) = l(K/X)$ (share of capital equals savings ratio).

(c) The assumption implies that the economy can increase its future output, and the rate of growth of that output, by reallocating resources from current production to the production of technology.